B A T M A N

LEGENDS OF
DARK KNIGHT

VOLUME 3

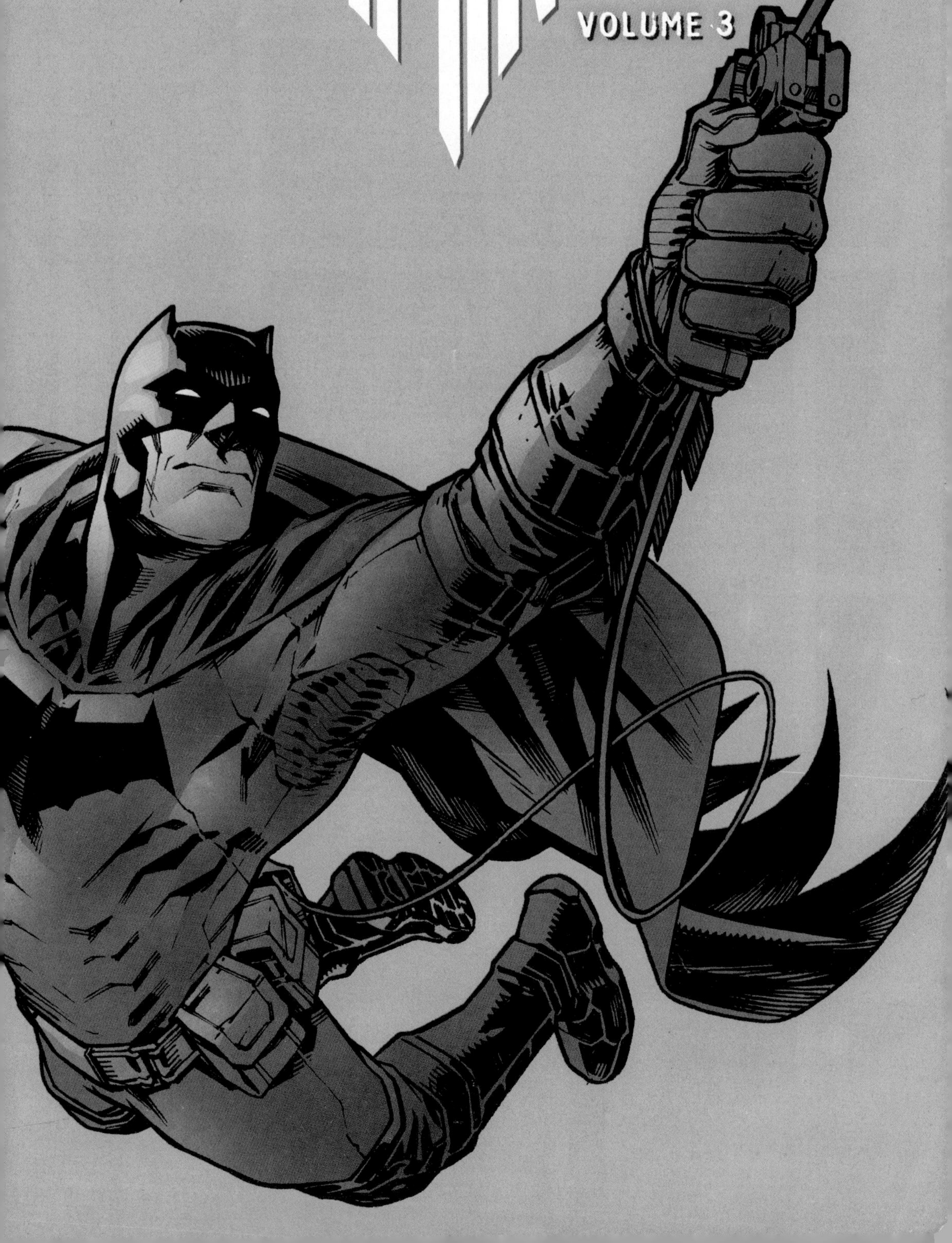

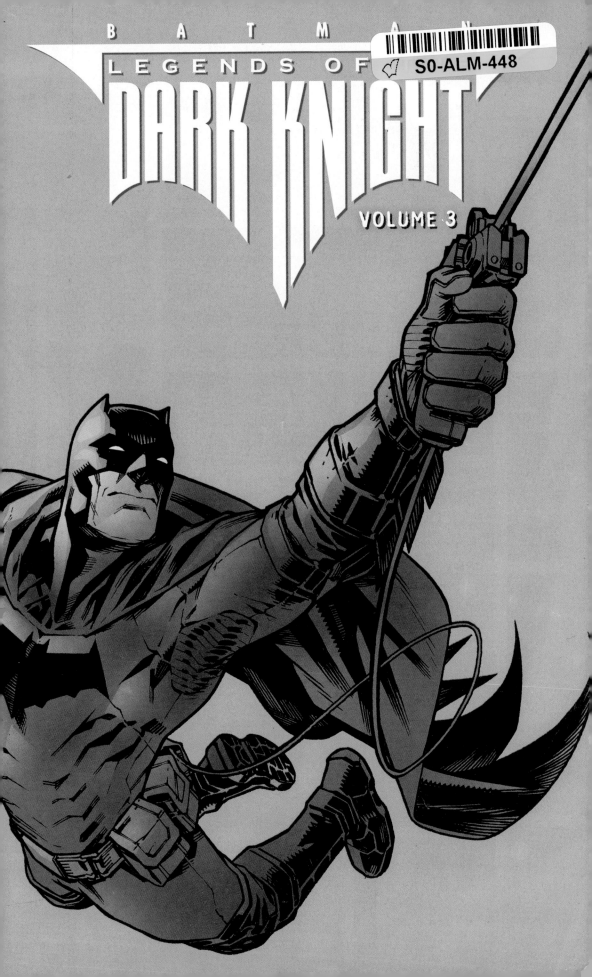

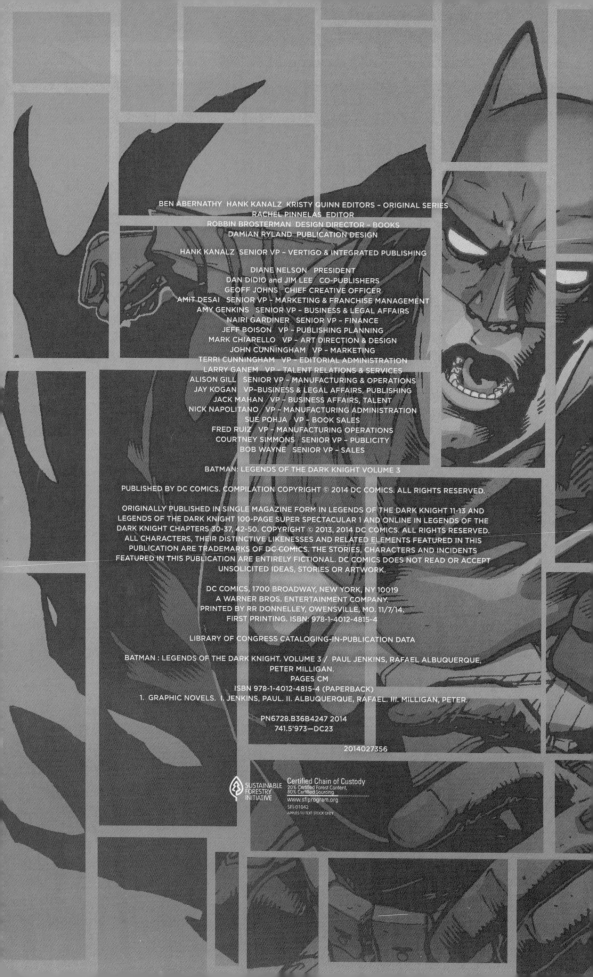

BEN ABERNATHY HANK KANALZ KRISTY QUINN EDITORS - ORIGINAL SERIES
RACHEL PINNELAS EDITOR
ROBBIN BROSTERMAN DESIGN DIRECTOR - BOOKS
DAMIAN RYLAND PUBLICATION DESIGN

HANK KANALZ SENIOR VP - VERTIGO & INTEGRATED PUBLISHING

DIANE NELSON PRESIDENT
DAN DIDIO and JIM LEE CO-PUBLISHERS
GEOFF JOHNS CHIEF CREATIVE OFFICER
AMIT DESAI SENIOR VP - MARKETING & FRANCHISE MANAGEMENT
AMY GENKINS SENIOR VP - BUSINESS & LEGAL AFFAIRS
NAIRI GARDINER SENIOR VP - FINANCE
JEFF BOISON VP - PUBLISHING PLANNING
MARK CHIARELLO VP - ART DIRECTION & DESIGN
JOHN CUNNINGHAM VP - MARKETING
TERRI CUNNINGHAM VP - EDITORIAL ADMINISTRATION
LARRY GANEM VP - TALENT RELATIONS & SERVICES
ALISON GILL SENIOR VP - MANUFACTURING & OPERATIONS
JAY KOGAN VP-BUSINESS & LEGAL AFFAIRS, PUBLISHING
JACK MAHAN VP - BUSINESS AFFAIRS, TALENT
NICK NAPOLITANO VP - MANUFACTURING ADMINISTRATION
SUE POHJA VP - BOOK SALES
FRED RUIZ VP - MANUFACTURING OPERATIONS
COURTNEY SIMMONS SENIOR VP - PUBLICITY
BOB WAYNE SENIOR VP - SALES

BATMAN: LEGENDS OF THE DARK KNIGHT VOLUME 3

DC COMICS, 1700 BROADWAY, NEW YORK, NY 10019
A WARNER BROS. ENTERTAINMENT COMPANY.
PRINTED BY RR DONNELLEY, OWENSVILLE, MO. 11/7/14.
FIRST PRINTING. ISBN: 978-1-4012-4815-4

LIBRARY OF CONGRESS CATALOGING-IN-PUBLICATION DATA

BATMAN : LEGENDS OF THE DARK KNIGHT. VOLUME 3 / PAUL JENKINS, RAFAEL ALBUQUERQUE,
PETER MILLIGAN.
PAGES CM
ISBN 978-1-4012-4815-4 (PAPERBACK)
1. GRAPHIC NOVELS. I. JENKINS, PAUL. II. ALBUQUERQUE, RAFAEL. III. MILLIGAN, PETER.

PN6728.B36B4247 2014
741.5'973—DC23

2014027356

BATMAN
LEGENDS OF THE
DARK KNIGHT

VOLUME 3

Paul JENKINS · Rafael ALBUQUERQUE · Peter MILLIGAN
Tim SEELEY · Dan MISHKIN · Jim ZUBKAVICH
WRITERS

OMAR FRANCIA · RAFAEL ALBUQUERQUE · RICCARDO BURCHIELLI
FREDDIE E. WILLIAMS II · TOM MANDRAKE · NEIL GOOGE
ARTISTS

REX LOKUS · DAVE McCAIG · WENDY BROOME · KATHRYN LAYNO
COLORISTS

Saida TEMOFONTE
LETTERER

Rafael ALBUQUERQUE
COLLECTION COVER ARTIST

BATMAN created by BOB KANE

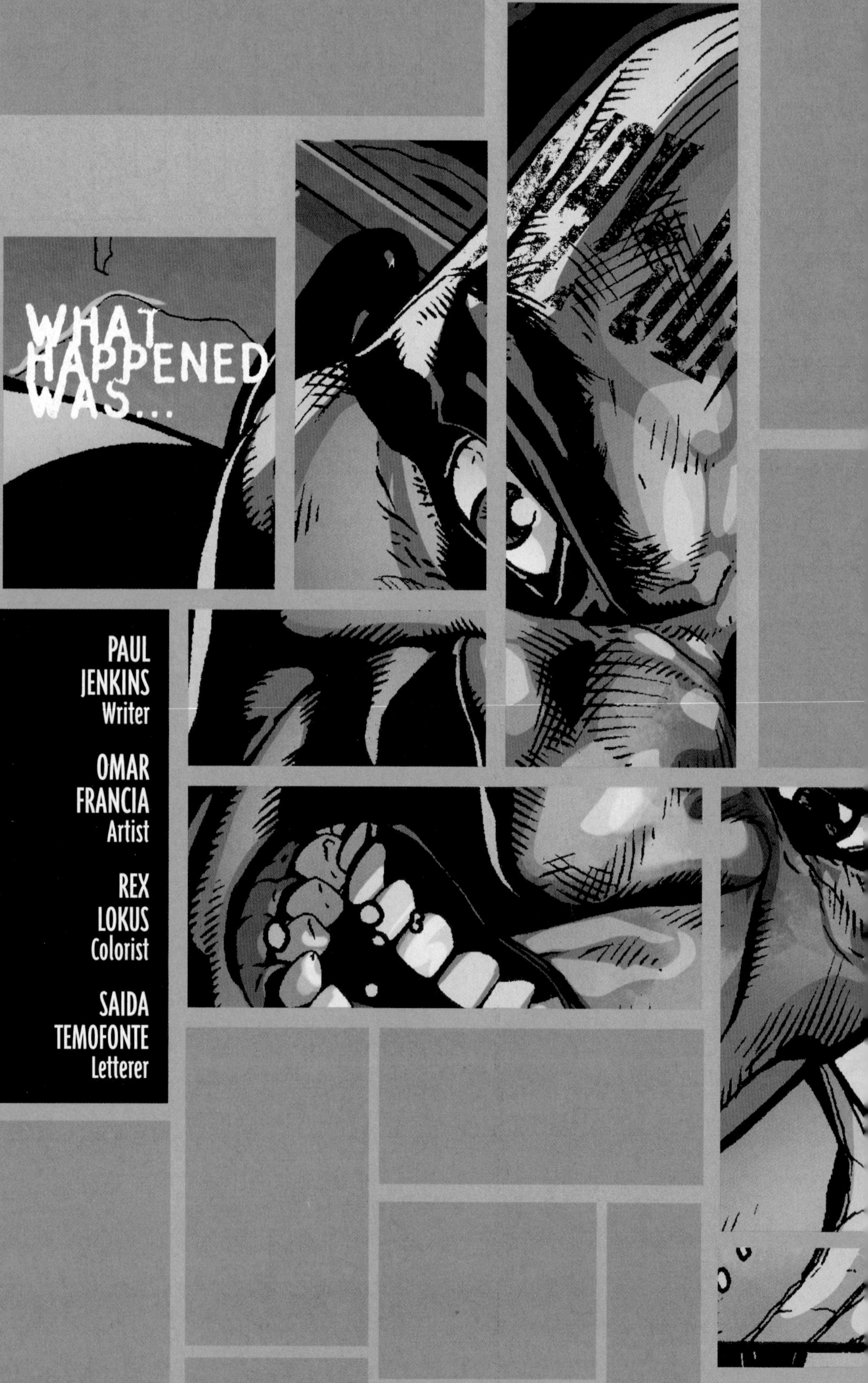
WHAT HAPPENED WAS...

PAUL JENKINS
Writer

OMAR FRANCIA
Artist

REX LOKUS
Colorist

SAIDA TEMOFONTE
Letterer

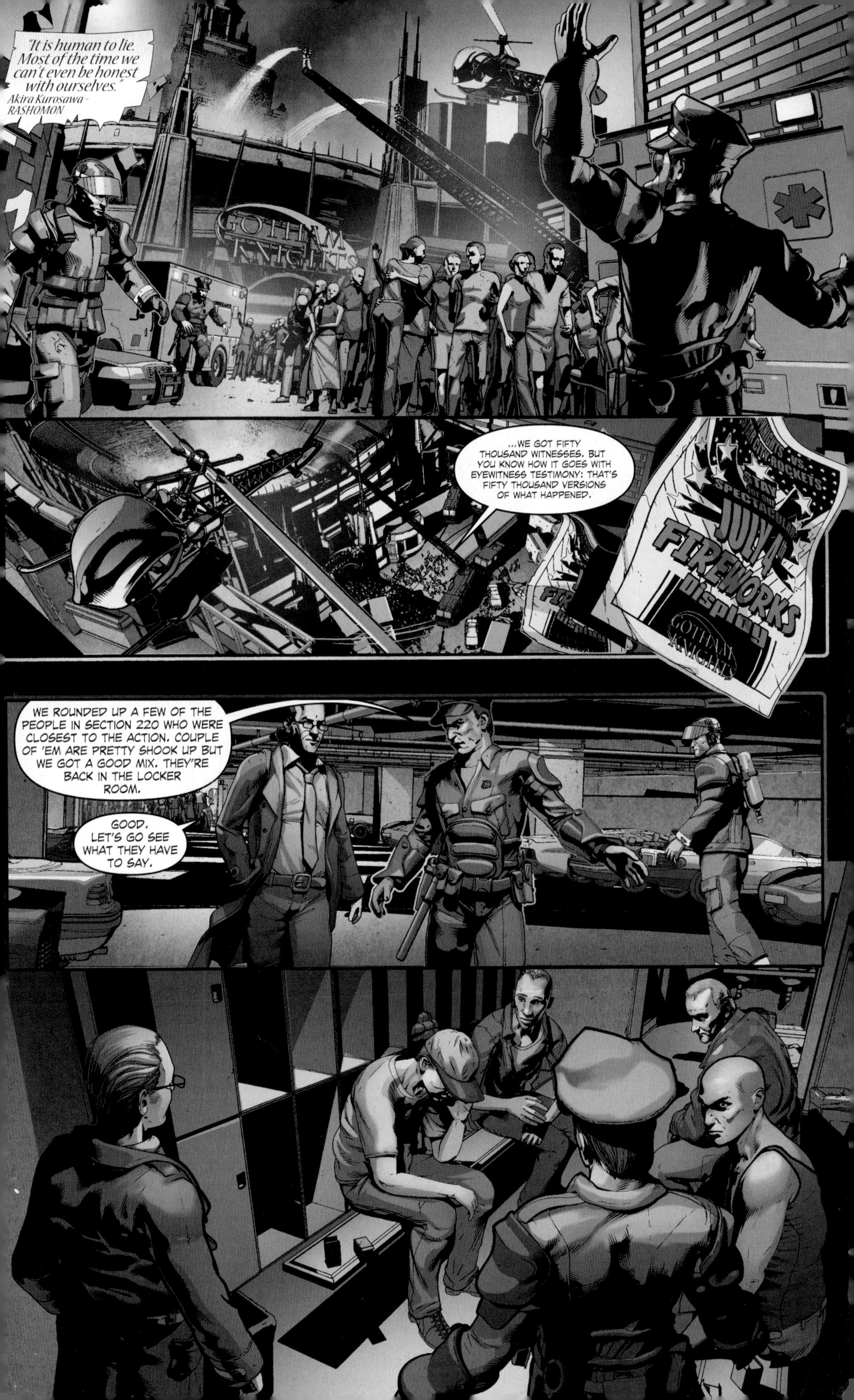
"It is human to lie. Most of the time we can't even be honest with ourselves."
Akira Kurosawa - RASHOMON
GOTHAM KNIGHTS
...WE GOT FIFTY THOUSAND WITNESSES. BUT YOU KNOW HOW IT GOES WITH EYEWITNESS TESTIMONY: THAT'S FIFTY THOUSAND VERSIONS OF WHAT HAPPENED.
STAY
SPECTACULAR
JULY 4
FIREWORKS
Display
GOTHAM KNIGHTS
WE ROUNDED UP A FEW OF THE PEOPLE IN SECTION 220 WHO WERE CLOSEST TO THE ACTION. COUPLE OF 'EM ARE PRETTY SHOOK UP BUT WE GOT A GOOD MIX. THEY'RE BACK IN THE LOCKER ROOM.
GOOD. LET'S GO SEE WHAT THEY HAVE TO SAY.

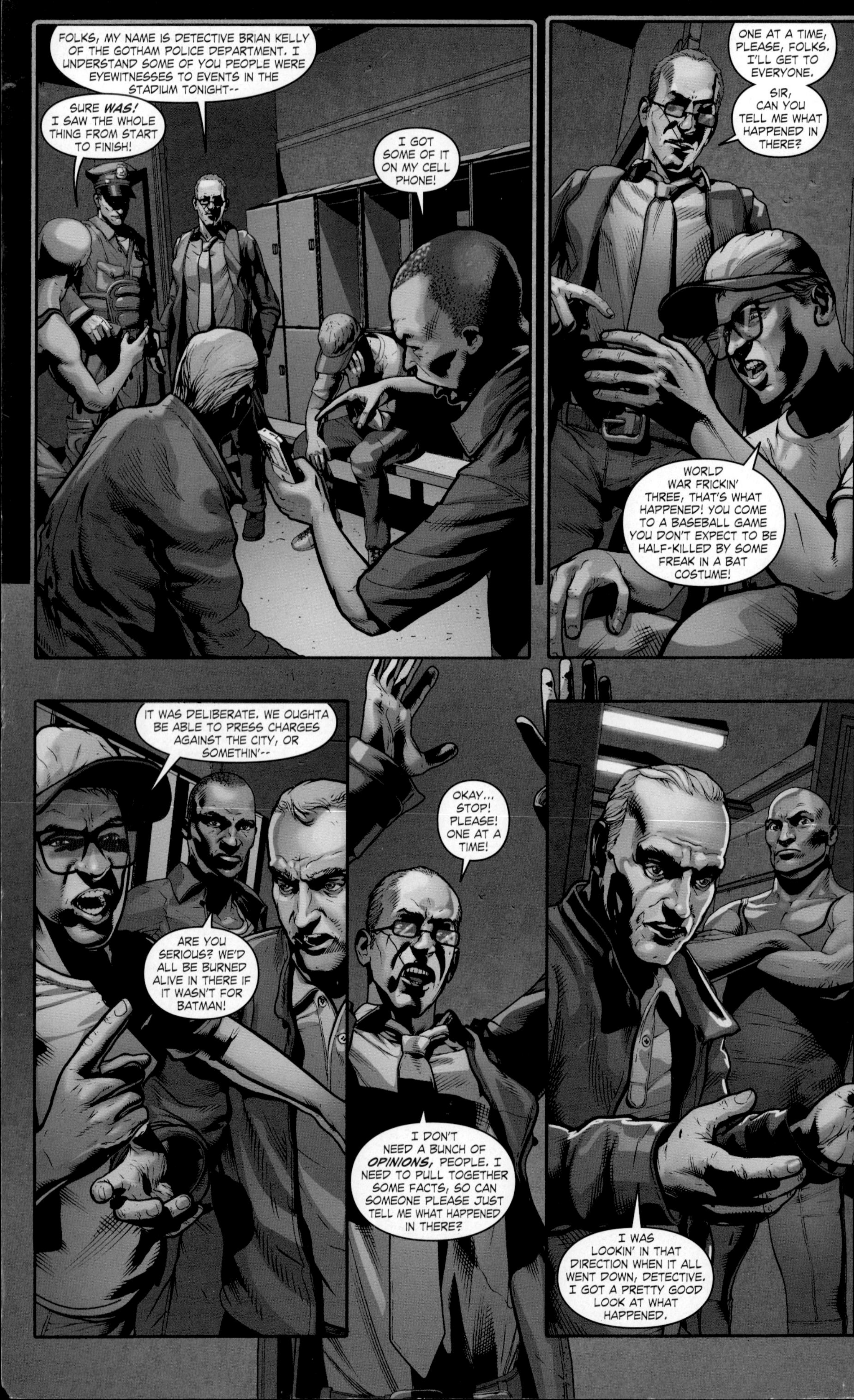

FOLKS, MY NAME IS DETECTIVE BRIAN KELLY OF THE GOTHAM POLICE DEPARTMENT. I UNDERSTAND SOME OF YOU PEOPLE WERE EYEWITNESSES TO EVENTS IN THE STADIUM TONIGHT--
SURE WAS! I SAW THE WHOLE THING FROM START TO FINISH!
I GOT SOME OF IT ON MY CELL PHONE!
ONE AT A TIME, PLEASE, FOLKS. I'LL GET TO EVERYONE.
SIR, CAN YOU TELL ME WHAT HAPPENED IN THERE?
WORLD WAR FRICKIN' THREE, THAT'S WHAT HAPPENED! YOU COME TO A BASEBALL GAME YOU DON'T EXPECT TO BE HALF-KILLED BY SOME FREAK IN A BAT COSTUME!
IT WAS DELIBERATE. WE OUGHTA BE ABLE TO PRESS CHARGES AGAINST THE CITY, OR SOMETHIN'--
ARE YOU SERIOUS? WE'D ALL BE BURNED ALIVE IN THERE IF IT WASN'T FOR BATMAN!
OKAY... STOP! PLEASE! ONE AT A TIME!
I DON'T NEED A BUNCH OF OPINIONS, PEOPLE. I NEED TO PULL TOGETHER SOME FACTS, SO CAN SOMEONE PLEASE JUST TELL ME WHAT HAPPENED IN THERE?
I WAS LOOKIN' IN THAT DIRECTION WHEN IT ALL WENT DOWN, DETECTIVE. I GOT A PRETTY GOOD LOOK AT WHAT HAPPENED.

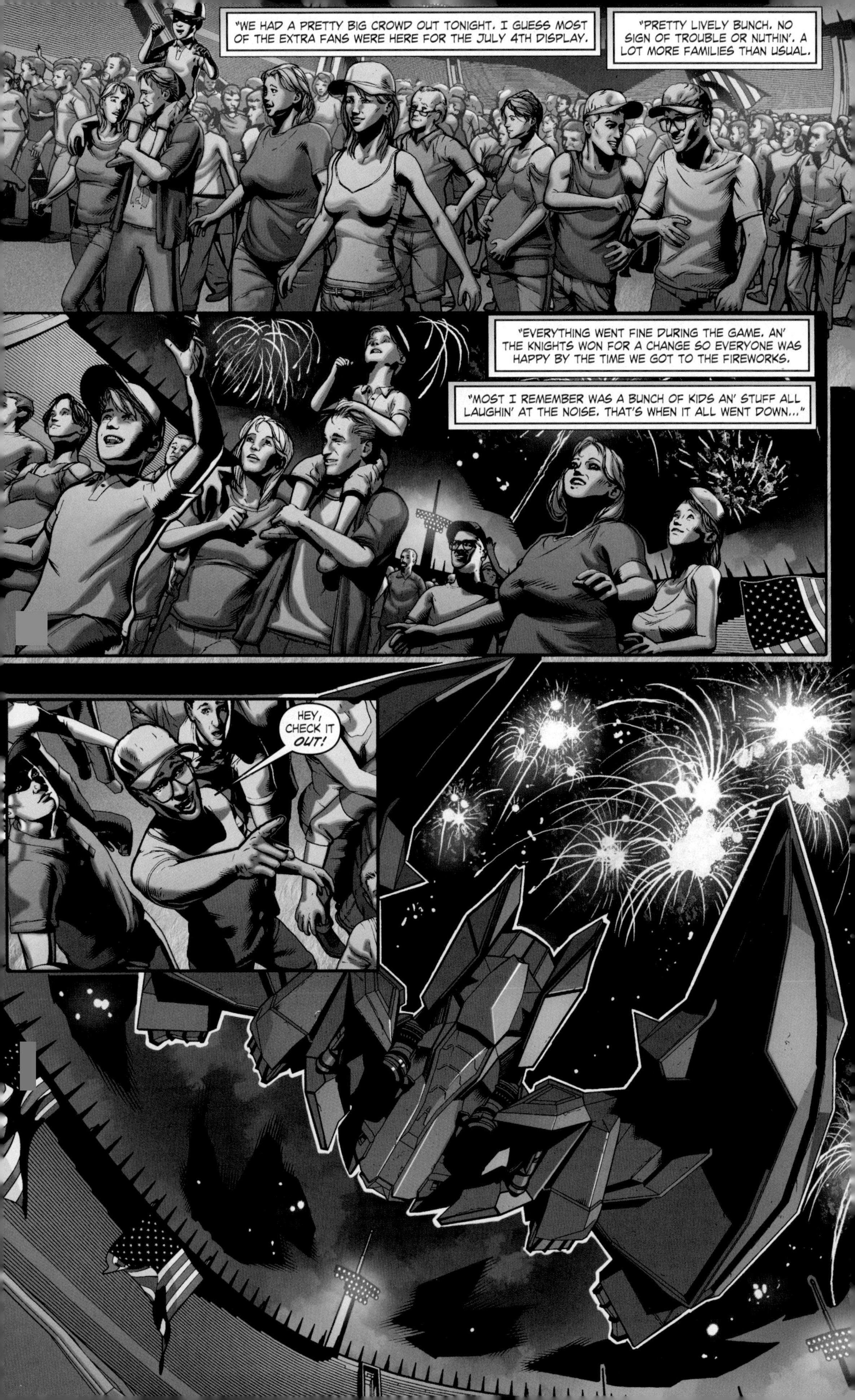
"WE HAD A PRETTY BIG CROWD OUT TONIGHT. I GUESS MOST OF THE EXTRA FANS WERE HERE FOR THE JULY 4TH DISPLAY.
"PRETTY LIVELY BUNCH. NO SIGN OF TROUBLE OR NUTHIN'. A LOT MORE FAMILIES THAN USUAL.
"EVERYTHING WENT FINE DURING THE GAME. AN' THE KNIGHTS WON FOR A CHANGE SO EVERYONE WAS HAPPY BY THE TIME WE GOT TO THE FIREWORKS.
"MOST I REMEMBER WAS A BUNCH OF KIDS AN' STUFF ALL LAUGHIN' AT THE NOISE. THAT'S WHEN IT ALL WENT DOWN..."
HEY, CHECK IT OUT!

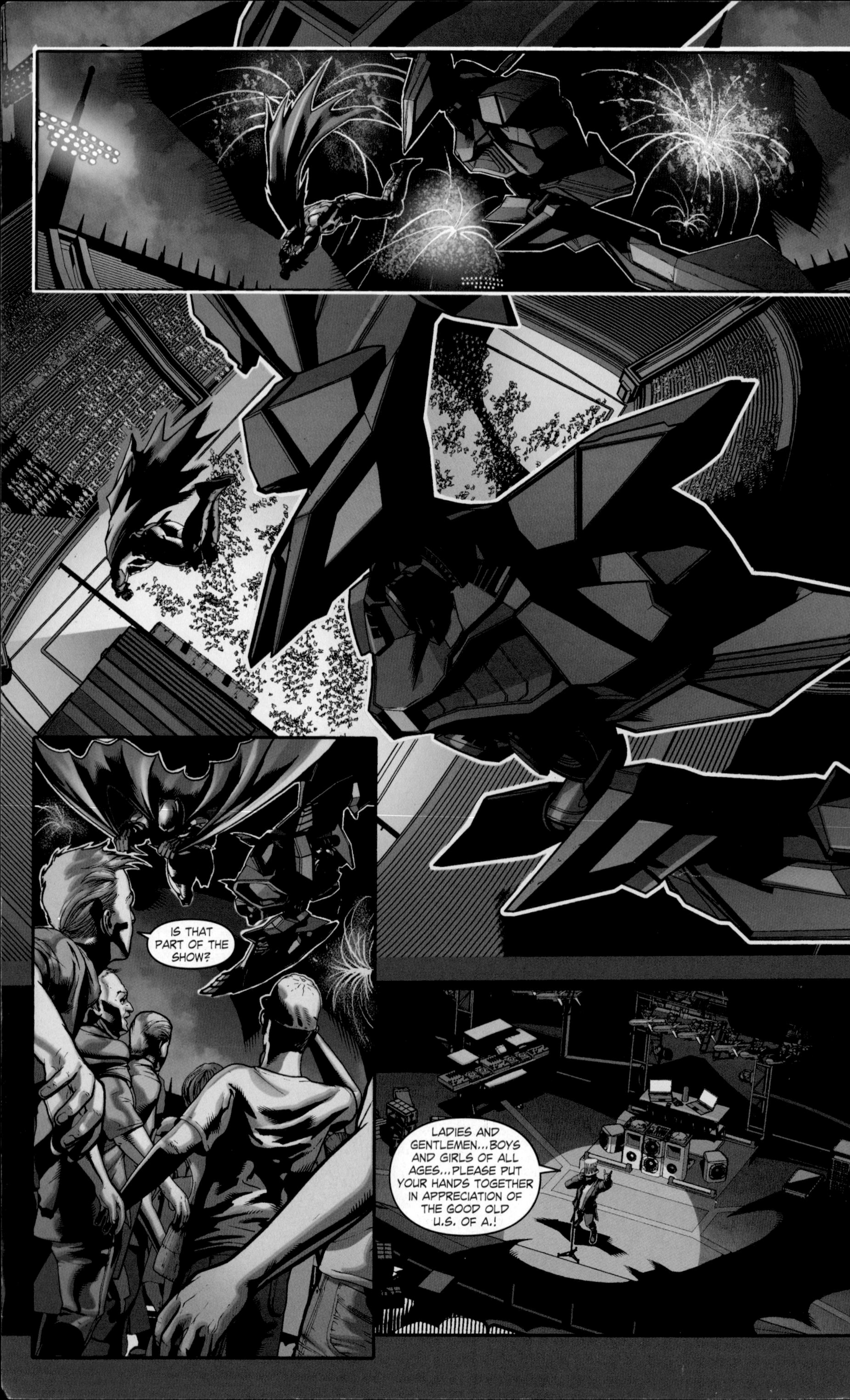
IS THAT PART OF THE SHOW?
LADIES AND GENTLEMEN...BOYS AND GIRLS OF ALL AGES...PLEASE PUT YOUR HANDS TOGETHER IN APPRECIATION OF THE GOOD OLD U.S. OF A.!

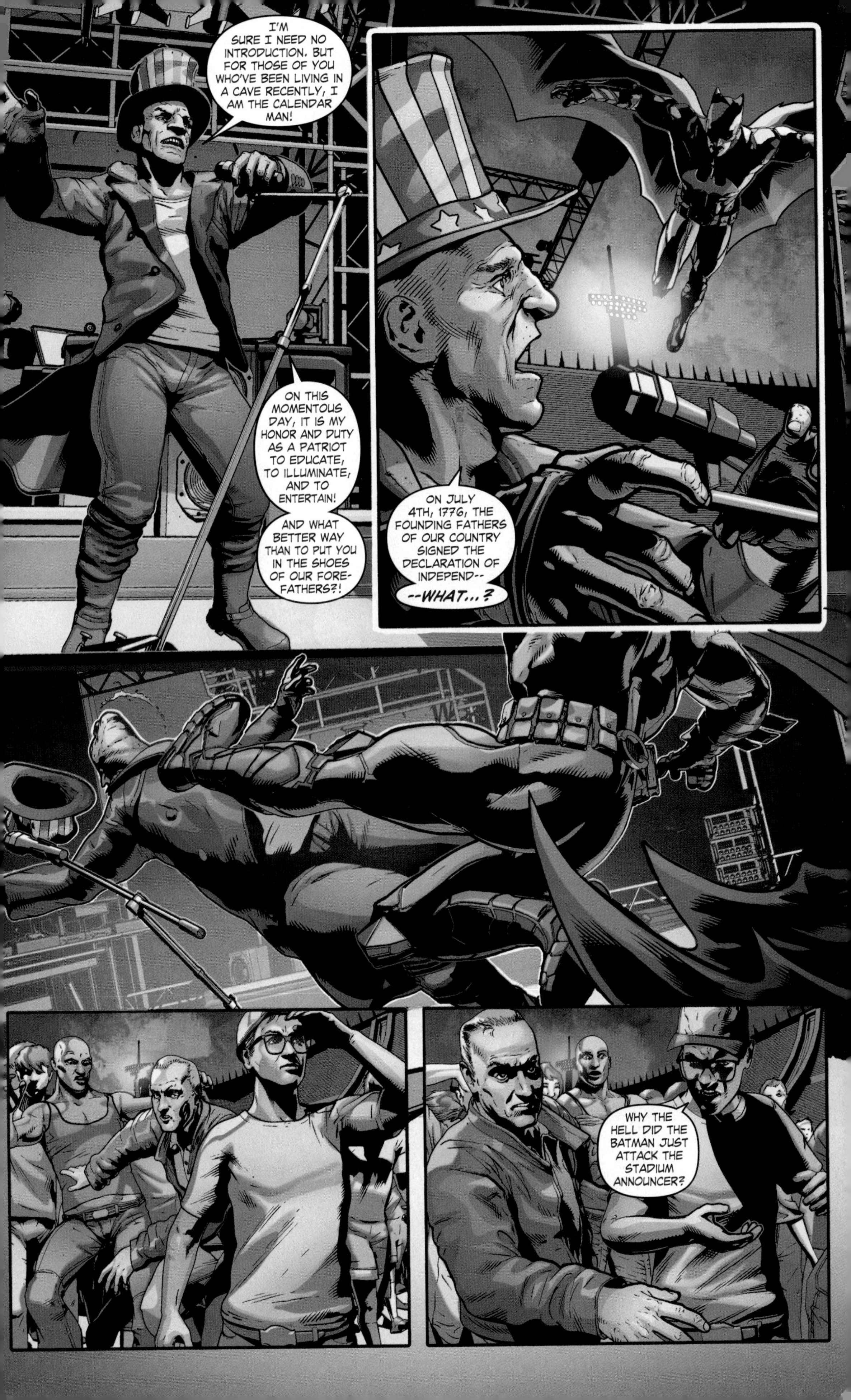
I'M SURE I NEED NO INTRODUCTION. BUT FOR THOSE OF YOU WHO'VE BEEN LIVING IN A CAVE RECENTLY, I AM THE CALENDAR MAN!
ON THIS MOMENTOUS DAY, IT IS MY HONOR AND DUTY AS A PATRIOT TO EDUCATE, TO ILLUMINATE, AND TO ENTERTAIN!
AND WHAT BETTER WAY THAN TO PUT YOU IN THE SHOES OF OUR FORE-FATHERS?!
ON JULY 4TH, 1776, THE FOUNDING FATHERS OF OUR COUNTRY SIGNED THE DECLARATION OF INDEPEND--
--WHAT...?
WHY THE HELL DID THE BATMAN JUST ATTACK THE STADIUM ANNOUNCER?

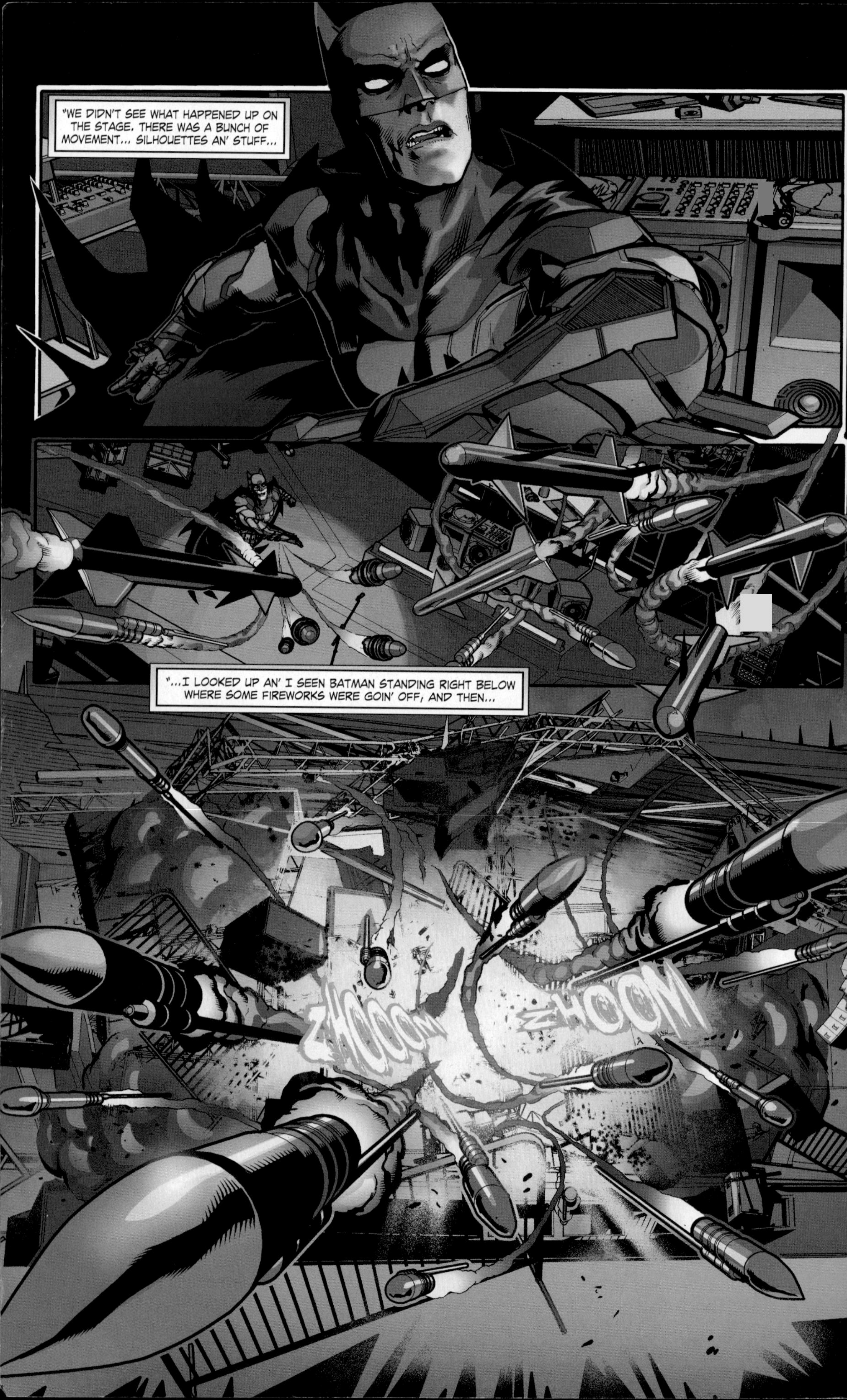
"WE DIDN'T SEE WHAT HAPPENED UP ON THE STAGE. THERE WAS A BUNCH OF MOVEMENT... SILHOUETTES AN' STUFF...
"...I LOOKED UP AN' I SEEN BATMAN STANDING RIGHT BELOW WHERE SOME FIREWORKS WERE GOIN' OFF, AND THEN...
ZHOOOM
ZHOOM

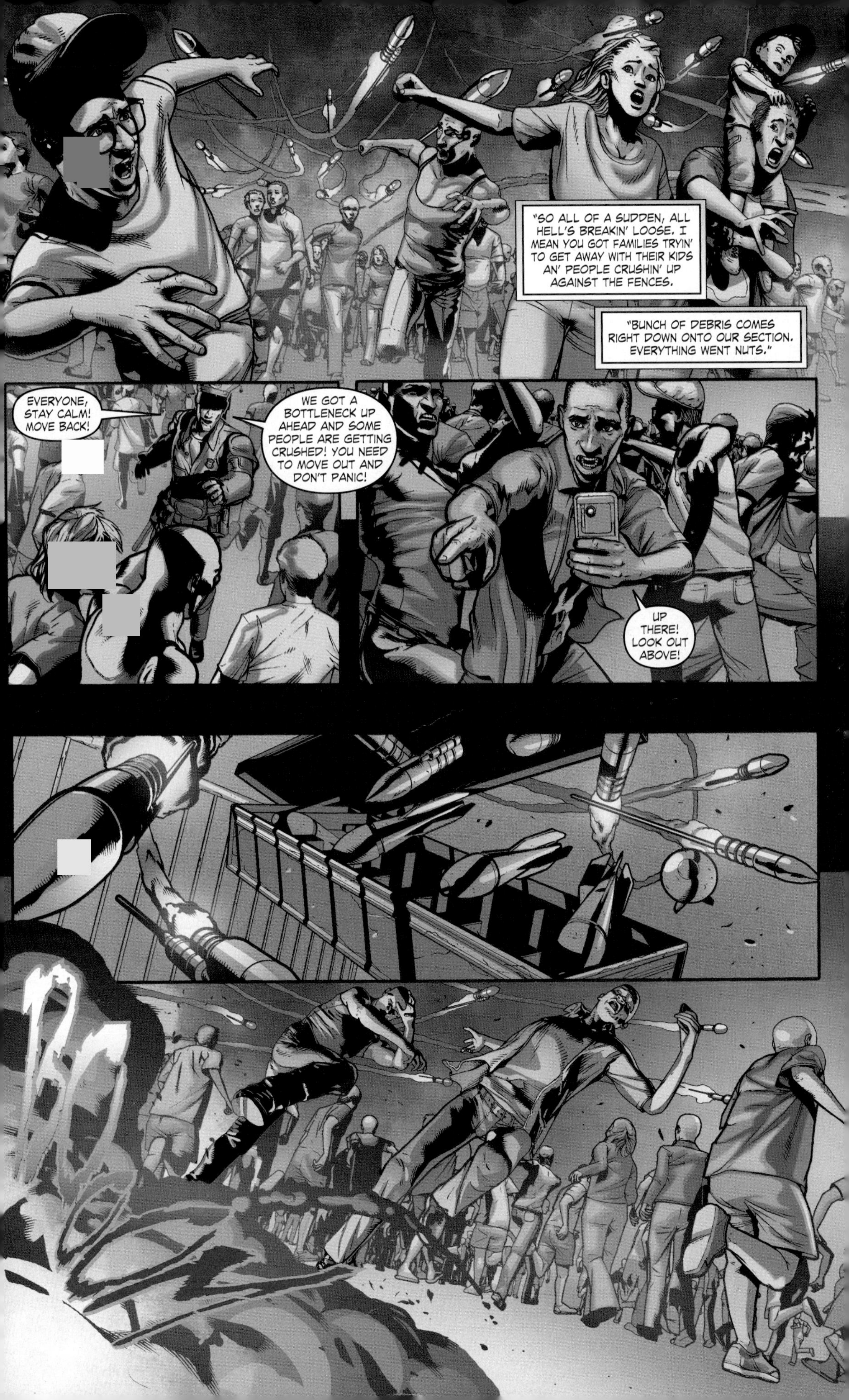
"SO ALL OF A SUDDEN, ALL HELL'S BREAKIN' LOOSE. I MEAN YOU GOT FAMILIES TRYIN' TO GET AWAY WITH THEIR KIDS AN' PEOPLE CRUSHIN' UP AGAINST THE FENCES.
"BUNCH OF DEBRIS COMES RIGHT DOWN ONTO OUR SECTION. EVERYTHING WENT NUTS."
EVERYONE, STAY CALM! MOVE BACK!
WE GOT A BOTTLENECK UP AHEAD AND SOME PEOPLE ARE GETTING CRUSHED! YOU NEED TO MOVE OUT AND DON'T PANIC!
UP THERE! LOOK OUT ABOVE!

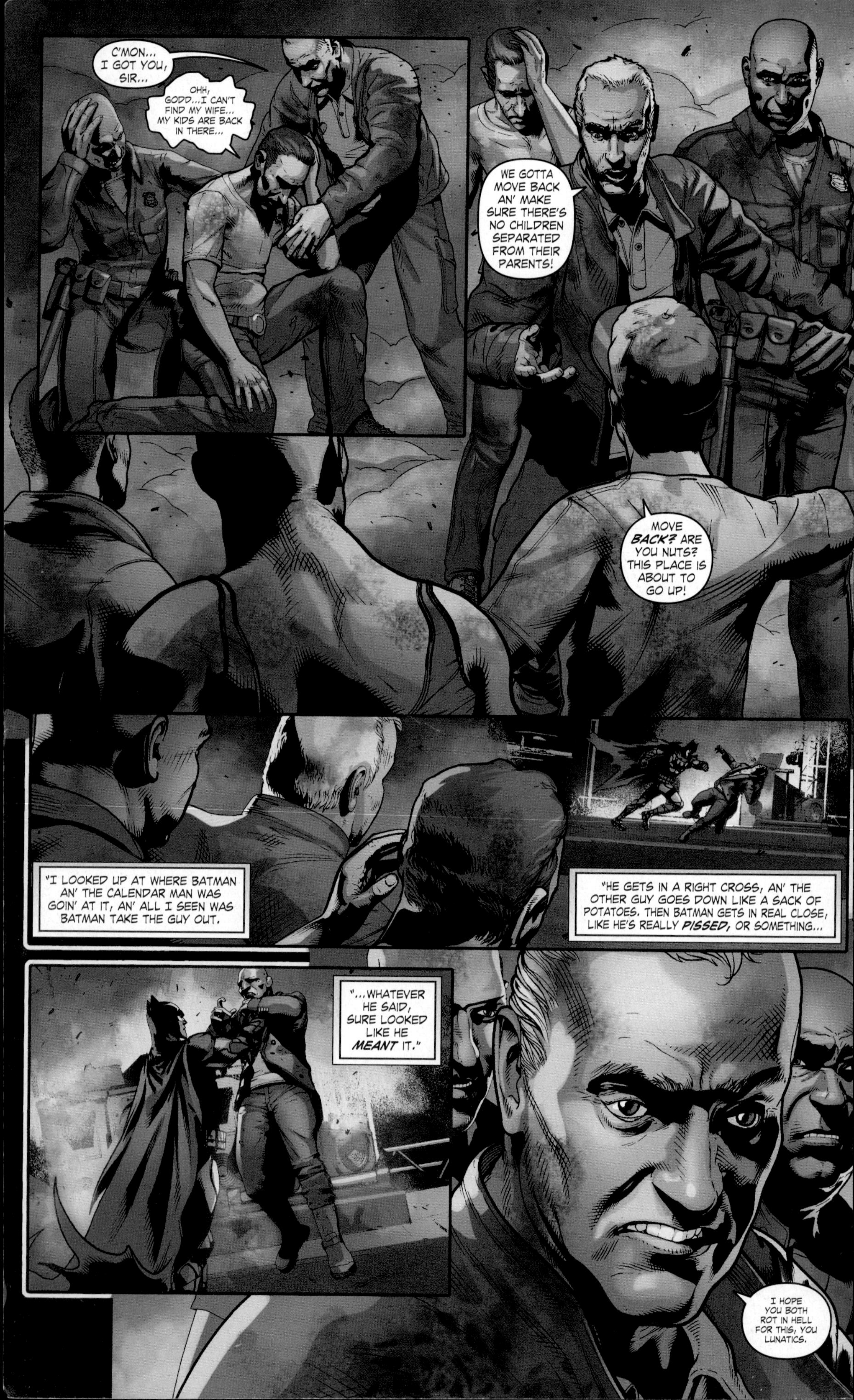
C'MON... I GOT YOU, SIR...
OHH, GODD...I CAN'T FIND MY WIFE... MY KIDS ARE BACK IN THERE...
WE GOTTA MOVE BACK AN' MAKE SURE THERE'S NO CHILDREN SEPARATED FROM THEIR PARENTS!
MOVE BACK? ARE YOU NUTS? THIS PLACE IS ABOUT TO GO UP!
"I LOOKED UP AT WHERE BATMAN AN' THE CALENDAR MAN WAS GOIN' AT IT, AN' ALL I SEEN WAS BATMAN TAKE THE GUY OUT.
"HE GETS IN A RIGHT CROSS, AN' THE OTHER GUY GOES DOWN LIKE A SACK OF POTATOES. THEN BATMAN GETS IN REAL CLOSE, LIKE HE'S REALLY PISSED, OR SOMETHING...
"...WHATEVER HE SAID, SURE LOOKED LIKE HE MEANT IT."
I HOPE YOU BOTH ROT IN HELL FOR THIS, YOU LUNATICS.

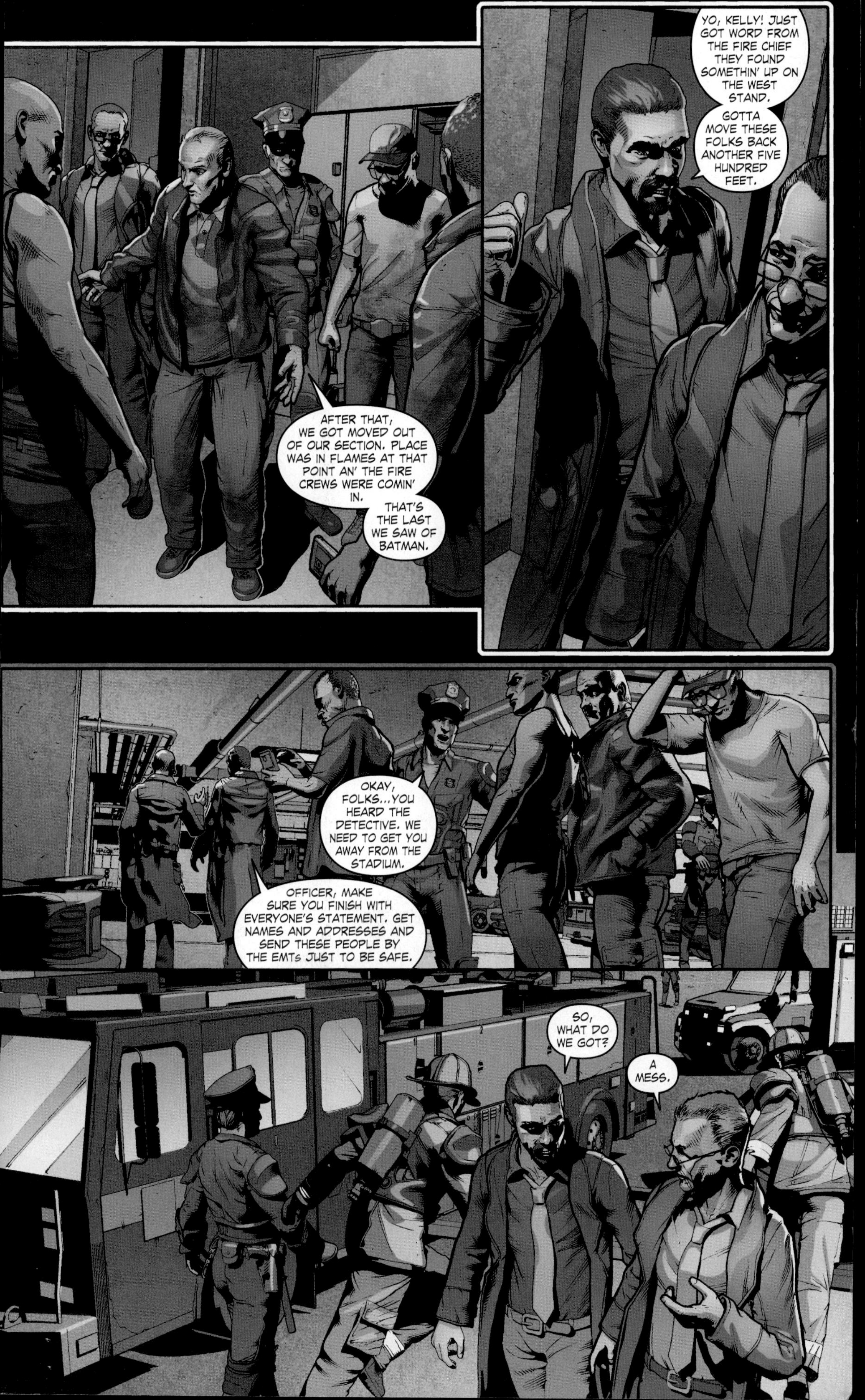
AFTER THAT, WE GOT MOVED OUT OF OUR SECTION. PLACE WAS IN FLAMES AT THAT POINT AN' THE FIRE CREWS WERE COMIN' IN.
THAT'S THE LAST WE SAW OF BATMAN.
YO, KELLY! JUST GOT WORD FROM THE FIRE CHIEF THEY FOUND SOMETHIN' UP ON THE WEST STAND.
GOTTA MOVE THESE FOLKS BACK ANOTHER FIVE HUNDRED FEET.
OKAY, FOLKS...YOU HEARD THE DETECTIVE. WE NEED TO GET YOU AWAY FROM THE STADIUM.
OFFICER, MAKE SURE YOU FINISH WITH EVERYONE'S STATEMENT. GET NAMES AND ADDRESSES AND SEND THESE PEOPLE BY THE EMTs JUST TO BE SAFE.
SO, WHAT DO WE GOT?
A MESS.

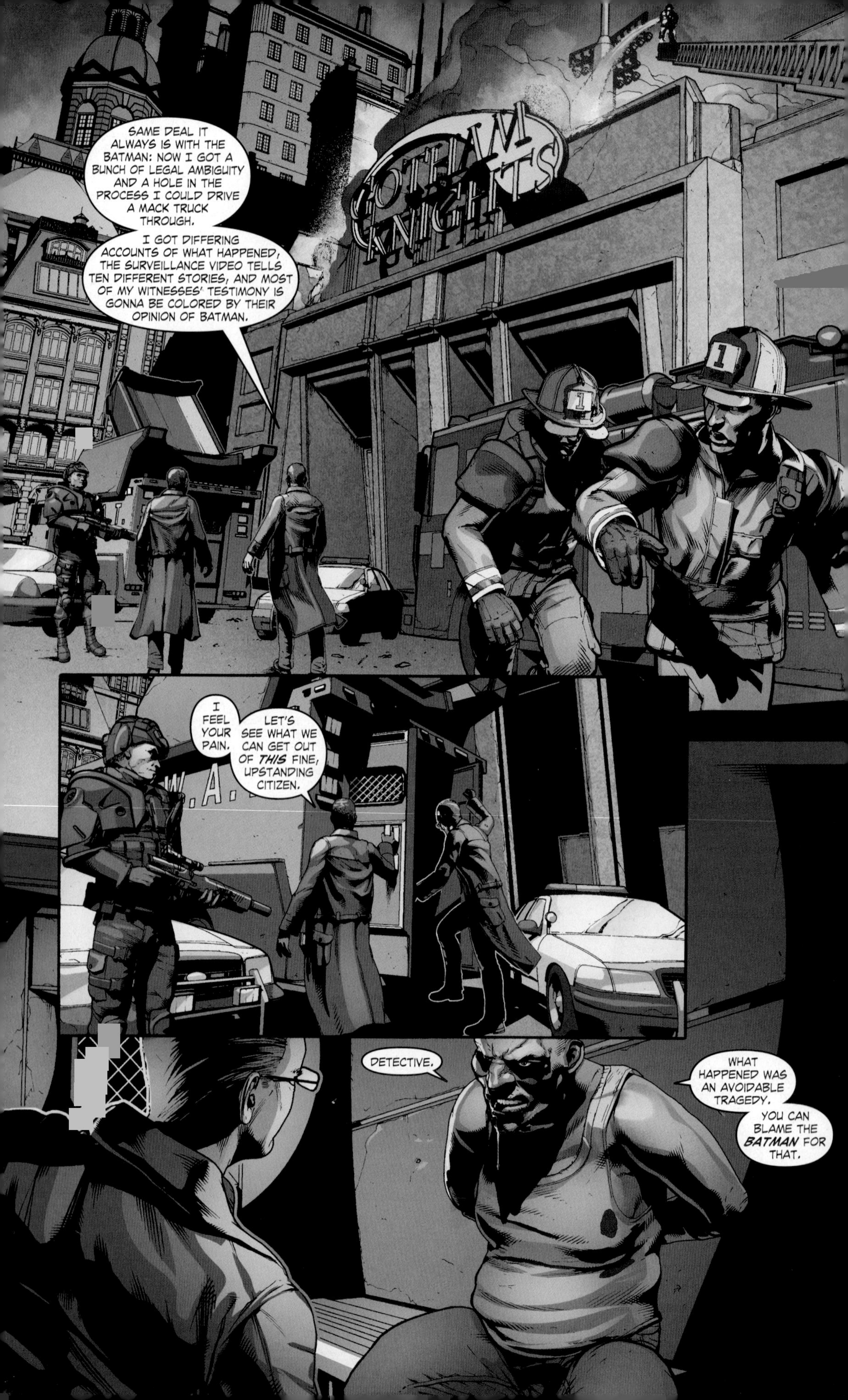
SAME DEAL IT ALWAYS IS WITH THE BATMAN: NOW I GOT A BUNCH OF LEGAL AMBIGUITY AND A HOLE IN THE PROCESS I COULD DRIVE A MACK TRUCK THROUGH.
I GOT DIFFERING ACCOUNTS OF WHAT HAPPENED, THE SURVEILLANCE VIDEO TELLS TEN DIFFERENT STORIES, AND MOST OF MY WITNESSES' TESTIMONY IS GONNA BE COLORED BY THEIR OPINION OF BATMAN.
GOTHAM KNIGHTS
I FEEL YOUR PAIN.
LET'S SEE WHAT WE CAN GET OUT OF *THIS* FINE, UPSTANDING CITIZEN.
DETECTIVE.
WHAT HAPPENED WAS AN AVOIDABLE TRAGEDY.
YOU CAN BLAME THE ***BATMAN*** FOR THAT.

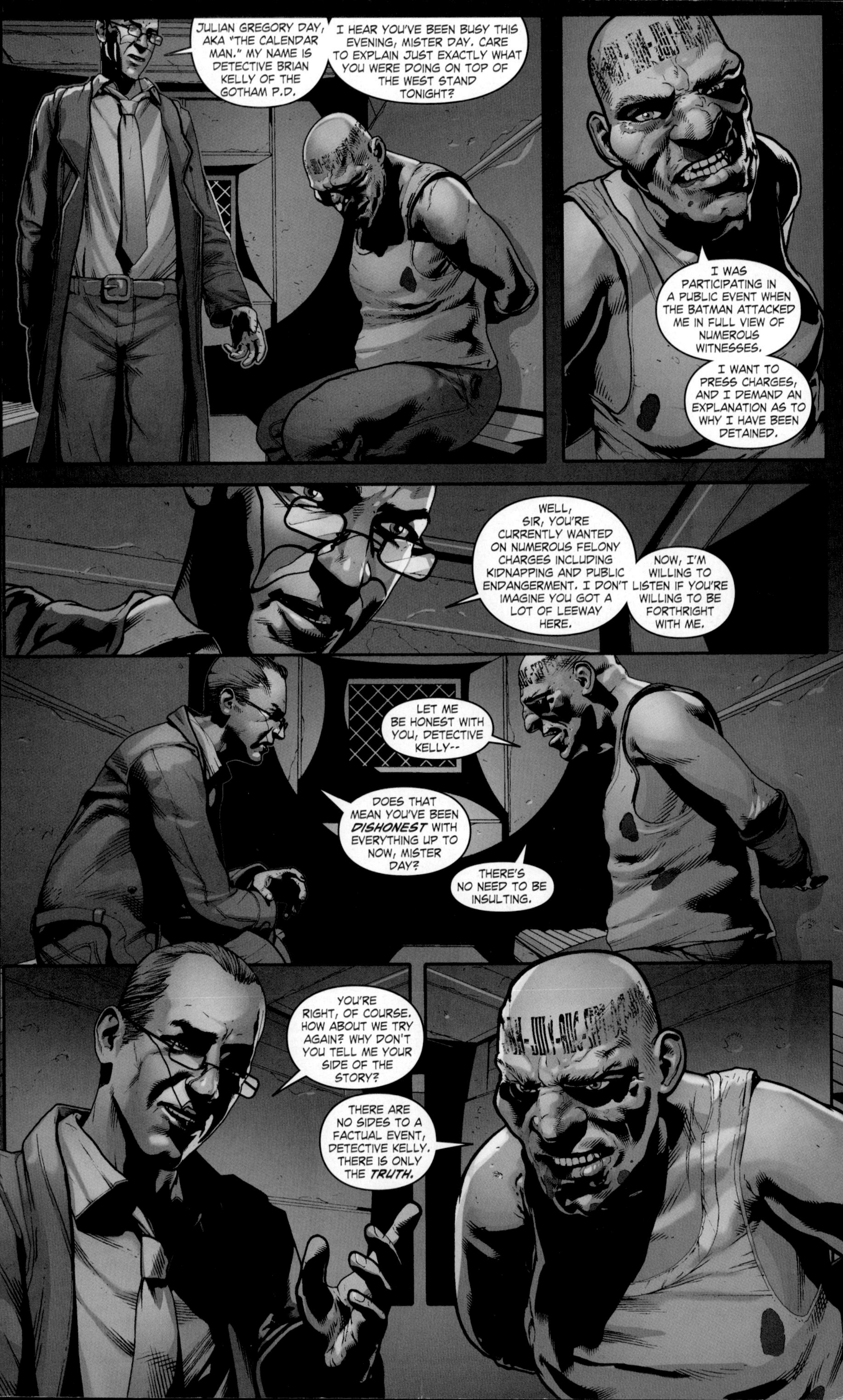
JULIAN GREGORY DAY, AKA "THE CALENDAR MAN." MY NAME IS DETECTIVE BRIAN KELLY OF THE GOTHAM P.D.
I HEAR YOU'VE BEEN BUSY THIS EVENING, MISTER DAY. CARE TO EXPLAIN JUST EXACTLY WHAT YOU WERE DOING ON TOP OF THE WEST STAND TONIGHT?
I WAS PARTICIPATING IN A PUBLIC EVENT WHEN THE BATMAN ATTACKED ME IN FULL VIEW OF NUMEROUS WITNESSES.
I WANT TO PRESS CHARGES, AND I DEMAND AN EXPLANATION AS TO WHY I HAVE BEEN DETAINED.
WELL, SIR, YOU'RE CURRENTLY WANTED ON NUMEROUS FELONY CHARGES INCLUDING KIDNAPPING AND PUBLIC ENDANGERMENT. I DON'T IMAGINE YOU GOT A LOT OF LEEWAY HERE.
NOW, I'M WILLING TO LISTEN IF YOU'RE WILLING TO BE FORTHRIGHT WITH ME.
LET ME BE HONEST WITH YOU, DETECTIVE KELLY--
DOES THAT MEAN YOU'VE BEEN DISHONEST WITH EVERYTHING UP TO NOW, MISTER DAY?
THERE'S NO NEED TO BE INSULTING.
YOU'RE RIGHT, OF COURSE. HOW ABOUT WE TRY AGAIN? WHY DON'T YOU TELL ME YOUR SIDE OF THE STORY?
THERE ARE NO SIDES TO A FACTUAL EVENT, DETECTIVE KELLY. THERE IS ONLY THE TRUTH.

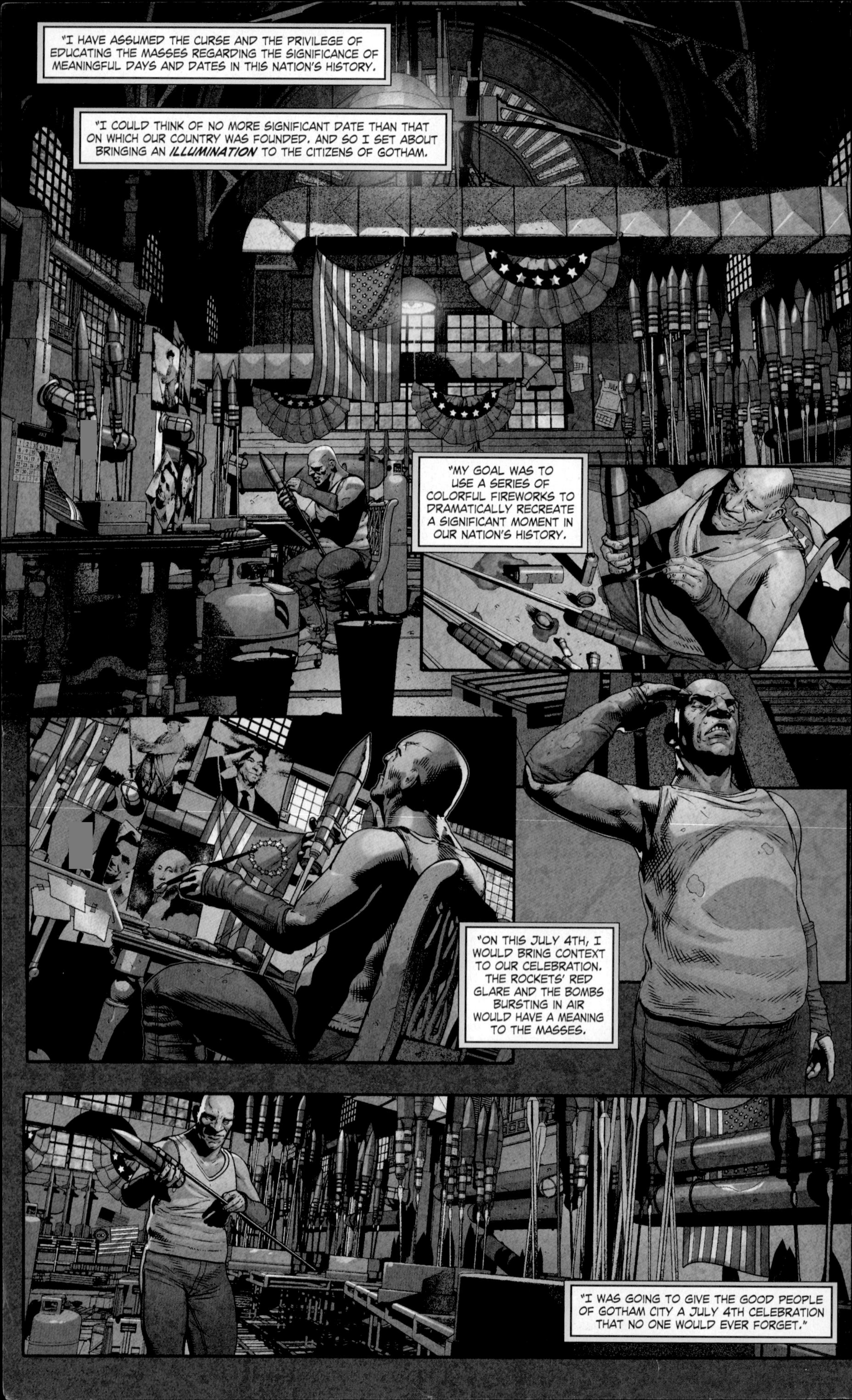
"I HAVE ASSUMED THE CURSE AND THE PRIVILEGE OF EDUCATING THE MASSES REGARDING THE SIGNIFICANCE OF MEANINGFUL DAYS AND DATES IN THIS NATION'S HISTORY.
"I COULD THINK OF NO MORE SIGNIFICANT DATE THAN THAT ON WHICH OUR COUNTRY WAS FOUNDED. AND SO I SET ABOUT BRINGING AN *ILLUMINATION* TO THE CITIZENS OF GOTHAM.
"MY GOAL WAS TO USE A SERIES OF COLORFUL FIREWORKS TO DRAMATICALLY RECREATE A SIGNIFICANT MOMENT IN OUR NATION'S HISTORY.
"ON THIS JULY 4TH, I WOULD BRING CONTEXT TO OUR CELEBRATION. THE ROCKETS' RED GLARE AND THE BOMBS BURSTING IN AIR WOULD HAVE A MEANING TO THE MASSES.
"I WAS GOING TO GIVE THE GOOD PEOPLE OF GOTHAM CITY A JULY 4TH CELEBRATION THAT NO ONE WOULD EVER FORGET."

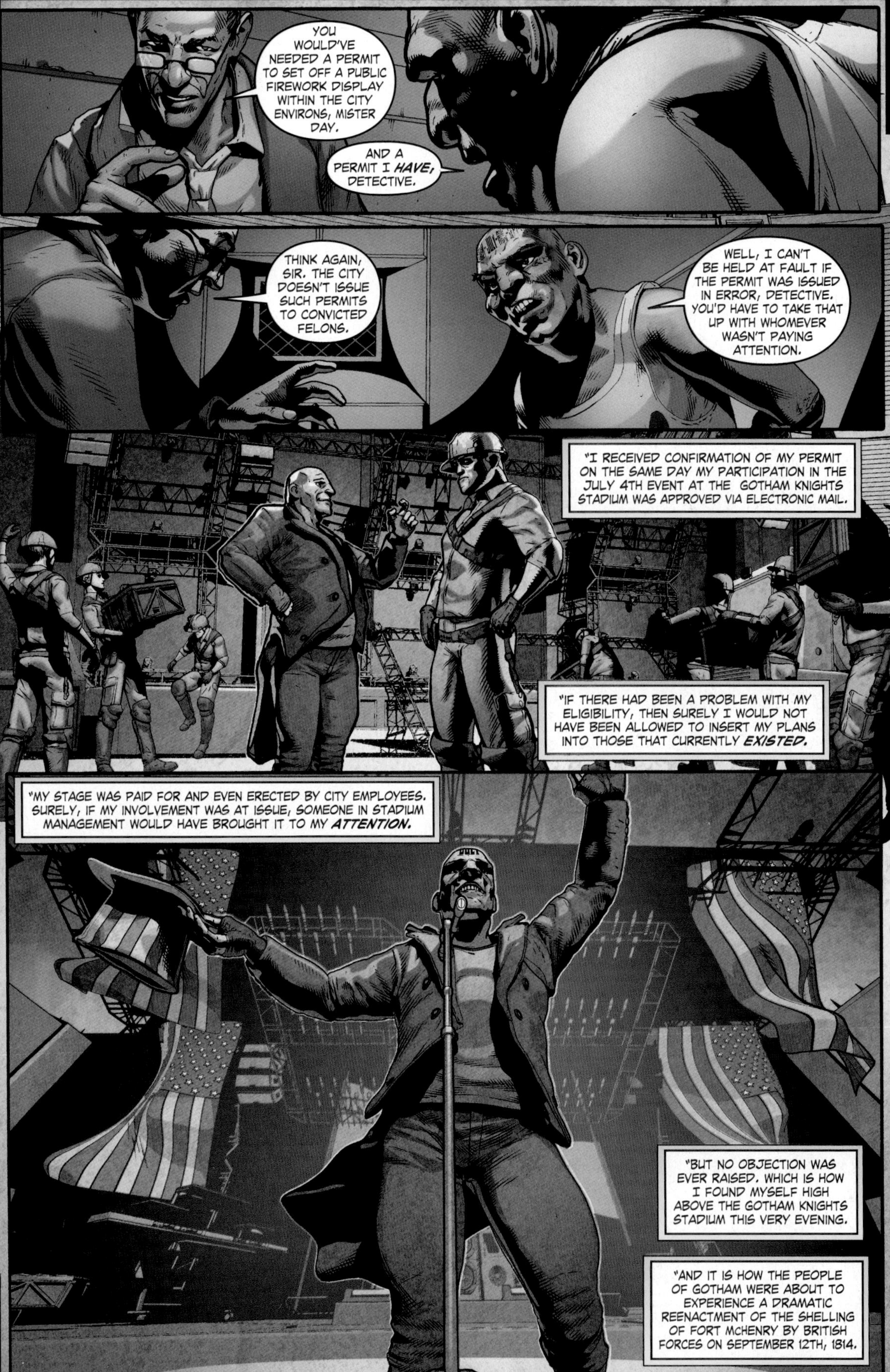
YOU WOULD'VE NEEDED A PERMIT TO SET OFF A PUBLIC FIREWORK DISPLAY WITHIN THE CITY ENVIRONS, MISTER DAY.
AND A PERMIT I *HAVE,* DETECTIVE.
THINK AGAIN, SIR. THE CITY DOESN'T ISSUE SUCH PERMITS TO CONVICTED FELONS.
WELL, I CAN'T BE HELD AT FAULT IF THE PERMIT WAS ISSUED IN ERROR, DETECTIVE. YOU'D HAVE TO TAKE THAT UP WITH WHOMEVER WASN'T PAYING ATTENTION.
"I RECEIVED CONFIRMATION OF MY PERMIT ON THE SAME DAY MY PARTICIPATION IN THE JULY 4TH EVENT AT THE GOTHAM KNIGHTS STADIUM WAS APPROVED VIA ELECTRONIC MAIL.
"IF THERE HAD BEEN A PROBLEM WITH MY ELIGIBILITY, THEN SURELY I WOULD NOT HAVE BEEN ALLOWED TO INSERT MY PLANS INTO THOSE THAT CURRENTLY *EXISTED.*
"MY STAGE WAS PAID FOR AND EVEN ERECTED BY CITY EMPLOYEES. SURELY, IF MY INVOLVEMENT WAS AT ISSUE, SOMEONE IN STADIUM MANAGEMENT WOULD HAVE BROUGHT IT TO MY *ATTENTION.*
"BUT NO OBJECTION WAS EVER RAISED. WHICH IS HOW I FOUND MYSELF HIGH ABOVE THE GOTHAM KNIGHTS STADIUM THIS VERY EVENING.
"AND IT IS HOW THE PEOPLE OF GOTHAM WERE ABOUT TO EXPERIENCE A DRAMATIC REENACTMENT OF THE SHELLING OF FORT MCHENRY BY BRITISH FORCES ON SEPTEMBER 12TH, 1814.

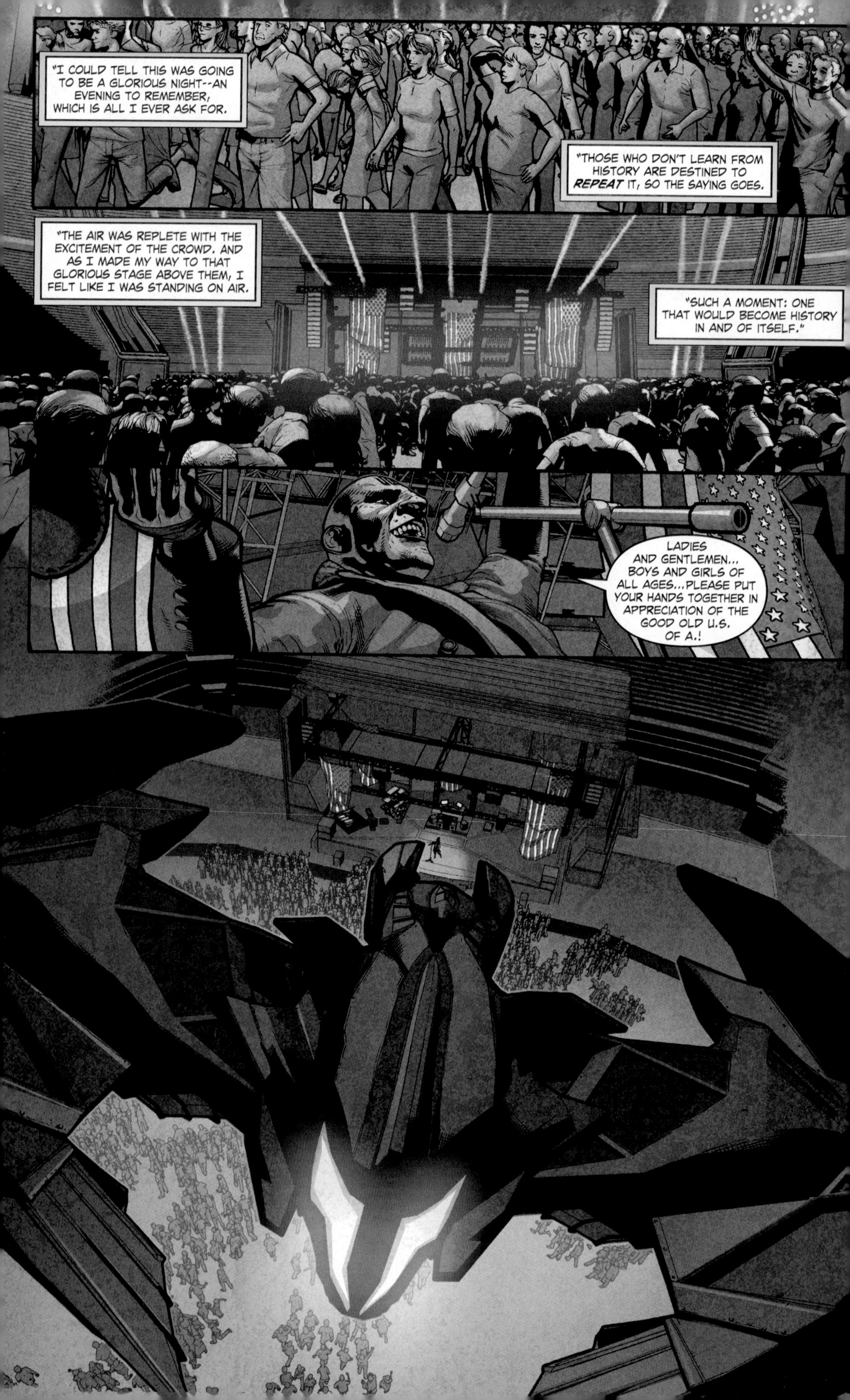
"I COULD TELL THIS WAS GOING TO BE A GLORIOUS NIGHT--AN EVENING TO REMEMBER, WHICH IS ALL I EVER ASK FOR.
"THOSE WHO DON'T LEARN FROM HISTORY ARE DESTINED TO REPEAT IT, SO THE SAYING GOES.
"THE AIR WAS REPLETE WITH THE EXCITEMENT OF THE CROWD. AND AS I MADE MY WAY TO THAT GLORIOUS STAGE ABOVE THEM, I FELT LIKE I WAS STANDING ON AIR.
"SUCH A MOMENT: ONE THAT WOULD BECOME HISTORY IN AND OF ITSELF."
LADIES AND GENTLEMEN... BOYS AND GIRLS OF ALL AGES...PLEASE PUT YOUR HANDS TOGETHER IN APPRECIATION OF THE GOOD OLD U.S. OF A.!

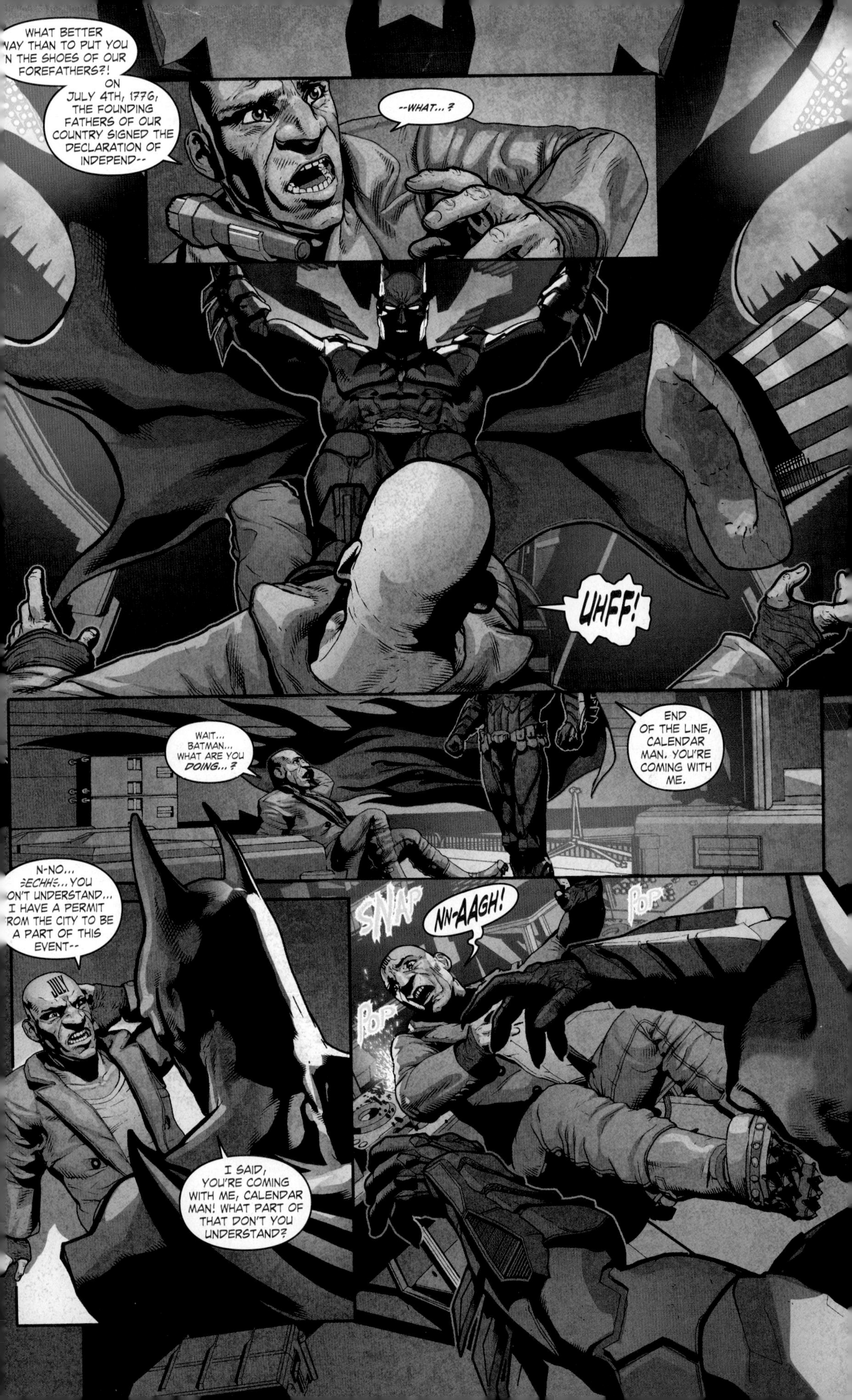

WHAT BETTER WAY THAN TO PUT YOU IN THE SHOES OF OUR FOREFATHERS?!
ON JULY 4TH, 1776, THE FOUNDING FATHERS OF OUR COUNTRY SIGNED THE DECLARATION OF INDEPEND--
--WHAT...?
UHFF!
WAIT... BATMAN... WHAT ARE YOU *DOING*...?
END OF THE LINE, CALENDAR MAN. YOU'RE COMING WITH ME.
N-NO... ECHHS... YOU ON'T UNDERSTAND... I HAVE A PERMIT ROM THE CITY TO BE A PART OF THIS EVENT--
I SAID, YOU'RE COMING WITH ME, CALENDAR MAN! WHAT PART OF THAT DON'T YOU UNDERSTAND?
SNAP
NN-AAGH!
POP
POP
JULY

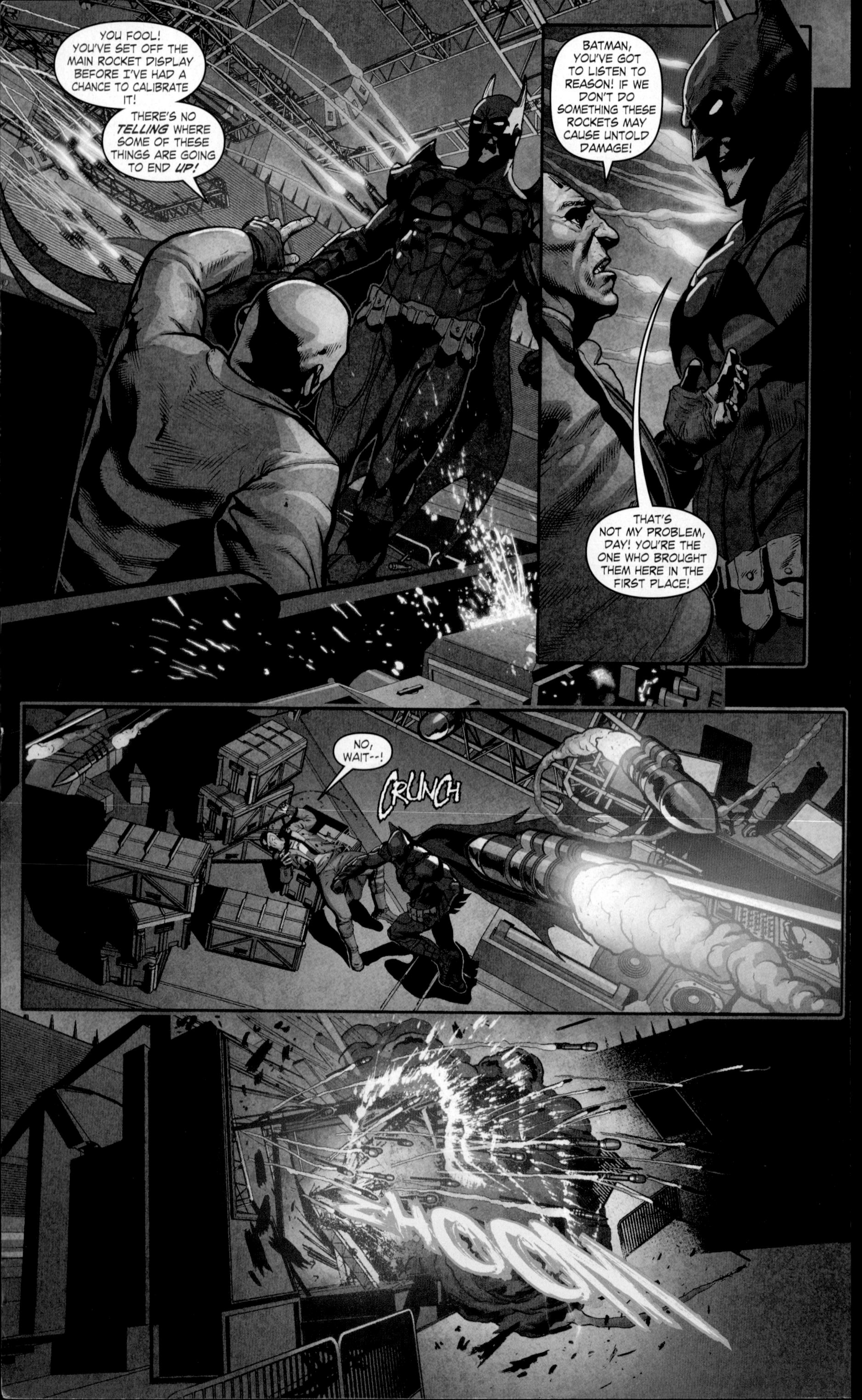
YOU FOOL! YOU'VE SET OFF THE MAIN ROCKET DISPLAY BEFORE I'VE HAD A CHANCE TO CALIBRATE IT!
THERE'S NO TELLING WHERE SOME OF THESE THINGS ARE GOING TO END UP!
BATMAN, YOU'VE GOT TO LISTEN TO REASON! IF WE DON'T DO SOMETHING THESE ROCKETS MAY CAUSE UNTOLD DAMAGE!
THAT'S NOT MY PROBLEM, DAY! YOU'RE THE ONE WHO BROUGHT THEM HERE IN THE FIRST PLACE!
NO, WAIT--!
CRUNCH
ZHOOM

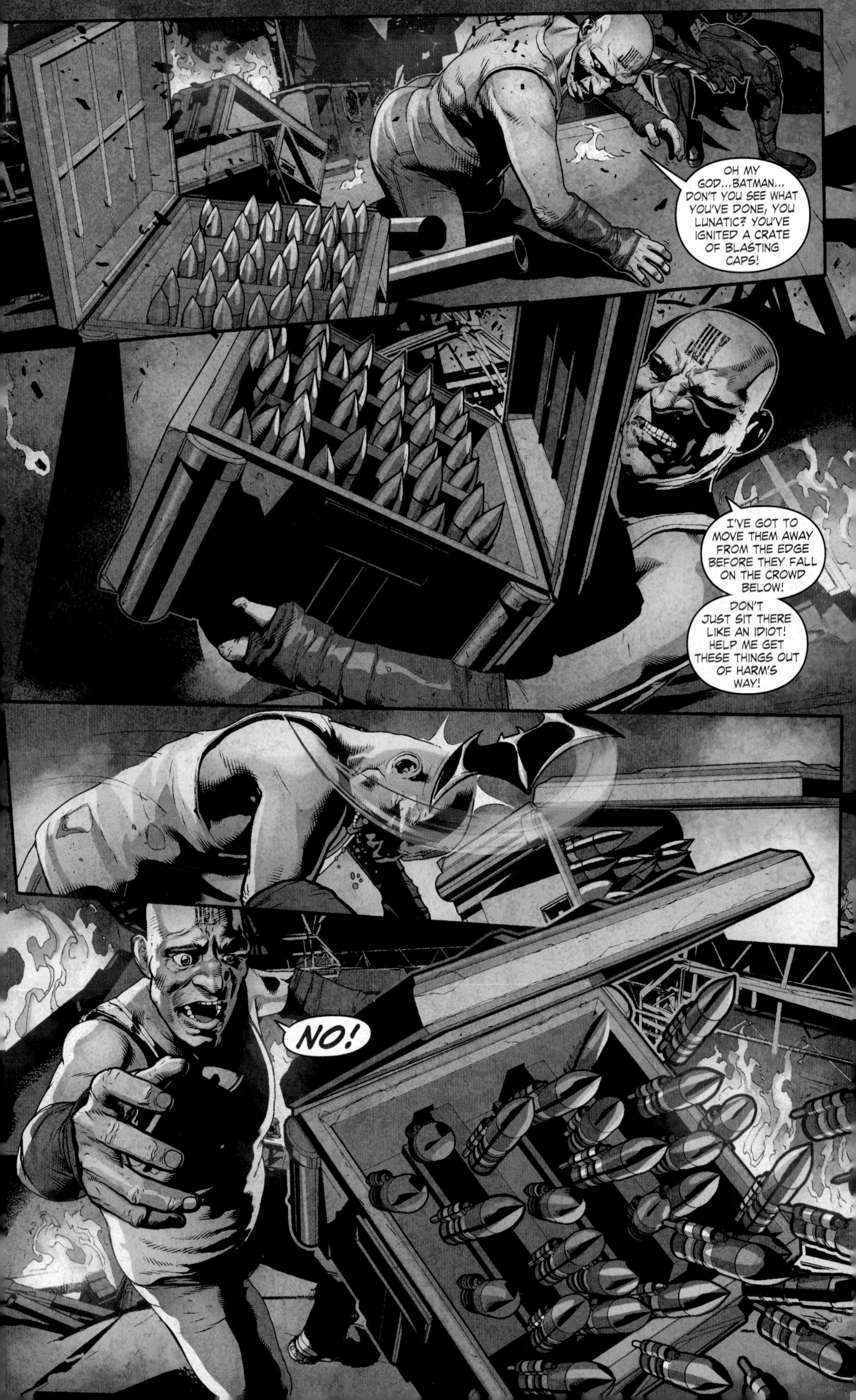
OH MY GOD...BATMAN... DON'T YOU SEE WHAT YOU'VE DONE, YOU LUNATIC? YOU'VE IGNITED A CRATE OF BLASTING CAPS!
I'VE GOT TO MOVE THEM AWAY FROM THE EDGE BEFORE THEY FALL ON THE CROWD BELOW!
DON'T JUST SIT THERE LIKE AN IDIOT! HELP ME GET THESE THINGS OUT OF HARM'S WAY!
NO!

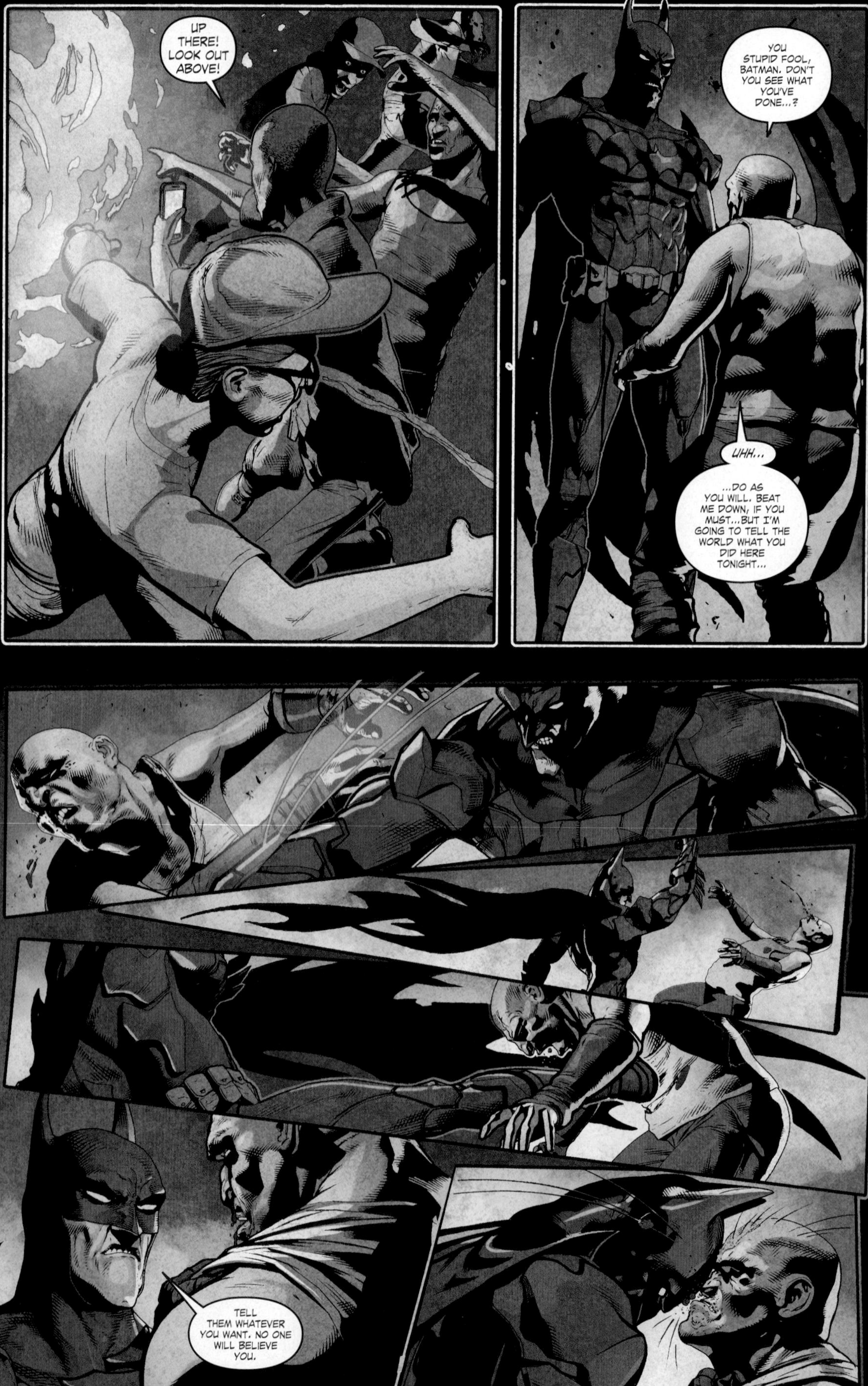
UP THERE! LOOK OUT ABOVE!
YOU STUPID FOOL, BATMAN. DON'T YOU SEE WHAT YOU'VE DONE...?
UHH...
...DO AS YOU WILL. BEAT ME DOWN, IF YOU MUST...BUT I'M GOING TO TELL THE WORLD WHAT YOU DID HERE TONIGHT...
TELL THEM WHATEVER YOU WANT. NO ONE WILL BELIEVE YOU.

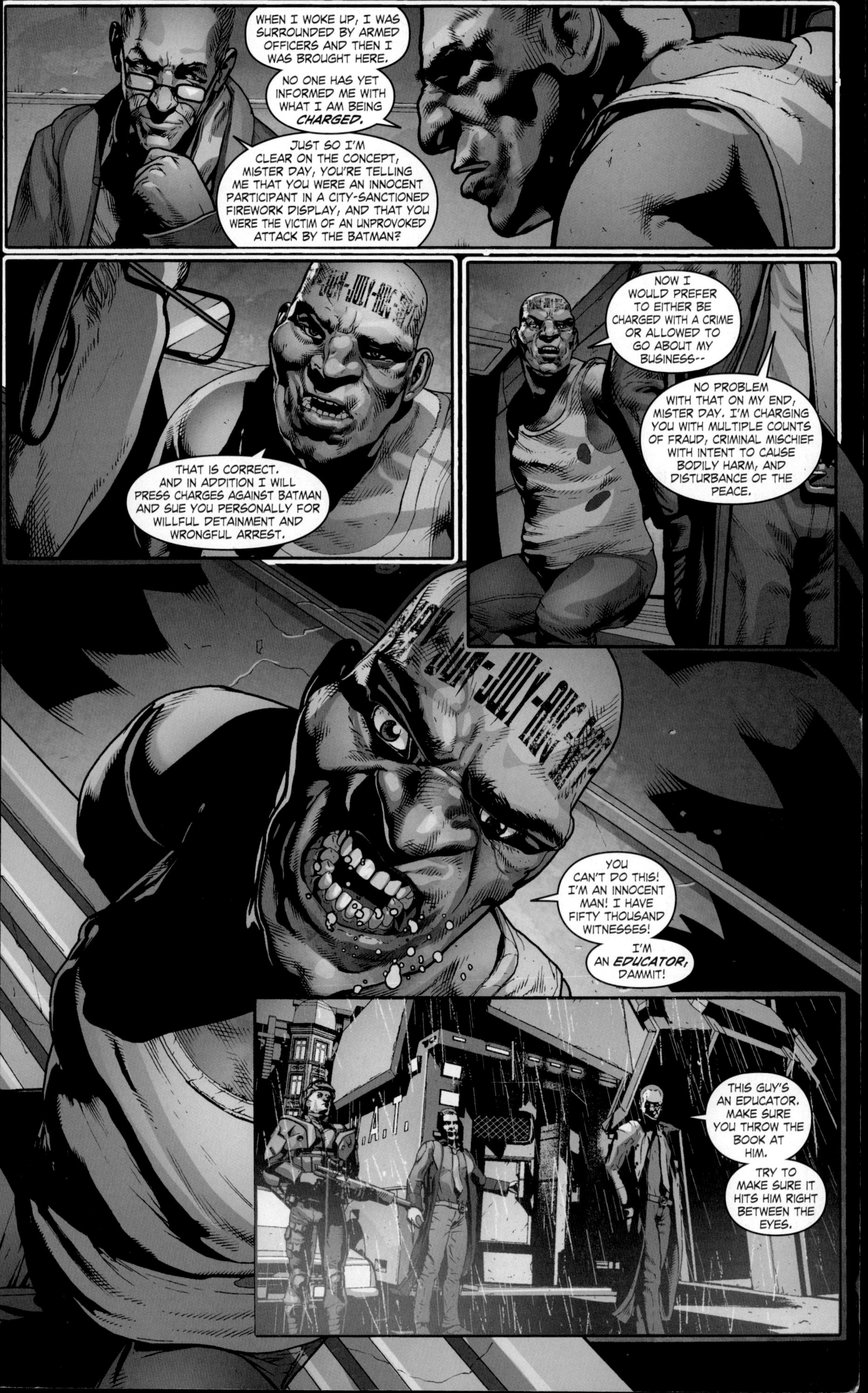
WHEN I WOKE UP, I WAS SURROUNDED BY ARMED OFFICERS AND THEN I WAS BROUGHT HERE.
NO ONE HAS YET INFORMED ME WITH WHAT I AM BEING *CHARGED.*
JUST SO I'M CLEAR ON THE CONCEPT, MISTER DAY, YOU'RE TELLING ME THAT YOU WERE AN INNOCENT PARTICIPANT IN A CITY-SANCTIONED FIREWORK DISPLAY, AND THAT YOU WERE THE VICTIM OF AN UNPROVOKED ATTACK BY THE BATMAN?
THAT IS CORRECT. AND IN ADDITION I WILL PRESS CHARGES AGAINST BATMAN AND SUE YOU PERSONALLY FOR WILLFUL DETAINMENT AND WRONGFUL ARREST.
NOW I WOULD PREFER TO EITHER BE CHARGED WITH A CRIME OR ALLOWED TO GO ABOUT MY BUSINESS--
NO PROBLEM WITH THAT ON MY END, MISTER DAY. I'M CHARGING YOU WITH MULTIPLE COUNTS OF FRAUD, CRIMINAL MISCHIEF WITH INTENT TO CAUSE BODILY HARM, AND DISTURBANCE OF THE PEACE.
YOU CAN'T DO THIS! I'M AN INNOCENT MAN! I HAVE FIFTY THOUSAND WITNESSES!
I'M AN *EDUCATOR,* DAMMIT!
THIS GUY'S AN EDUCATOR. MAKE SURE YOU THROW THE BOOK AT HIM.
TRY TO MAKE SURE IT HITS HIM RIGHT BETWEEN THE EYES.

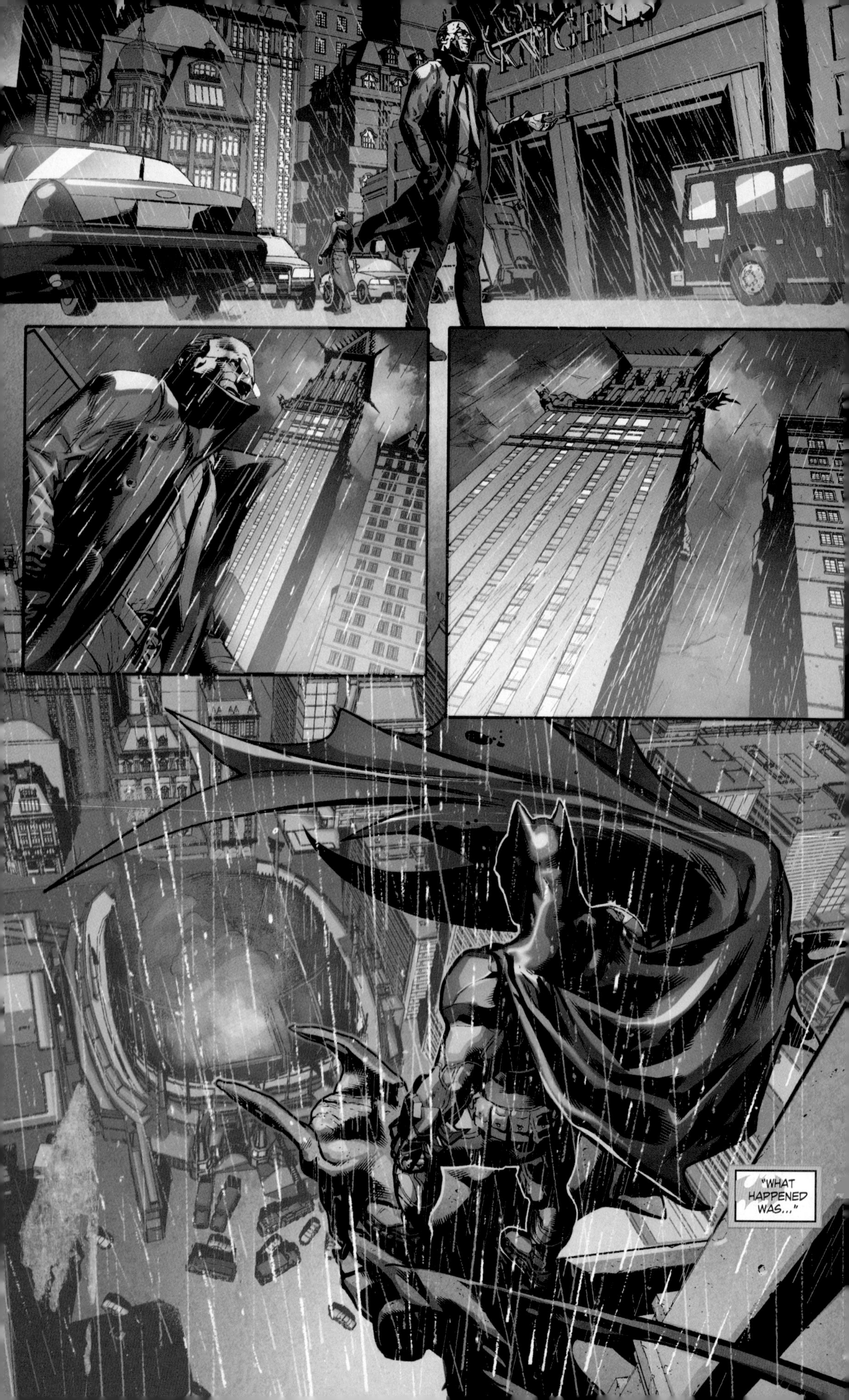
KNIGHTS
"WHAT HAPPENED WAS..."

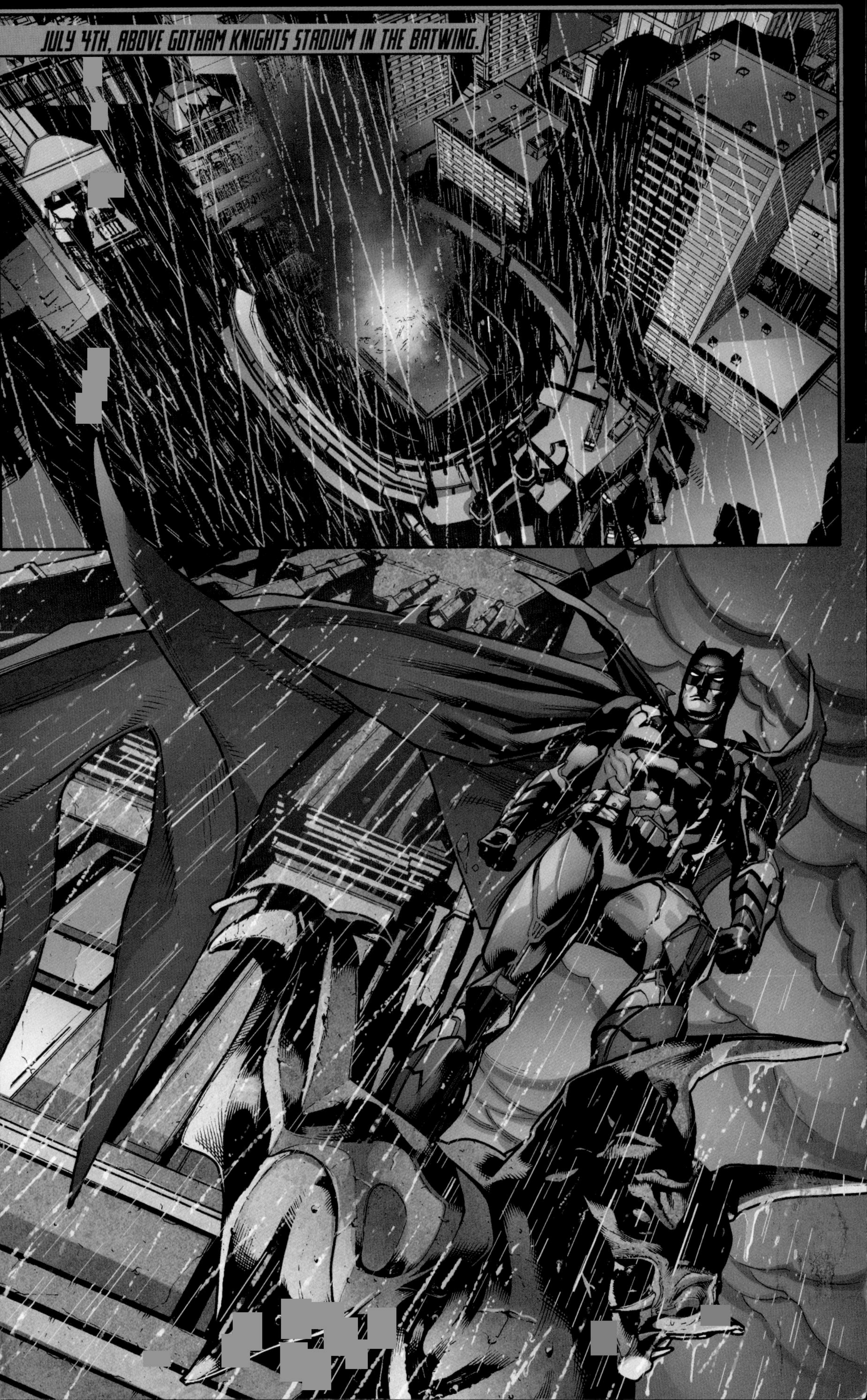
JULY 4TH, ABOVE GOTHAM KNIGHTS STADIUM IN THE BATWING.

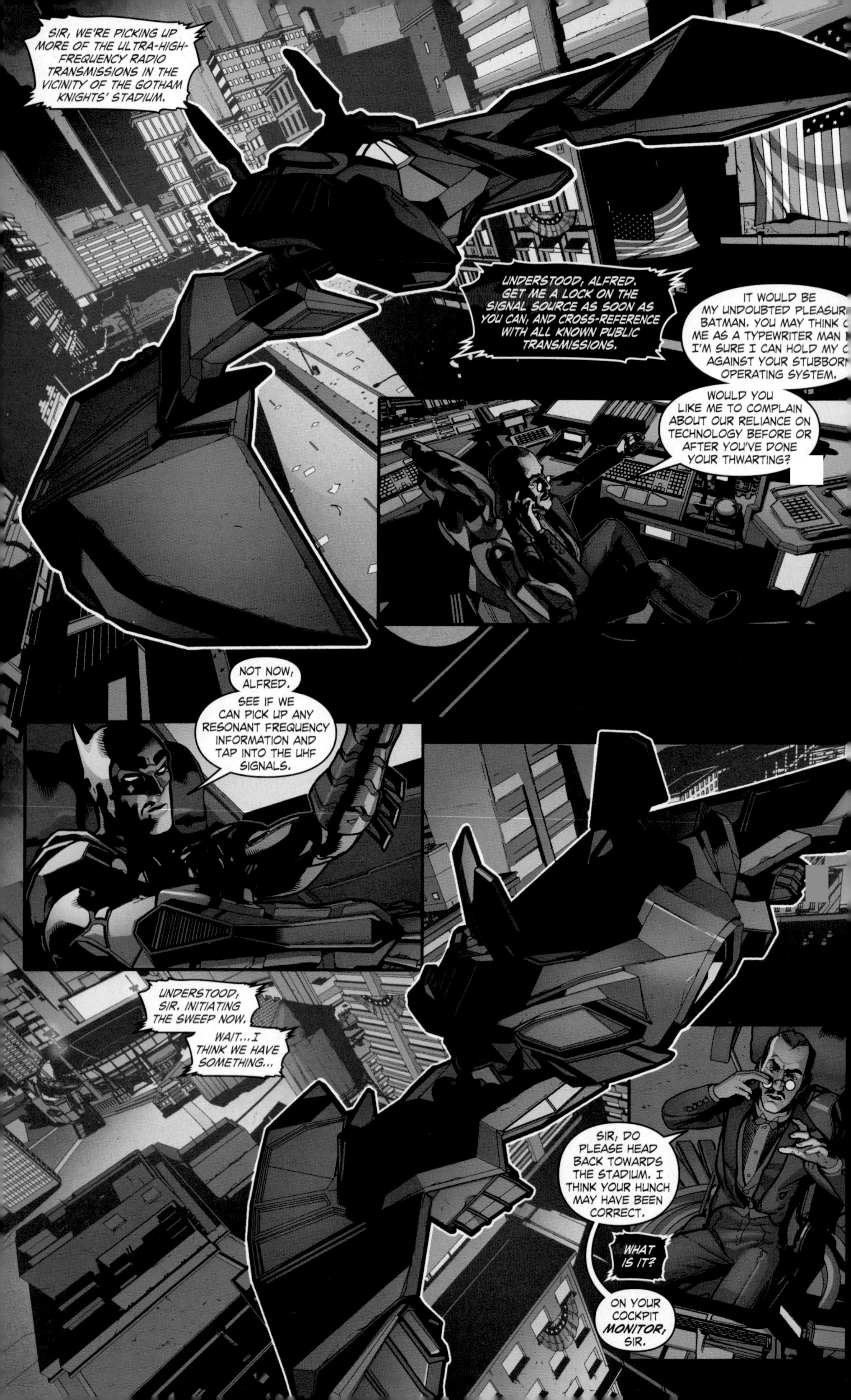
SIR, WE'RE PICKING UP MORE OF THE ULTRA-HIGH-FREQUENCY RADIO TRANSMISSIONS IN THE VICINITY OF THE GOTHAM KNIGHTS' STADIUM.
UNDERSTOOD, ALFRED. GET ME A LOCK ON THE SIGNAL SOURCE AS SOON AS YOU CAN, AND CROSS-REFERENCE WITH ALL KNOWN PUBLIC TRANSMISSIONS.
IT WOULD BE MY UNDOUBTED PLEASUR BATMAN. YOU MAY THINK MY ME AS A TYPEWRITER MAN I'M SURE I CAN HOLD MY AGAINST YOUR STUBBOR OPERATING SYSTEM.
WOULD YOU LIKE ME TO COMPLAIN ABOUT OUR RELIANCE ON TECHNOLOGY BEFORE OR AFTER YOU'VE DONE YOUR THWARTING?
NOT NOW, ALFRED.
SEE IF WE CAN PICK UP ANY RESONANT FREQUENCY INFORMATION AND TAP INTO THE UHF SIGNALS.
UNDERSTOOD, SIR. INITIATING THE SWEEP NOW.
WAIT...I THINK WE HAVE SOMETHING...
SIR, DO PLEASE HEAD BACK TOWARDS THE STADIUM. I THINK YOUR HUNCH MAY HAVE BEEN CORRECT.
WHAT IS IT?
ON YOUR COCKPIT MONITOR, SIR.

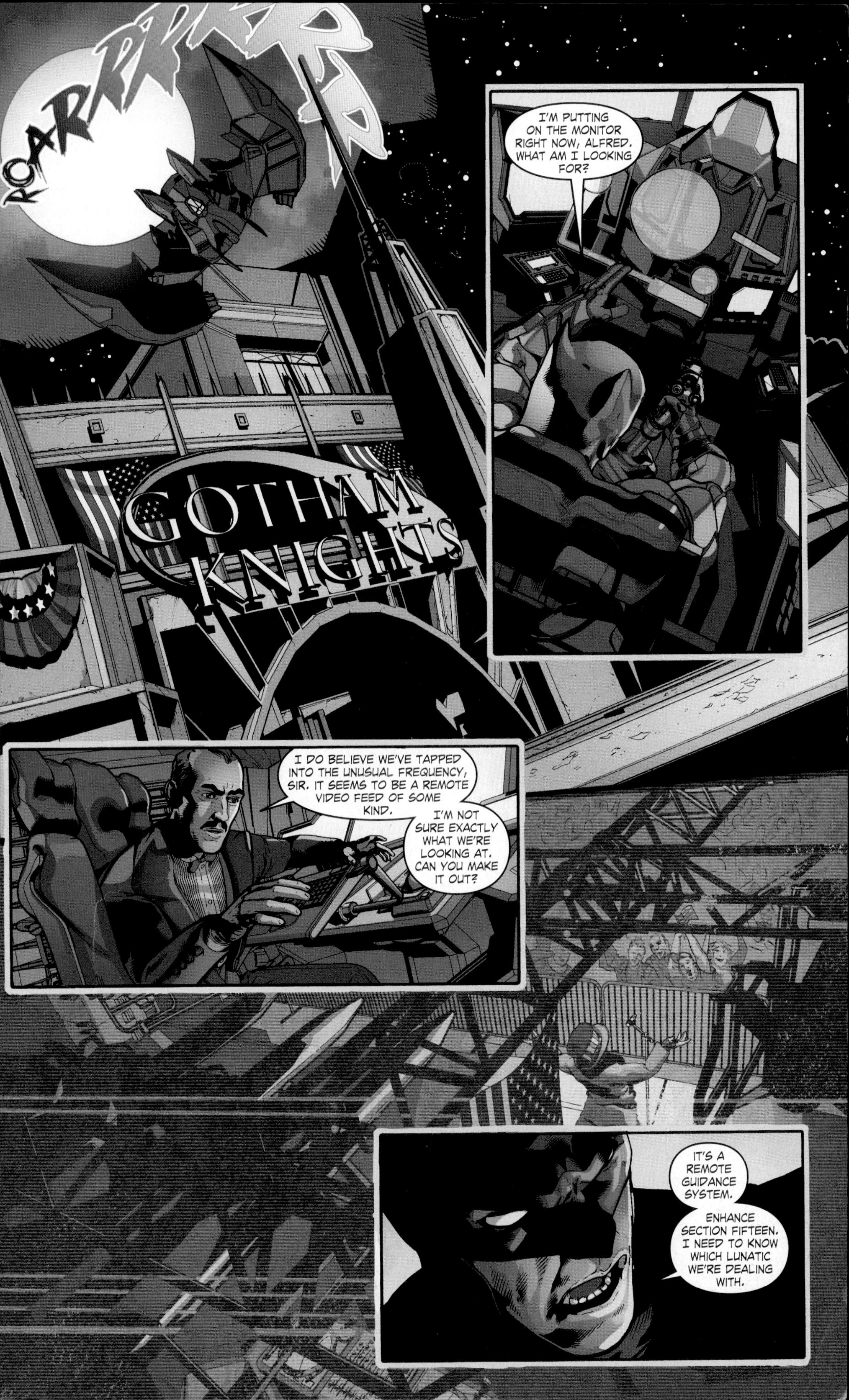
ROARRRRRR
GOTHAM KNIGHTS
I'M PUTTING ON THE MONITOR RIGHT NOW, ALFRED. WHAT AM I LOOKING FOR?
I DO BELIEVE WE'VE TAPPED INTO THE UNUSUAL FREQUENCY, SIR. IT SEEMS TO BE A REMOTE VIDEO FEED OF SOME KIND.
I'M NOT SURE EXACTLY WHAT WE'RE LOOKING AT. CAN YOU MAKE IT OUT?
IT'S A REMOTE GUIDANCE SYSTEM.
ENHANCE SECTION FIFTEEN. I NEED TO KNOW WHICH LUNATIC WE'RE DEALING WITH.

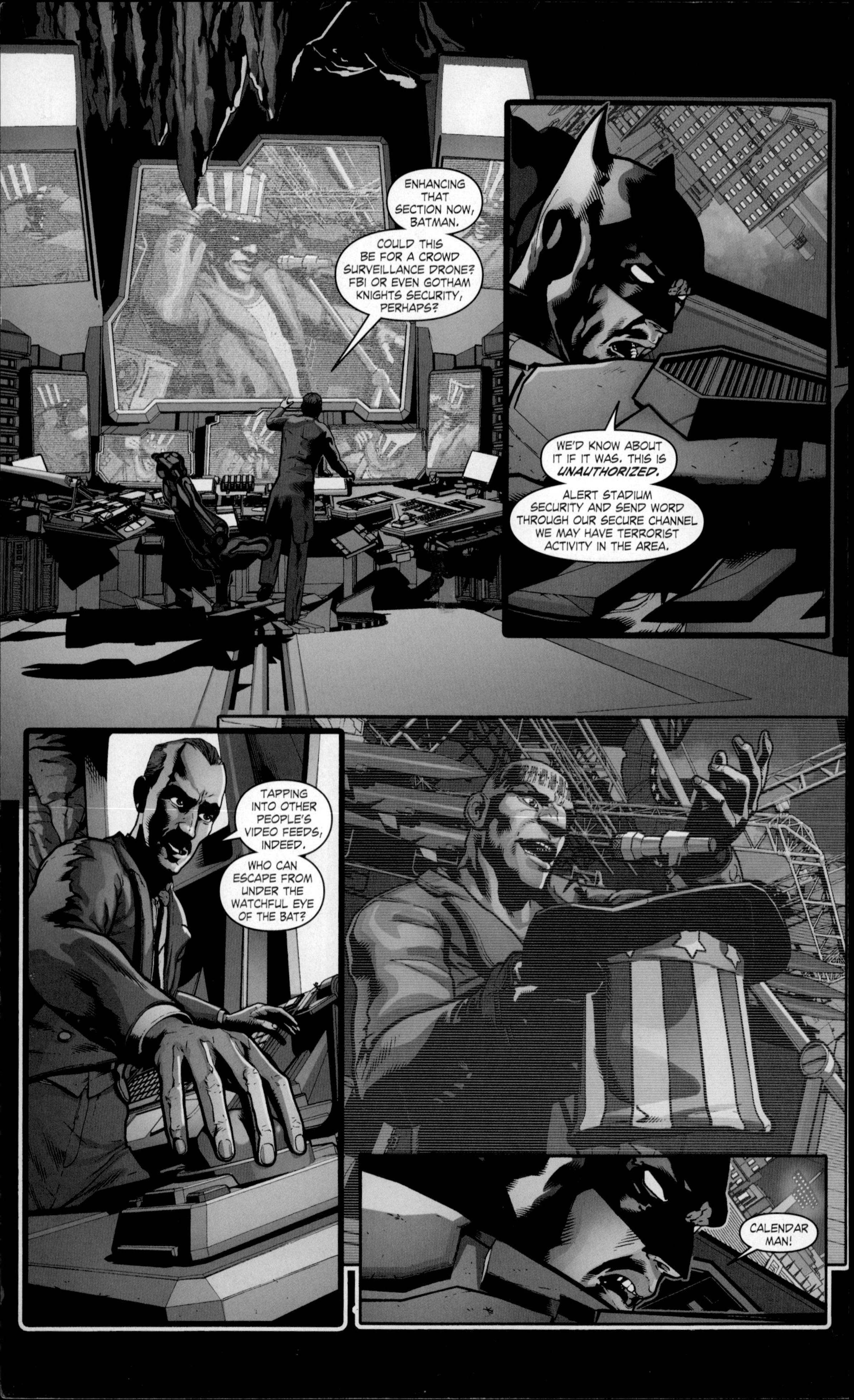
ENHANCING THAT SECTION NOW, BATMAN.
COULD THIS BE FOR A CROWD SURVEILLANCE DRONE? FBI OR EVEN GOTHAM KNIGHTS SECURITY, PERHAPS?
WE'D KNOW ABOUT IT IF IT WAS. THIS IS *UNAUTHORIZED.*
ALERT STADIUM SECURITY AND SEND WORD THROUGH OUR SECURE CHANNEL WE MAY HAVE TERRORIST ACTIVITY IN THE AREA.
TAPPING INTO OTHER PEOPLE'S VIDEO FEEDS, INDEED.
WHO CAN ESCAPE FROM UNDER THE WATCHFUL EYE OF THE BAT?
CALENDAR MAN!

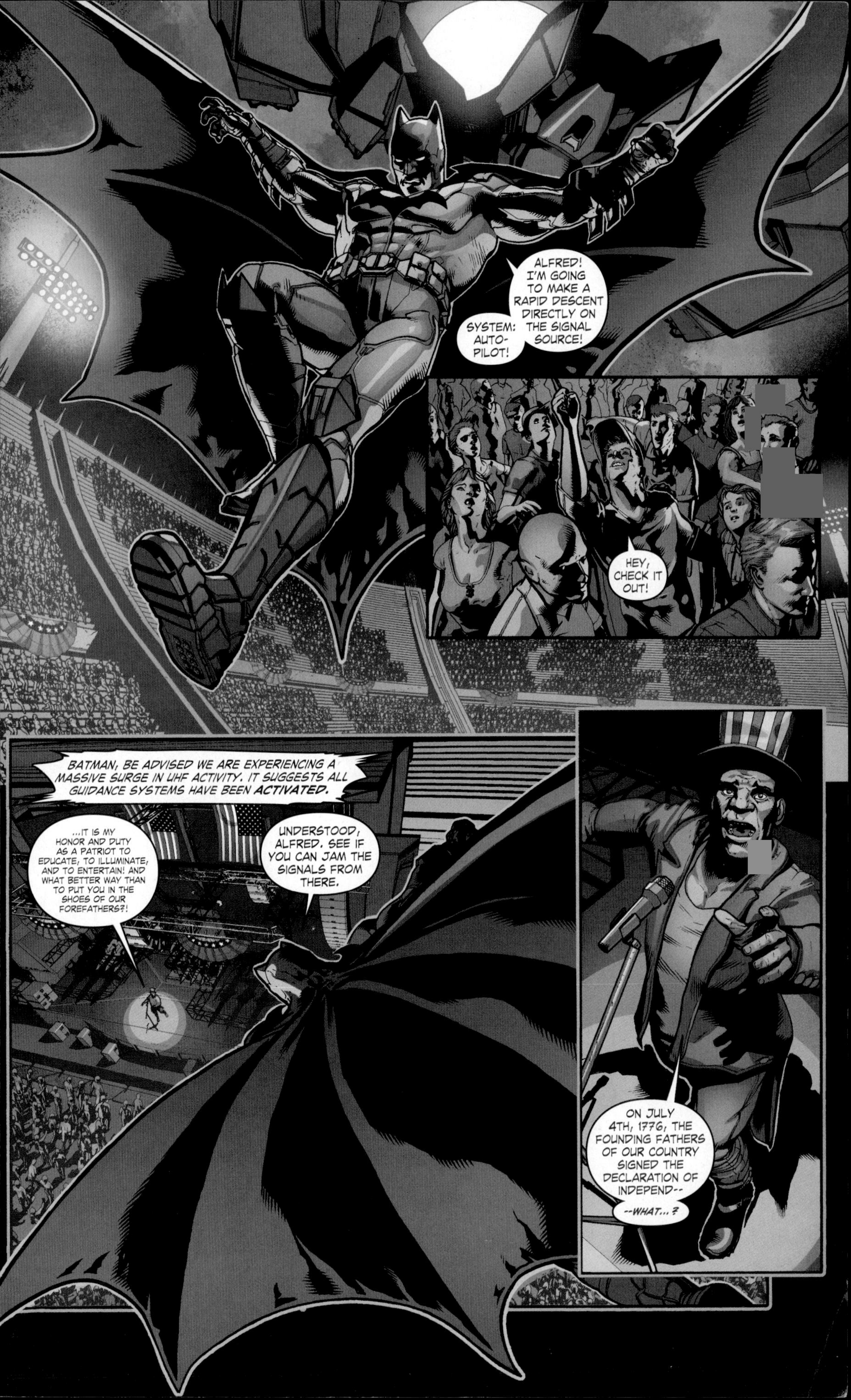
SYSTEM: AUTO-PILOT!
ALFRED! I'M GOING TO MAKE A RAPID DESCENT DIRECTLY ON THE SIGNAL SOURCE!
HEY, CHECK IT OUT!
BATMAN, BE ADVISED WE ARE EXPERIENCING A MASSIVE SURGE IN UHF ACTIVITY. IT SUGGESTS ALL GUIDANCE SYSTEMS HAVE BEEN ACTIVATED.
...IT IS MY HONOR AND DUTY AS A PATRIOT TO EDUCATE, TO ILLUMINATE, AND TO ENTERTAIN! AND WHAT BETTER WAY THAN TO PUT YOU IN THE SHOES OF OUR FOREFATHERS?!
UNDERSTOOD, ALFRED. SEE IF YOU CAN JAM THE SIGNALS FROM THERE.
ON JULY 4TH, 1776, THE FOUNDING FATHERS OF OUR COUNTRY SIGNED THE DECLARATION OF INDEPEND--
--WHAT...?

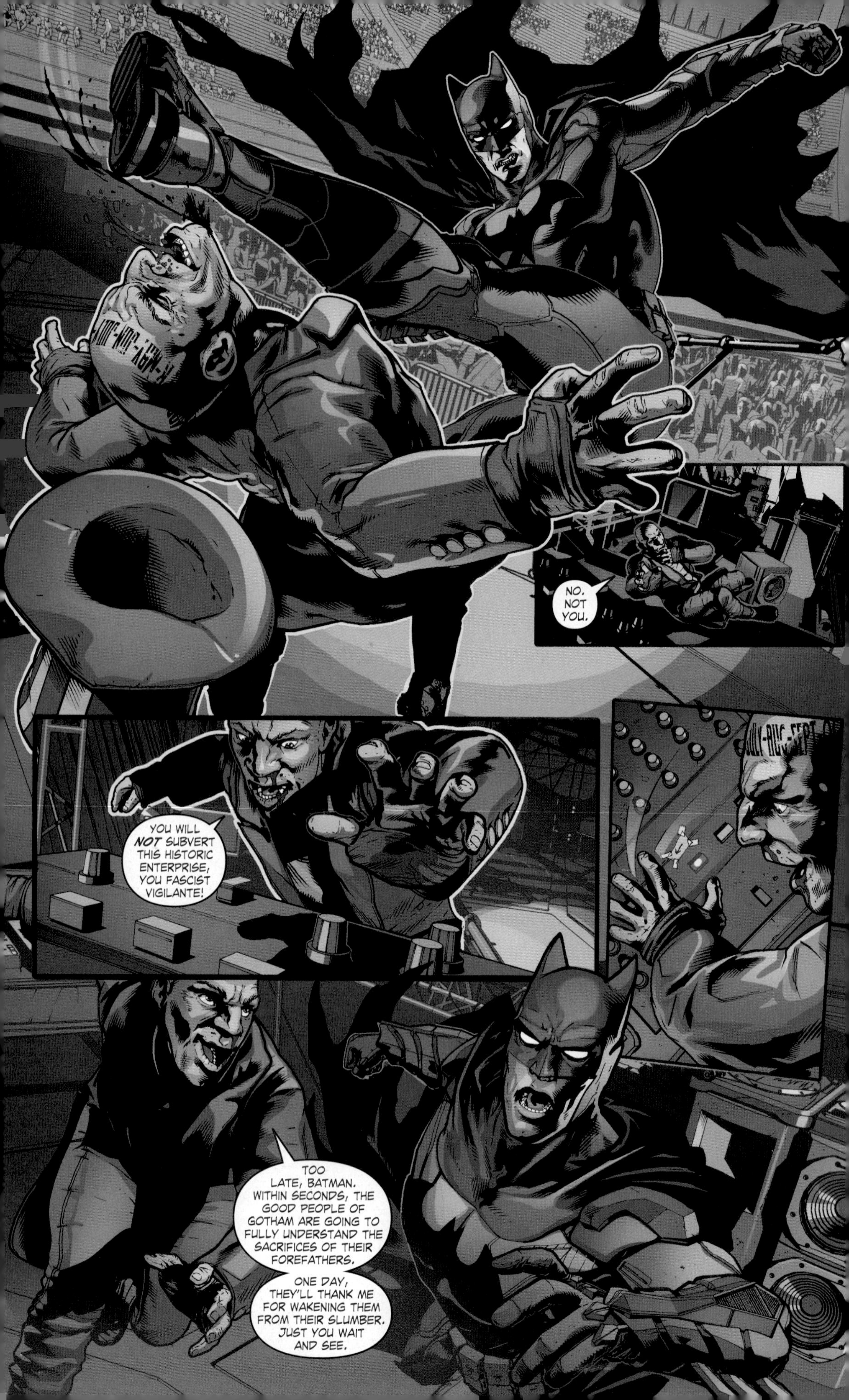
NO. NOT YOU.
YOU WILL **NOT** SUBVERT THIS HISTORIC ENTERPRISE, YOU FASCIST VIGILANTE!
TOO LATE, BATMAN. WITHIN SECONDS, THE GOOD PEOPLE OF GOTHAM ARE GOING TO FULLY UNDERSTAND THE SACRIFICES OF THEIR FOREFATHERS.
ONE DAY, THEY'LL THANK ME FOR WAKENING THEM FROM THEIR SLUMBER. JUST YOU WAIT AND SEE.

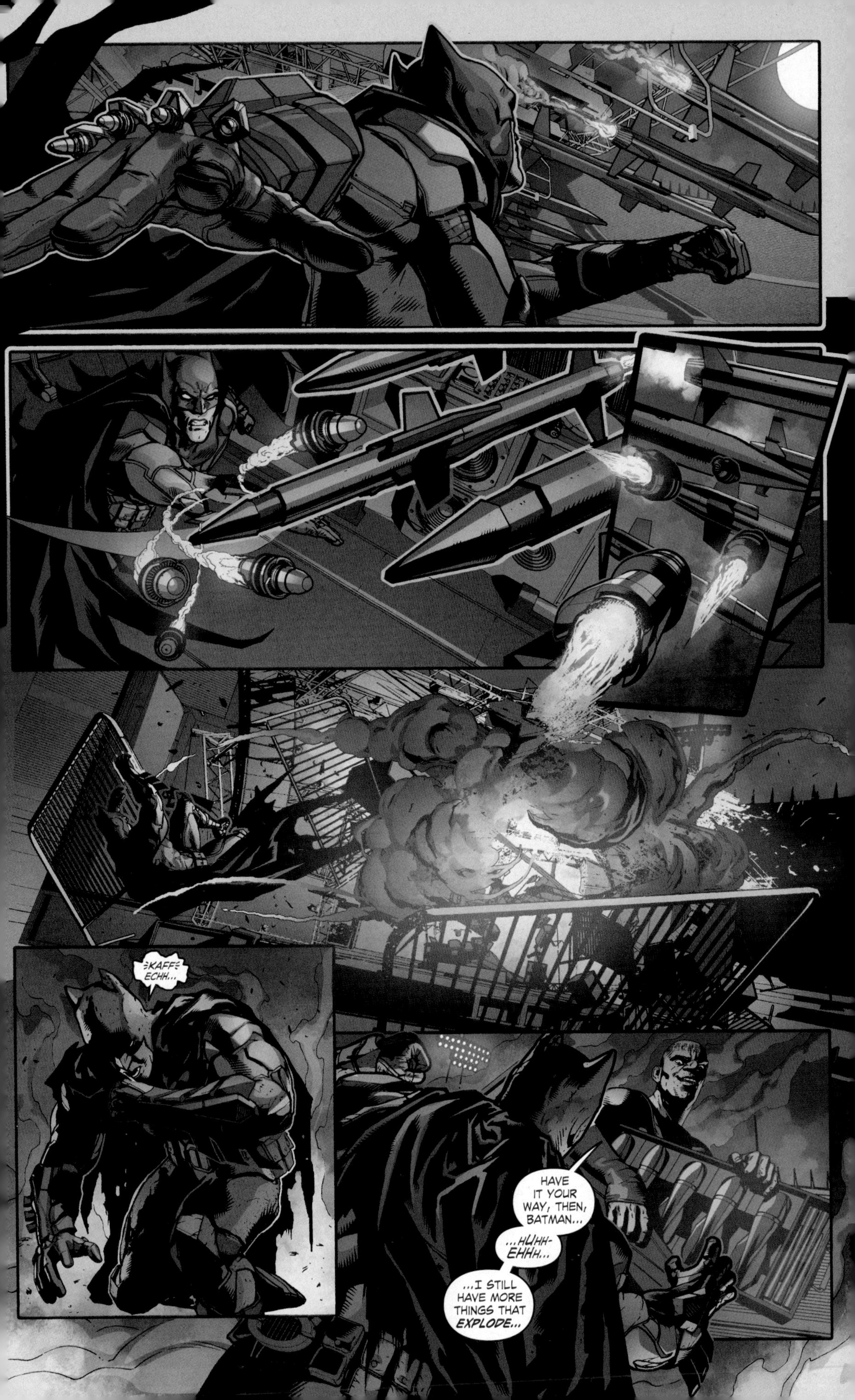
KAFF ECHH...
HAVE IT YOUR WAY, THEN, BATMAN...
...HUHH-EHHH...
...I STILL HAVE MORE THINGS THAT EXPLODE...

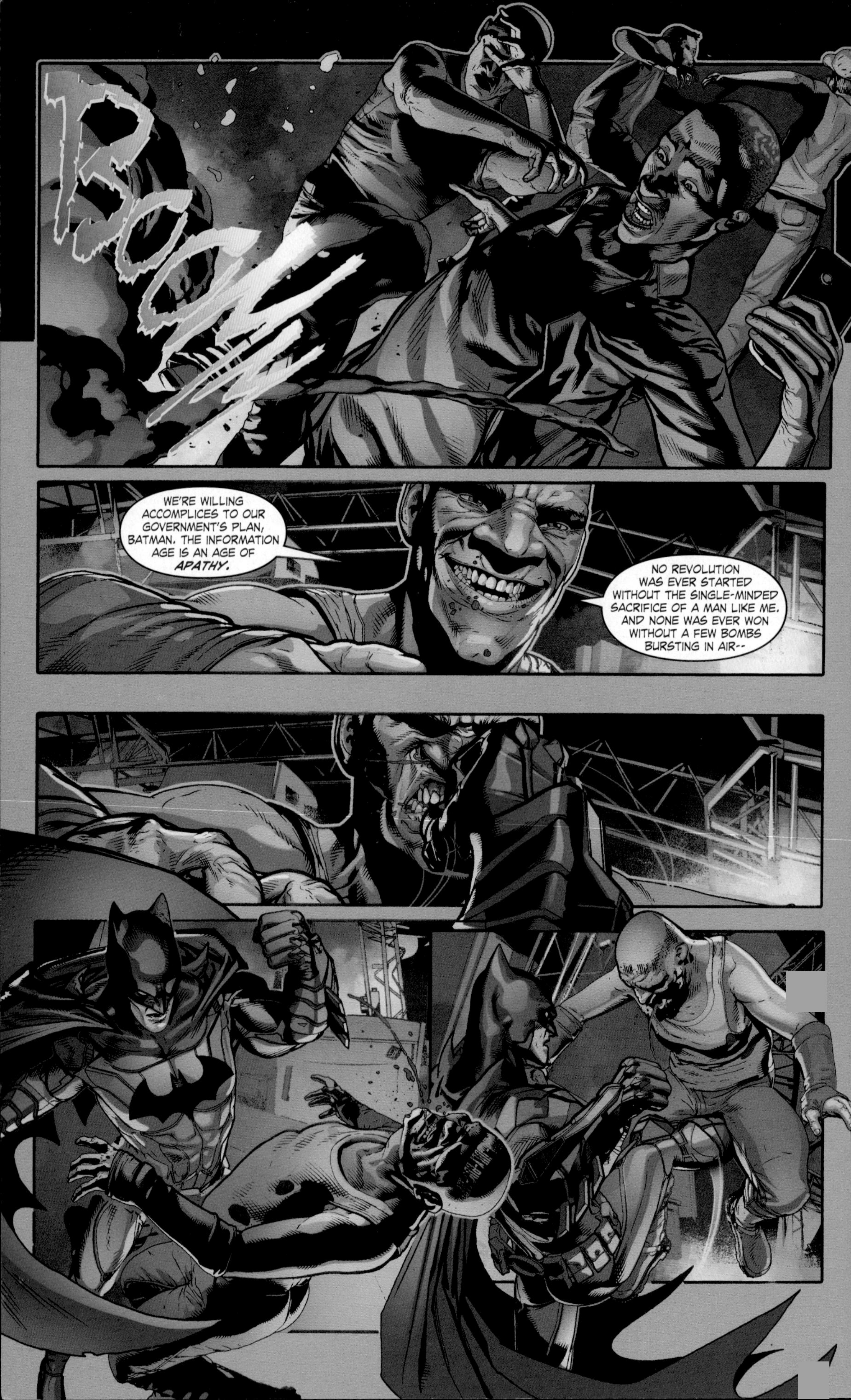
BOOM
WE'RE WILLING ACCOMPLICES TO OUR GOVERNMENT'S PLAN, BATMAN. THE INFORMATION AGE IS AN AGE OF APATHY.
NO REVOLUTION WAS EVER STARTED WITHOUT THE SINGLE-MINDED SACRIFICE OF A MAN LIKE ME. AND NONE WAS EVER WON WITHOUT A FEW BOMBS BURSTING IN AIR--

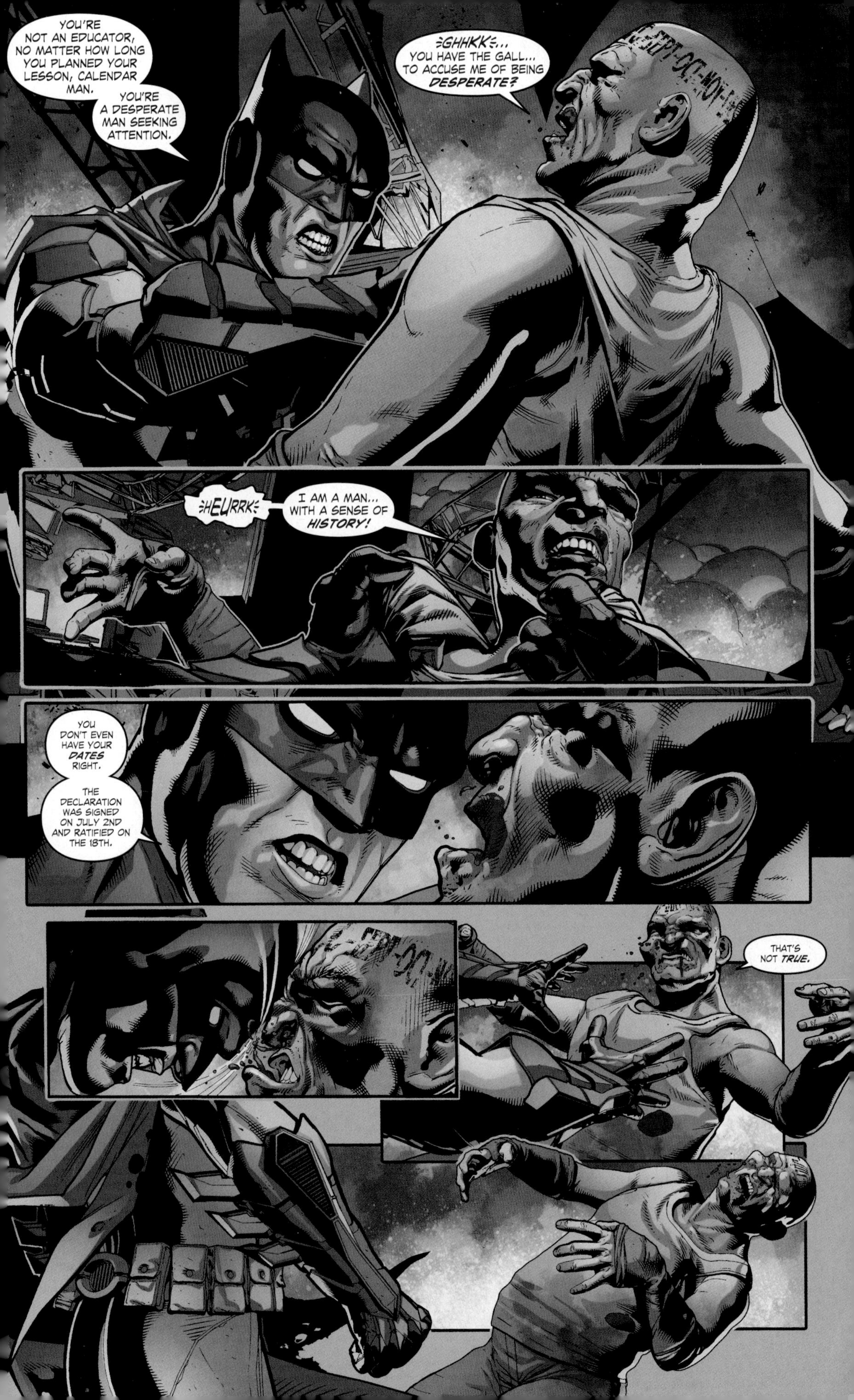
YOU'RE NOT AN EDUCATOR, NO MATTER HOW LONG YOU PLANNED YOUR LESSON, CALENDAR MAN.
YOU'RE A DESPERATE MAN SEEKING ATTENTION.
GHHKK... YOU HAVE THE GALL... TO ACCUSE ME OF BEING DESPERATE?
HEURRK
I AM A MAN... WITH A SENSE OF HISTORY!
YOU DON'T EVEN HAVE YOUR DATES RIGHT.
THE DECLARATION WAS SIGNED ON JULY 2ND AND RATIFIED ON THE 18TH.
THAT'S NOT TRUE.

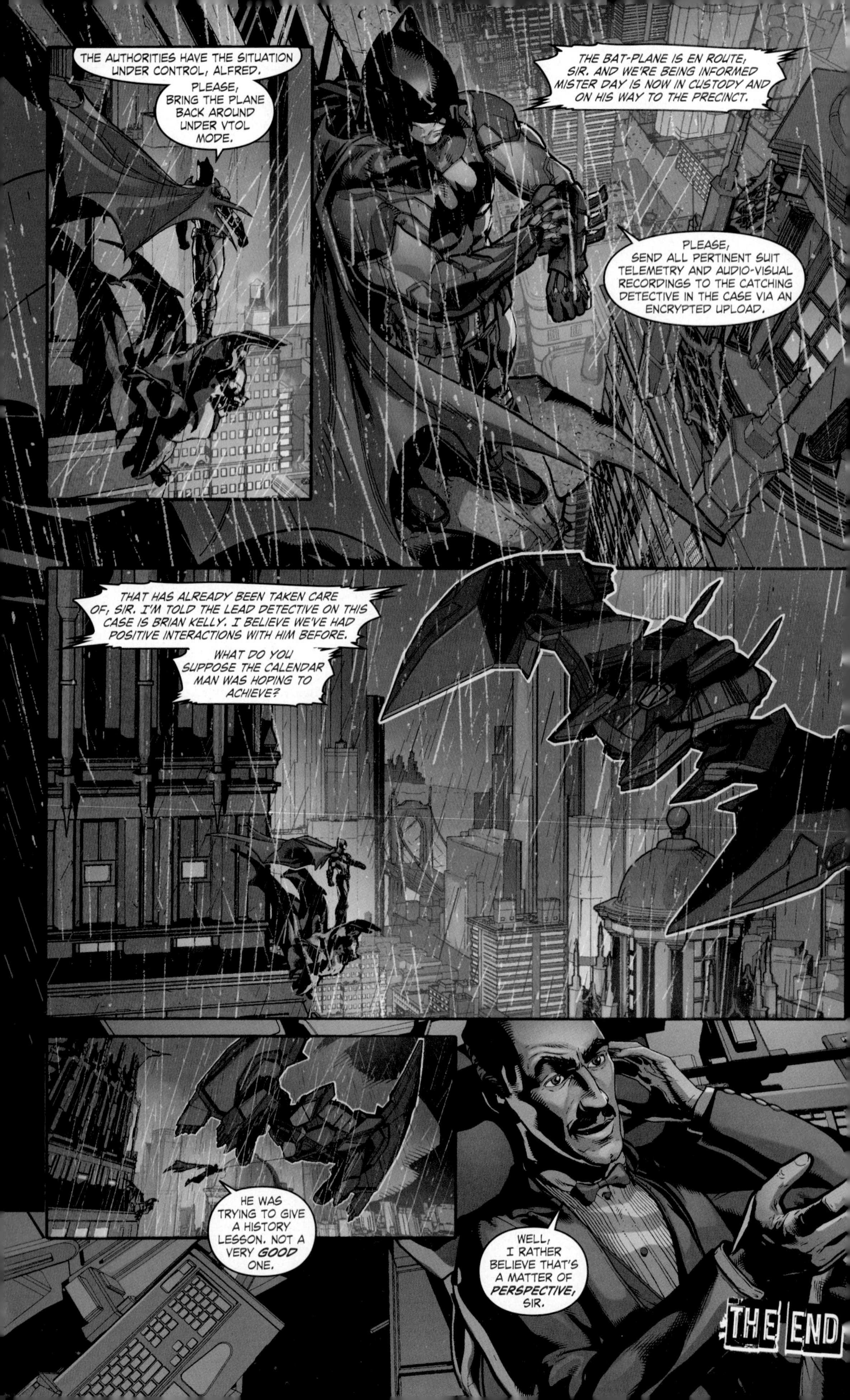
THE AUTHORITIES HAVE THE SITUATION UNDER CONTROL, ALFRED.
PLEASE, BRING THE PLANE BACK AROUND UNDER VTOL MODE.
THE BAT-PLANE IS EN ROUTE, SIR. AND WE'RE BEING INFORMED MISTER DAY IS NOW IN CUSTODY AND ON HIS WAY TO THE PRECINCT.
PLEASE, SEND ALL PERTINENT SUIT TELEMETRY AND AUDIO-VISUAL RECORDINGS TO THE CATCHING DETECTIVE IN THE CASE VIA AN ENCRYPTED UPLOAD.
THAT HAS ALREADY BEEN TAKEN CARE OF, SIR. I'M TOLD THE LEAD DETECTIVE ON THIS CASE IS BRIAN KELLY. I BELIEVE WE'VE HAD POSITIVE INTERACTIONS WITH HIM BEFORE.
WHAT DO YOU SUPPOSE THE CALENDAR MAN WAS HOPING TO ACHIEVE?
HE WAS TRYING TO GIVE A HISTORY LESSON. NOT A VERY GOOD ONE.
WELL, I RATHER BELIEVE THAT'S A MATTER OF PERSPECTIVE, SIR.
THE END

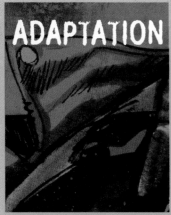

ADAPTATION

RAFAEL ALBUQUERQUE
Writer
&
Artist

DAVE McCAIG
Colorist

SAIDA TEMOFONTE
Letterer

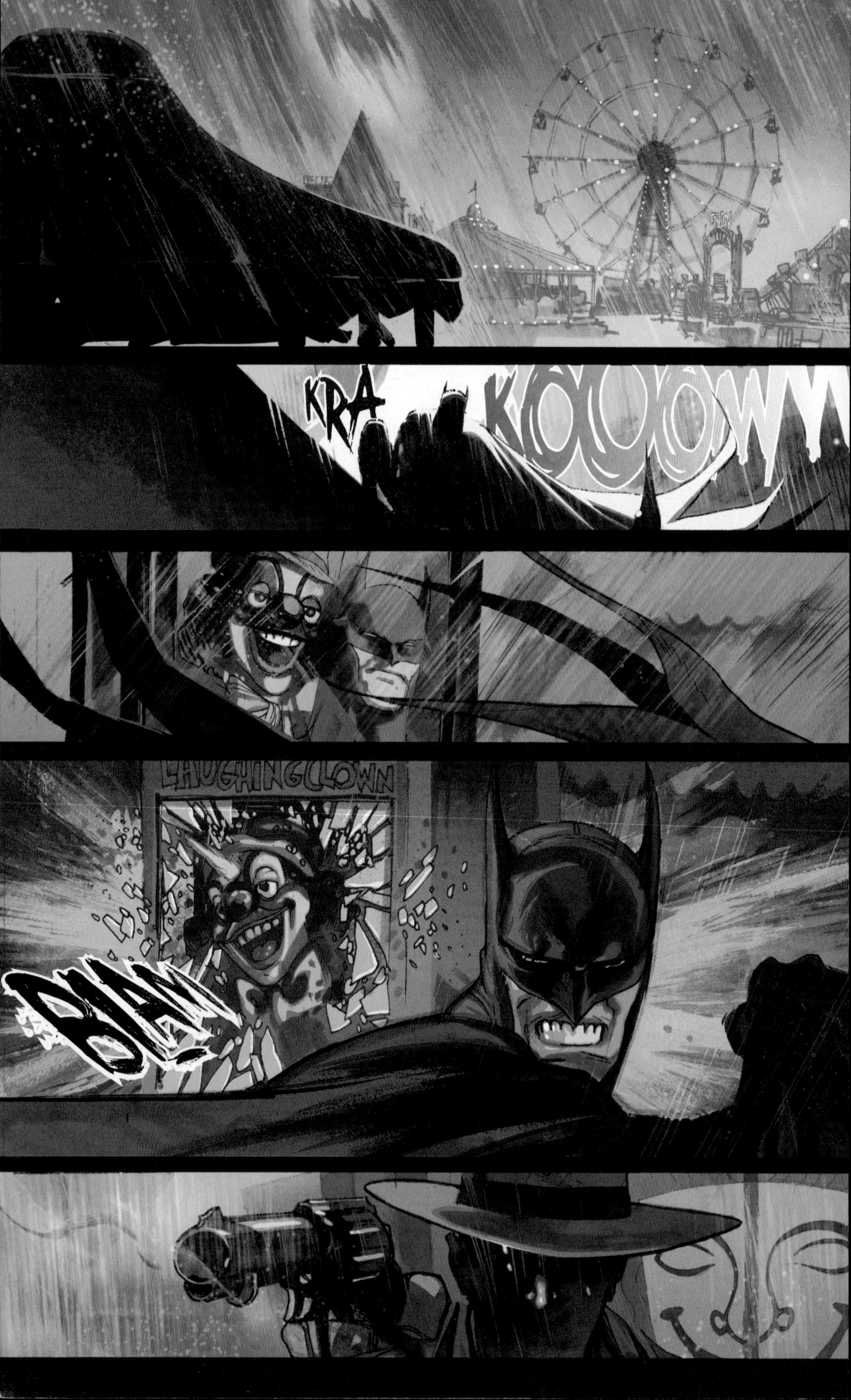
FUN
KRA
KOOOOW
LAUGHINGCLOWN
BLAM

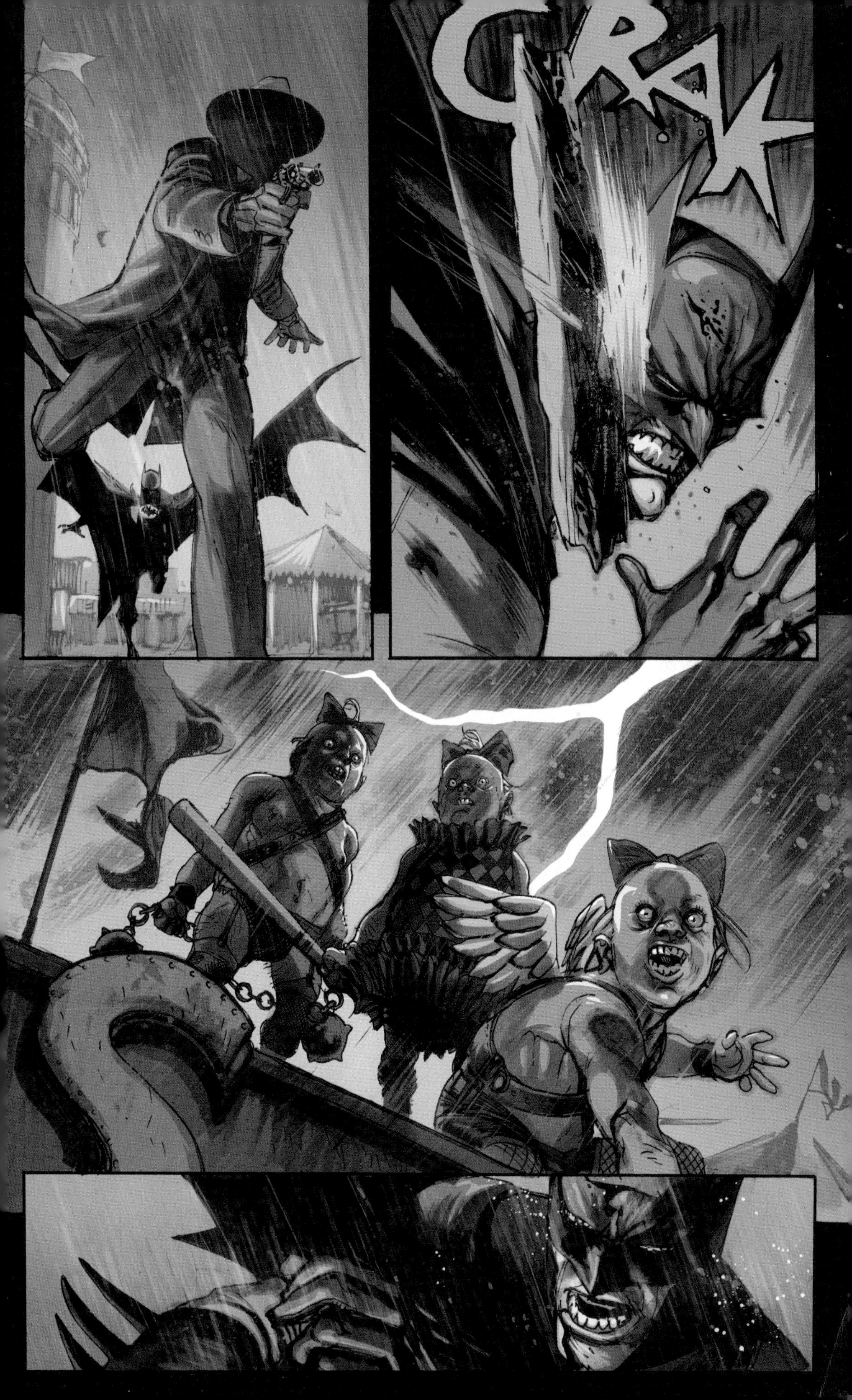
CRAK

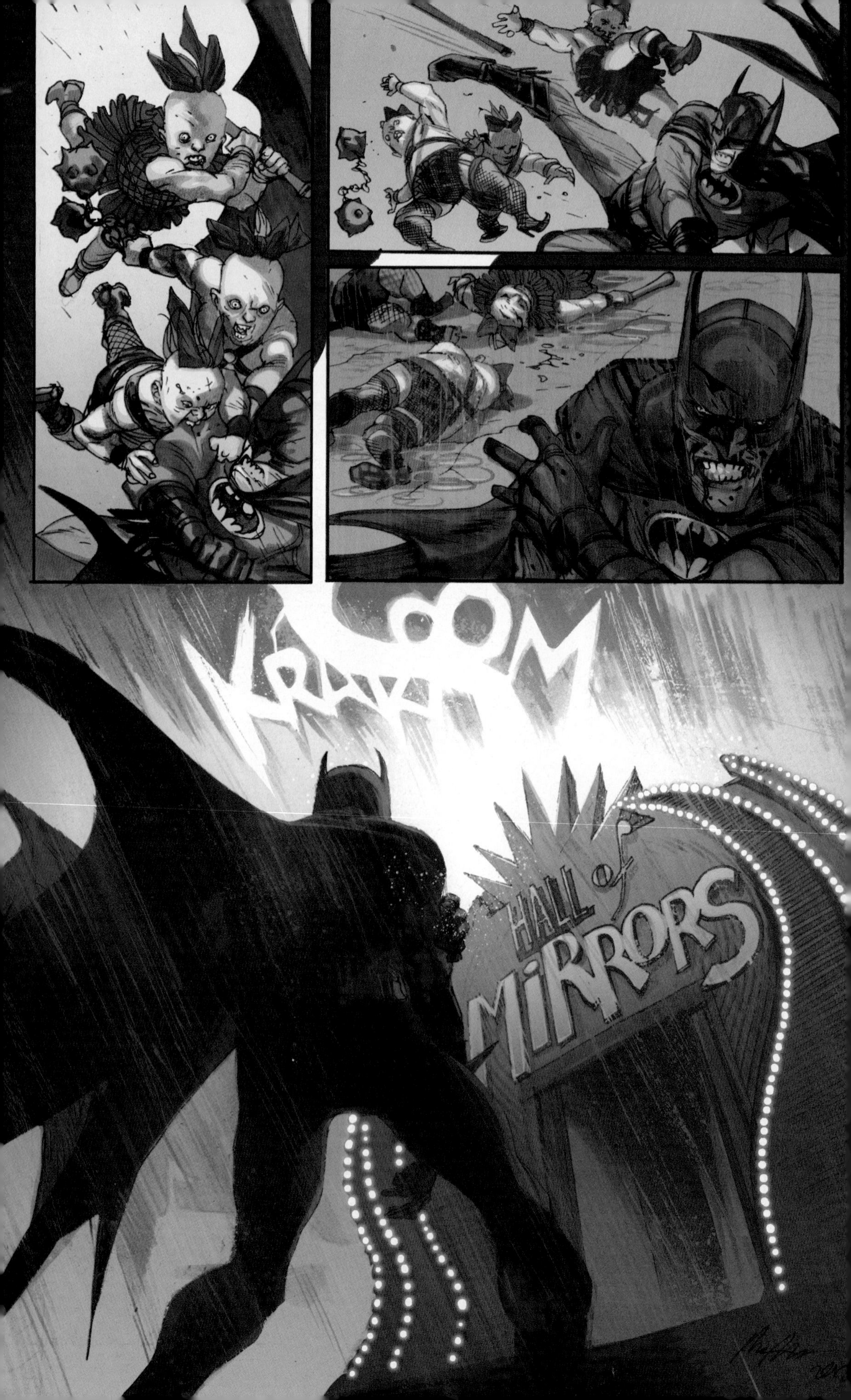
HALL of MIRRORS

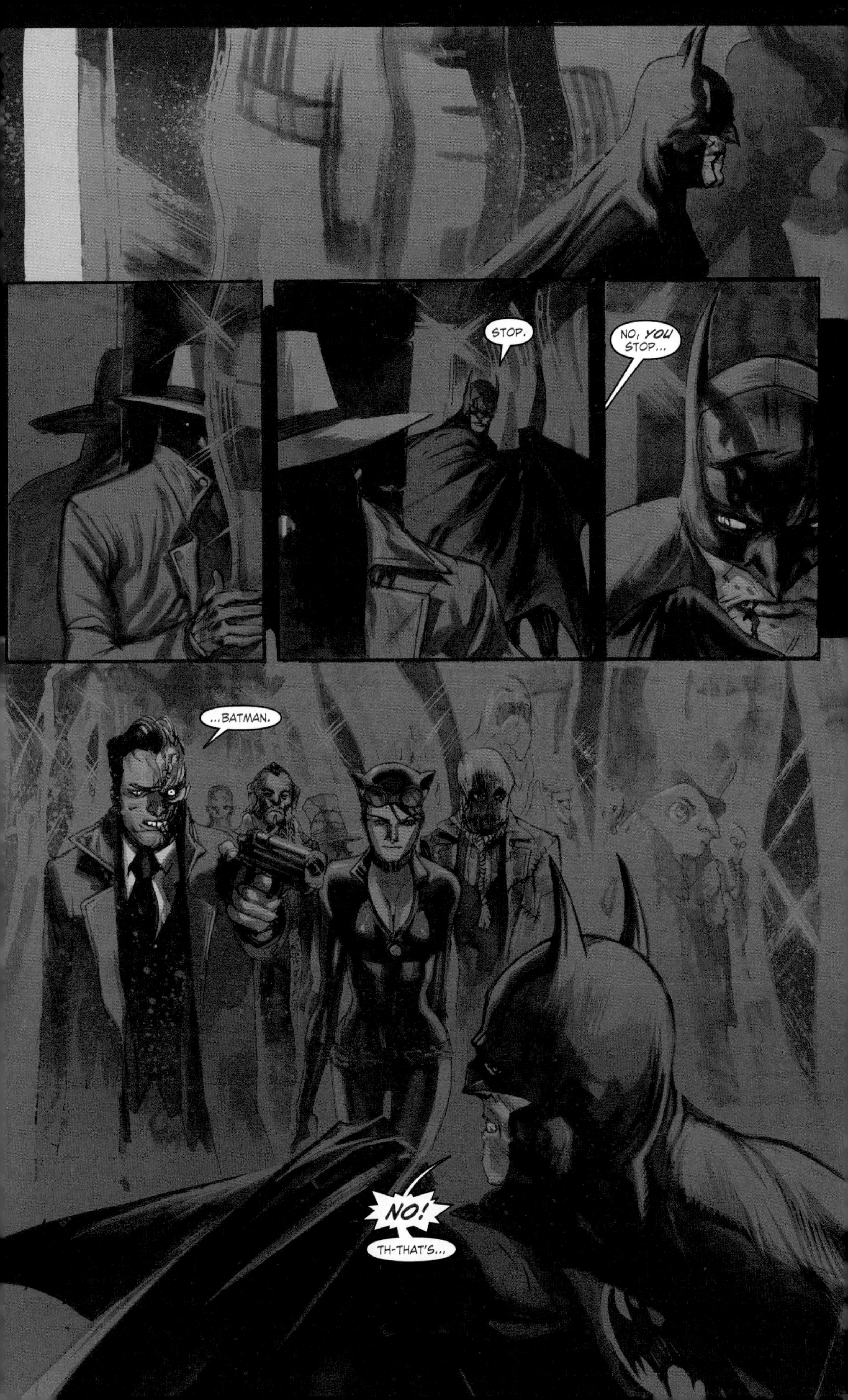
STOP.
NO, YOU STOP...
...BATMAN.
NO!
TH-THAT'S...

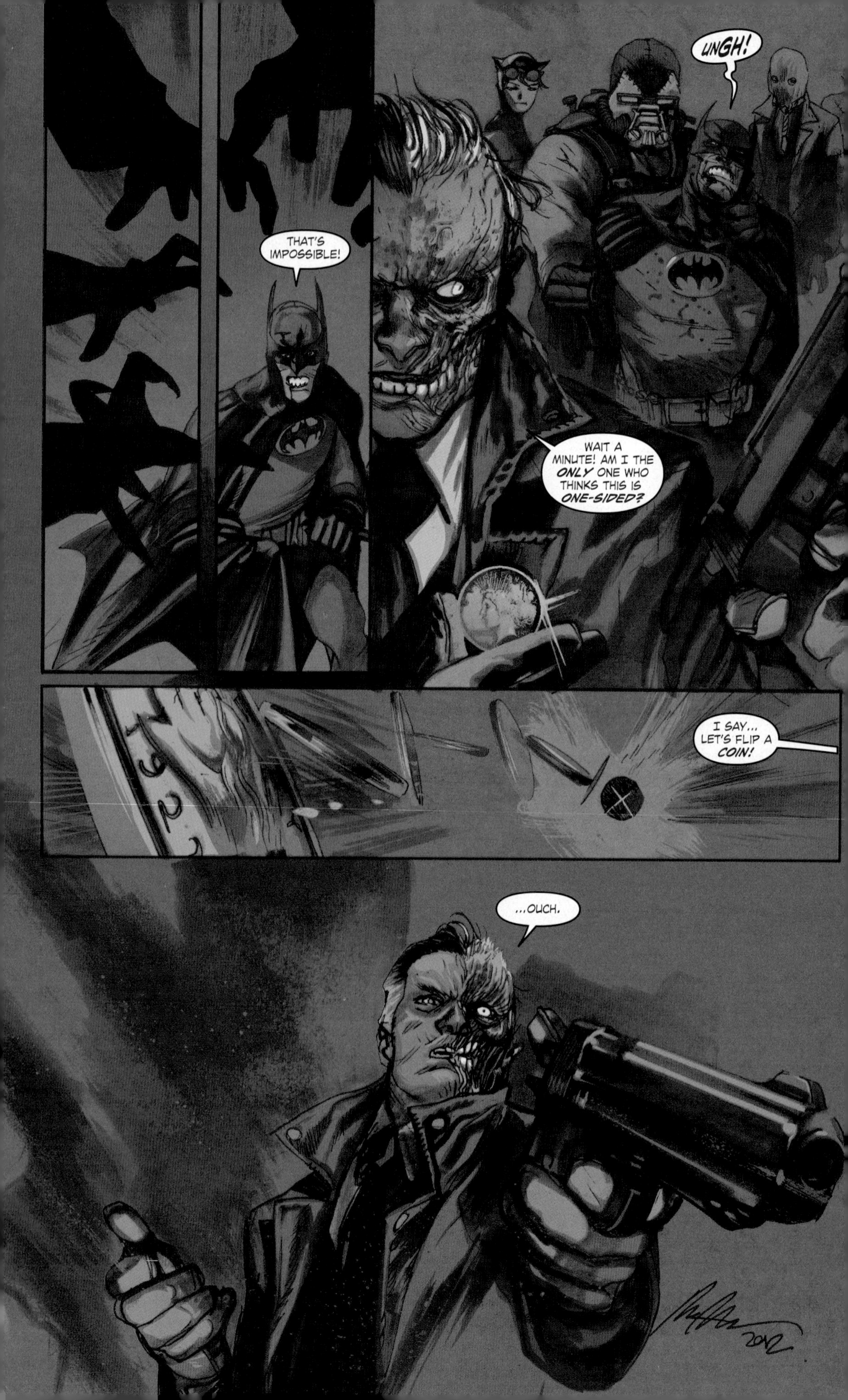
THAT'S IMPOSSIBLE!
UNGH!
WAIT A MINUTE! AM I THE ONLY ONE WHO THINKS THIS IS ONE-SIDED?
I SAY... LET'S FLIP A COIN!
...OUCH.

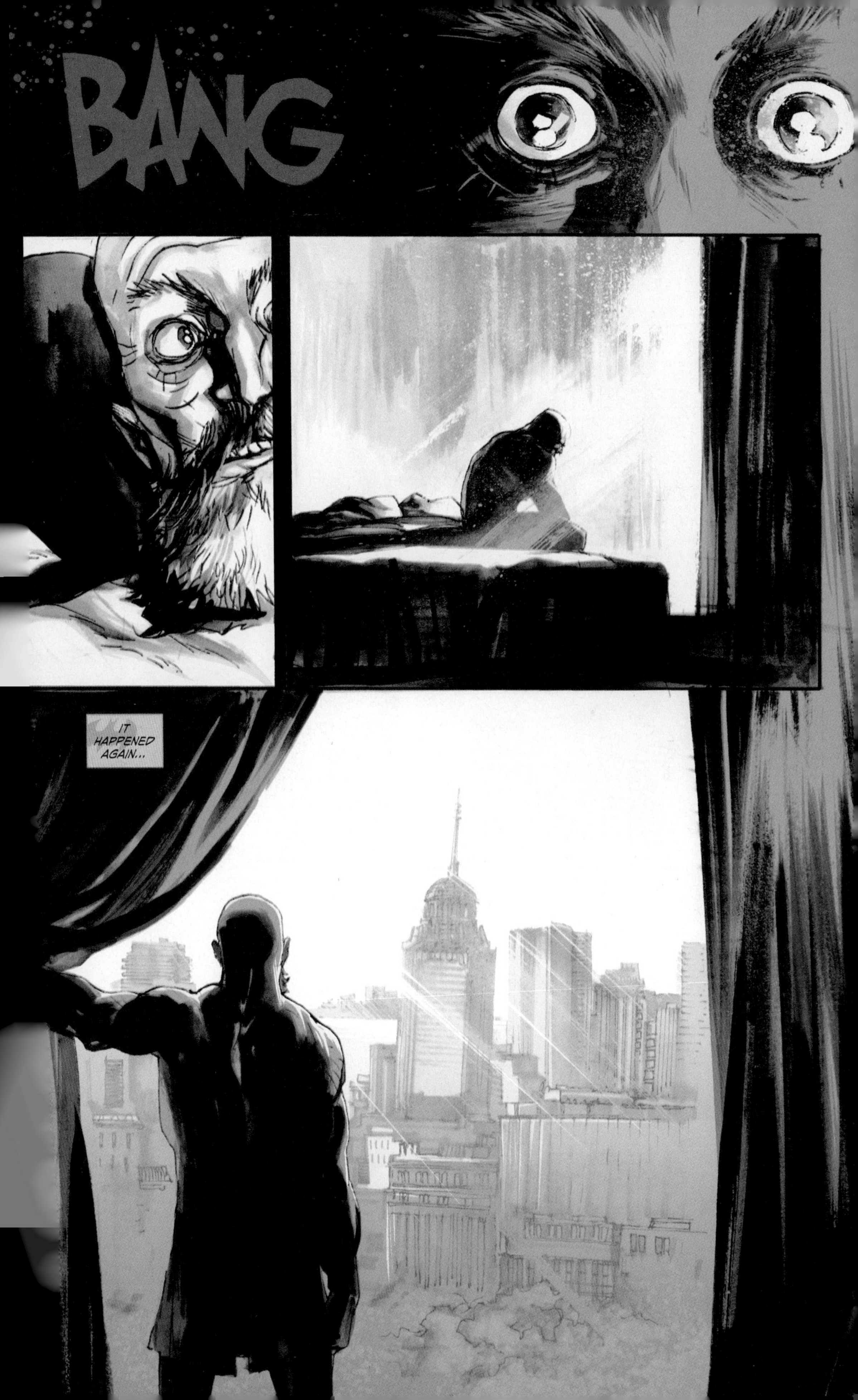
BANG
IT HAPPENED AGAIN...

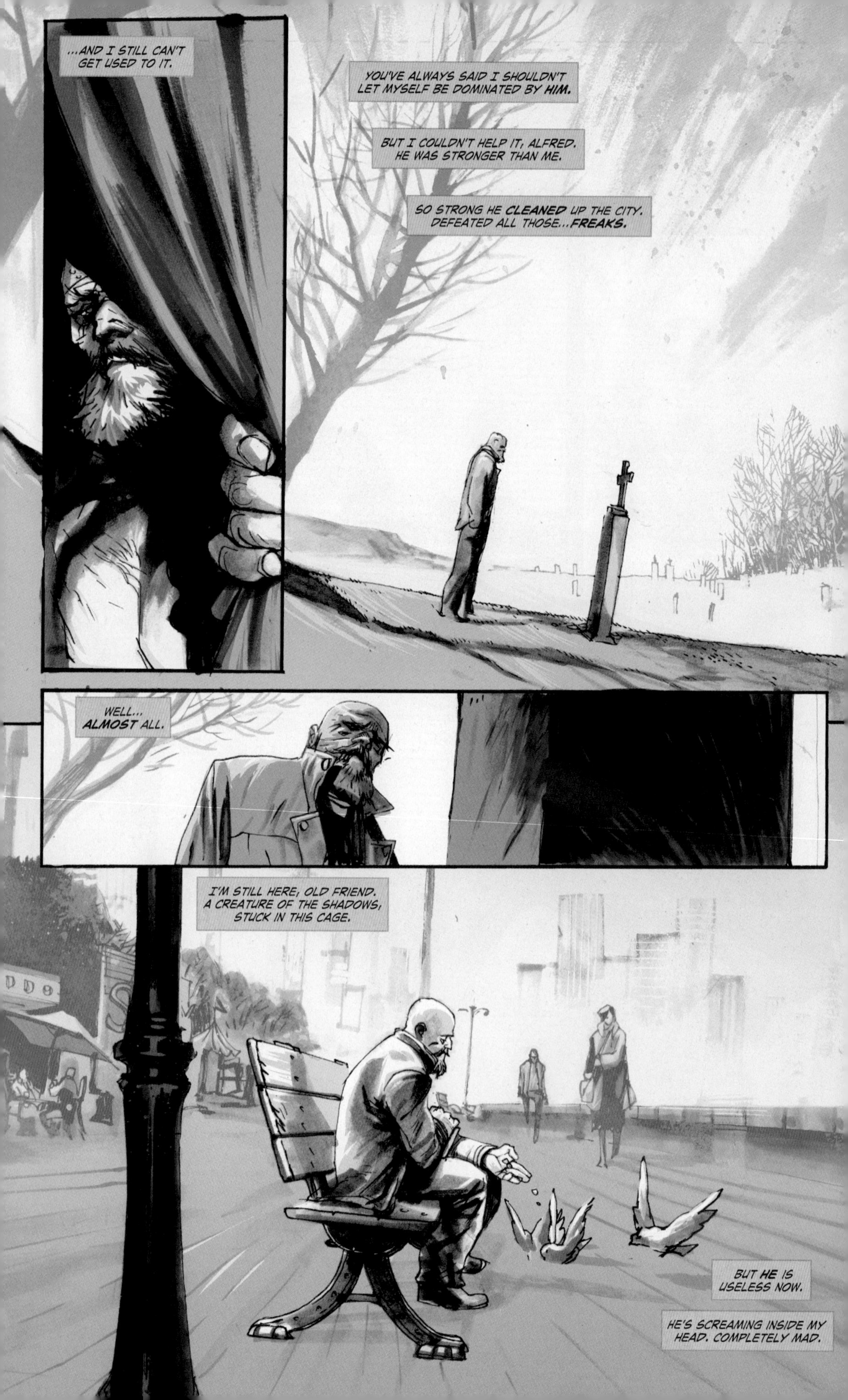
...AND I STILL CAN'T GET USED TO IT.
YOU'VE ALWAYS SAID I SHOULDN'T LET MYSELF BE DOMINATED BY **HIM.**
BUT I COULDN'T HELP IT, ALFRED. HE WAS STRONGER THAN ME.
SO STRONG HE **CLEANED** UP THE CITY. DEFEATED ALL THOSE... **FREAKS.**
WELL... **ALMOST** ALL.
I'M STILL HERE, OLD FRIEND. A CREATURE OF THE SHADOWS, STUCK IN THIS CAGE.
BUT **HE** IS USELESS NOW.
HE'S SCREAMING INSIDE MY HEAD. COMPLETELY MAD.

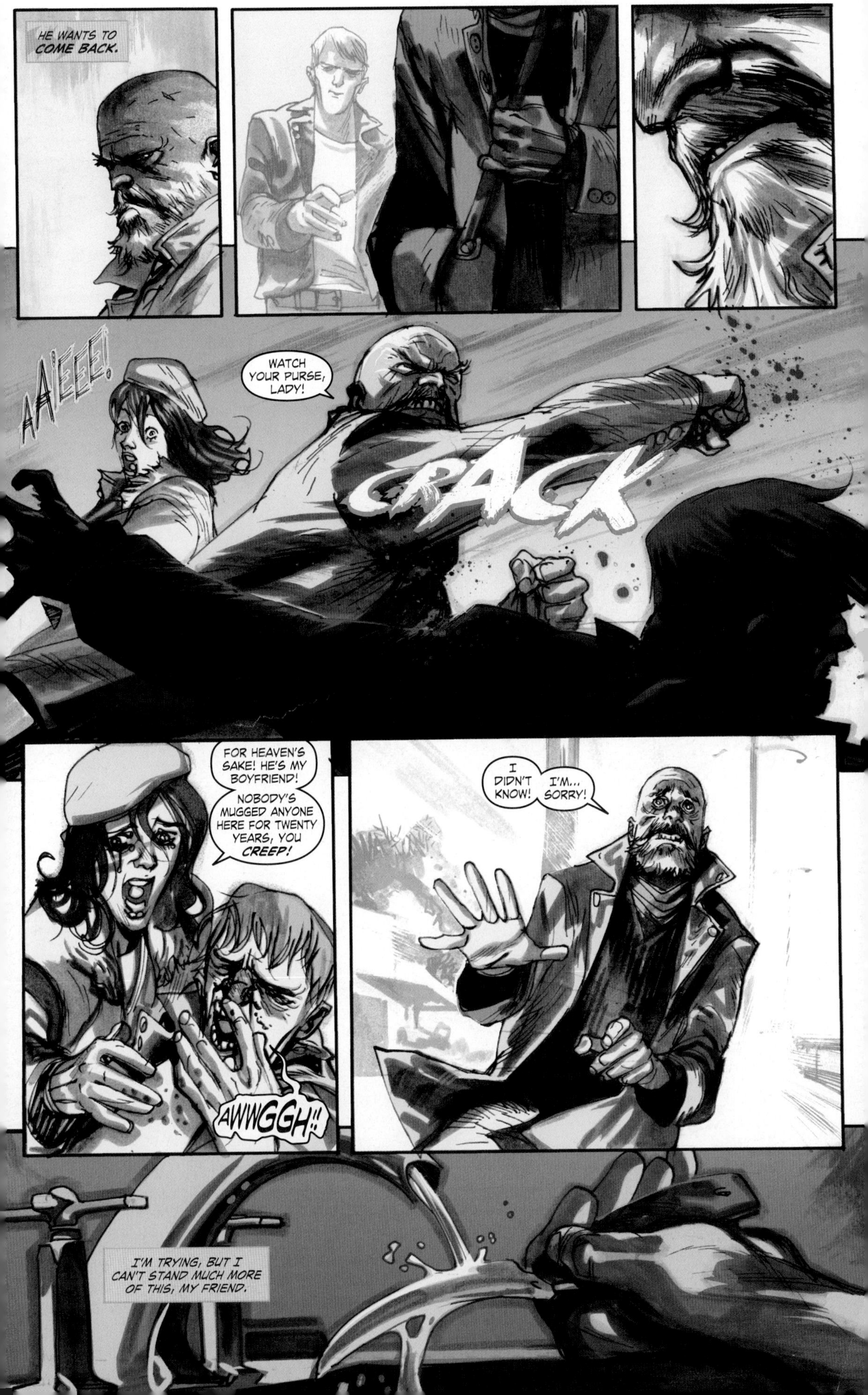
HE WANTS TO COME BACK.
AAIEEE!
WATCH YOUR PURSE, LADY!
CRACK
FOR HEAVEN'S SAKE! HE'S MY BOYFRIEND!
NOBODY'S MUGGED ANYONE HERE FOR TWENTY YEARS, YOU CREEP!
AWWGGH!!
I DIDN'T KNOW!
I'M... SORRY!
I'M TRYING, BUT I CAN'T STAND MUCH MORE OF THIS, MY FRIEND.

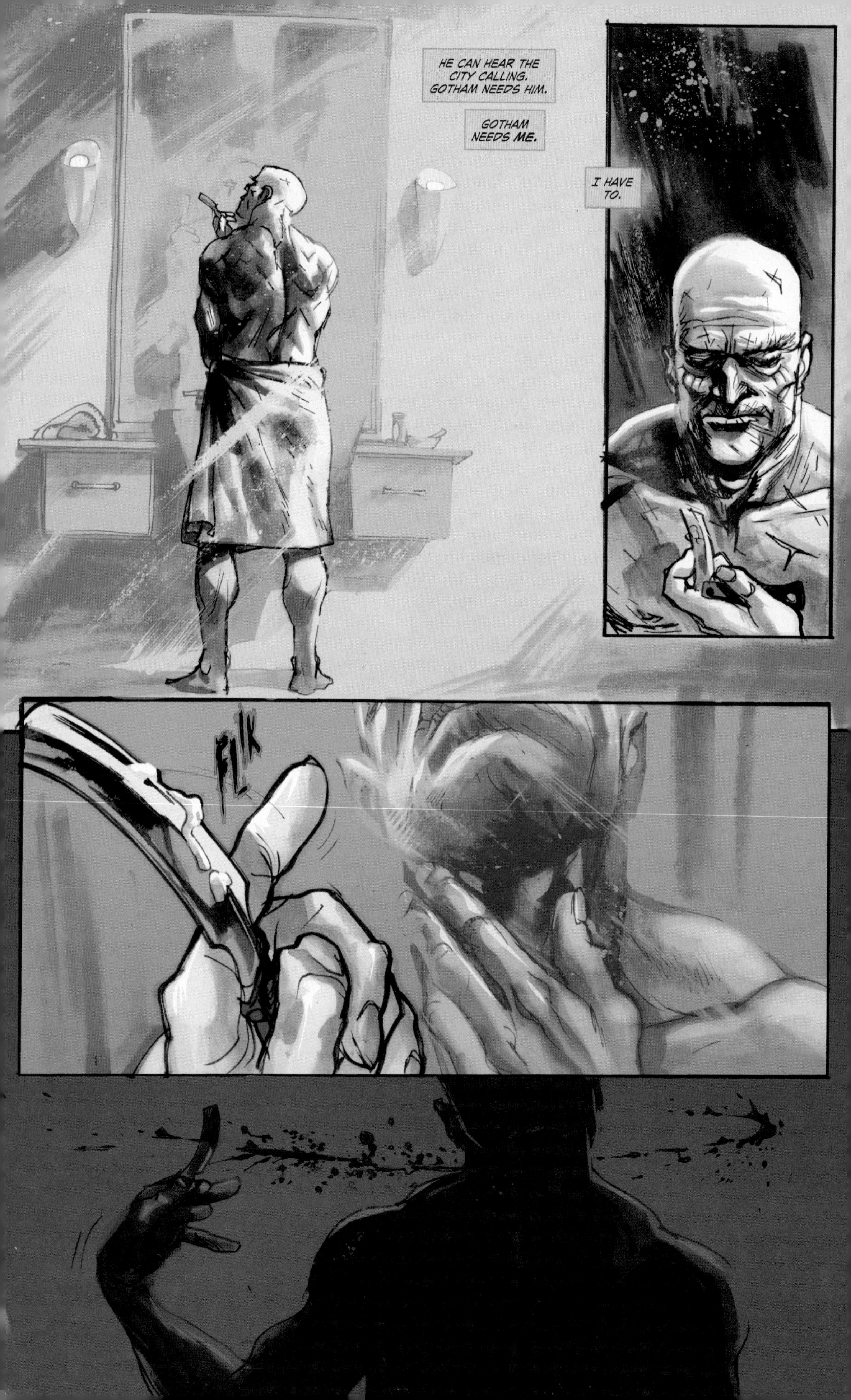
HE CAN HEAR THE CITY CALLING. GOTHAM NEEDS HIM.
GOTHAM NEEDS ME.
I HAVE TO.
FLIK

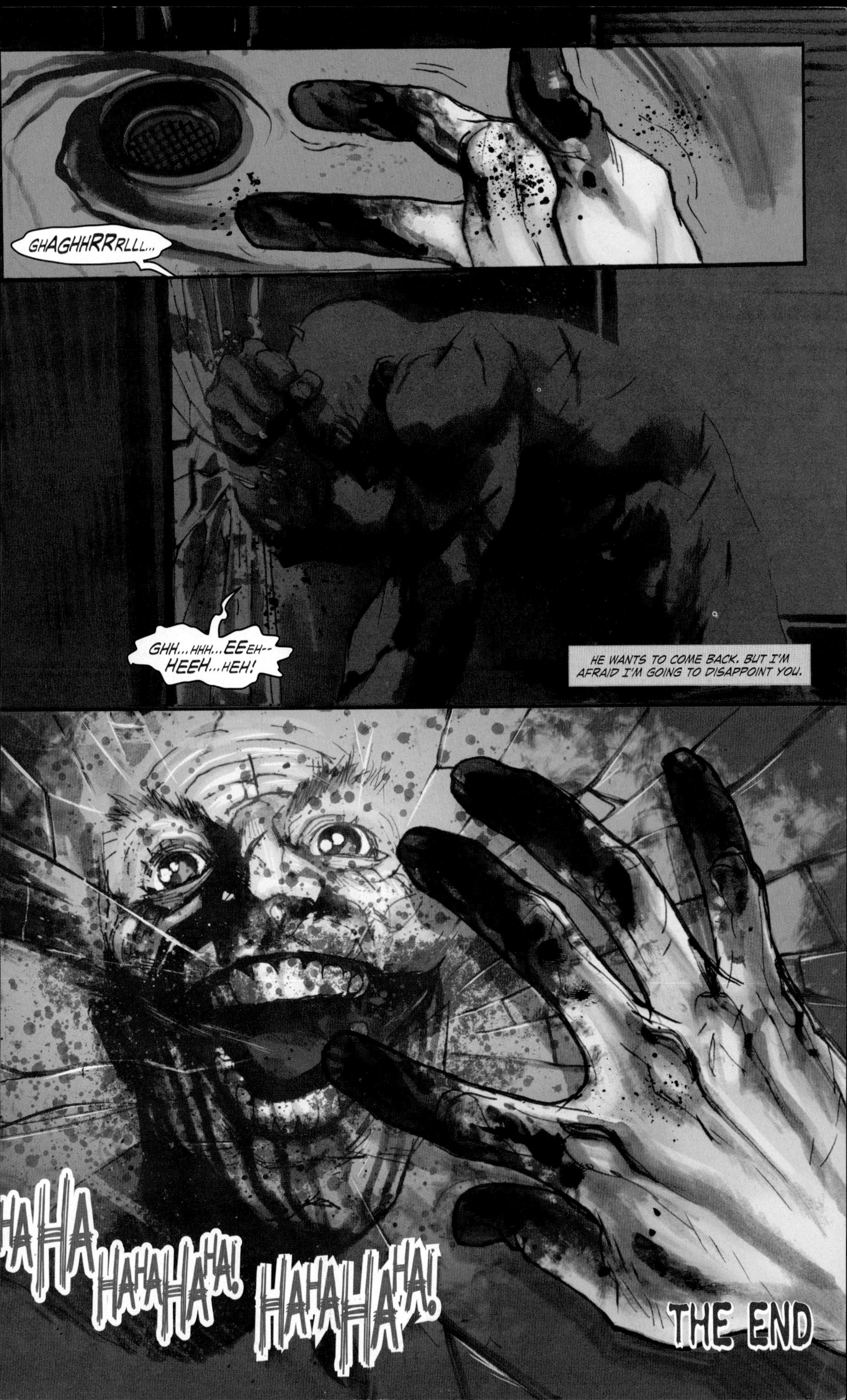
GHAGHHRRrlll...
GHH...HHH...EEeh--HEEH...HEH!
HE WANTS TO COME BACK. BUT I'M AFRAID I'M GOING TO DISAPPOINT YOU.
HAHA HAHAHAHA! HAHAHAHA!
THE END

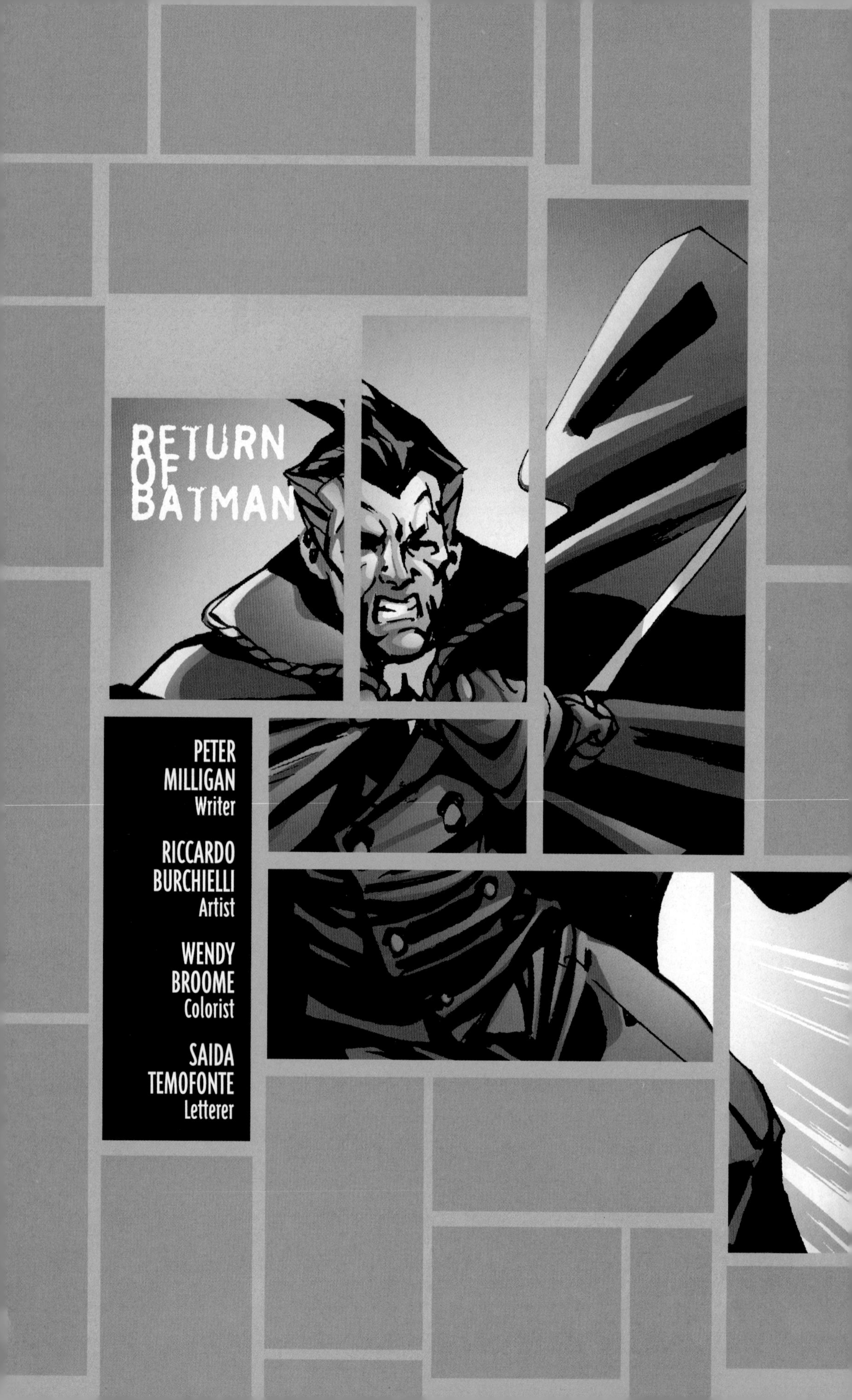
RETURN OF BATMAN
PETER MILLIGAN Writer
RICCARDO BURCHIELLI Artist
WENDY BROOME Colorist
SAIDA TEMOFONTE Letterer

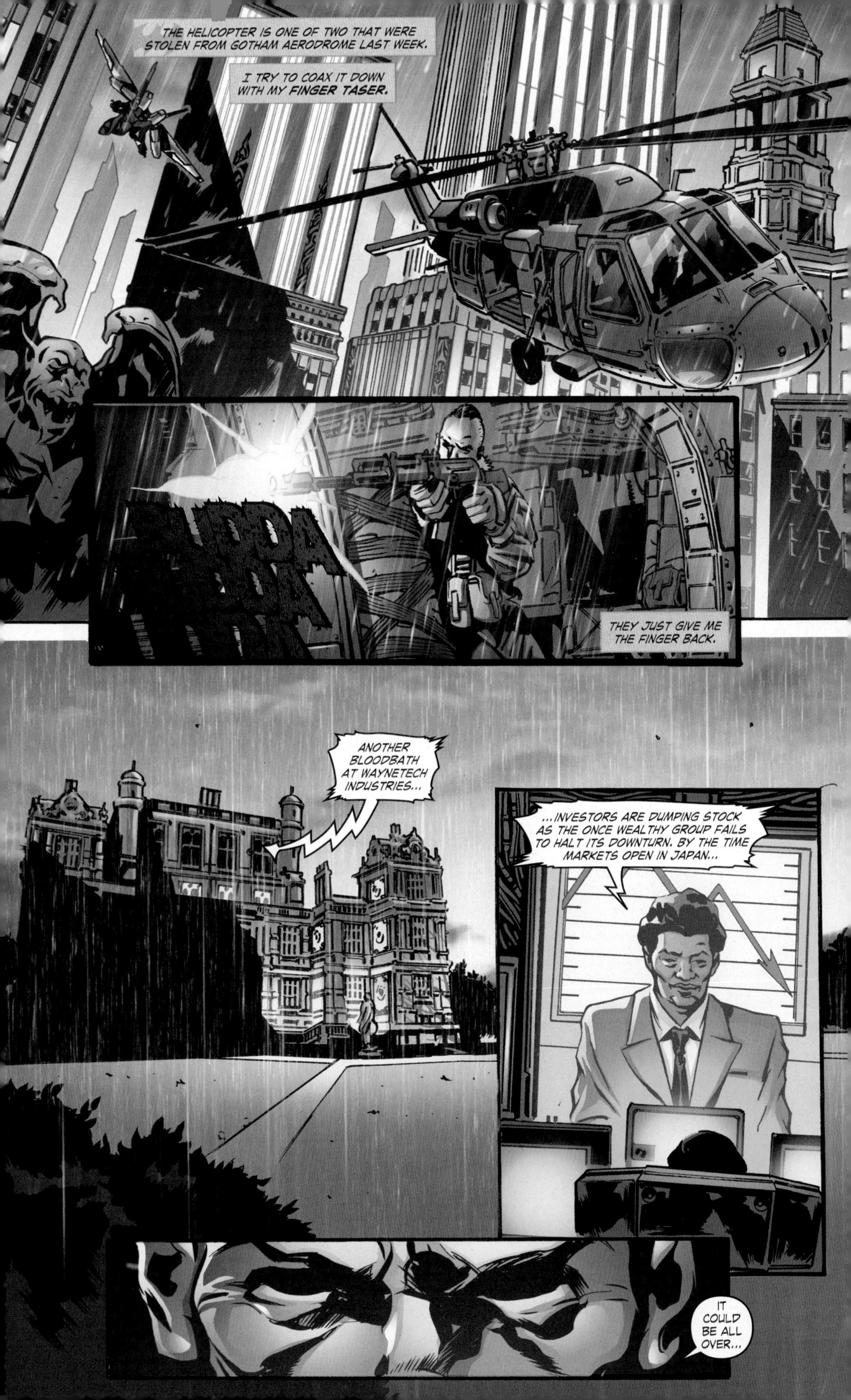
THE HELICOPTER IS ONE OF TWO THAT WERE STOLEN FROM GOTHAM AERODROME LAST WEEK.
I TRY TO COAX IT DOWN WITH MY FINGER TASER.
THEY JUST GIVE ME THE FINGER BACK.
ANOTHER BLOODBATH AT WAYNETECH INDUSTRIES...
...INVESTORS ARE DUMPING STOCK AS THE ONCE WEALTHY GROUP FAILS TO HALT ITS DOWNTURN. BY THE TIME MARKETS OPEN IN JAPAN...
IT COULD BE ALL OVER...

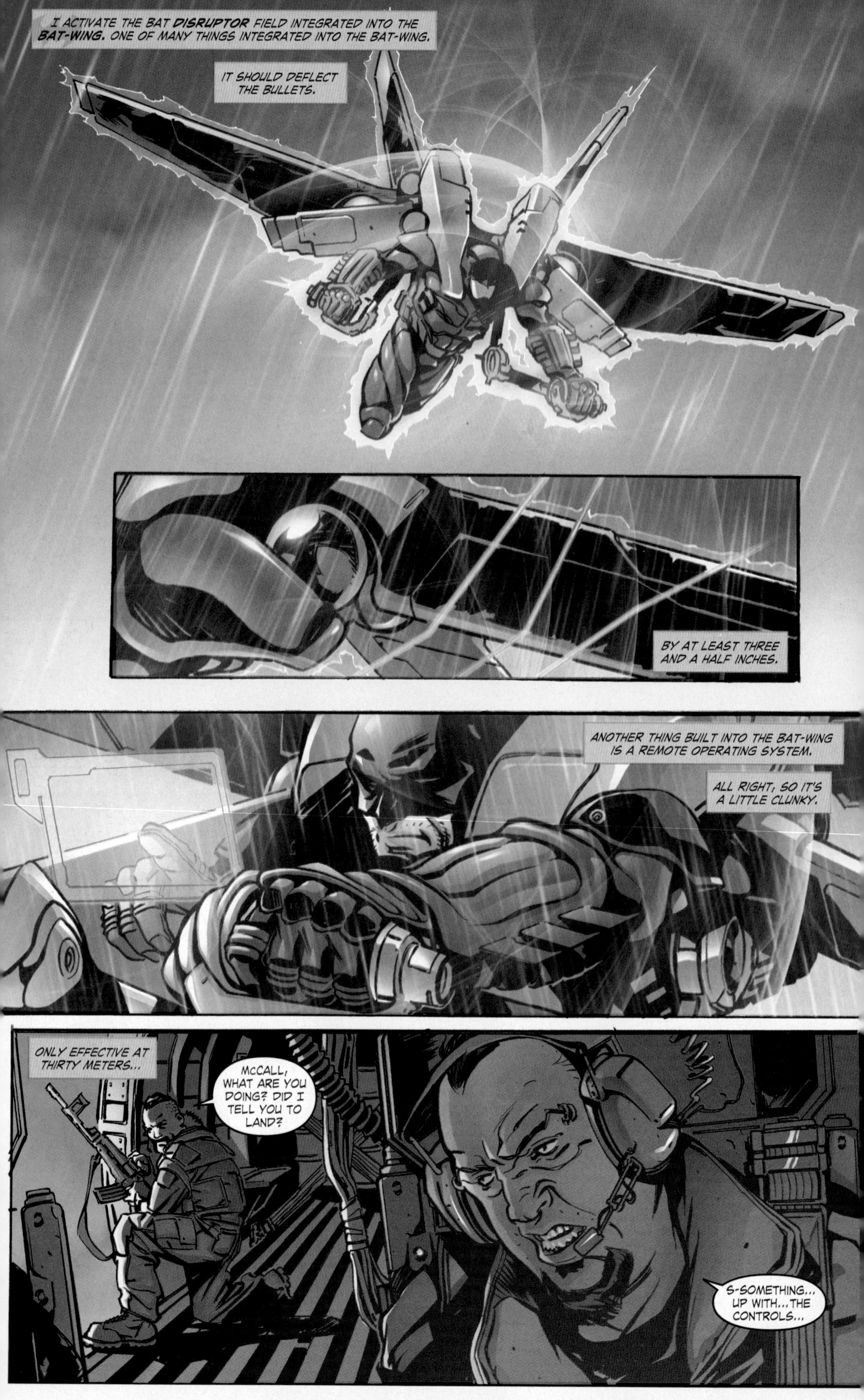
I ACTIVATE THE BAT DISRUPTOR FIELD INTEGRATED INTO THE BAT-WING. ONE OF MANY THINGS INTEGRATED INTO THE BAT-WING.
IT SHOULD DEFLECT THE BULLETS.
BY AT LEAST THREE AND A HALF INCHES.
ANOTHER THING BUILT INTO THE BAT-WING IS A REMOTE OPERATING SYSTEM.
ALL RIGHT, SO IT'S A LITTLE CLUNKY.
ONLY EFFECTIVE AT THIRTY METERS...
McCALL, WHAT ARE YOU DOING? DID I TELL YOU TO LAND?
S-SOMETHING... UP WITH... THE CONTROLS...

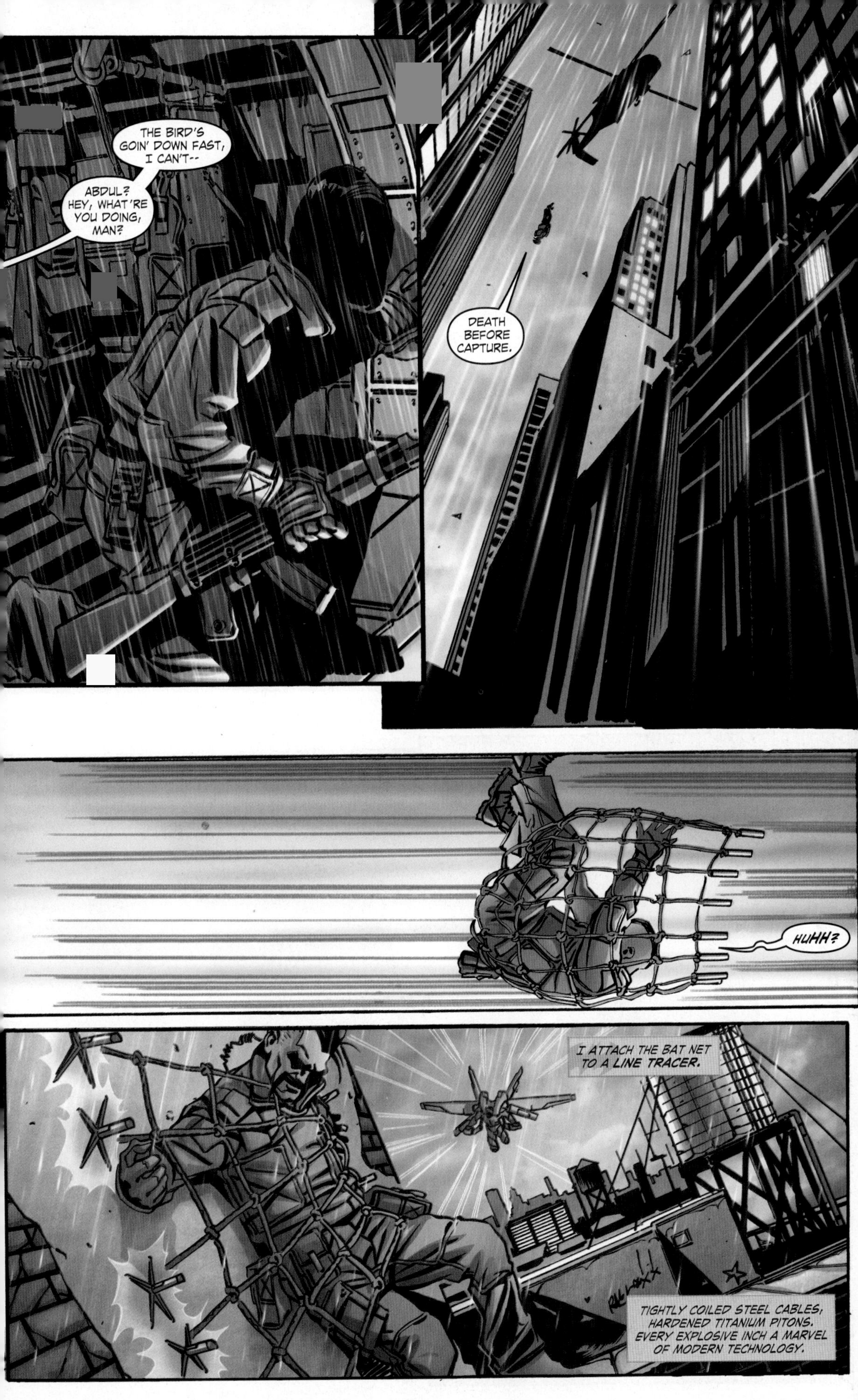
THE BIRD'S GOIN' DOWN FAST, I CAN'T--
ABDUL? HEY, WHAT'RE YOU DOING, MAN?
DEATH BEFORE CAPTURE.
HUHH?
I ATTACH THE BAT NET TO A LINE TRACER.
TIGHTLY COILED STEEL CABLES; HARDENED TITANIUM PITONS. EVERY EXPLOSIVE INCH A MARVEL OF MODERN TECHNOLOGY.

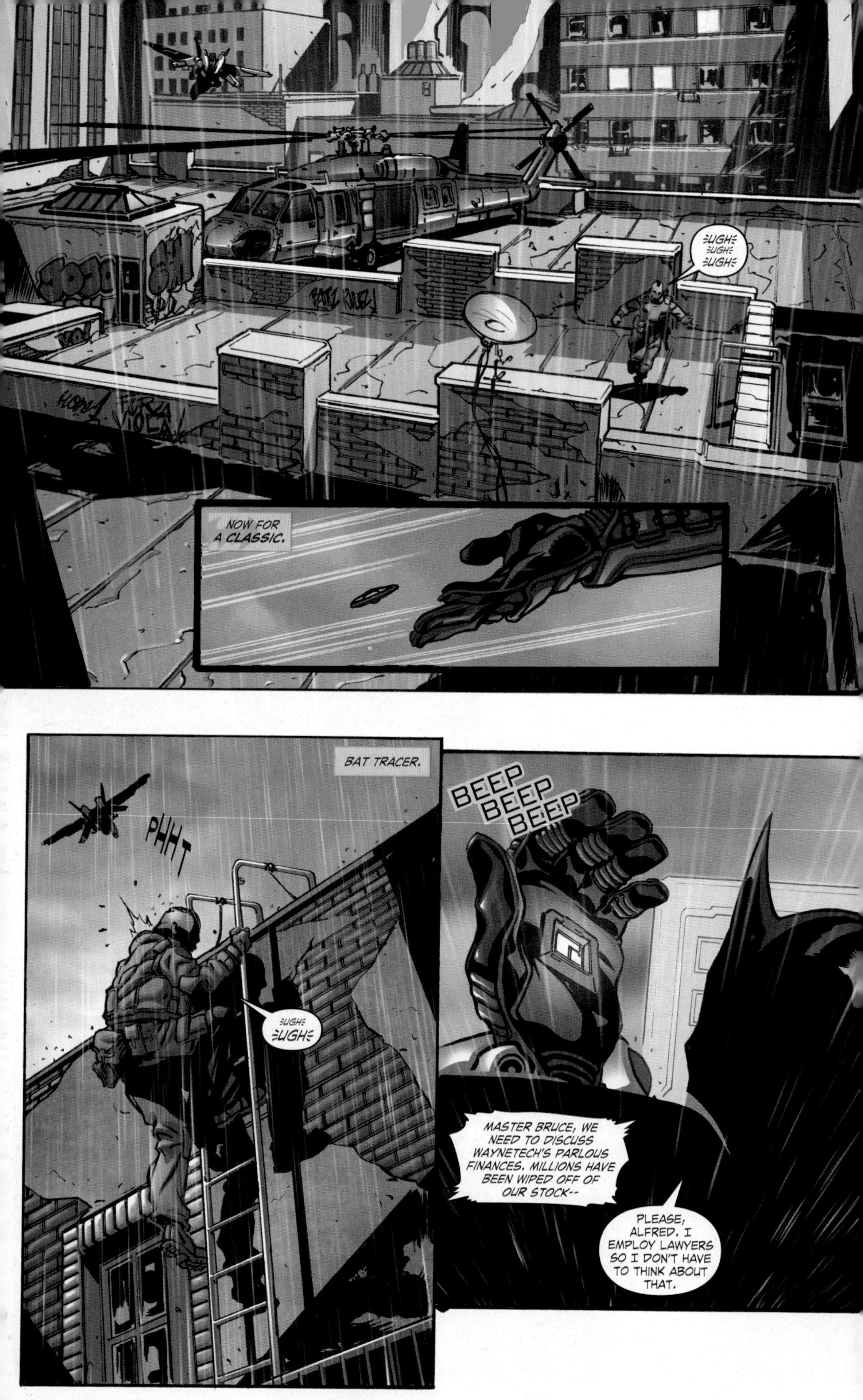
UGH UGH UGH
NOW FOR A CLASSIC.
BAT TRACER.
PHHT
UGH UGH
BEEP BEEP BEEP
MASTER BRUCE, WE NEED TO DISCUSS WAYNETECH'S PARLOUS FINANCES. MILLIONS HAVE BEEN WIPED OFF OF OUR STOCK--
PLEASE, ALFRED. I EMPLOY LAWYERS SO I DON'T HAVE TO THINK ABOUT THAT.

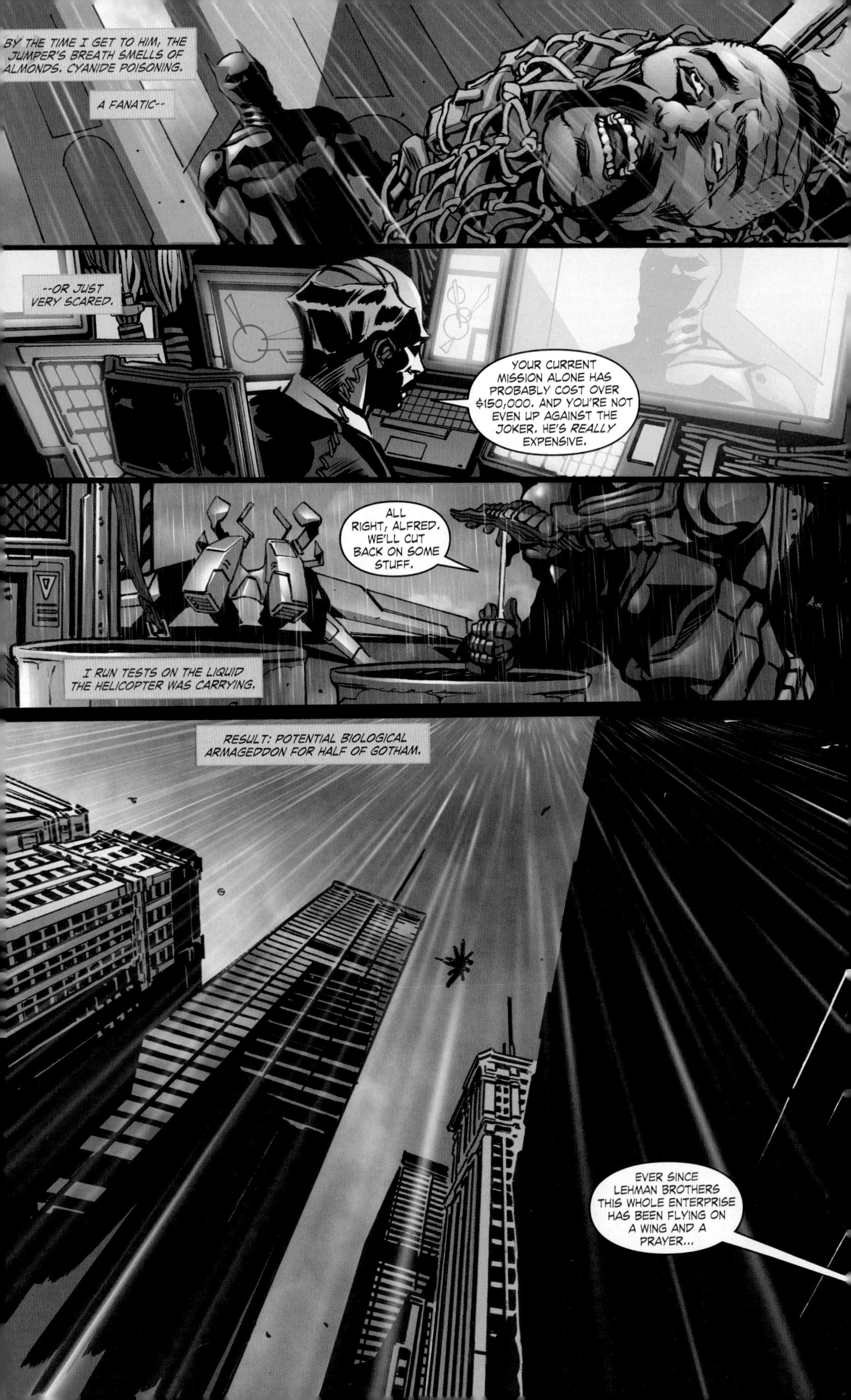
BY THE TIME I GET TO HIM, THE JUMPER'S BREATH SMELLS OF ALMONDS. CYANIDE POISONING.
A FANATIC--
--OR JUST VERY SCARED.
YOUR CURRENT MISSION ALONE HAS PROBABLY COST OVER $150,000. AND YOU'RE NOT EVEN UP AGAINST THE JOKER. HE'S REALLY EXPENSIVE.
ALL RIGHT, ALFRED. WE'LL CUT BACK ON SOME STUFF.
I RUN TESTS ON THE LIQUID THE HELICOPTER WAS CARRYING.
RESULT: POTENTIAL BIOLOGICAL ARMAGEDDON FOR HALF OF GOTHAM.
EVER SINCE LEHMAN BROTHERS THIS WHOLE ENTERPRISE HAS BEEN FLYING ON A WING AND A PRAYER...

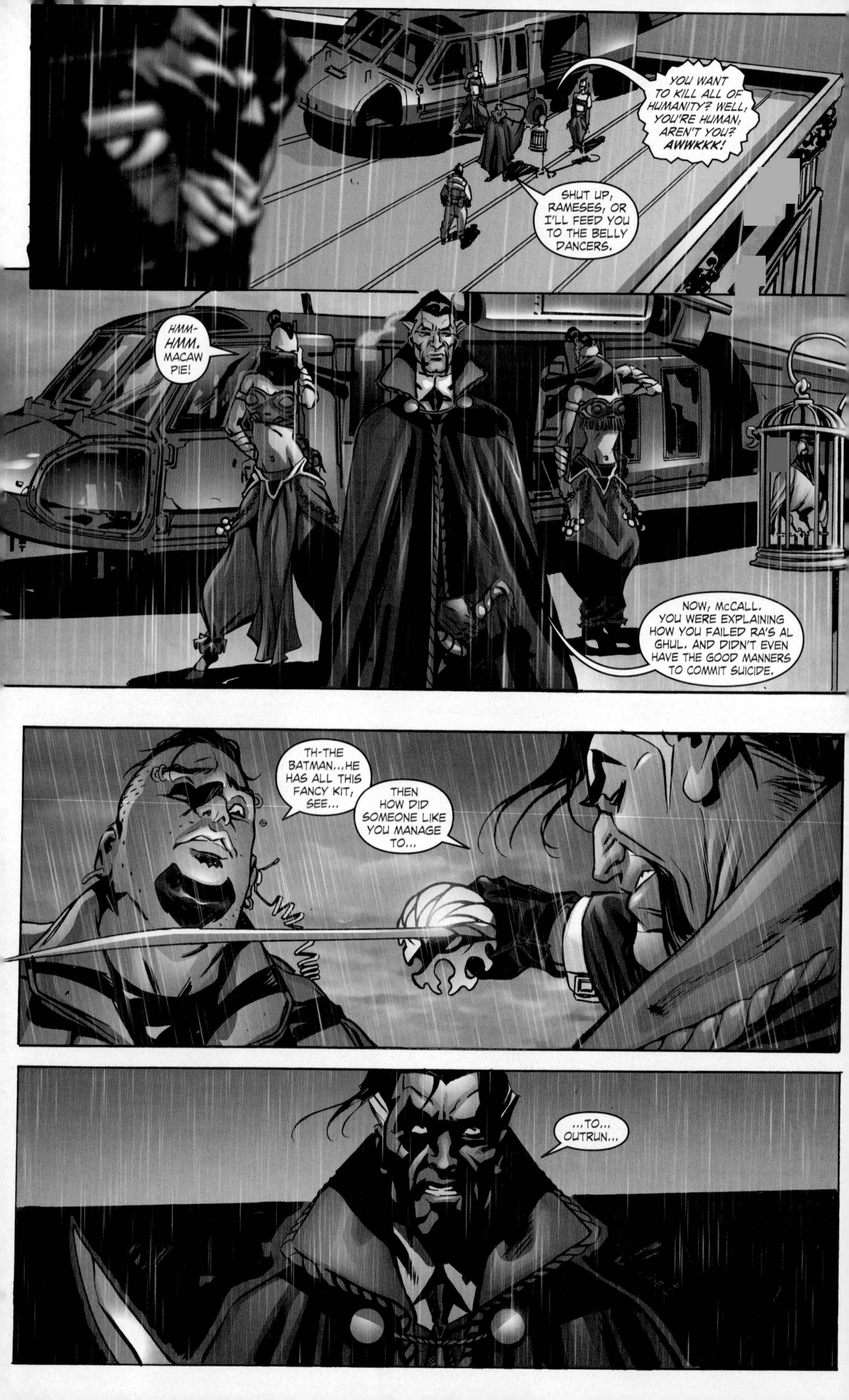
YOU WANT TO KILL ALL OF HUMANITY? WELL, YOU'RE HUMAN, AREN'T YOU? AWWKKK!
SHUT UP, RAMESES, OR I'LL FEED YOU TO THE BELLY DANCERS.
HMM-HMM. MACAW PIE!
NOW, McCALL. YOU WERE EXPLAINING HOW YOU FAILED RA'S AL GHUL. AND DIDN'T EVEN HAVE THE GOOD MANNERS TO COMMIT SUICIDE.
TH-THE BATMAN...HE HAS ALL THIS FANCY KIT, SEE...
THEN HOW DID SOMEONE LIKE YOU MANAGE TO...
...TO... OUTRUN...

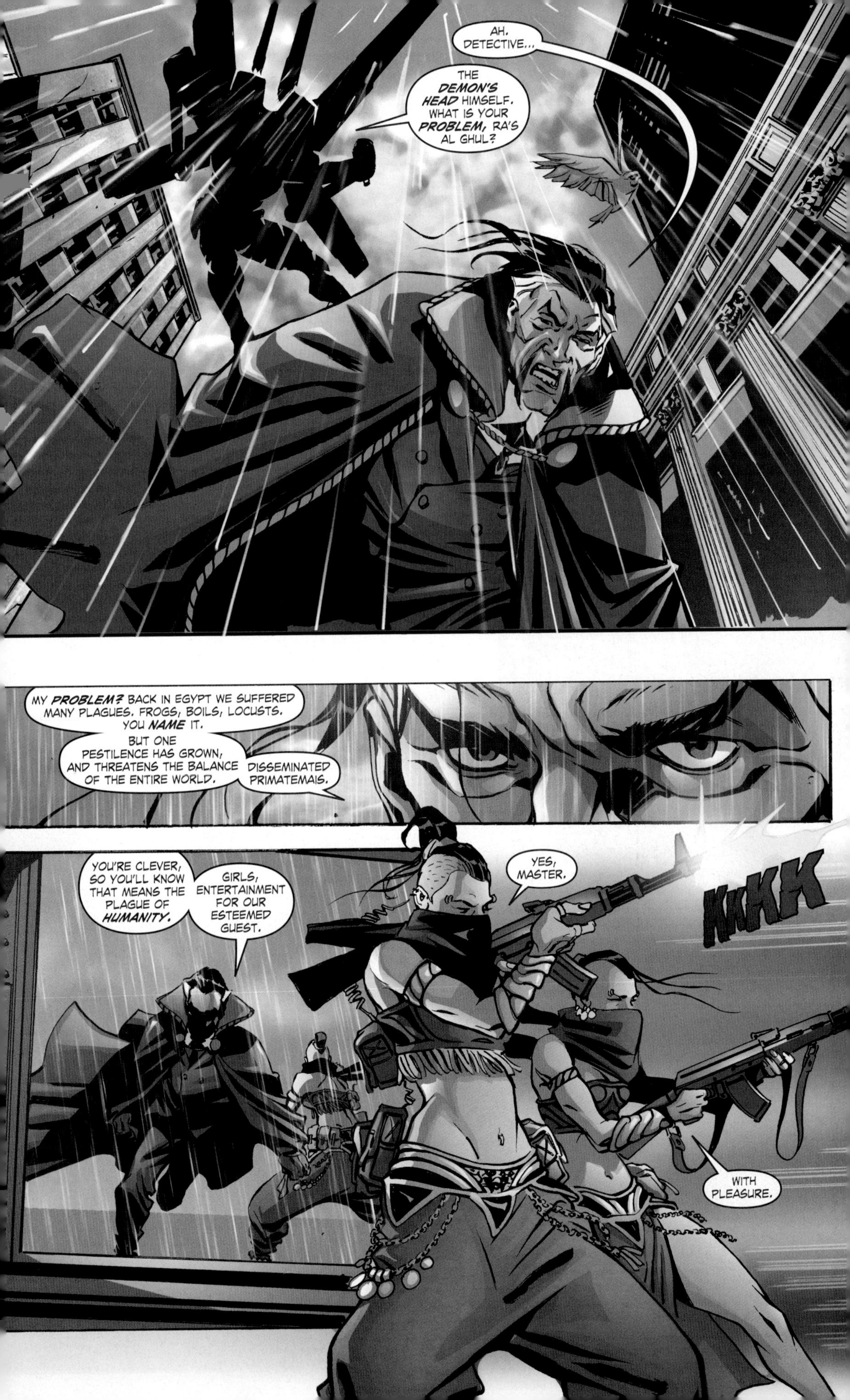
AH. DETECTIVE...
THE DEMON'S HEAD HIMSELF. WHAT IS YOUR PROBLEM, RA'S AL GHUL?
MY PROBLEM? BACK IN EGYPT WE SUFFERED MANY PLAGUES. FROGS, BOILS, LOCUSTS. YOU NAME IT.
BUT ONE PESTILENCE HAS GROWN, AND THREATENS THE BALANCE OF THE ENTIRE WORLD.
DISSEMINATED PRIMATEMAIS.
YOU'RE CLEVER, SO YOU'LL KNOW THAT MEANS THE PLAGUE OF HUMANITY.
GIRLS, ENTERTAINMENT FOR OUR ESTEEMED GUEST.
YES, MASTER.
KKKK
WITH PLEASURE.

HEAT SIGNATURE. SUPER RADAR. ELECTRO DISRUPTOR. BAT-WING ROCKET FUEL.

MINI BAT MISSILES.

KROOMM
KRTBOOMM
KRATBOO

SORRY, ALFRED...

...THAT'S PROBABLY ANOTHER 90 THOU...

CUT BACK ON STUFF, HE SAYS. WE'RE *ALREADY* CUTTING BACK...

ELECTRONICS MALFUNCTION!

KCKK
KCKK
KCKK

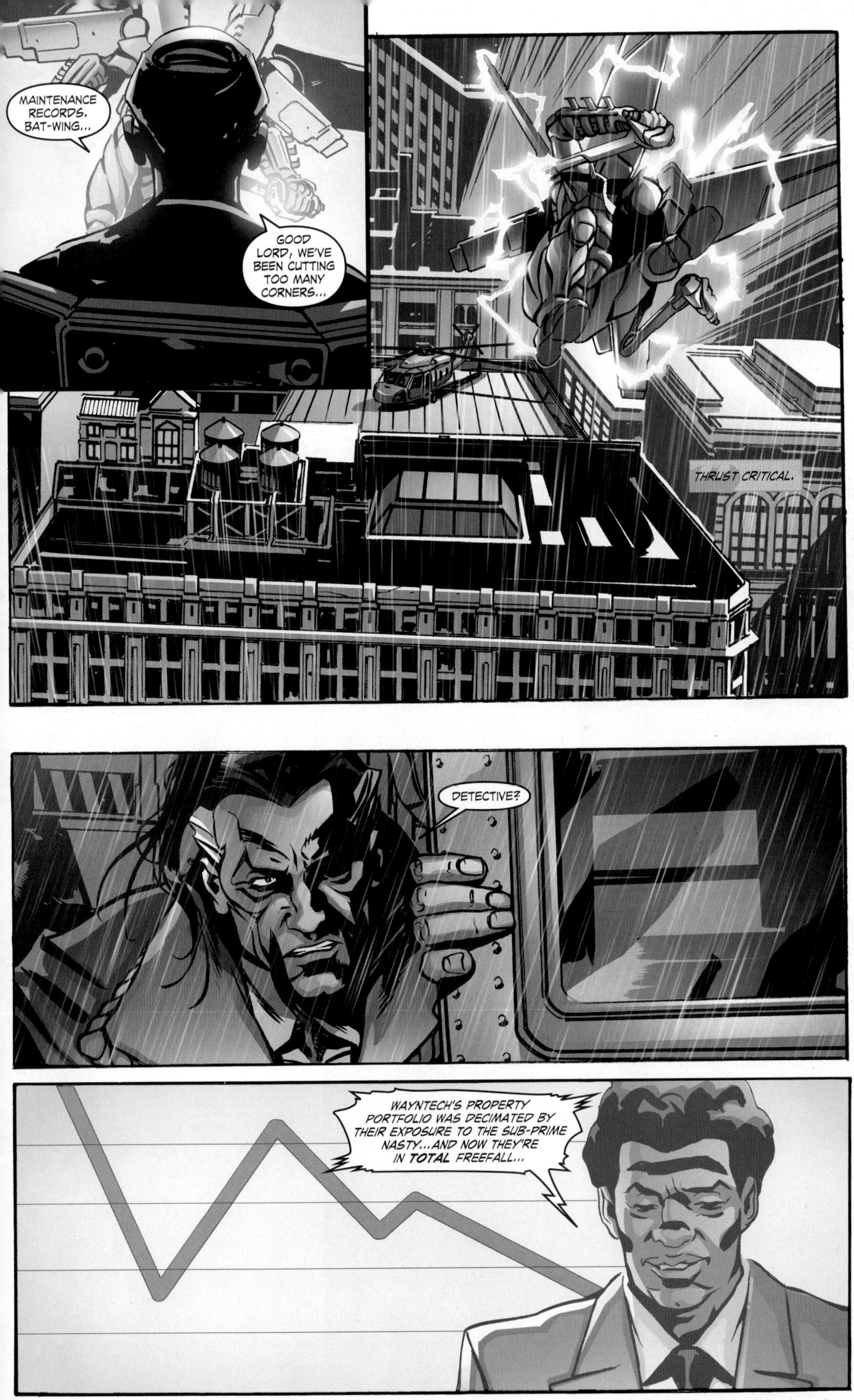
MAINTENANCE RECORDS. BAT-WING...
GOOD LORD, WE'VE BEEN CUTTING TOO MANY CORNERS...
THRUST CRITICAL.
DETECTIVE?
WAYNTECH'S PROPERTY PORTFOLIO WAS DECIMATED BY THEIR EXPOSURE TO THE SUB-PRIME NASTY...AND NOW THEY'RE IN TOTAL FREEFALL...

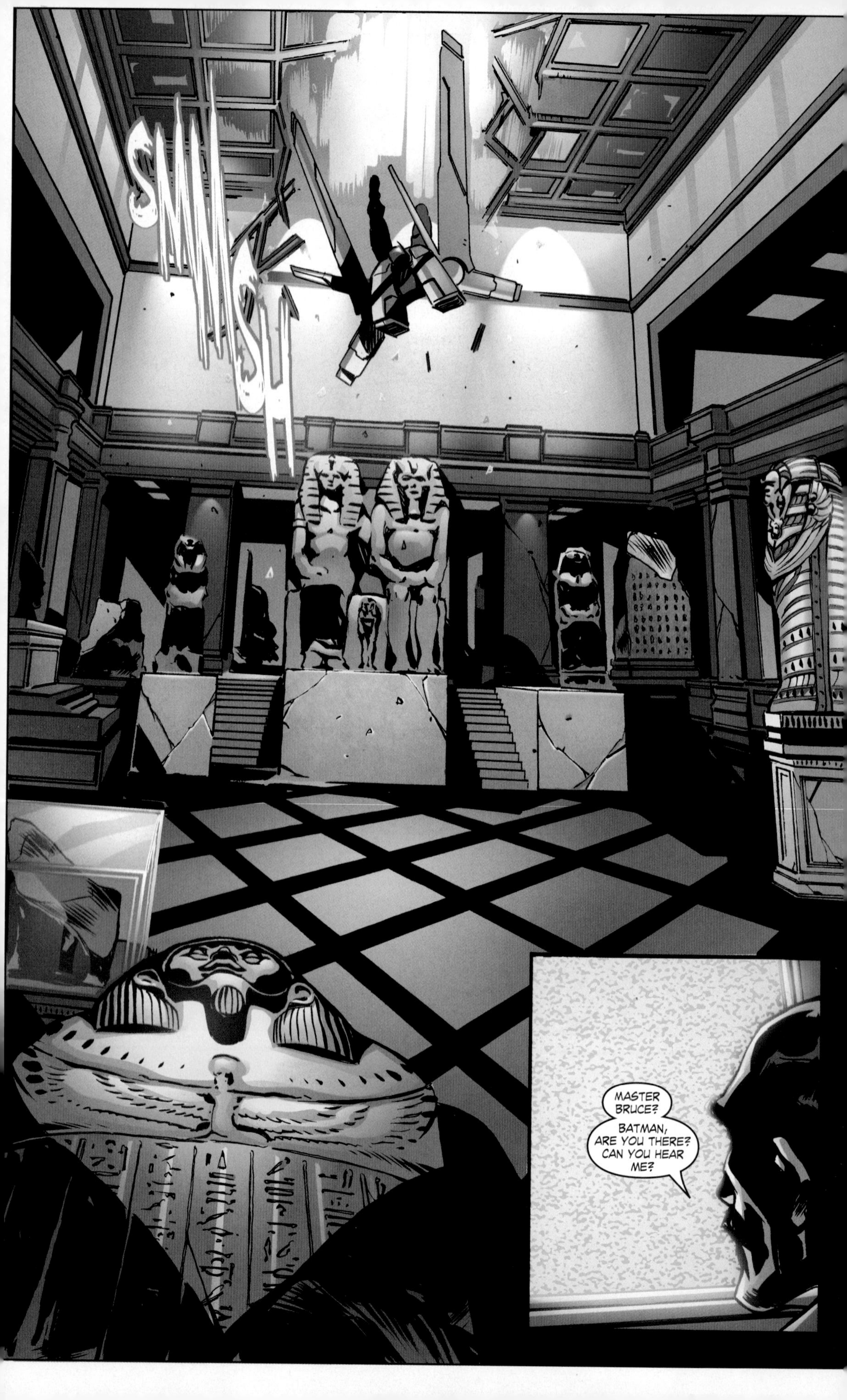
SMASH
MASTER BRUCE?
BATMAN, ARE YOU THERE? CAN YOU HEAR ME?

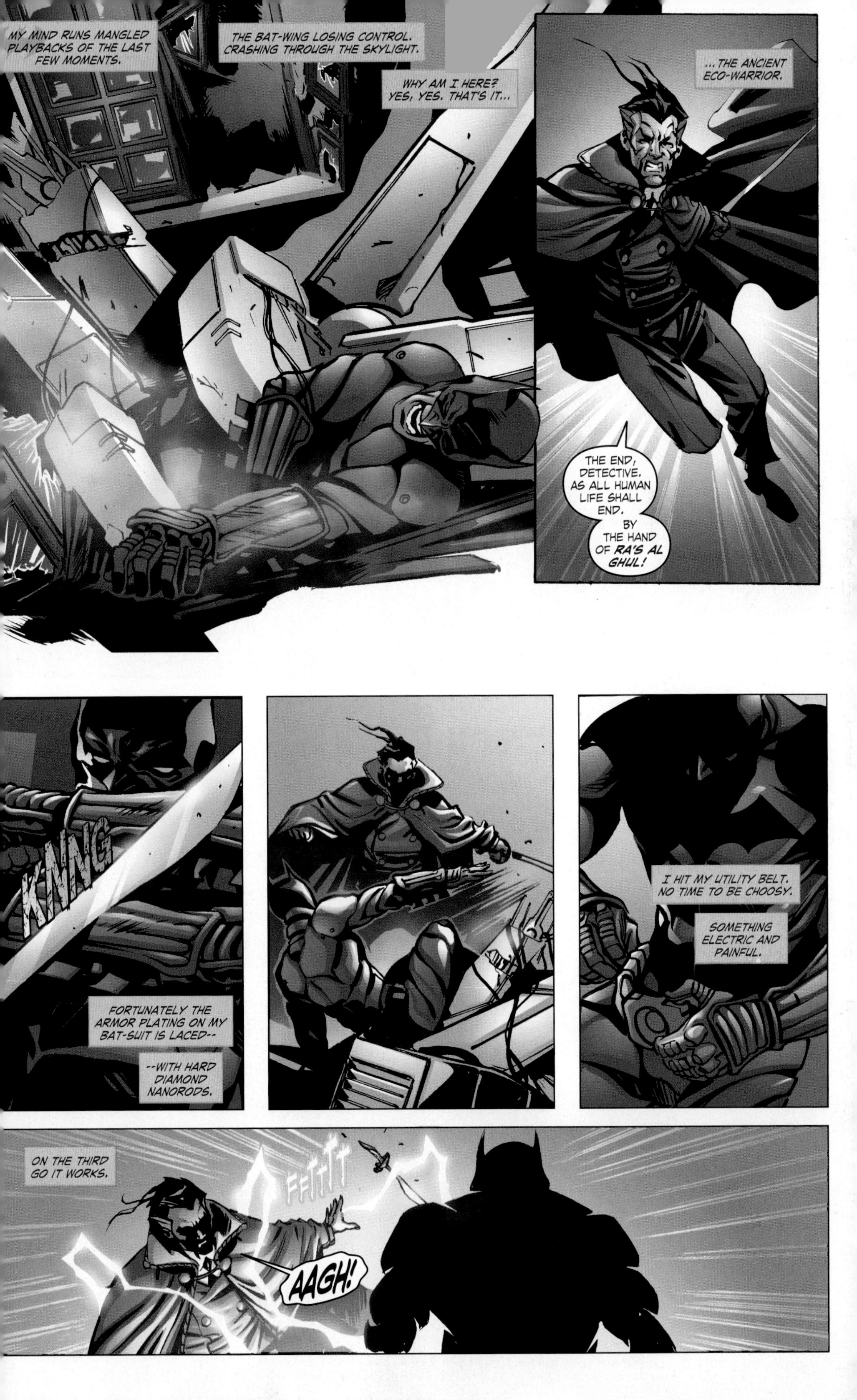
MY MIND RUNS MANGLED PLAYBACKS OF THE LAST FEW MOMENTS.
THE BAT-WING LOSING CONTROL. CRASHING THROUGH THE SKYLIGHT.
WHY AM I HERE? YES, YES. THAT'S IT...
...THE ANCIENT ECO-WARRIOR.
THE END, DETECTIVE. AS ALL HUMAN LIFE SHALL END.
BY THE HAND OF RA'S AL GHUL!
KNNG
FORTUNATELY THE ARMOR PLATING ON MY BAT-SUIT IS LACED--
--WITH HARD DIAMOND NANORODS.
I HIT MY UTILITY BELT. NO TIME TO BE CHOOSY.
SOMETHING ELECTRIC AND PAINFUL.
ON THE THIRD GO IT WORKS.
FFTTTT
AAGH!

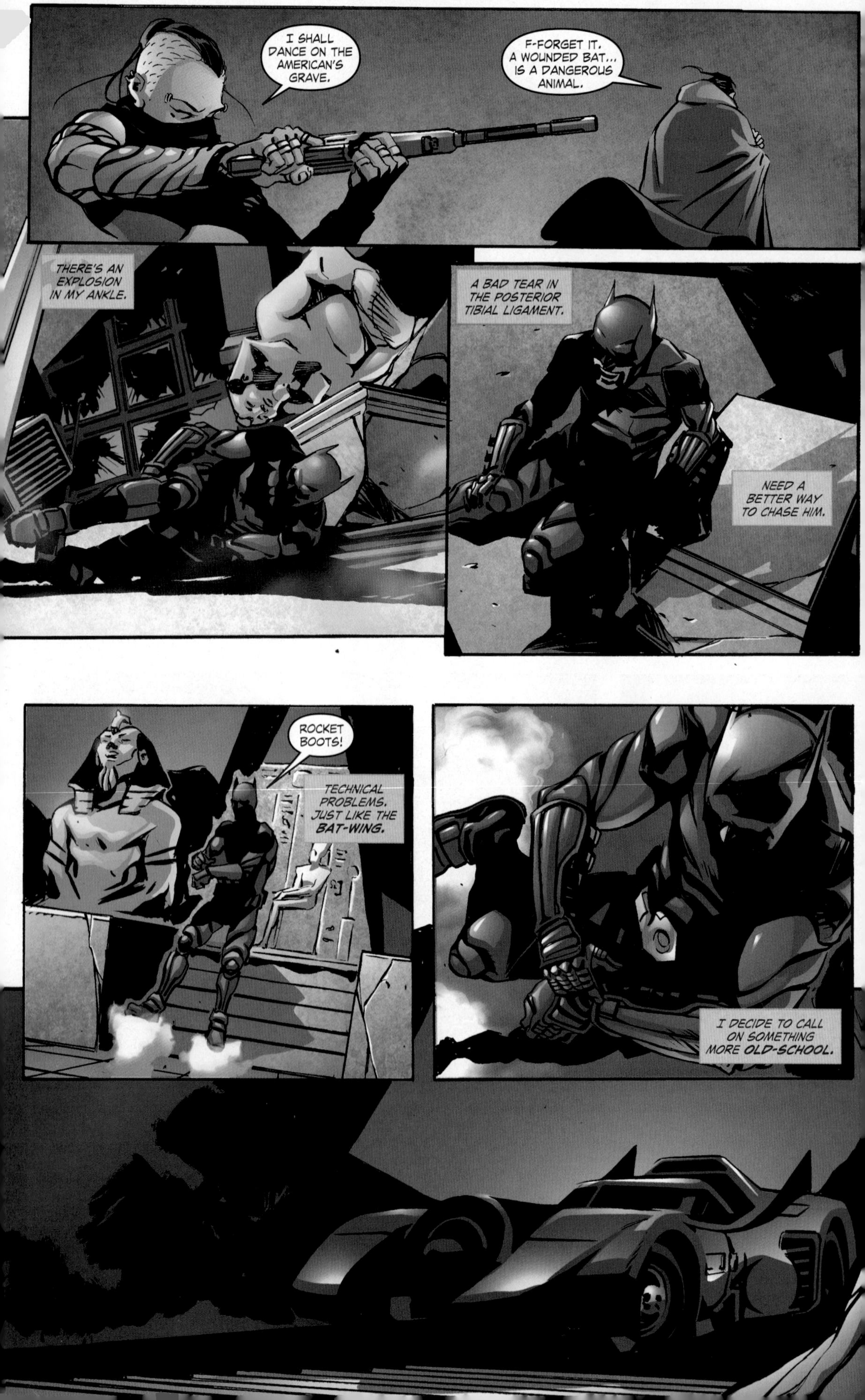
I SHALL DANCE ON THE AMERICAN'S GRAVE.
F-FORGET IT. A WOUNDED BAT... IS A DANGEROUS ANIMAL.
THERE'S AN EXPLOSION IN MY ANKLE.
A BAD TEAR IN THE POSTERIOR TIBIAL LIGAMENT.
NEED A BETTER WAY TO CHASE HIM.
ROCKET BOOTS!
TECHNICAL PROBLEMS. JUST LIKE THE BAT-WING.
I DECIDE TO CALL ON SOMETHING MORE OLD-SCHOOL.

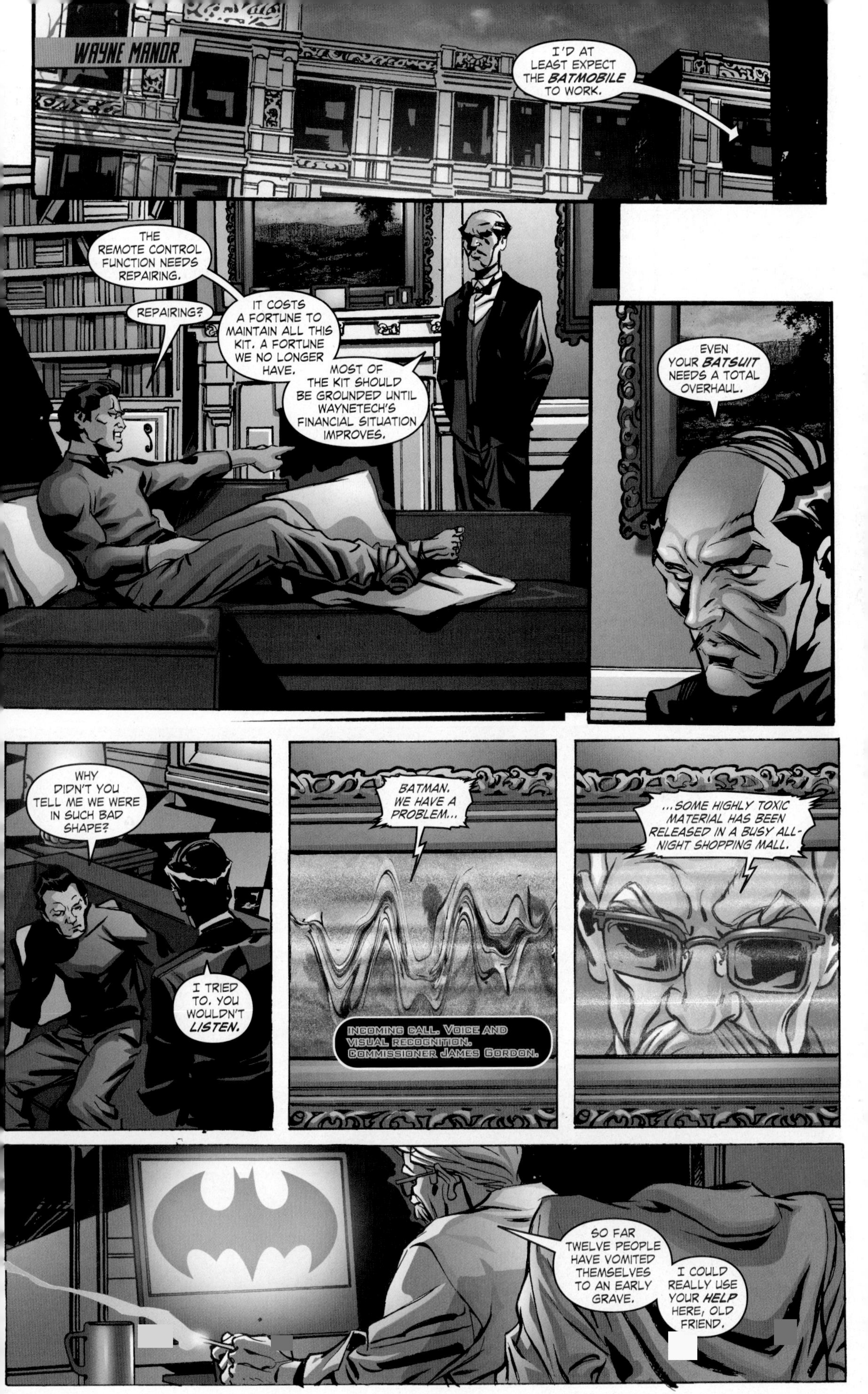
WAYNE MANOR.
I'D AT LEAST EXPECT THE BATMOBILE TO WORK.
THE REMOTE CONTROL FUNCTION NEEDS REPAIRING.
REPAIRING?
IT COSTS A FORTUNE TO MAINTAIN ALL THIS KIT. A FORTUNE WE NO LONGER HAVE.
MOST OF THE KIT SHOULD BE GROUNDED UNTIL WAYNETECH'S FINANCIAL SITUATION IMPROVES.
EVEN YOUR BATSUIT NEEDS A TOTAL OVERHAUL.
WHY DIDN'T YOU TELL ME WE WERE IN SUCH BAD SHAPE?
I TRIED TO. YOU WOULDN'T LISTEN.
BATMAN. WE HAVE A PROBLEM...
INCOMING CALL. VOICE AND VISUAL RECOGNITION. COMMISSIONER JAMES GORDON.
...SOME HIGHLY TOXIC MATERIAL HAS BEEN RELEASED IN A BUSY ALL-NIGHT SHOPPING MALL.
SO FAR TWELVE PEOPLE HAVE VOMITED THEMSELVES TO AN EARLY GRAVE.
I COULD REALLY USE YOUR HELP HERE, OLD FRIEND.

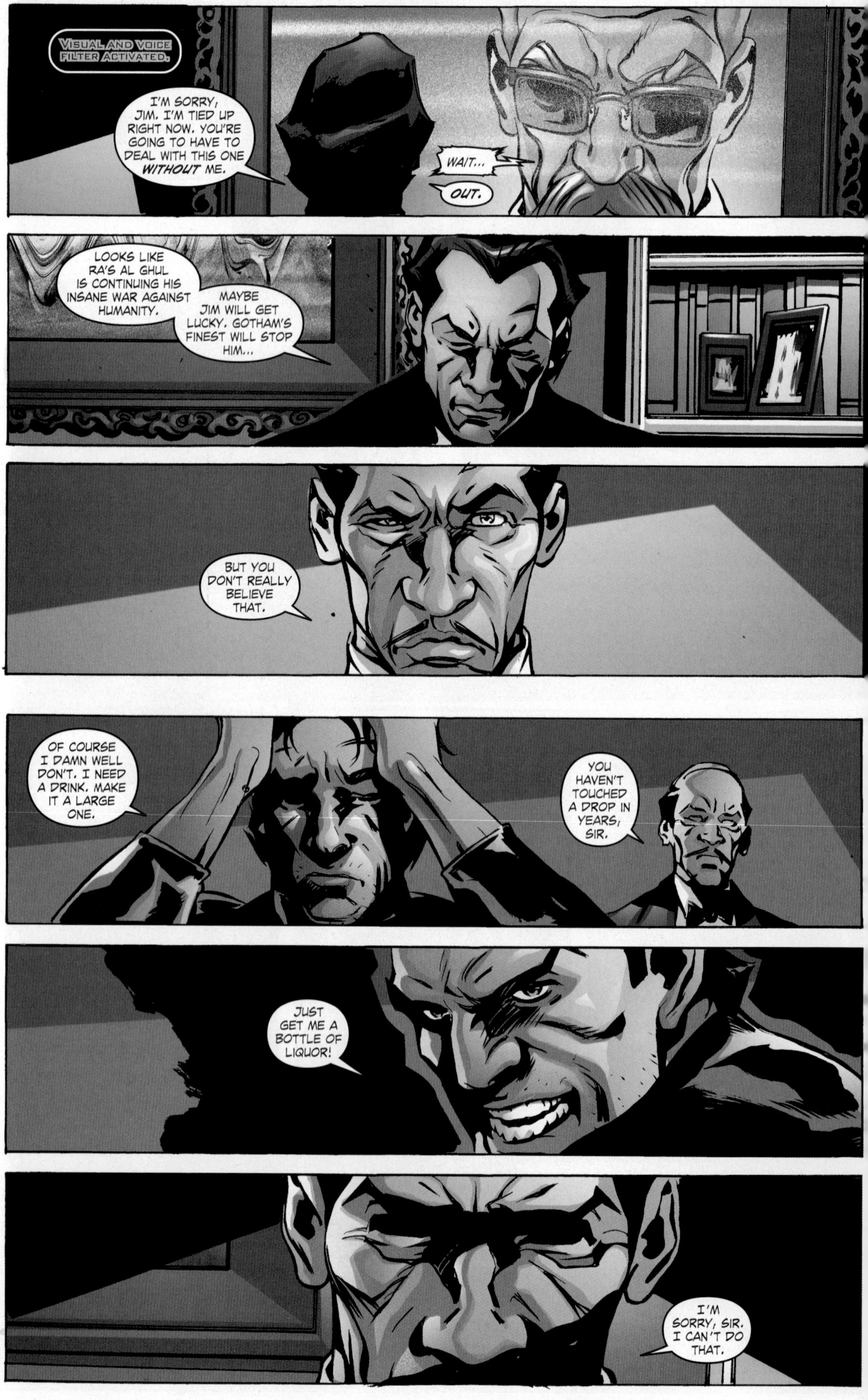
VISUAL AND VOICE FILTER ACTIVATED.
I'M SORRY, JIM. I'M TIED UP RIGHT NOW. YOU'RE GOING TO HAVE TO DEAL WITH THIS ONE *WITHOUT* ME.
WAIT...
OUT.
LOOKS LIKE RA'S AL GHUL IS CONTINUING HIS INSANE WAR AGAINST HUMANITY.
MAYBE JIM WILL GET LUCKY. GOTHAM'S FINEST WILL STOP HIM...
BUT YOU DON'T REALLY BELIEVE THAT.
OF COURSE I DAMN WELL DON'T. I NEED A DRINK. MAKE IT A LARGE ONE.
YOU HAVEN'T TOUCHED A DROP IN YEARS, SIR.
JUST GET ME A BOTTLE OF LIQUOR!
I'M SORRY, SIR. I CAN'T DO THAT.

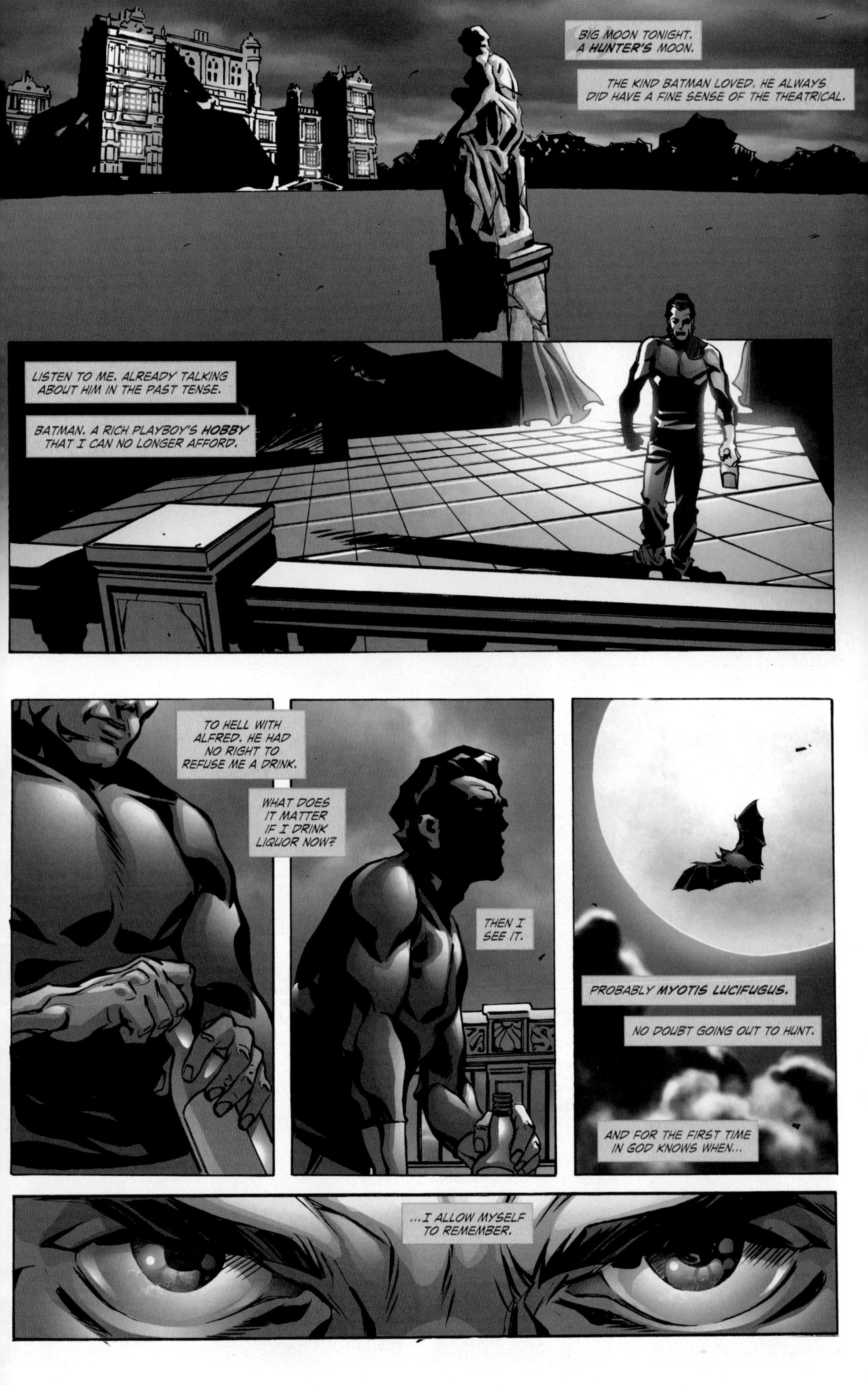
BIG MOON TONIGHT. A HUNTER'S MOON.
THE KIND BATMAN LOVED. HE ALWAYS DID HAVE A FINE SENSE OF THE THEATRICAL.
LISTEN TO ME. ALREADY TALKING ABOUT HIM IN THE PAST TENSE.
BATMAN. A RICH PLAYBOY'S HOBBY THAT I CAN NO LONGER AFFORD.
TO HELL WITH ALFRED. HE HAD NO RIGHT TO REFUSE ME A DRINK.
WHAT DOES IT MATTER IF I DRINK LIQUOR NOW?
THEN I SEE IT.
PROBABLY MYOTIS LUCIFUGUS.
NO DOUBT GOING OUT TO HUNT.
AND FOR THE FIRST TIME IN GOD KNOWS WHEN...
...I ALLOW MYSELF TO REMEMBER.

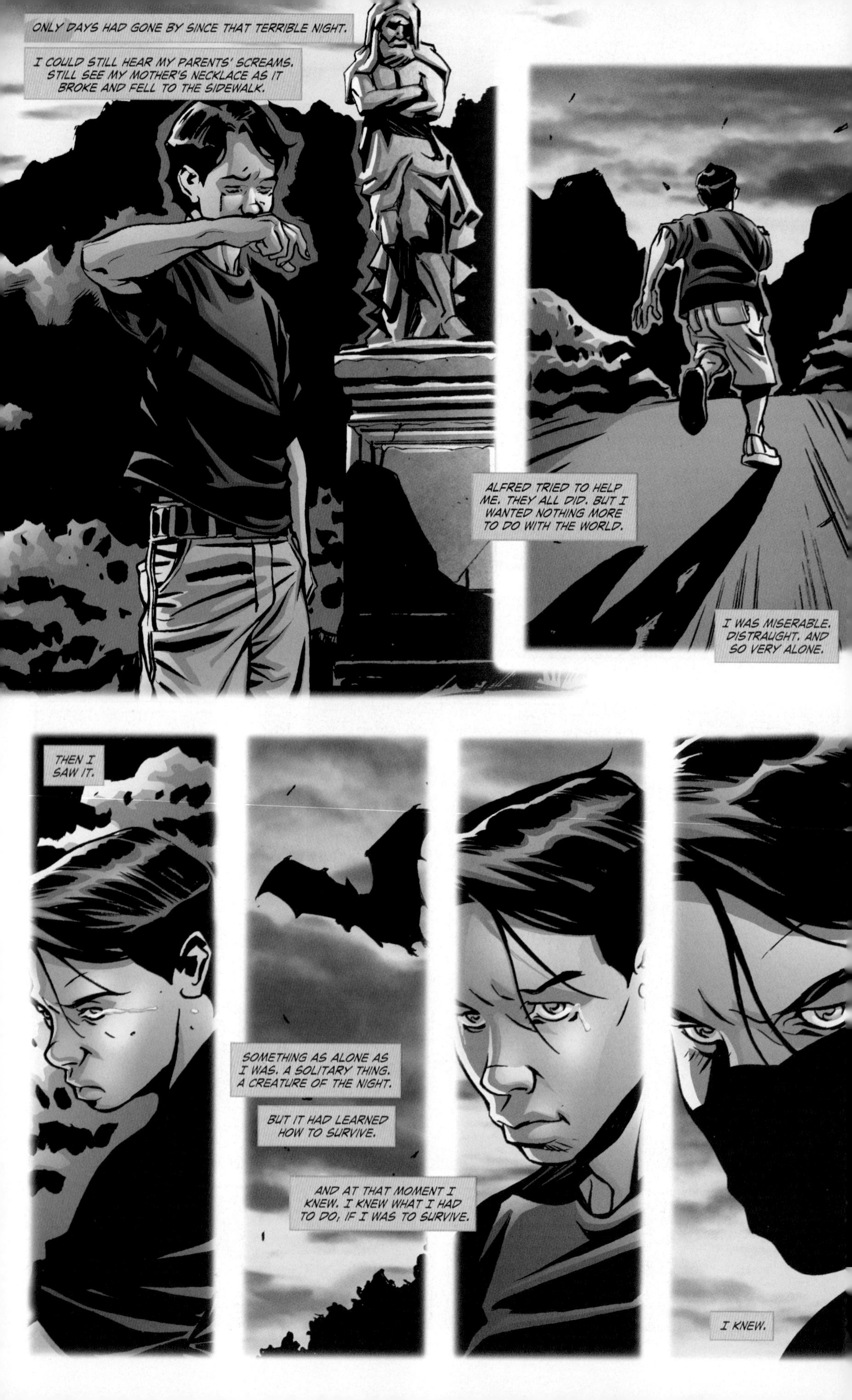

ONLY DAYS HAD GONE BY SINCE THAT TERRIBLE NIGHT.
I COULD STILL HEAR MY PARENTS' SCREAMS. STILL SEE MY MOTHER'S NECKLACE AS IT BROKE AND FELL TO THE SIDEWALK.
ALFRED TRIED TO HELP ME. THEY ALL DID. BUT I WANTED NOTHING MORE TO DO WITH THE WORLD.
I WAS MISERABLE. DISTRAUGHT. AND SO VERY ALONE.
THEN I SAW IT.
SOMETHING AS ALONE AS I WAS. A SOLITARY THING. A CREATURE OF THE NIGHT.
BUT IT HAD LEARNED HOW TO SURVIVE.
AND AT THAT MOMENT I KNEW. I KNEW WHAT I HAD TO DO, IF I WAS TO SURVIVE.
I KNEW.

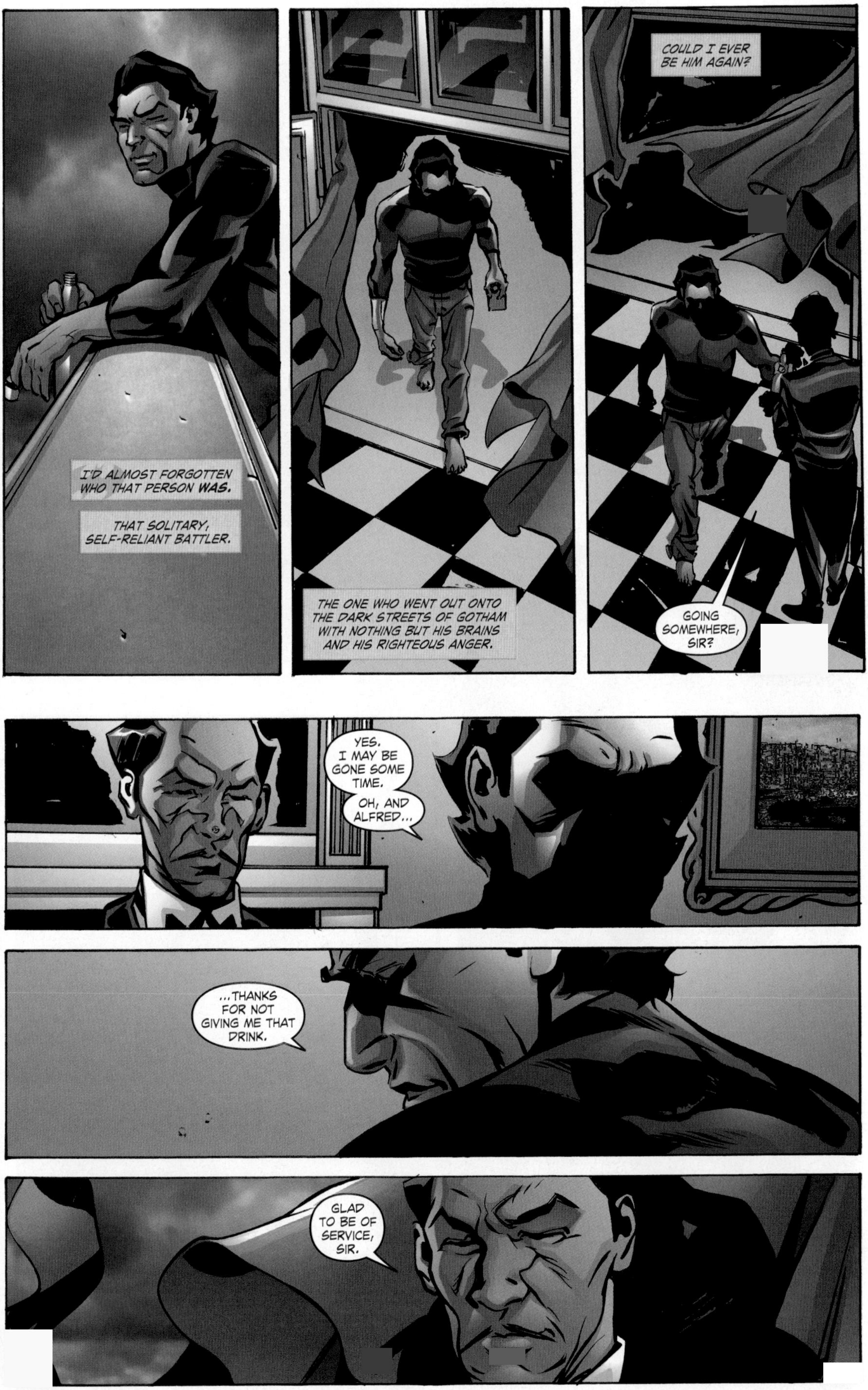
I'D ALMOST FORGOTTEN WHO THAT PERSON WAS.
THAT SOLITARY, SELF-RELIANT BATTLER.
THE ONE WHO WENT OUT ONTO THE DARK STREETS OF GOTHAM WITH NOTHING BUT HIS BRAINS AND HIS RIGHTEOUS ANGER.
COULD I EVER BE HIM AGAIN?
GOING SOMEWHERE, SIR?
YES. I MAY BE GONE SOME TIME.
OH, AND ALFRED...
...THANKS FOR NOT GIVING ME THAT DRINK.
GLAD TO BE OF SERVICE, SIR.

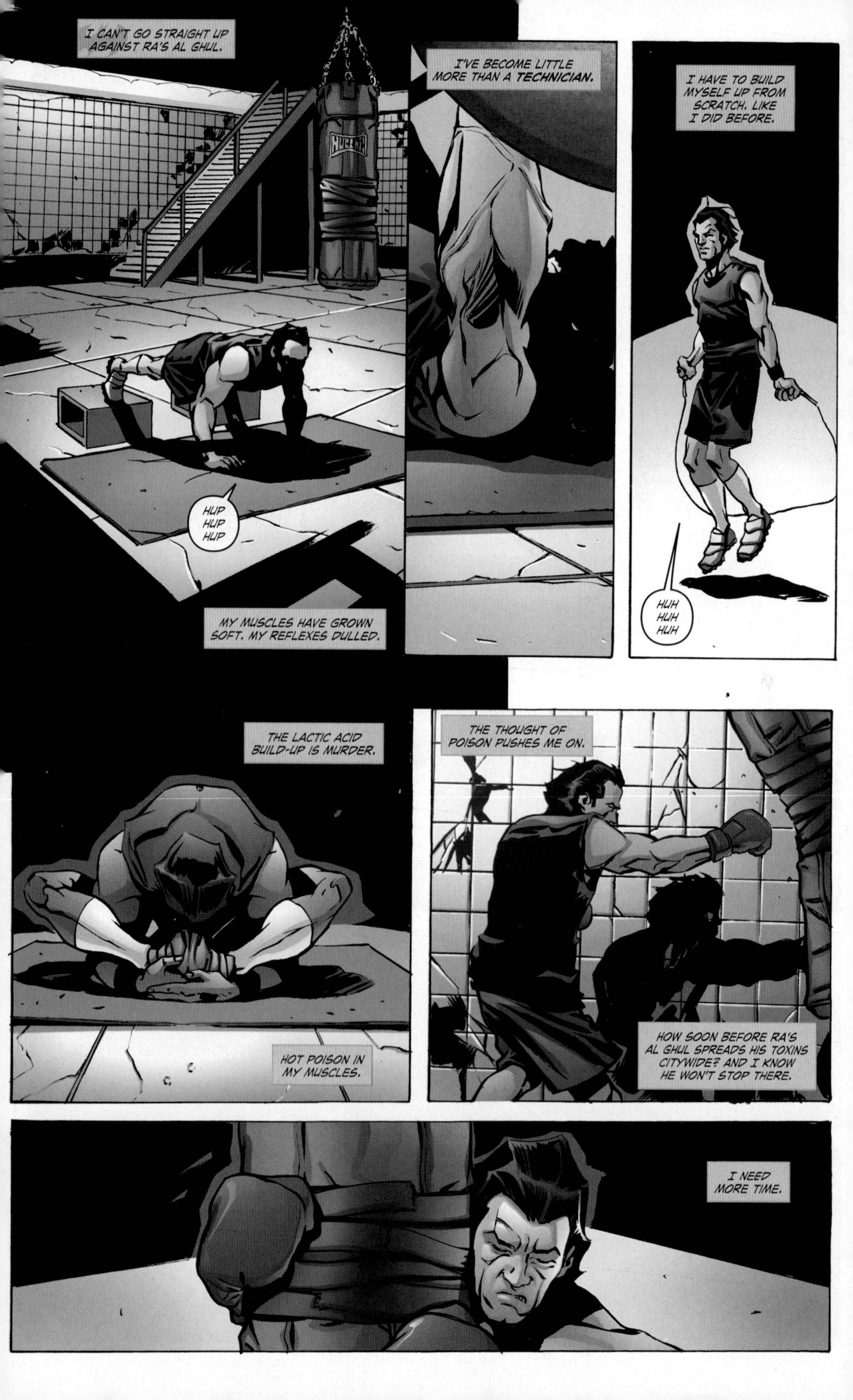
I CAN'T GO STRAIGHT UP AGAINST RA'S AL GHUL.
HUP HUP HUP
MY MUSCLES HAVE GROWN SOFT. MY REFLEXES DULLED.
I'VE BECOME LITTLE MORE THAN A **TECHNICIAN.**
I HAVE TO BUILD MYSELF UP FROM SCRATCH. LIKE I DID BEFORE.
HUH HUH HUH
THE LACTIC ACID BUILD-UP IS MURDER.
HOT POISON IN MY MUSCLES.
THE THOUGHT OF POISON PUSHES ME ON.
HOW SOON BEFORE RA'S AL GHUL SPREADS HIS TOXINS CITYWIDE? AND I KNOW HE WON'T STOP THERE.
I NEED MORE TIME.

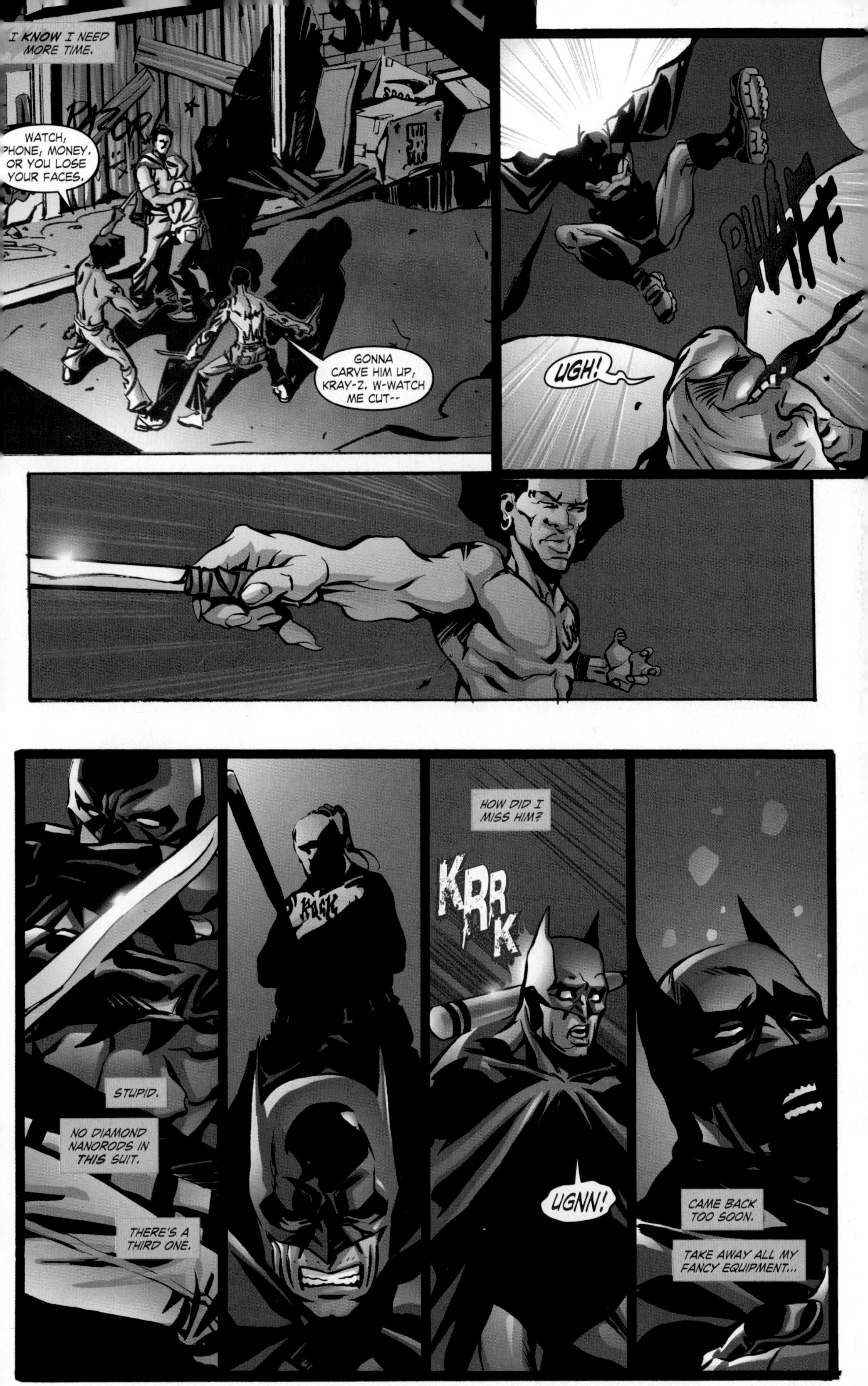
I KNOW I NEED MORE TIME.
PA-POP!
WATCH, PHONE, MONEY. OR YOU LOSE YOUR FACES.
GONNA CARVE HIM UP, KRAY-Z. W-WATCH ME CUT--
BHAFF
UGH!
STUPID.
NO DIAMOND NANORODS IN THIS SUIT.
THERE'S A THIRD ONE.
HOW DID I MISS HIM?
KRRK
UGNN!
CAME BACK TOO SOON.
TAKE AWAY ALL MY FANCY EQUIPMENT...

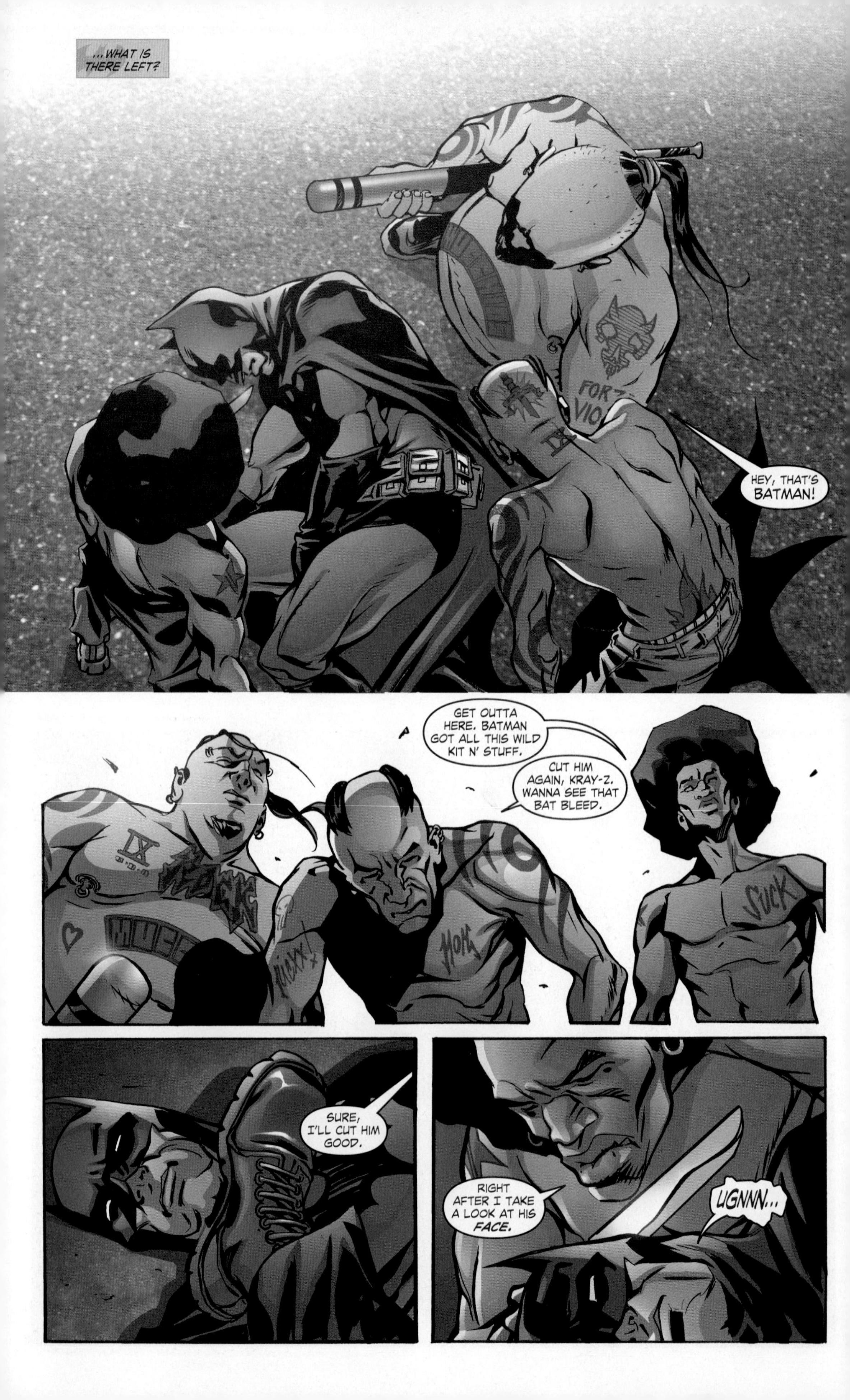
...WHAT IS THERE LEFT?
HEY, THAT'S BATMAN!
GET OUTTA HERE. BATMAN GOT ALL THIS WILD KIT N' STUFF.
CUT HIM AGAIN, KRAY-Z. WANNA SEE THAT BAT BLEED.
SURE, I'LL CUT HIM GOOD.
RIGHT AFTER I TAKE A LOOK AT HIS FACE.
UGNNN...

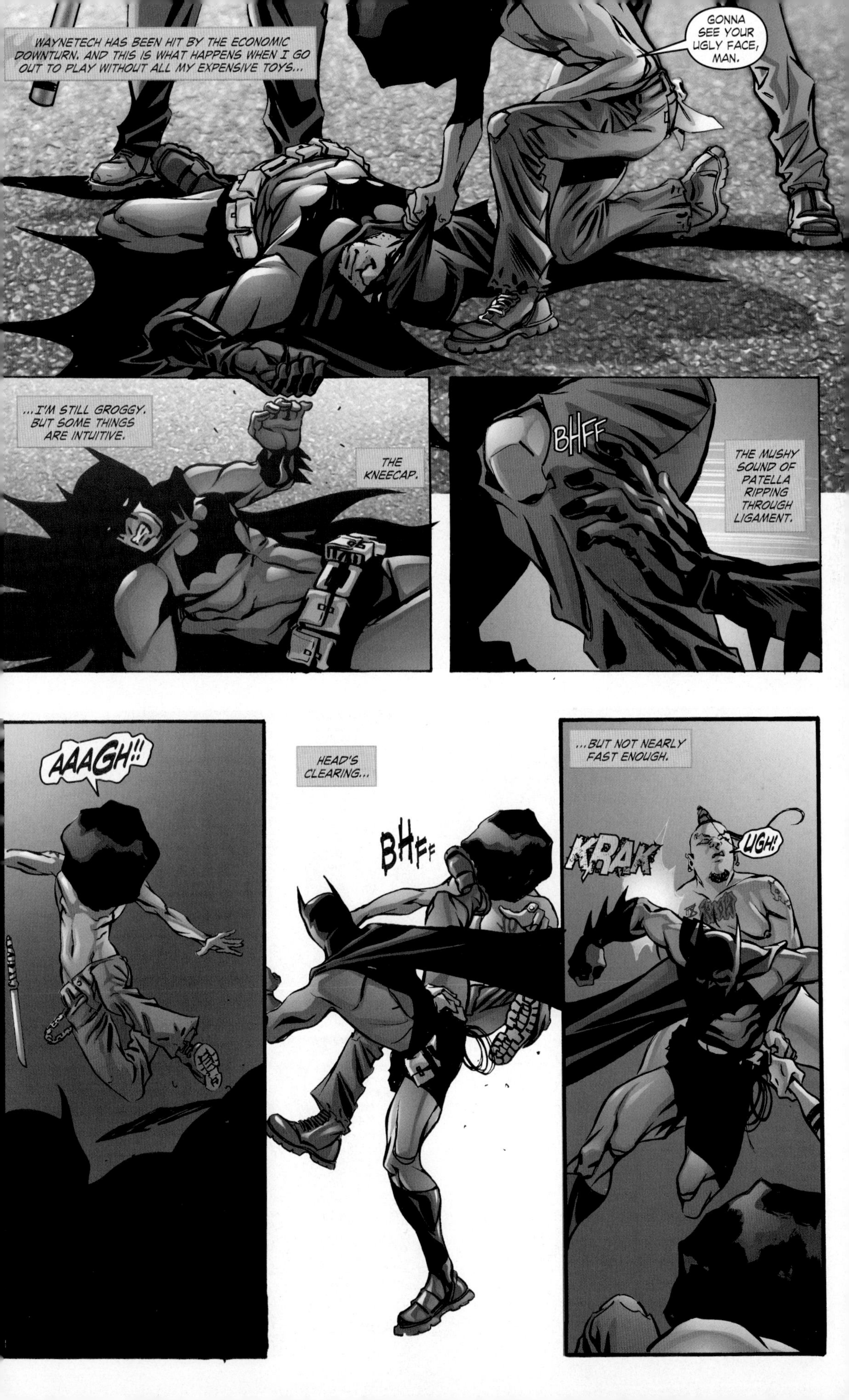
WAYNETECH HAS BEEN HIT BY THE ECONOMIC DOWNTURN. AND THIS IS WHAT HAPPENS WHEN I GO OUT TO PLAY WITHOUT ALL MY EXPENSIVE TOYS...
GONNA SEE YOUR UGLY FACE, MAN.
...I'M STILL GROGGY. BUT SOME THINGS ARE INTUITIVE.
THE KNEECAP.
BHFF
THE MUSHY SOUND OF PATELLA RIPPING THROUGH LIGAMENT.
AAAGH!!
HEAD'S CLEARING...
BHFF
...BUT NOT NEARLY FAST ENOUGH.
KRAK
UGH!

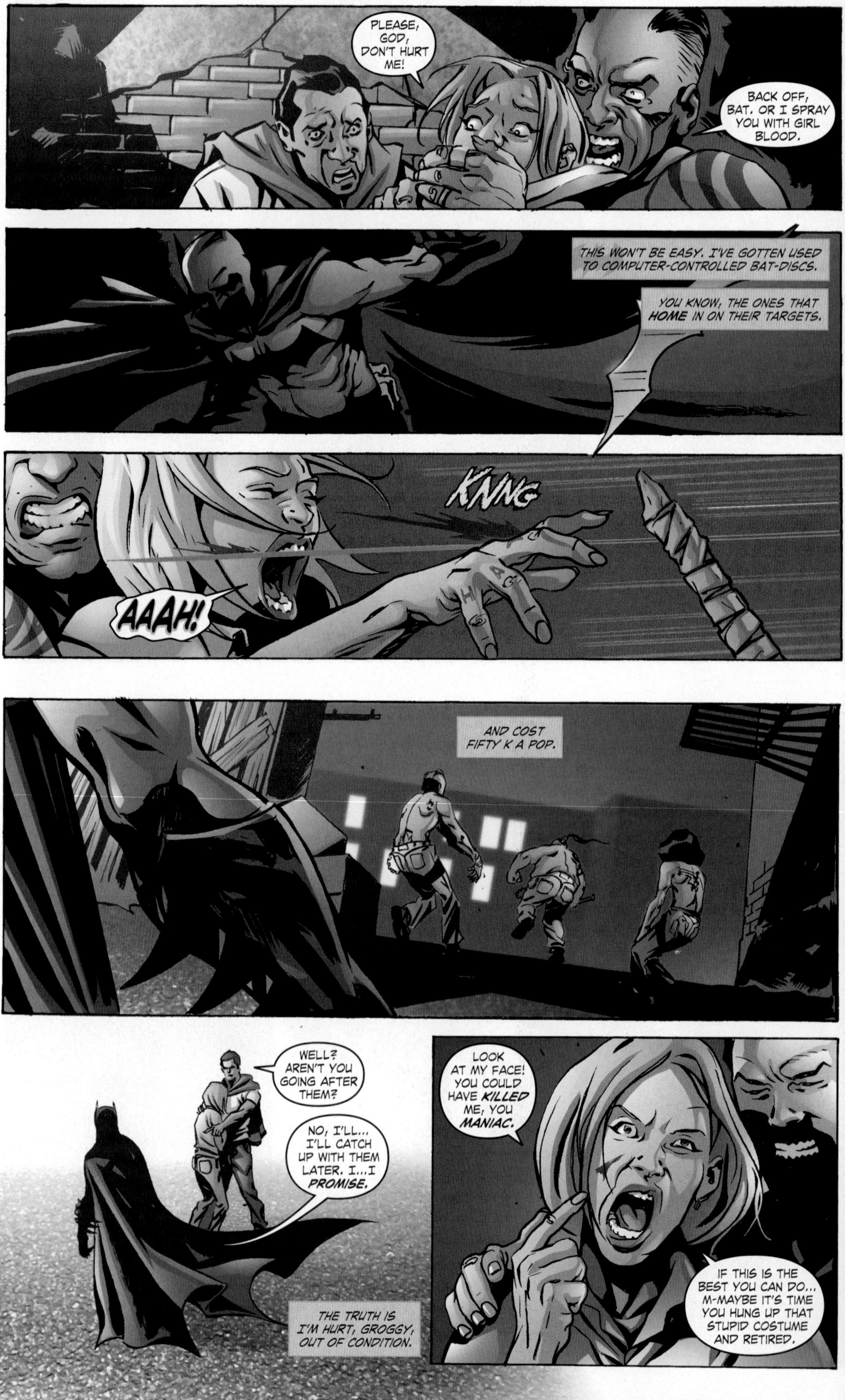
PLEASE, GOD, DON'T HURT ME!
BACK OFF, BAT. OR I SPRAY YOU WITH GIRL BLOOD.
THIS WON'T BE EASY. I'VE GOTTEN USED TO COMPUTER-CONTROLLED BAT-DISCS.
YOU KNOW, THE ONES THAT HOME IN ON THEIR TARGETS.
KNNG
AAAH!
AND COST FIFTY K A POP.
WELL? AREN'T YOU GOING AFTER THEM?
NO, I'LL... I'LL CATCH UP WITH THEM LATER. I...I PROMISE.
THE TRUTH IS I'M HURT, GROGGY, OUT OF CONDITION.
LOOK AT MY FACE! YOU COULD HAVE KILLED ME, YOU MANIAC.
IF THIS IS THE BEST YOU CAN DO... M-MAYBE IT'S TIME YOU HUNG UP THAT STUPID COSTUME AND RETIRED.

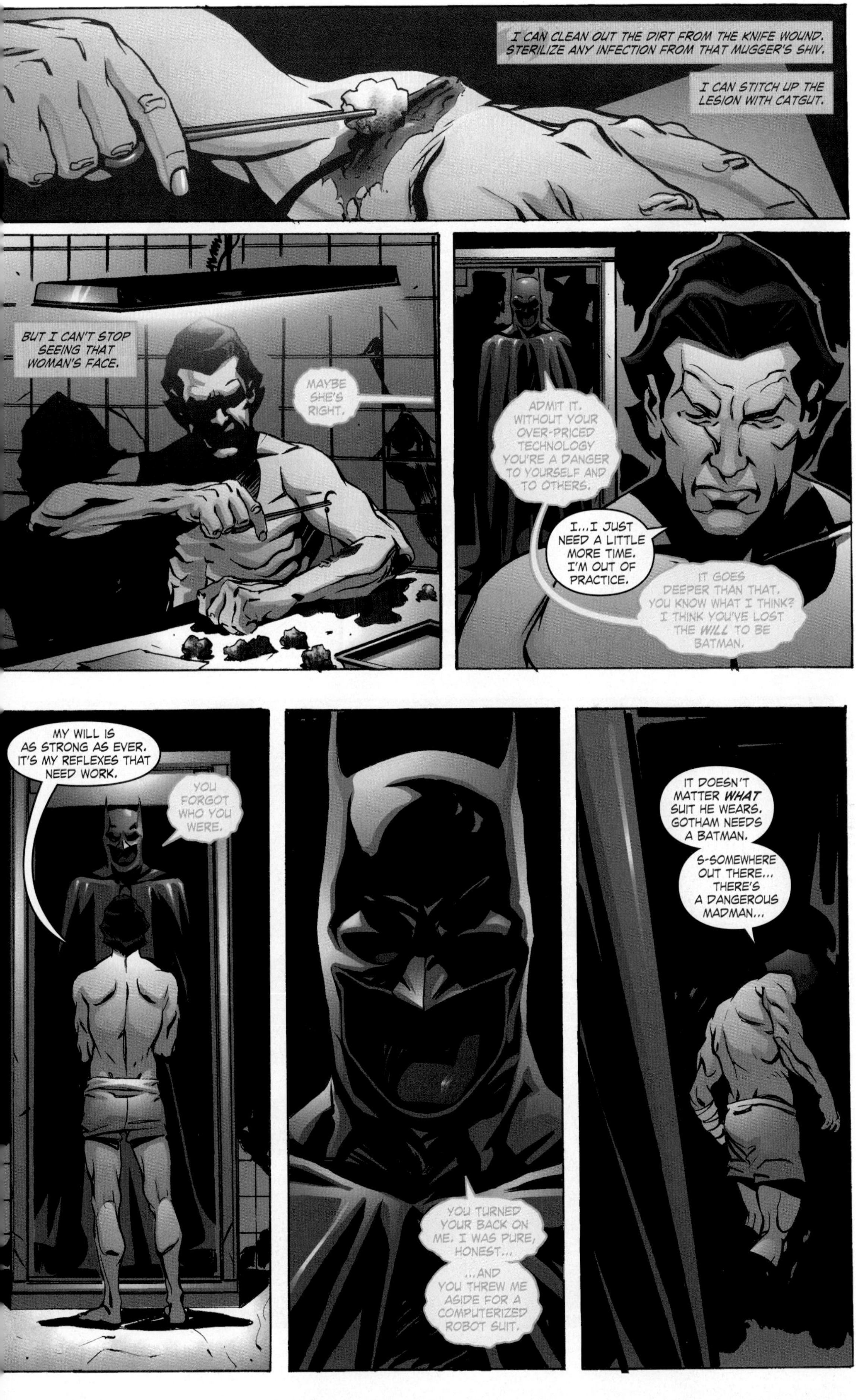
I CAN CLEAN OUT THE DIRT FROM THE KNIFE WOUND. STERILIZE ANY INFECTION FROM THAT MUGGER'S SHIV.
I CAN STITCH UP THE LESION WITH CATGUT.
BUT I CAN'T STOP SEEING THAT WOMAN'S FACE.
MAYBE SHE'S RIGHT.
ADMIT IT. WITHOUT YOUR OVER-PRICED TECHNOLOGY YOU'RE A DANGER TO YOURSELF AND TO OTHERS.
I...I JUST NEED A LITTLE MORE TIME. I'M OUT OF PRACTICE.
IT GOES DEEPER THAN THAT. YOU KNOW WHAT I THINK? I THINK YOU'VE LOST THE WILL TO BE BATMAN.
MY WILL IS AS STRONG AS EVER. IT'S MY REFLEXES THAT NEED WORK.
YOU FORGOT WHO YOU WERE.
YOU TURNED YOUR BACK ON ME. I WAS PURE, HONEST...
...AND YOU THREW ME ASIDE FOR A COMPUTERIZED ROBOT SUIT.
IT DOESN'T MATTER WHAT SUIT HE WEARS. GOTHAM NEEDS A BATMAN.
S-SOMEWHERE OUT THERE... THERE'S A DANGEROUS MADMAN...

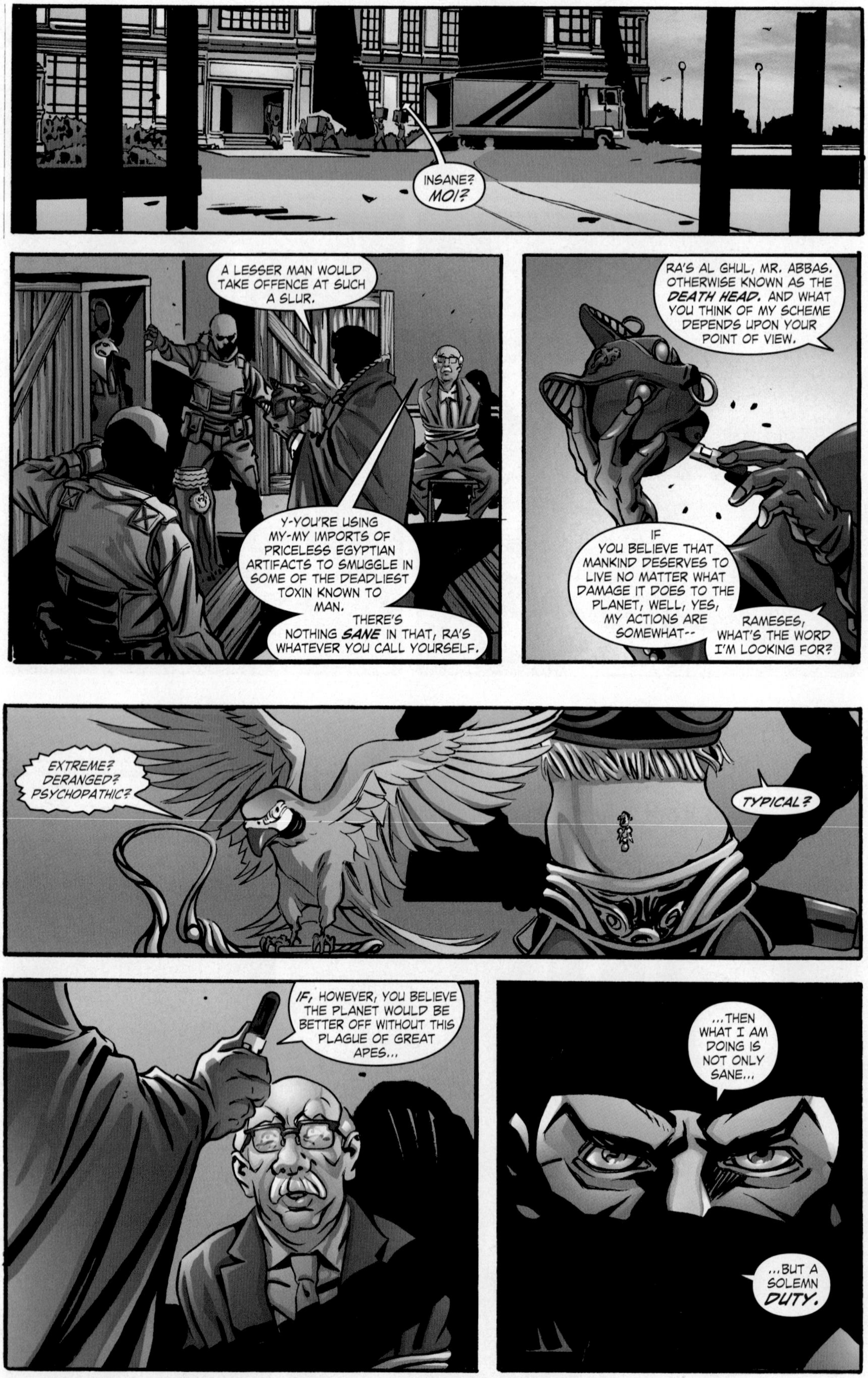
INSANE? MOI?
A LESSER MAN WOULD TAKE OFFENCE AT SUCH A SLUR.
Y-YOU'RE USING MY-MY IMPORTS OF PRICELESS EGYPTIAN ARTIFACTS TO SMUGGLE IN SOME OF THE DEADLIEST TOXIN KNOWN TO MAN.
THERE'S NOTHING SANE IN THAT, RA'S WHATEVER YOU CALL YOURSELF.
RA'S AL GHUL, MR. ABBAS. OTHERWISE KNOWN AS THE DEATH HEAD. AND WHAT YOU THINK OF MY SCHEME DEPENDS UPON YOUR POINT OF VIEW.
IF YOU BELIEVE THAT MANKIND DESERVES TO LIVE NO MATTER WHAT DAMAGE IT DOES TO THE PLANET, WELL, YES, MY ACTIONS ARE SOMEWHAT--
RAMESES, WHAT'S THE WORD I'M LOOKING FOR?
EXTREME? DERANGED? PSYCHOPATHIC?
TYPICAL?
IF, HOWEVER, YOU BELIEVE THE PLANET WOULD BE BETTER OFF WITHOUT THIS PLAGUE OF GREAT APES...
...THEN WHAT I AM DOING IS NOT ONLY SANE...
...BUT A SOLEMN DUTY.

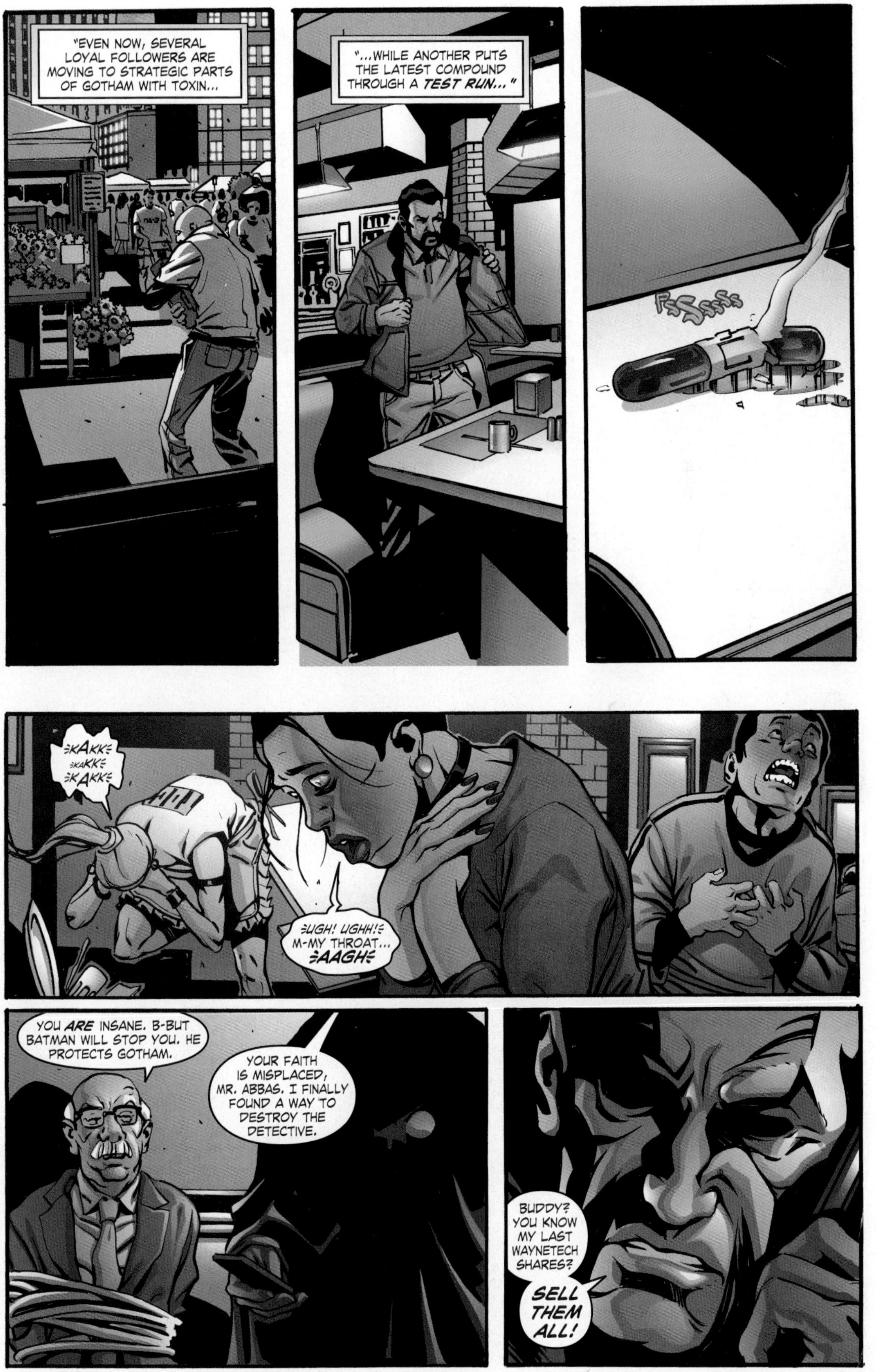

"EVEN NOW, SEVERAL LOYAL FOLLOWERS ARE MOVING TO STRATEGIC PARTS OF GOTHAM WITH TOXIN...
"...WHILE ANOTHER PUTS THE LATEST COMPOUND THROUGH A TEST RUN..."
PSSSSSS
KAKK KAKK KAKK
UGH! UGHH! M-MY THROAT... AAGH
YOU ARE INSANE. B-BUT BATMAN WILL STOP YOU. HE PROTECTS GOTHAM.
YOUR FAITH IS MISPLACED, MR. ABBAS. I FINALLY FOUND A WAY TO DESTROY THE DETECTIVE.
BUDDY? YOU KNOW MY LAST WAYNETECH SHARES?
SELL THEM ALL!

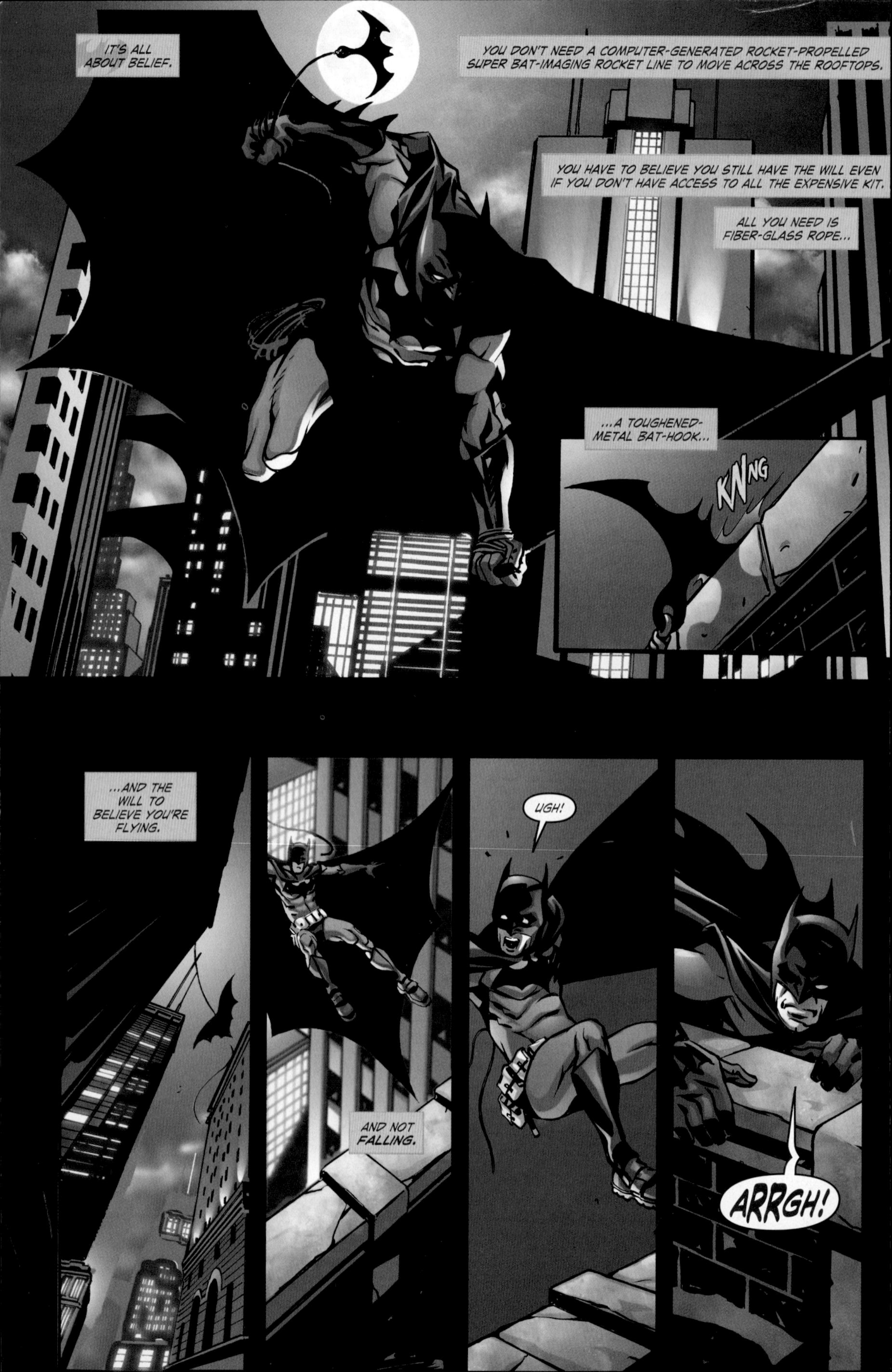

IT'S ALL ABOUT BELIEF.
YOU DON'T NEED A COMPUTER-GENERATED ROCKET-PROPELLED SUPER BAT-IMAGING ROCKET LINE TO MOVE ACROSS THE ROOFTOPS.
YOU HAVE TO BELIEVE YOU STILL HAVE THE WILL EVEN IF YOU DON'T HAVE ACCESS TO ALL THE EXPENSIVE KIT.
ALL YOU NEED IS FIBER-GLASS ROPE...
...A TOUGHENED-METAL BAT-HOOK...
KNNG
...AND THE WILL TO BELIEVE YOU'RE FLYING.
AND NOT FALLING.
UGH!
ARRGH!

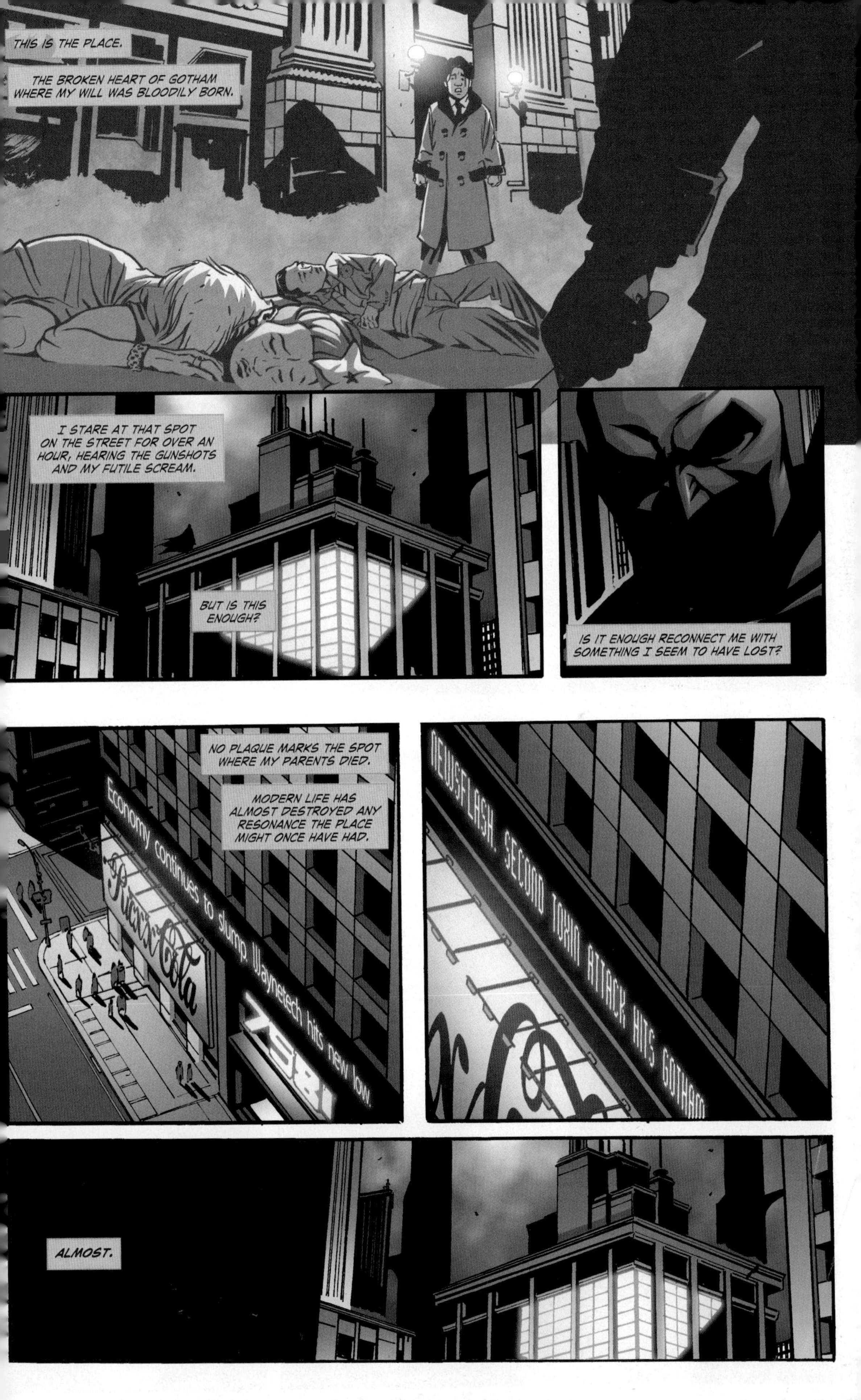
THIS IS THE PLACE.
THE BROKEN HEART OF GOTHAM WHERE MY WILL WAS BLOODILY BORN.
I STARE AT THAT SPOT ON THE STREET FOR OVER AN HOUR, HEARING THE GUNSHOTS AND MY FUTILE SCREAM.
BUT IS THIS ENOUGH?
IS IT ENOUGH RECONNECT ME WITH SOMETHING I SEEM TO HAVE LOST?
NO PLAQUE MARKS THE SPOT WHERE MY PARENTS DIED.
MODERN LIFE HAS ALMOST DESTROYED ANY RESONANCE THE PLACE MIGHT ONCE HAVE HAD.
Economy continues to slump. Waynetech hits new low.
NEWSFLASH. SECOND TOXIN ATTACK HITS GOTHAM
ALMOST.

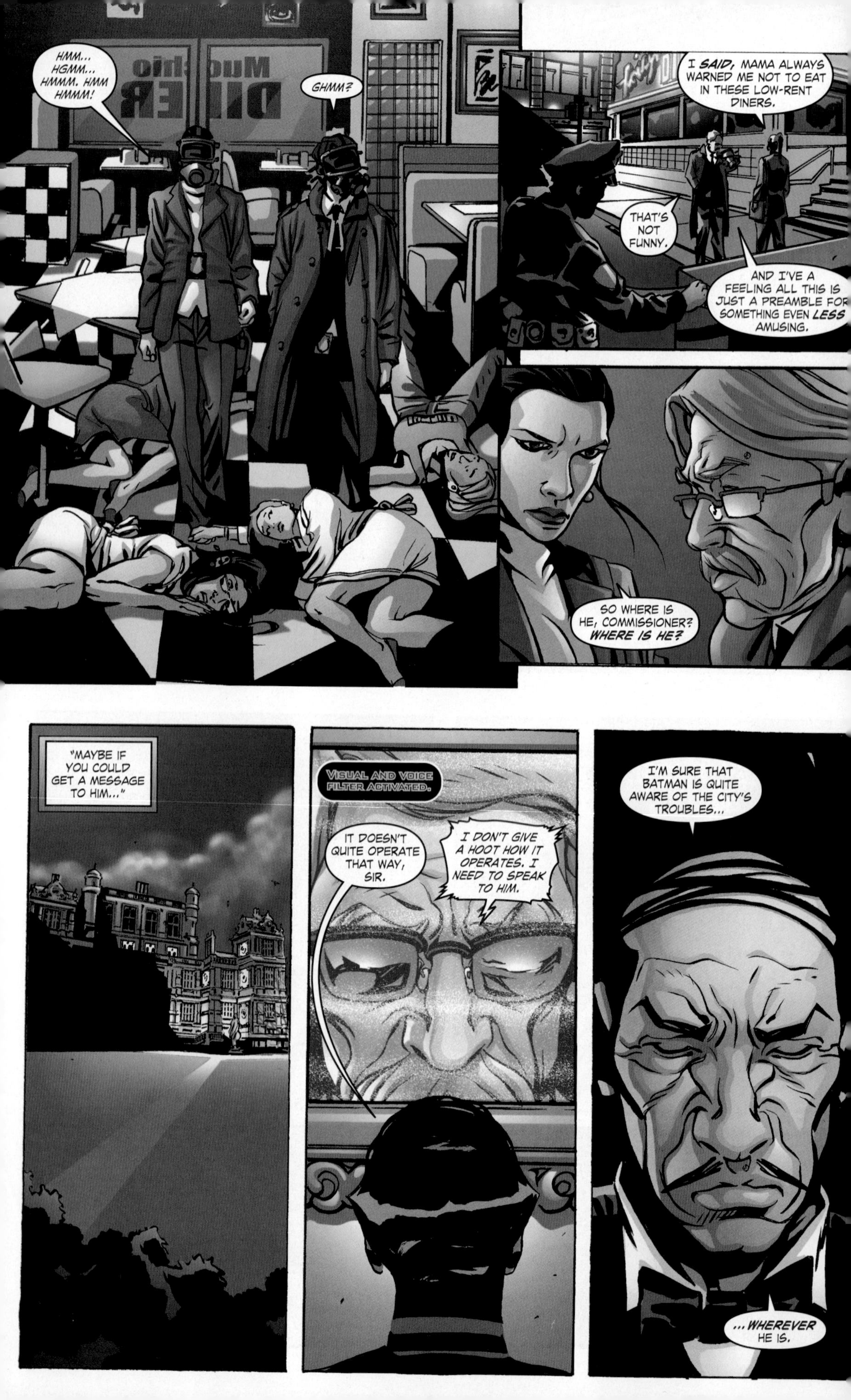

Mucchio
DINER
HMM... HGMM... HMMM. HMM HMMM!
GHMM?
I SAID, MAMA ALWAYS WARNED ME NOT TO EAT IN THESE LOW-RENT DINERS.
THAT'S NOT FUNNY.
AND I'VE A FEELING ALL THIS IS JUST A PREAMBLE FOR SOMETHING EVEN LESS AMUSING.
SO WHERE IS HE, COMMISSIONER? WHERE IS HE?
"MAYBE IF YOU COULD GET A MESSAGE TO HIM..."
VISUAL AND VOICE FILTER ACTIVATED.
IT DOESN'T QUITE OPERATE THAT WAY, SIR.
I DON'T GIVE A HOOT HOW IT OPERATES. I NEED TO SPEAK TO HIM.
I'M SURE THAT BATMAN IS QUITE AWARE OF THE CITY'S TROUBLES...
...WHEREVER HE IS.

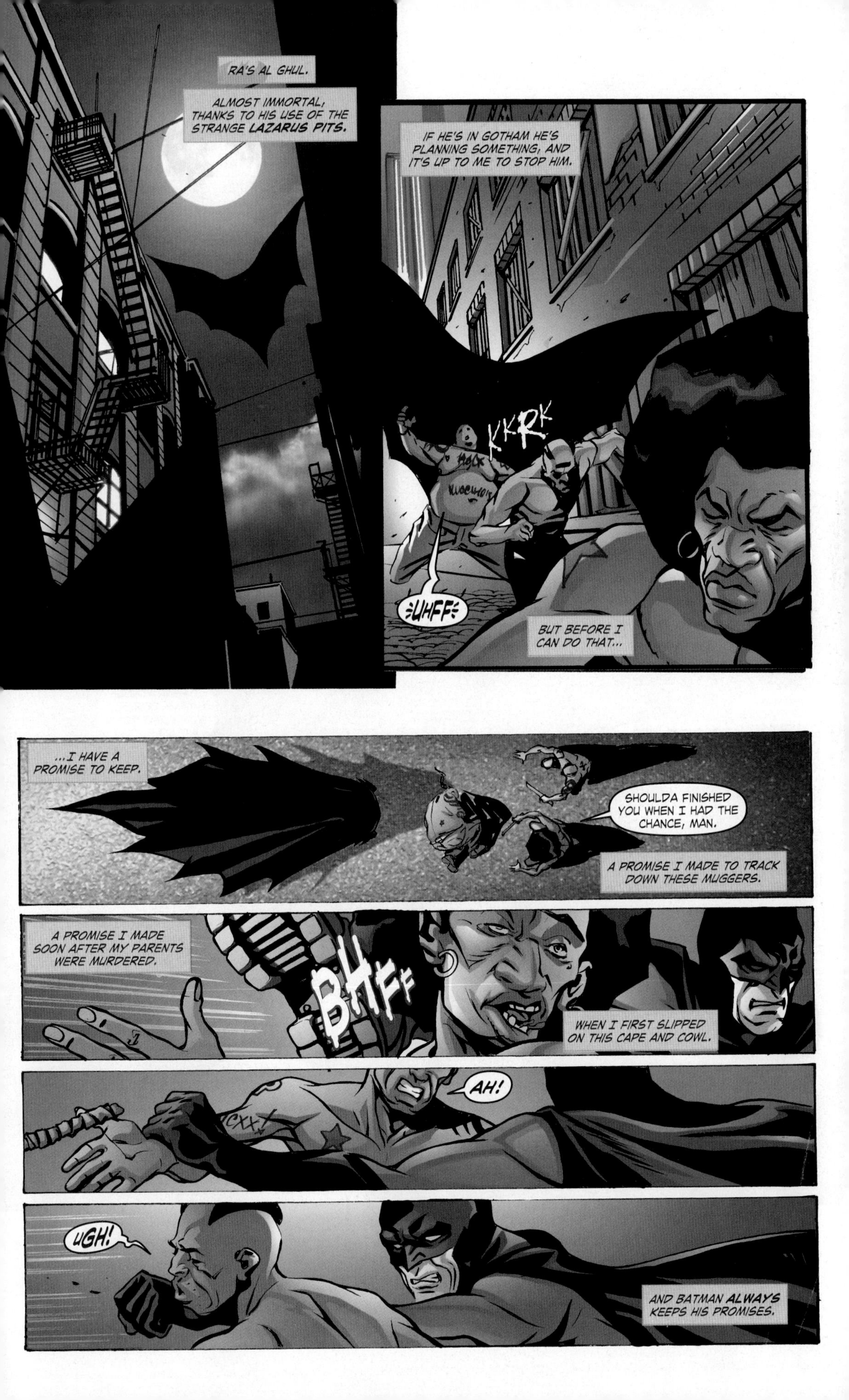

RA'S AL GHUL.
ALMOST IMMORTAL, THANKS TO HIS USE OF THE STRANGE **LAZARUS PITS.**
IF HE'S IN GOTHAM HE'S PLANNING SOMETHING, AND IT'S UP TO ME TO STOP HIM.
KKRK
UHFF
BUT BEFORE I CAN DO THAT...
...I HAVE A PROMISE TO KEEP.
SHOULDA FINISHED YOU WHEN I HAD THE CHANCE, MAN.
A PROMISE I MADE TO TRACK DOWN THESE MUGGERS.
A PROMISE I MADE SOON AFTER MY PARENTS WERE MURDERED.
BHFF
WHEN I FIRST SLIPPED ON THIS CAPE AND COWL.
AH!
UGH!
AND BATMAN **ALWAYS** KEEPS HIS PROMISES.

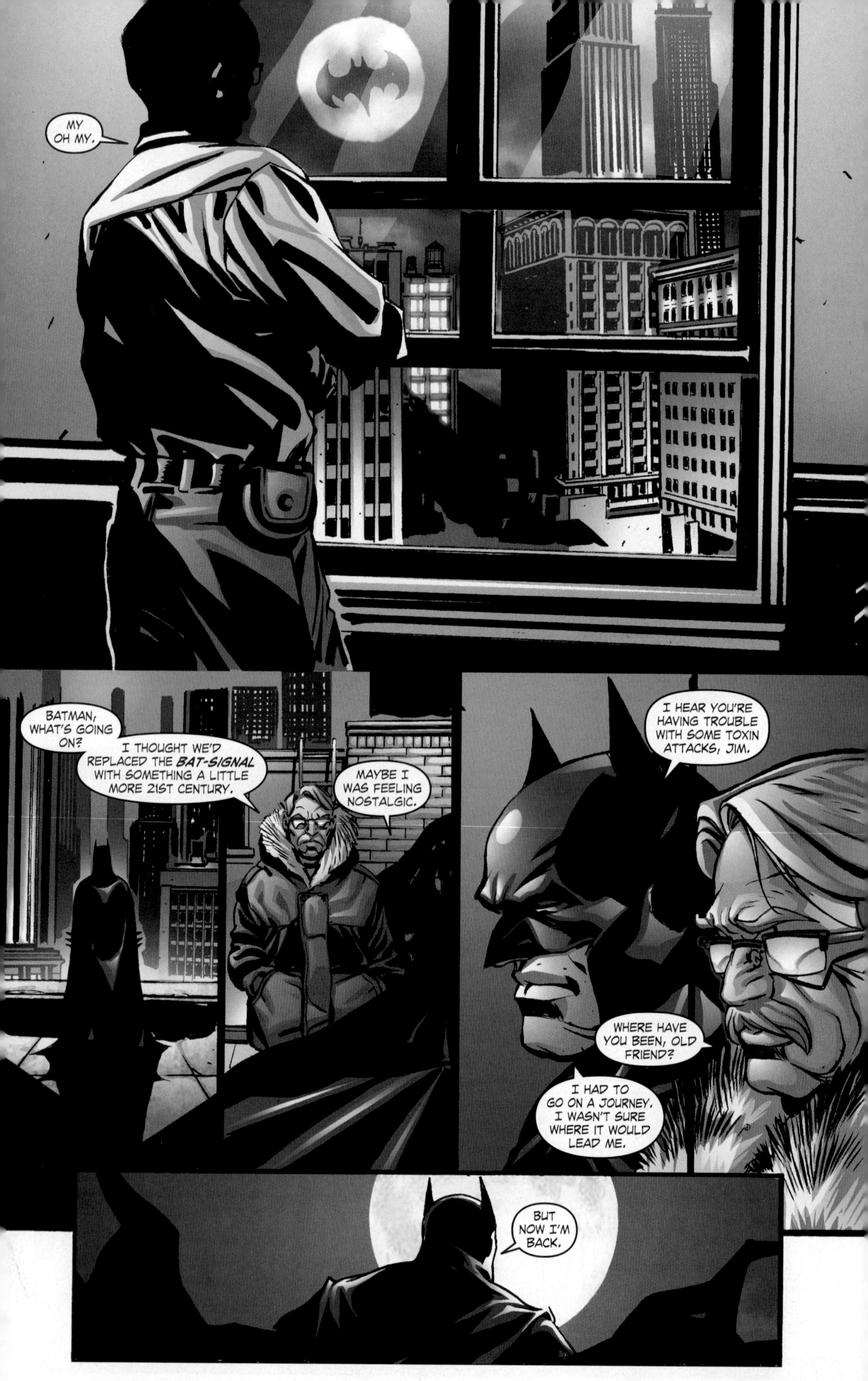
MY OH MY.
BATMAN, WHAT'S GOING ON?
I THOUGHT WE'D REPLACED THE BAT-SIGNAL WITH SOMETHING A LITTLE MORE 21ST CENTURY.
MAYBE I WAS FEELING NOSTALGIC.
I HEAR YOU'RE HAVING TROUBLE WITH SOME TOXIN ATTACKS, JIM.
WHERE HAVE YOU BEEN, OLD FRIEND?
I HAD TO GO ON A JOURNEY. I WASN'T SURE WHERE IT WOULD LEAD ME.
BUT NOW I'M BACK.

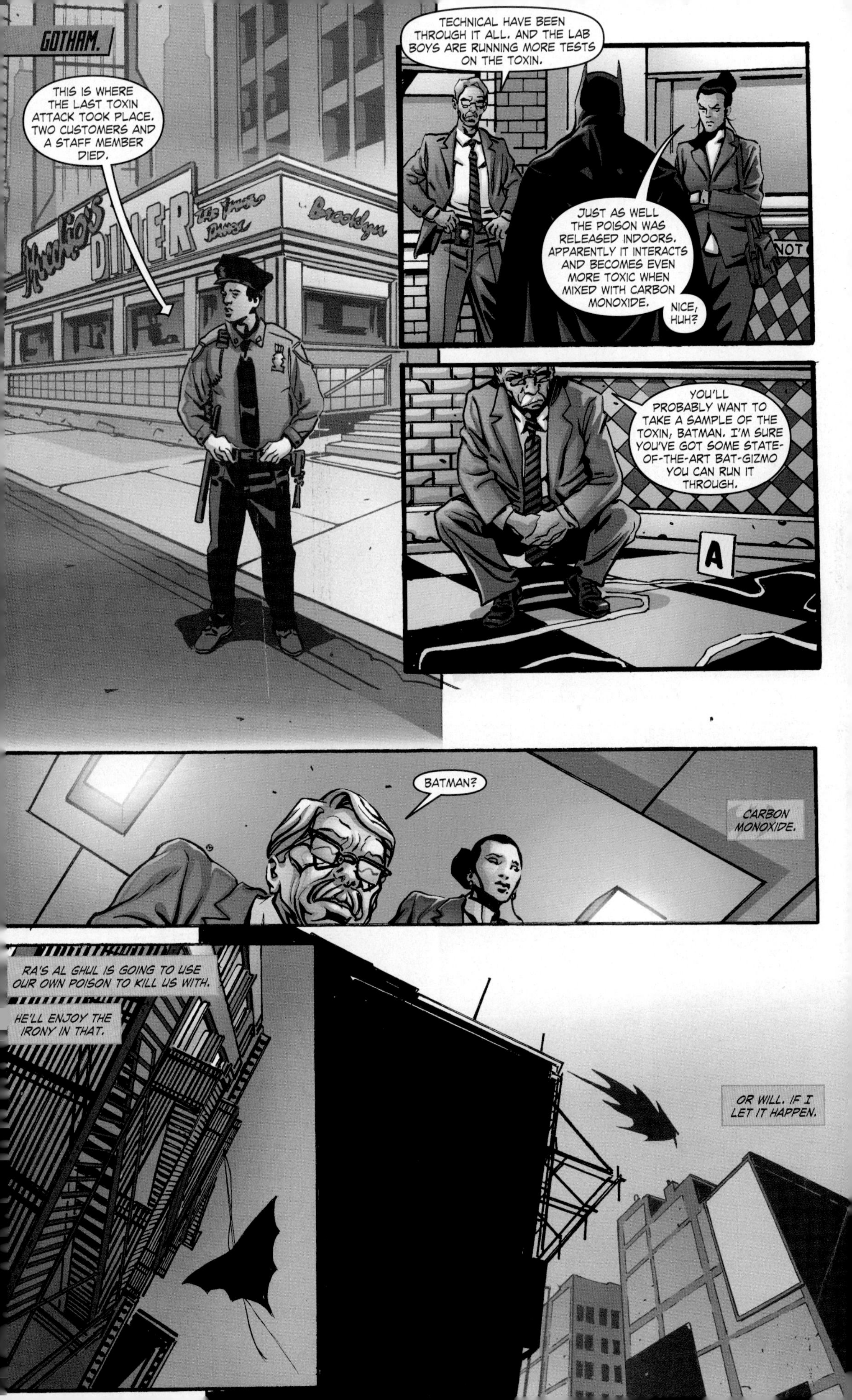
GOTHAM.
THIS IS WHERE THE LAST TOXIN ATTACK TOOK PLACE. TWO CUSTOMERS AND A STAFF MEMBER DIED.
DINER
Brooklyn
TECHNICAL HAVE BEEN THROUGH IT ALL. AND THE LAB BOYS ARE RUNNING MORE TESTS ON THE TOXIN.
JUST AS WELL THE POISON WAS RELEASED INDOORS. APPARENTLY IT INTERACTS AND BECOMES EVEN MORE TOXIC WHEN MIXED WITH CARBON MONOXIDE.
NICE, HUH?
YOU'LL PROBABLY WANT TO TAKE A SAMPLE OF THE TOXIN, BATMAN. I'M SURE YOU'VE GOT SOME STATE-OF-THE-ART BAT-GIZMO YOU CAN RUN IT THROUGH.
A
BATMAN?
CARBON MONOXIDE.
RA'S AL GHUL IS GOING TO USE OUR OWN POISON TO KILL US WITH.
HE'LL ENJOY THE IRONY IN THAT.
OR WILL. IF I LET IT HAPPEN.

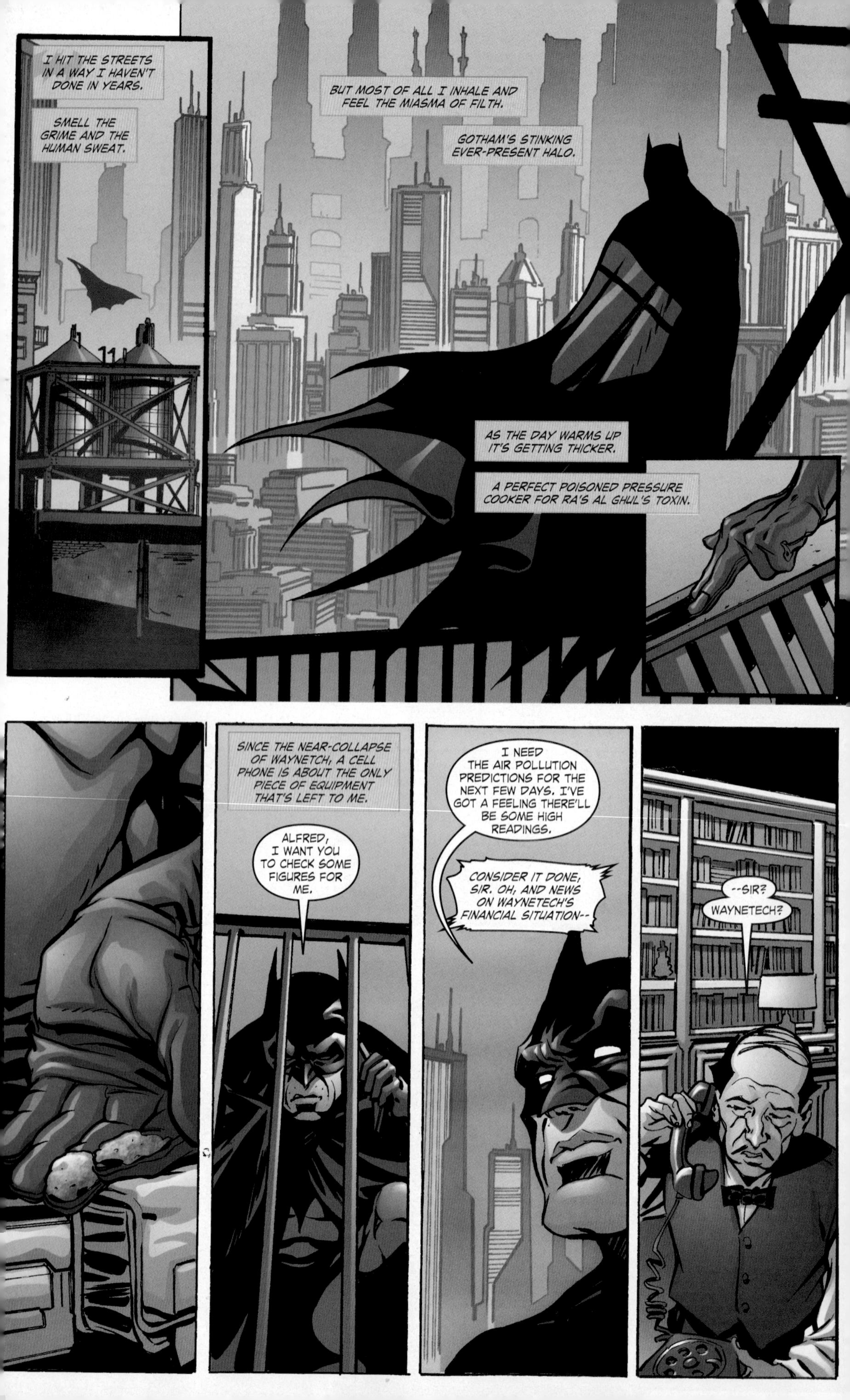
I HIT THE STREETS IN A WAY I HAVEN'T DONE IN YEARS.
SMELL THE GRIME AND THE HUMAN SWEAT.
BUT MOST OF ALL I INHALE AND FEEL THE MIASMA OF FILTH.
GOTHAM'S STINKING EVER-PRESENT HALO.
AS THE DAY WARMS UP IT'S GETTING THICKER.
A PERFECT POISONED PRESSURE COOKER FOR RA'S AL GHUL'S TOXIN.
SINCE THE NEAR-COLLAPSE OF WAYNETECH, A CELL PHONE IS ABOUT THE ONLY PIECE OF EQUIPMENT THAT'S LEFT TO ME.
ALFRED, I WANT YOU TO CHECK SOME FIGURES FOR ME.
I NEED THE AIR POLLUTION PREDICTIONS FOR THE NEXT FEW DAYS. I'VE GOT A FEELING THERE'LL BE SOME HIGH READINGS.
CONSIDER IT DONE, SIR. OH, AND NEWS ON WAYNETECH'S FINANCIAL SITUATION--
--SIR? WAYNETECH?

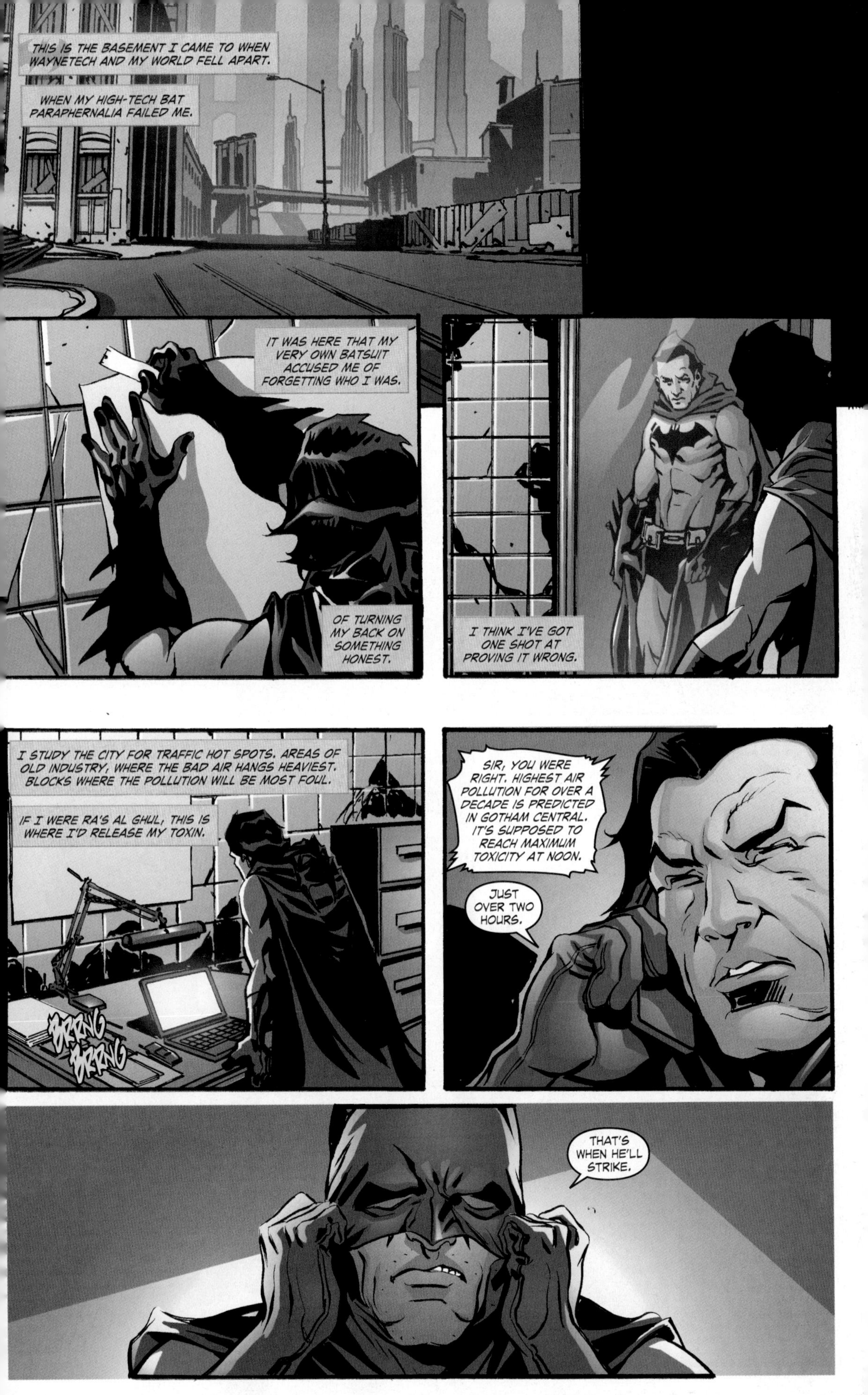
THIS IS THE BASEMENT I CAME TO WHEN WAYNETECH AND MY WORLD FELL APART.
WHEN MY HIGH-TECH BAT PARAPHERNALIA FAILED ME.
IT WAS HERE THAT MY VERY OWN BATSUIT ACCUSED ME OF FORGETTING WHO I WAS.
OF TURNING MY BACK ON SOMETHING HONEST.
I THINK I'VE GOT ONE SHOT AT PROVING IT WRONG.
I STUDY THE CITY FOR TRAFFIC HOT SPOTS. AREAS OF OLD INDUSTRY, WHERE THE BAD AIR HANGS HEAVIEST. BLOCKS WHERE THE POLLUTION WILL BE MOST FOUL.
IF I WERE RA'S AL GHUL, THIS IS WHERE I'D RELEASE MY TOXIN.
BRRNG BRRNG
SIR, YOU WERE RIGHT. HIGHEST AIR POLLUTION FOR OVER A DECADE IS PREDICTED IN GOTHAM CENTRAL. IT'S SUPPOSED TO REACH MAXIMUM TOXICITY AT NOON.
JUST OVER TWO HOURS.
THAT'S WHEN HE'LL STRIKE.

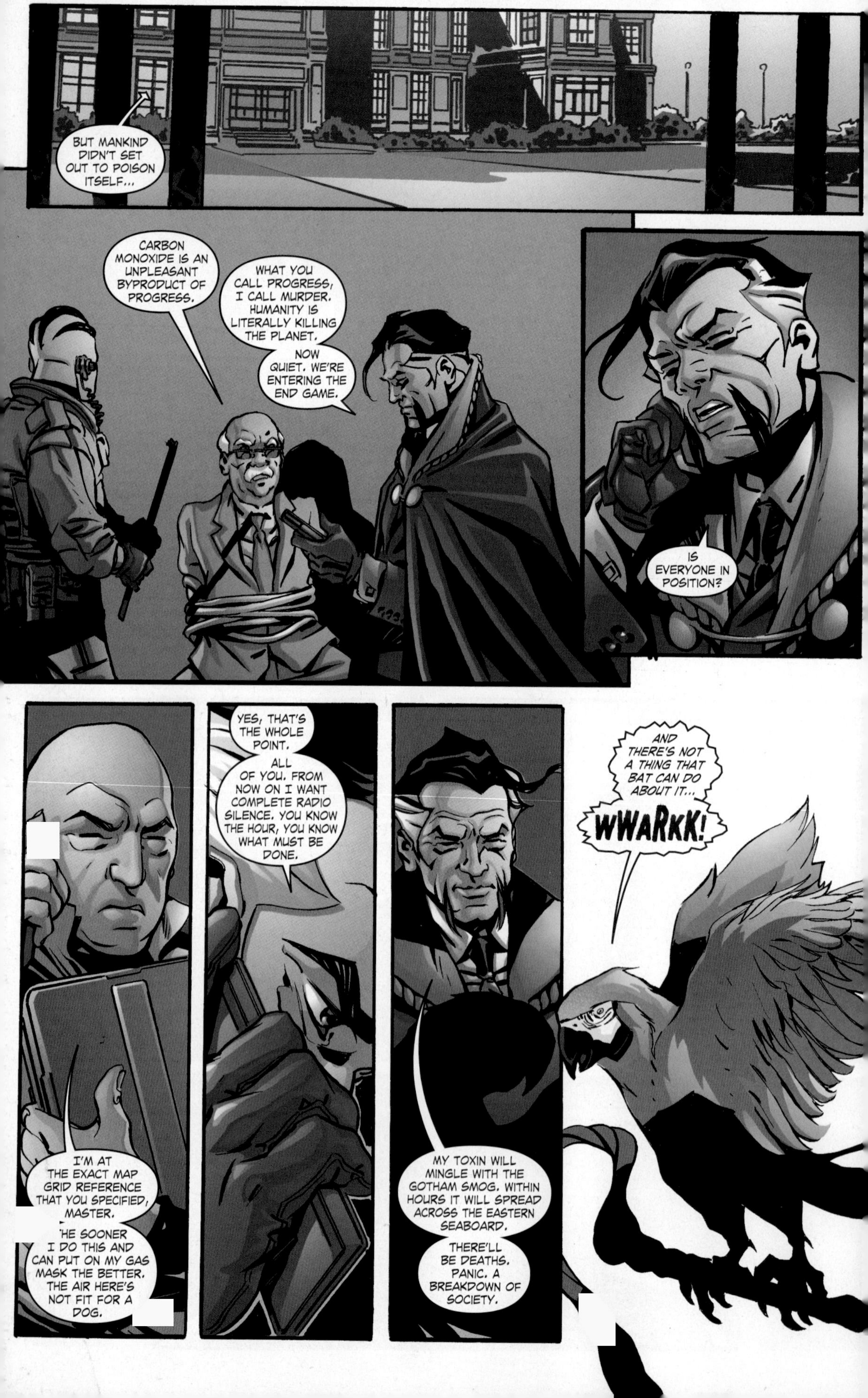
BUT MANKIND DIDN'T SET OUT TO POISON ITSELF...
CARBON MONOXIDE IS AN UNPLEASANT BYPRODUCT OF PROGRESS.
WHAT YOU CALL PROGRESS, I CALL MURDER. HUMANITY IS LITERALLY KILLING THE PLANET.
NOW QUIET. WE'RE ENTERING THE END GAME.
IS EVERYONE IN POSITION?
I'M AT THE EXACT MAP GRID REFERENCE THAT YOU SPECIFIED, MASTER.
THE SOONER I DO THIS AND CAN PUT ON MY GAS MASK THE BETTER. THE AIR HERE'S NOT FIT FOR A DOG.
YES, THAT'S THE WHOLE POINT.
ALL OF YOU. FROM NOW ON I WANT COMPLETE RADIO SILENCE. YOU KNOW THE HOUR, YOU KNOW WHAT MUST BE DONE.
MY TOXIN WILL MINGLE WITH THE GOTHAM SMOG. WITHIN HOURS IT WILL SPREAD ACROSS THE EASTERN SEABOARD.
THERE'LL BE DEATHS. PANIC. A BREAKDOWN OF SOCIETY.
AND THERE'S NOT A THING THAT BAT CAN DO ABOUT IT...
WWARKK!

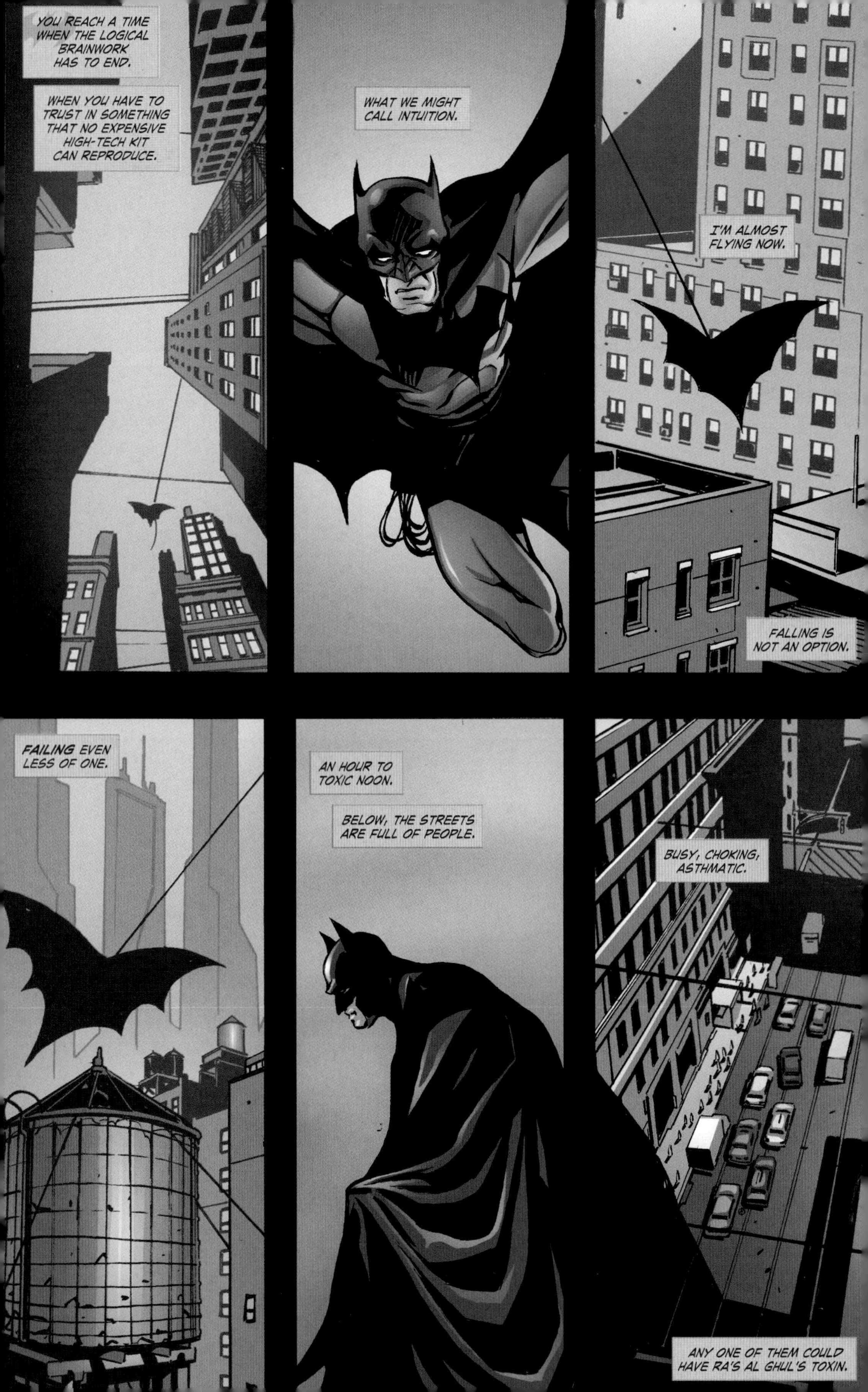
YOU REACH A TIME WHEN THE LOGICAL BRAINWORK HAS TO END.
WHEN YOU HAVE TO TRUST IN SOMETHING THAT NO EXPENSIVE HIGH-TECH KIT CAN REPRODUCE.
WHAT WE MIGHT CALL INTUITION.
I'M ALMOST FLYING NOW.
FALLING IS NOT AN OPTION.
FAILING EVEN LESS OF ONE.
AN HOUR TO TOXIC NOON.
BELOW, THE STREETS ARE FULL OF PEOPLE.
BUSY, CHOKING, ASTHMATIC.
ANY ONE OF THEM COULD HAVE RA'S AL GHUL'S TOXIN.

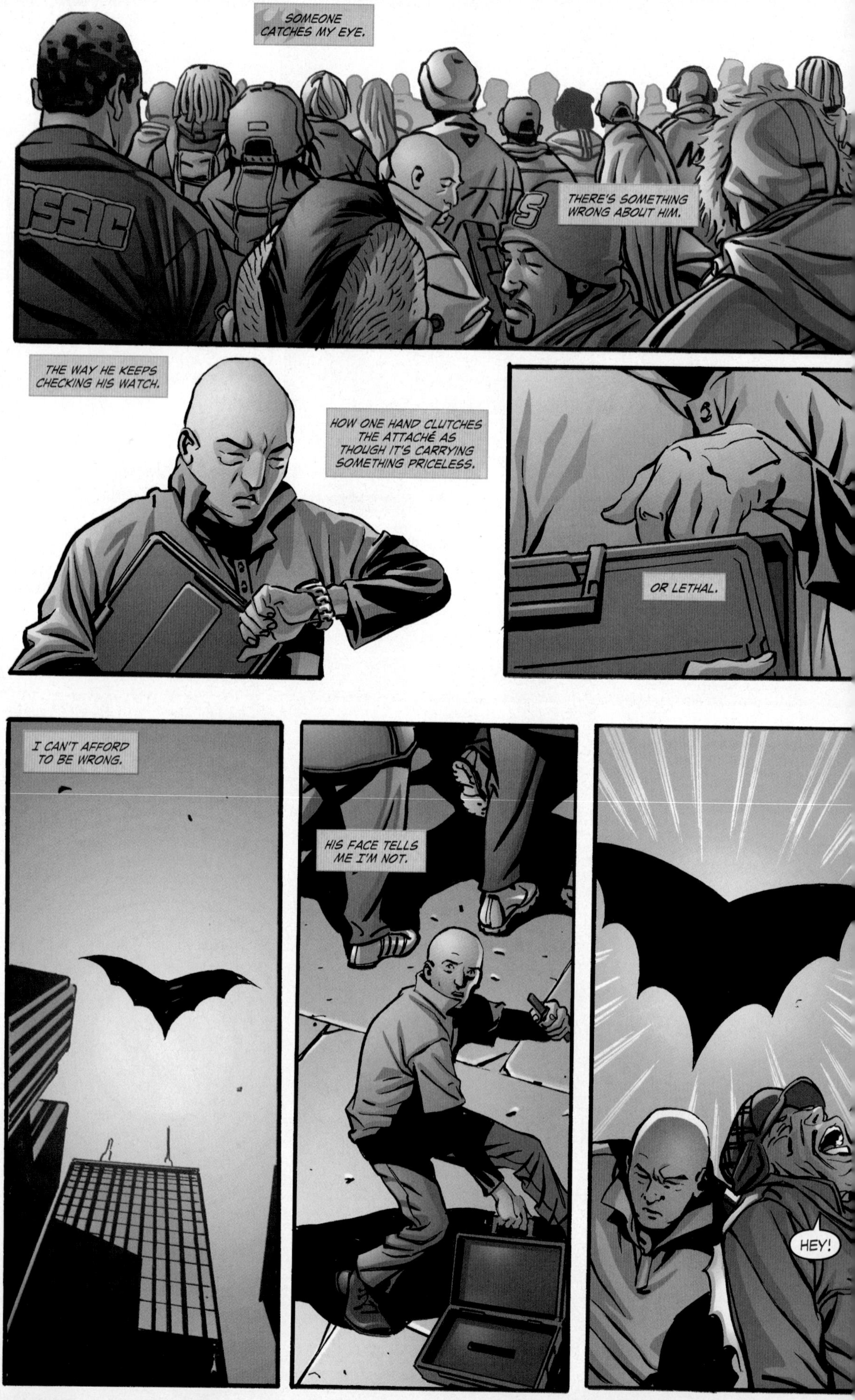
SOMEONE CATCHES MY EYE.
THERE'S SOMETHING WRONG ABOUT HIM.
THE WAY HE KEEPS CHECKING HIS WATCH.
HOW ONE HAND CLUTCHES THE ATTACHÉ AS THOUGH IT'S CARRYING SOMETHING PRICELESS.
OR LETHAL.
I CAN'T AFFORD TO BE WRONG.
HIS FACE TELLS ME I'M NOT.
HEY!

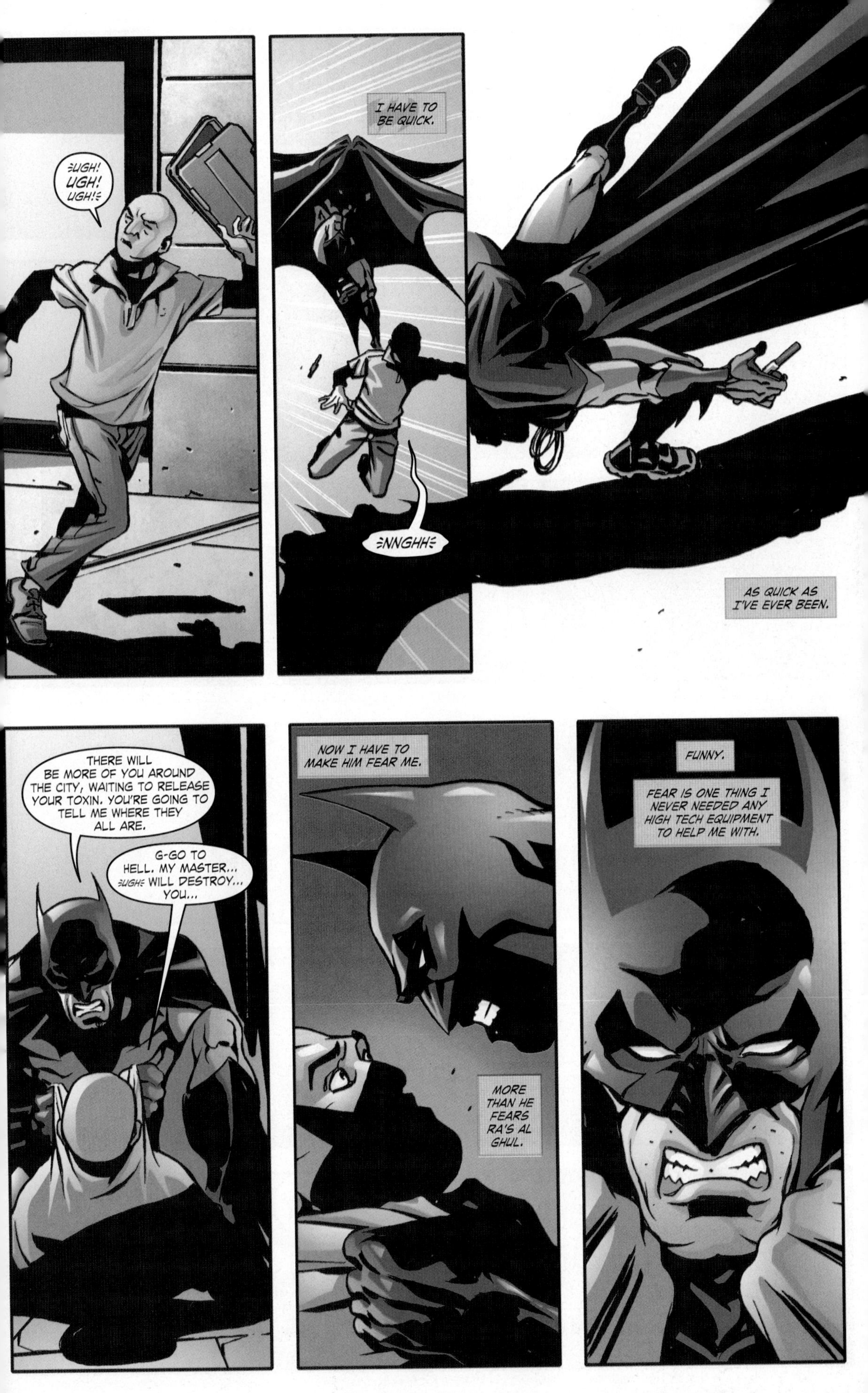
UGH!
UGH!
UGH!
I HAVE TO BE QUICK.
NNGHH
AS QUICK AS I'VE EVER BEEN.
THERE WILL BE MORE OF YOU AROUND THE CITY, WAITING TO RELEASE YOUR TOXIN. YOU'RE GOING TO TELL ME WHERE THEY ALL ARE.
G-GO TO HELL. MY MASTER... UGH WILL DESTROY... YOU...
NOW I HAVE TO MAKE HIM FEAR ME.
MORE THAN HE FEARS RA'S AL GHUL.
FUNNY.
FEAR IS ONE THING I NEVER NEEDED ANY HIGH TECH EQUIPMENT TO HELP ME WITH.

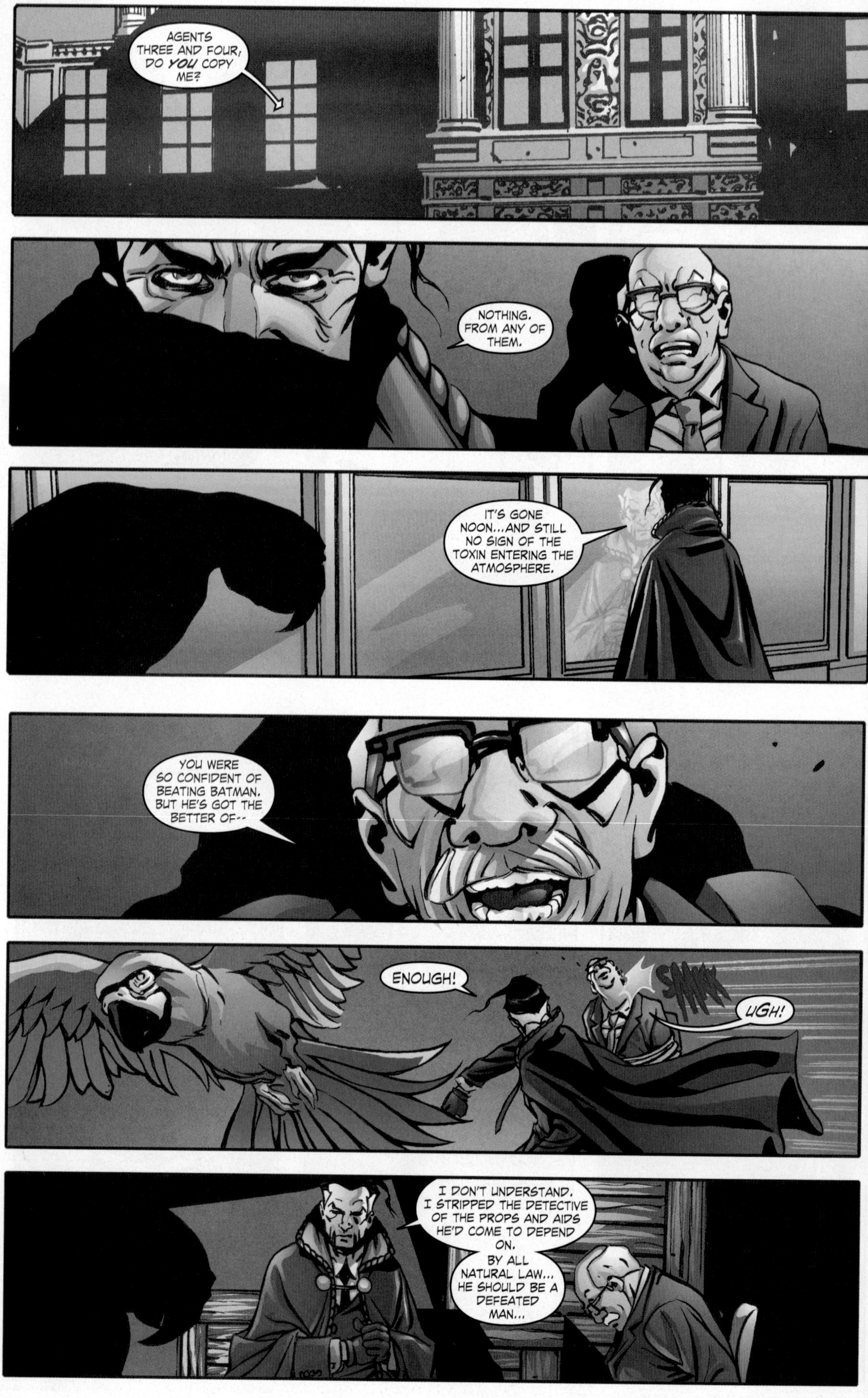
AGENTS THREE AND FOUR, DO YOU COPY ME?
NOTHING. FROM ANY OF THEM.
IT'S GONE NOON...AND STILL NO SIGN OF THE TOXIN ENTERING THE ATMOSPHERE.
YOU WERE SO CONFIDENT OF BEATING BATMAN. BUT HE'S GOT THE BETTER OF--
ENOUGH!
UGH!
I DON'T UNDERSTAND. I STRIPPED THE DETECTIVE OF THE PROPS AND AIDS HE'D COME TO DEPEND ON.
BY ALL NATURAL LAW... HE SHOULD BE A DEFEATED MAN...

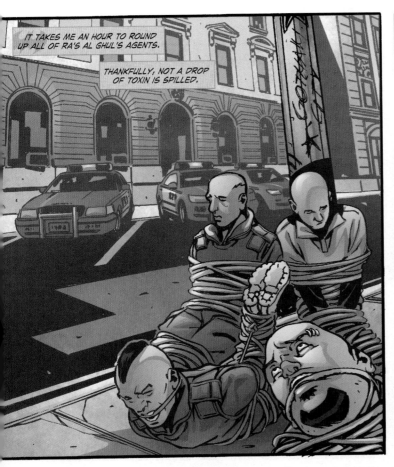

IT TAKES ME AN HOUR TO ROUND UP ALL OF RA'S AL GHUL'S AGENTS.

THANKFULLY, NOT A DROP OF TOXIN IS SPILLED.

AS I ENTER HIS HEADQUARTERS I KNOW WHAT TO EXPECT.

COME ON, RA'S AL GHUL HASN'T SURVIVED FOR COUNTLESS CENTURIES...

...WITHOUT BEING ONE SLIPPERY BASTARD.

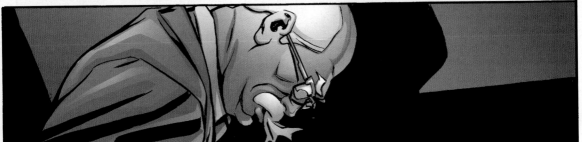

UNTIL NEXT TIME, DETECTIVE.

"CAN YOU BE SO CERTAIN THAT IT WAS RA'S AL GHUL WHO ALMOST BROUGHT WAYNETECH TO FINANCIAL RUIN?"

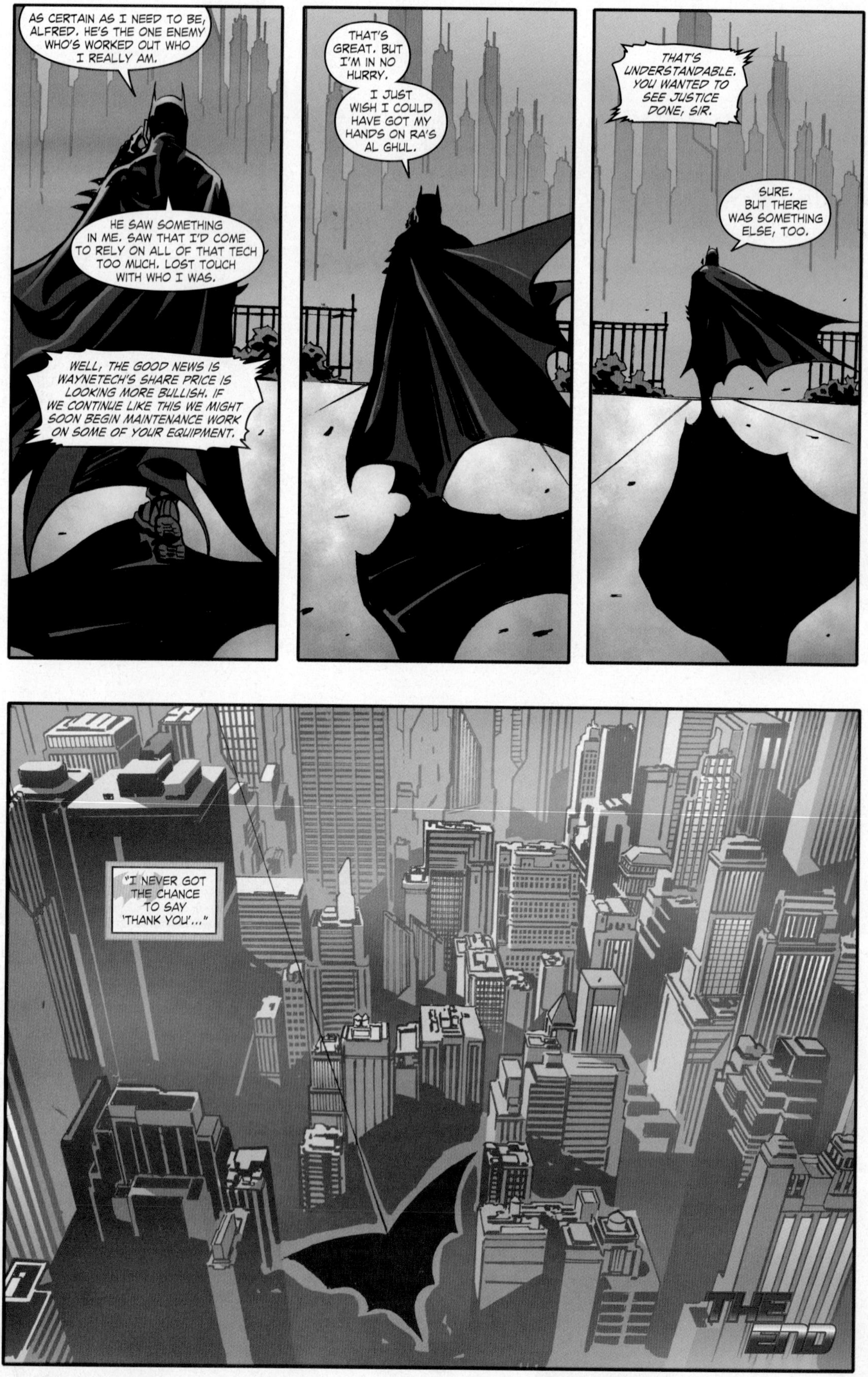
AS CERTAIN AS I NEED TO BE, ALFRED. HE'S THE ONE ENEMY WHO'S WORKED OUT WHO I REALLY AM.
HE SAW SOMETHING IN ME. SAW THAT I'D COME TO RELY ON ALL OF THAT TECH TOO MUCH. LOST TOUCH WITH WHO I WAS.
WELL, THE GOOD NEWS IS WAYNETECH'S SHARE PRICE IS LOOKING MORE BULLISH. IF WE CONTINUE LIKE THIS WE MIGHT SOON BEGIN MAINTENANCE WORK ON SOME OF YOUR EQUIPMENT.
THAT'S GREAT. BUT I'M IN NO HURRY.
I JUST WISH I COULD HAVE GOT MY HANDS ON RA'S AL GHUL.
THAT'S UNDERSTANDABLE. YOU WANTED TO SEE JUSTICE DONE, SIR.
SURE. BUT THERE WAS SOMETHING ELSE, TOO.
"I NEVER GOT THE CHANCE TO SAY 'THANK YOU'..."
THE END

UNLUCKY THIRTEEN

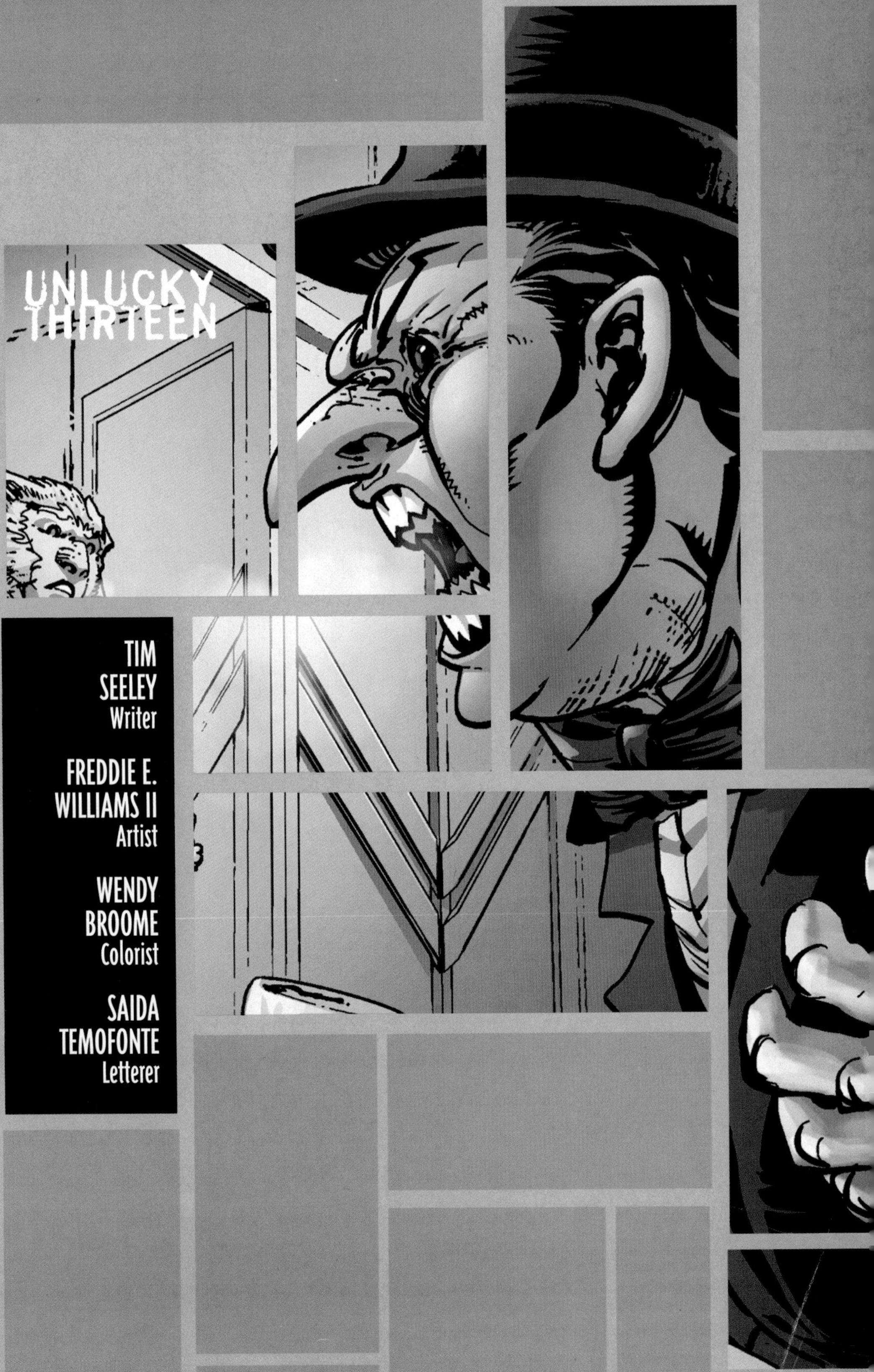

TIM SEELEY
Writer

FREDDIE E. WILLIAMS II
Artist

WENDY BROOME
Colorist

SAIDA TEMOFONTE
Letterer

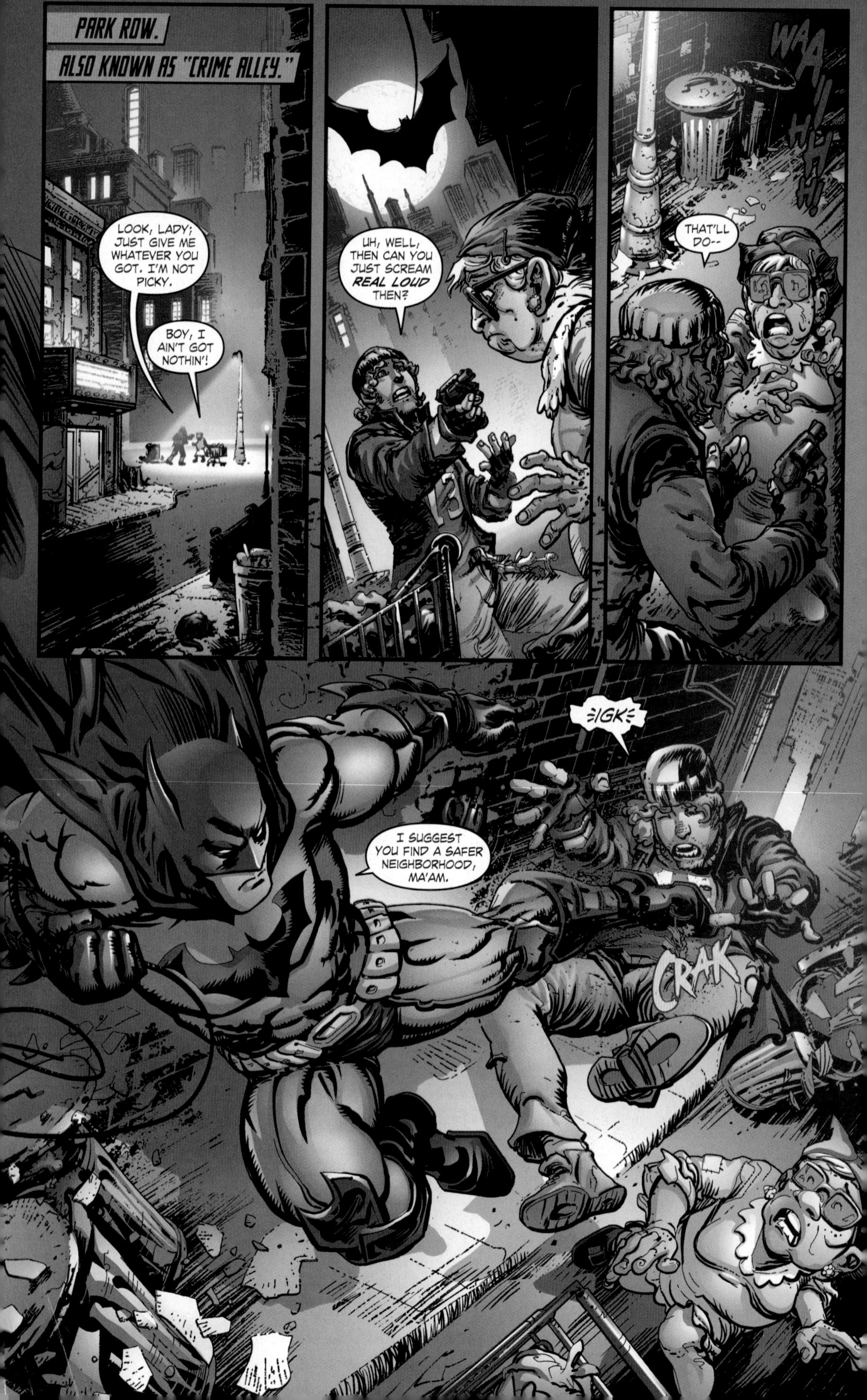
PARK ROW.
ALSO KNOWN AS "CRIME ALLEY."
LOOK, LADY; JUST GIVE ME WHATEVER YOU GOT. I'M NOT PICKY.
BOY, I AIN'T GOT NOTHIN'!
UH, WELL, THEN CAN YOU JUST SCREAM REAL LOUD THEN?
WAAAHHH!
THAT'LL DO--
IGK
I SUGGEST YOU FIND A SAFER NEIGHBORHOOD, MA'AM.
CRAK

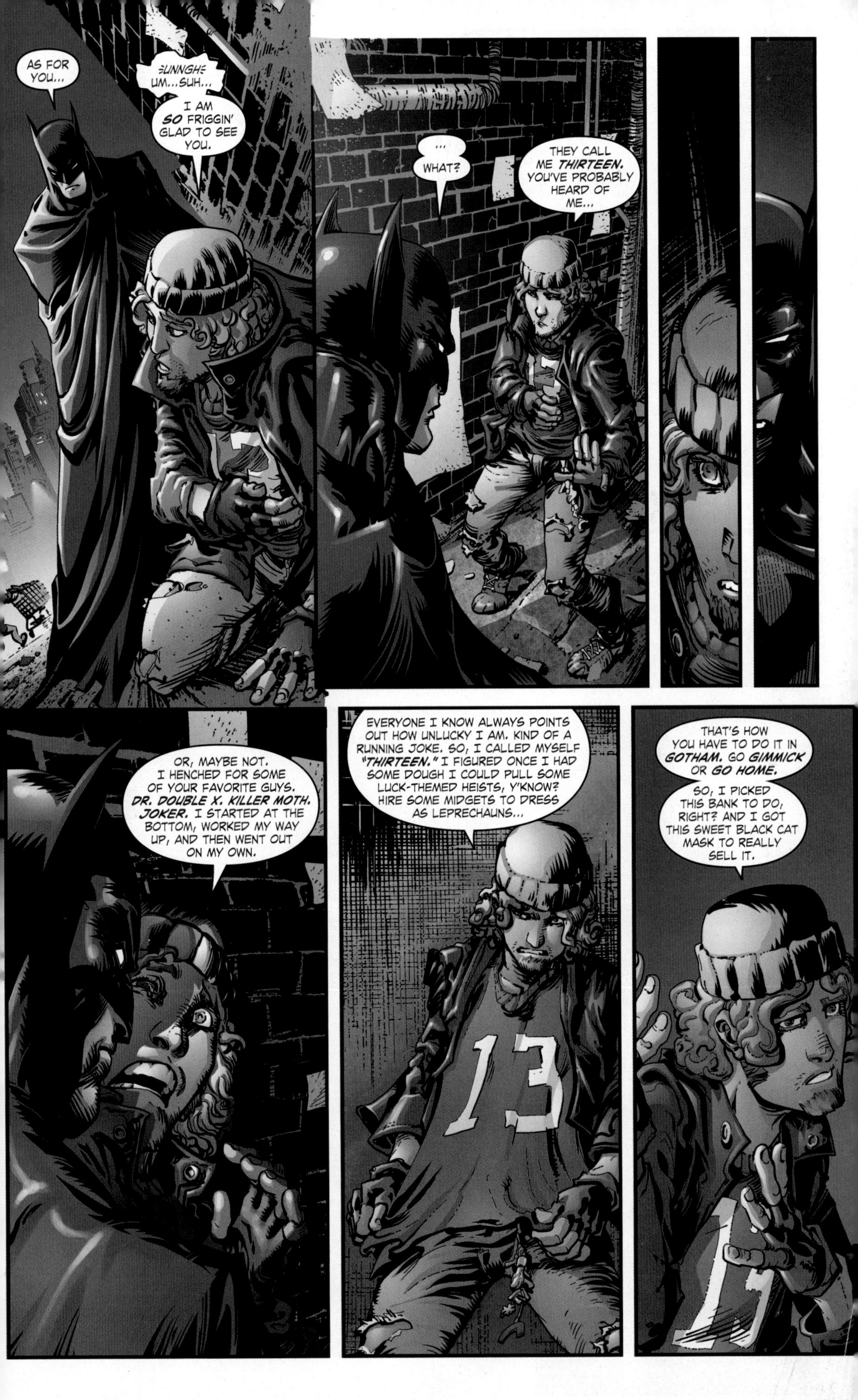
AS FOR YOU...
UNNGH UM...SUH...
I AM SO FRIGGIN' GLAD TO SEE YOU.
... WHAT?
THEY CALL ME THIRTEEN. YOU'VE PROBABLY HEARD OF ME...
OR, MAYBE NOT. I HENCHED FOR SOME OF YOUR FAVORITE GUYS. DR. DOUBLE X. KILLER MOTH. JOKER. I STARTED AT THE BOTTOM, WORKED MY WAY UP, AND THEN WENT OUT ON MY OWN.
EVERYONE I KNOW ALWAYS POINTS OUT HOW UNLUCKY I AM. KIND OF A RUNNING JOKE. SO, I CALLED MYSELF "THIRTEEN." I FIGURED ONCE I HAD SOME DOUGH I COULD PULL SOME LUCK-THEMED HEISTS, Y'KNOW? HIRE SOME MIDGETS TO DRESS AS LEPRECHAUNS...
THAT'S HOW YOU HAVE TO DO IT IN GOTHAM. GO GIMMICK OR GO HOME.
SO, I PICKED THIS BANK TO DO, RIGHT? AND I GOT THIS SWEET BLACK CAT MASK TO REALLY SELL IT.

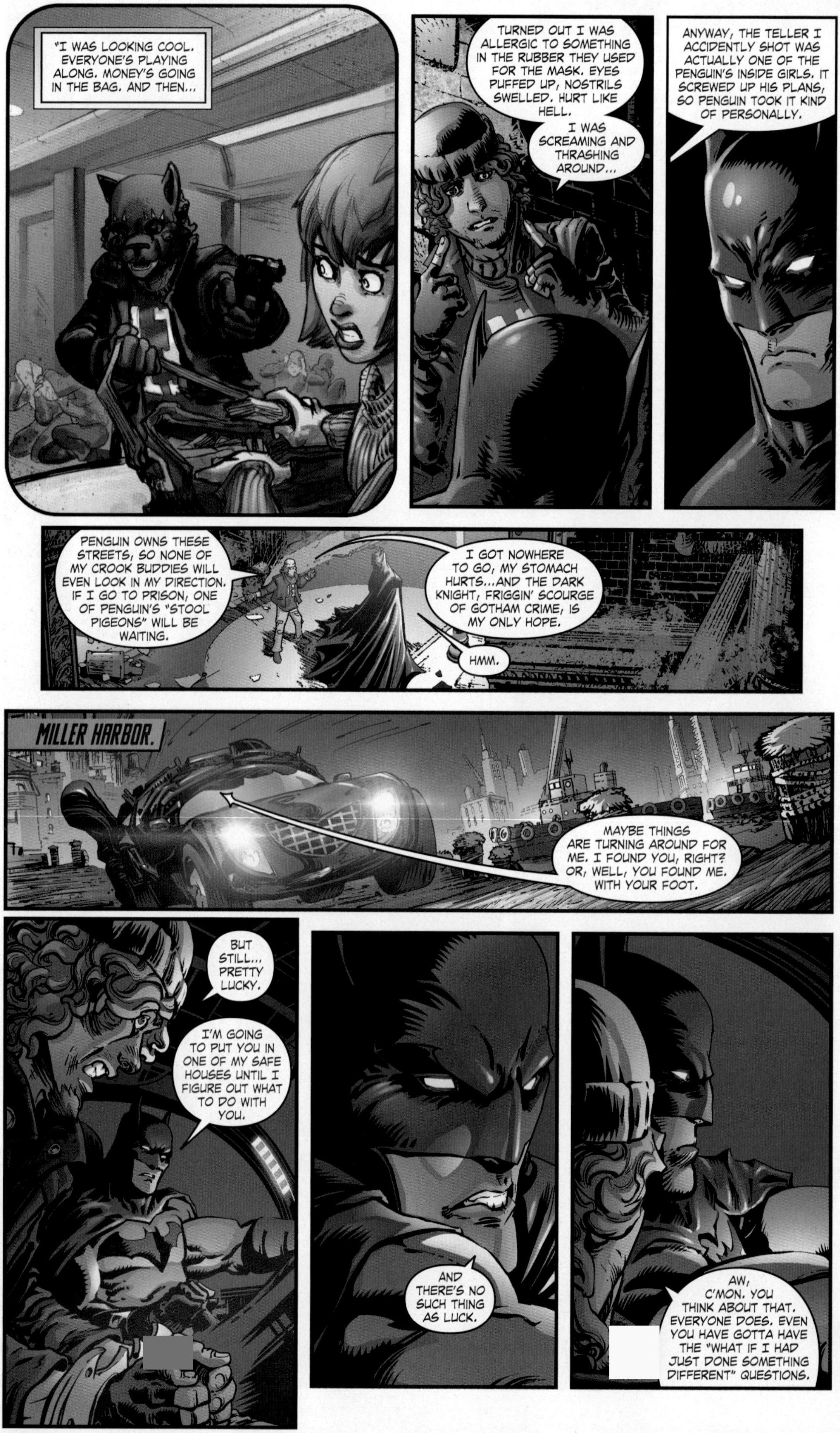
"I WAS LOOKING COOL. EVERYONE'S PLAYING ALONG. MONEY'S GOING IN THE BAG. AND THEN...
TURNED OUT I WAS ALLERGIC TO SOMETHING IN THE RUBBER THEY USED FOR THE MASK. EYES PUFFED UP, NOSTRILS SWELLED. HURT LIKE HELL.
I WAS SCREAMING AND THRASHING AROUND...
ANYWAY, THE TELLER I ACCIDENTLY SHOT WAS ACTUALLY ONE OF THE PENGUIN'S INSIDE GIRLS. IT SCREWED UP HIS PLANS, SO PENGUIN TOOK IT KIND OF PERSONALLY.
PENGUIN OWNS THESE STREETS, SO NONE OF MY CROOK BUDDIES WILL EVEN LOOK IN MY DIRECTION. IF I GO TO PRISON, ONE OF PENGUIN'S "STOOL PIGEONS" WILL BE WAITING.
I GOT NOWHERE TO GO, MY STOMACH HURTS...AND THE DARK KNIGHT, FRIGGIN' SCOURGE OF GOTHAM CRIME, IS MY ONLY HOPE.
HMM.
MILLER HARBOR.
MAYBE THINGS ARE TURNING AROUND FOR ME. I FOUND YOU, RIGHT? OR, WELL, YOU FOUND ME. WITH YOUR FOOT.
BUT STILL... PRETTY LUCKY.
I'M GOING TO PUT YOU IN ONE OF MY SAFE HOUSES UNTIL I FIGURE OUT WHAT TO DO WITH YOU.
AND THERE'S NO SUCH THING AS LUCK.
AW, C'MON. YOU THINK ABOUT THAT. EVERYONE DOES. EVEN YOU HAVE GOTTA HAVE THE "WHAT IF I HAD JUST DONE SOMETHING DIFFERENT" QUESTIONS.

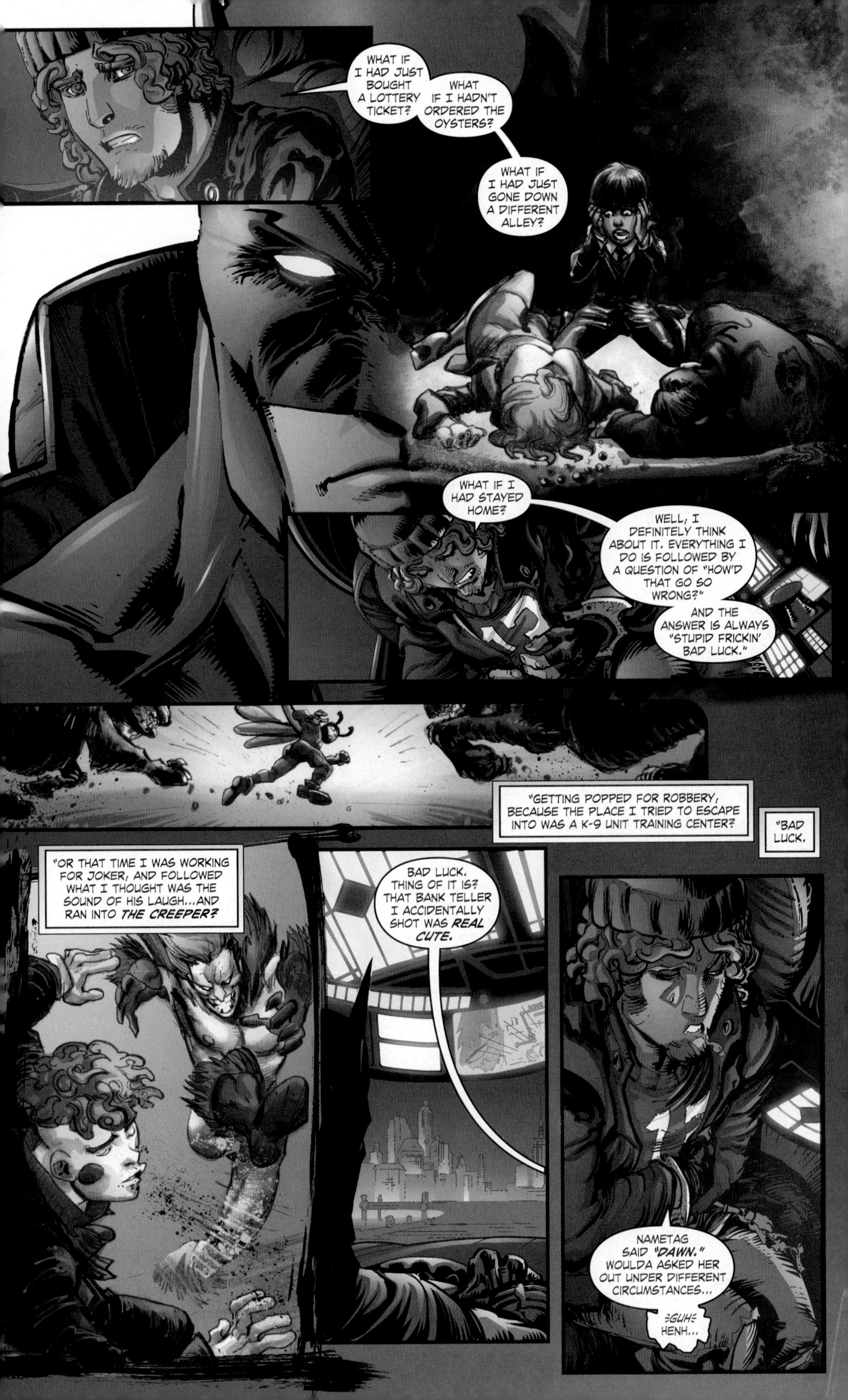
WHAT IF I HAD JUST BOUGHT A LOTTERY TICKET?
WHAT IF I HADN'T ORDERED THE OYSTERS?
WHAT IF I HAD JUST GONE DOWN A DIFFERENT ALLEY?
WHAT IF I HAD STAYED HOME?
WELL, I DEFINITELY THINK ABOUT IT. EVERYTHING I DO IS FOLLOWED BY A QUESTION OF "HOW'D THAT GO SO WRONG?"
AND THE ANSWER IS ALWAYS "STUPID FRICKIN' BAD LUCK."
"GETTING POPPED FOR ROBBERY, BECAUSE THE PLACE I TRIED TO ESCAPE INTO WAS A K-9 UNIT TRAINING CENTER?
"BAD LUCK.
"OR THAT TIME I WAS WORKING FOR JOKER, AND FOLLOWED WHAT I THOUGHT WAS THE SOUND OF HIS LAUGH...AND RAN INTO THE CREEPER?
BAD LUCK. THING OF IT IS? THAT BANK TELLER I ACCIDENTALLY SHOT WAS REAL CUTE.
NAMETAG SAID "DAWN." WOULDA ASKED HER OUT UNDER DIFFERENT CIRCUMSTANCES...
GUH HENH...

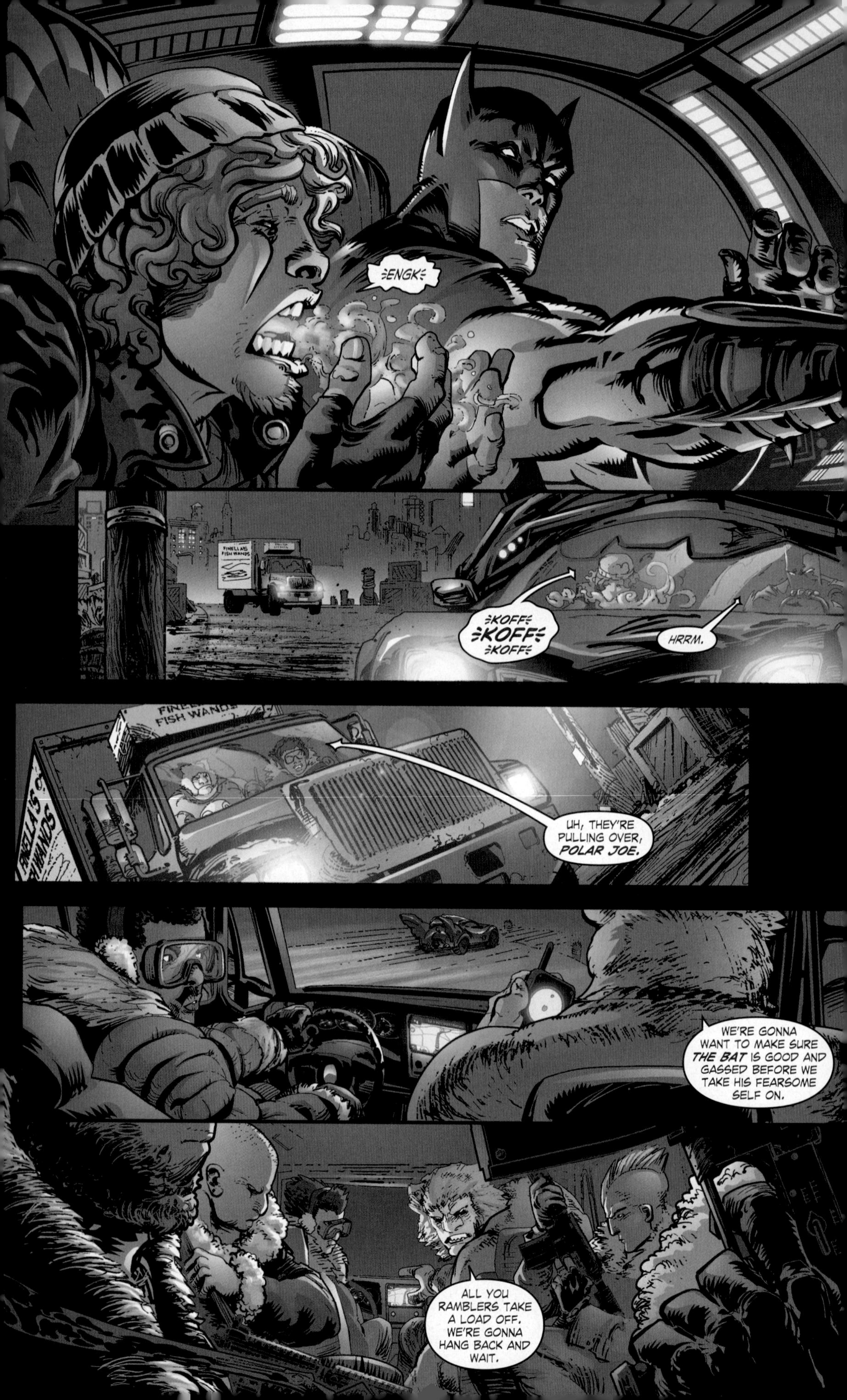
ENGK
FINELLA'S FISH WANDS
KOFF KOFF KOFF
HRRM.
FINELLA'S FISH WANDS
UH, THEY'RE PULLING OVER, POLAR JOE.
WE'RE GONNA WANT TO MAKE SURE THE BAT IS GOOD AND GASSED BEFORE WE TAKE HIS FEARSOME SELF ON.
ALL YOU RAMBLERS TAKE A LOAD OFF. WE'RE GONNA HANG BACK AND WAIT.

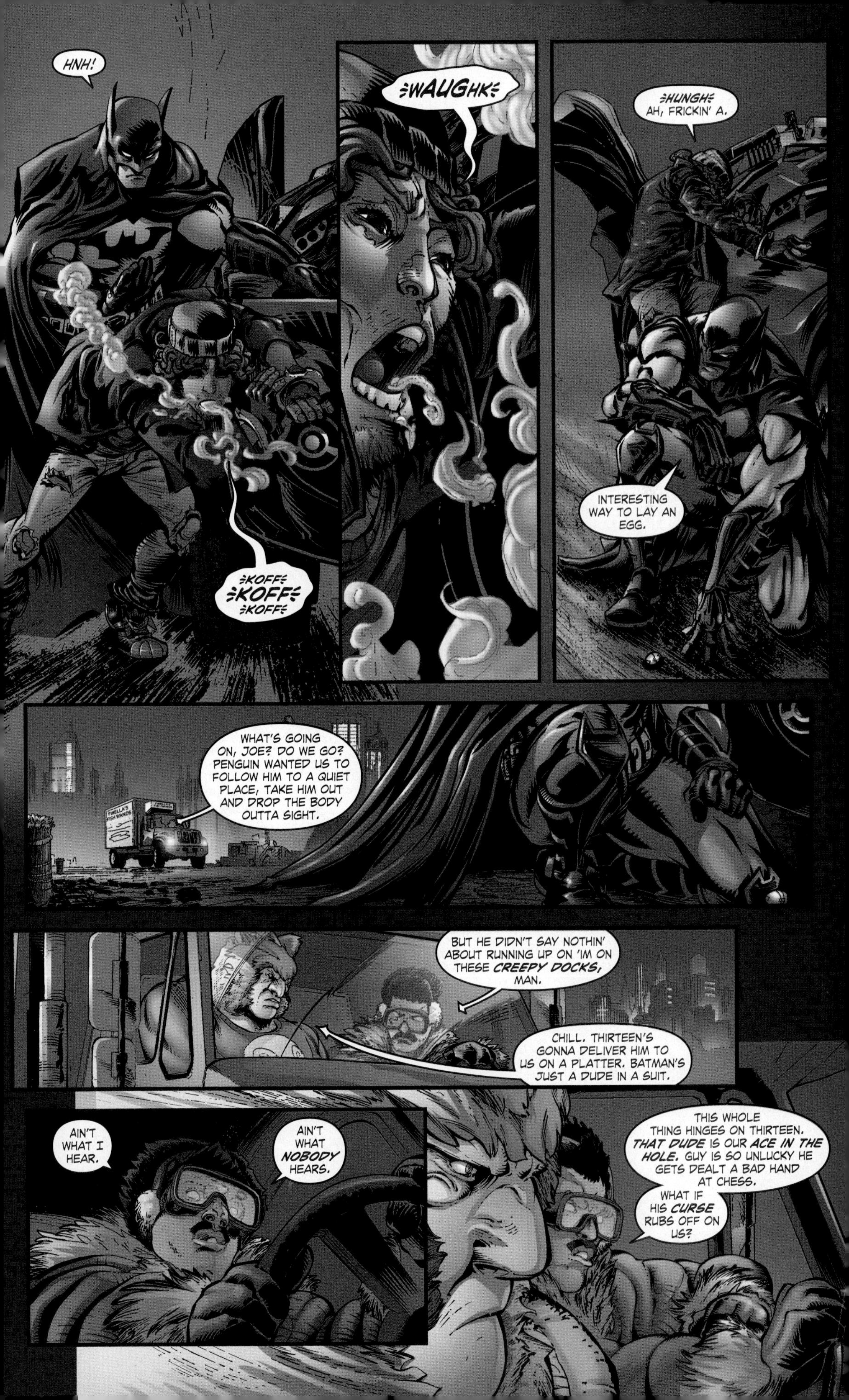
HNH!
WAUGHK
KOFF KOFF KOFF
HUNGH AH, FRICKIN' A.
INTERESTING WAY TO LAY AN EGG.
WHAT'S GOING ON, JOE? DO WE GO? PENGUIN WANTED US TO FOLLOW HIM TO A QUIET PLACE, TAKE HIM OUT AND DROP THE BODY OUTTA SIGHT.
FINELLA'S FISH WANDS
BUT HE DIDN'T SAY NOTHIN' ABOUT RUNNING UP ON 'IM ON THESE CREEPY DOCKS, MAN.
CHILL. THIRTEEN'S GONNA DELIVER HIM TO US ON A PLATTER. BATMAN'S JUST A DUDE IN A SUIT.
AIN'T WHAT I HEAR.
AIN'T WHAT NOBODY HEARS.
THIS WHOLE THING HINGES ON THIRTEEN. THAT DUDE IS OUR ACE IN THE HOLE. GUY IS SO UNLUCKY HE GETS DEALT A BAD HAND AT CHESS.
WHAT IF HIS CURSE RUBS OFF ON US?

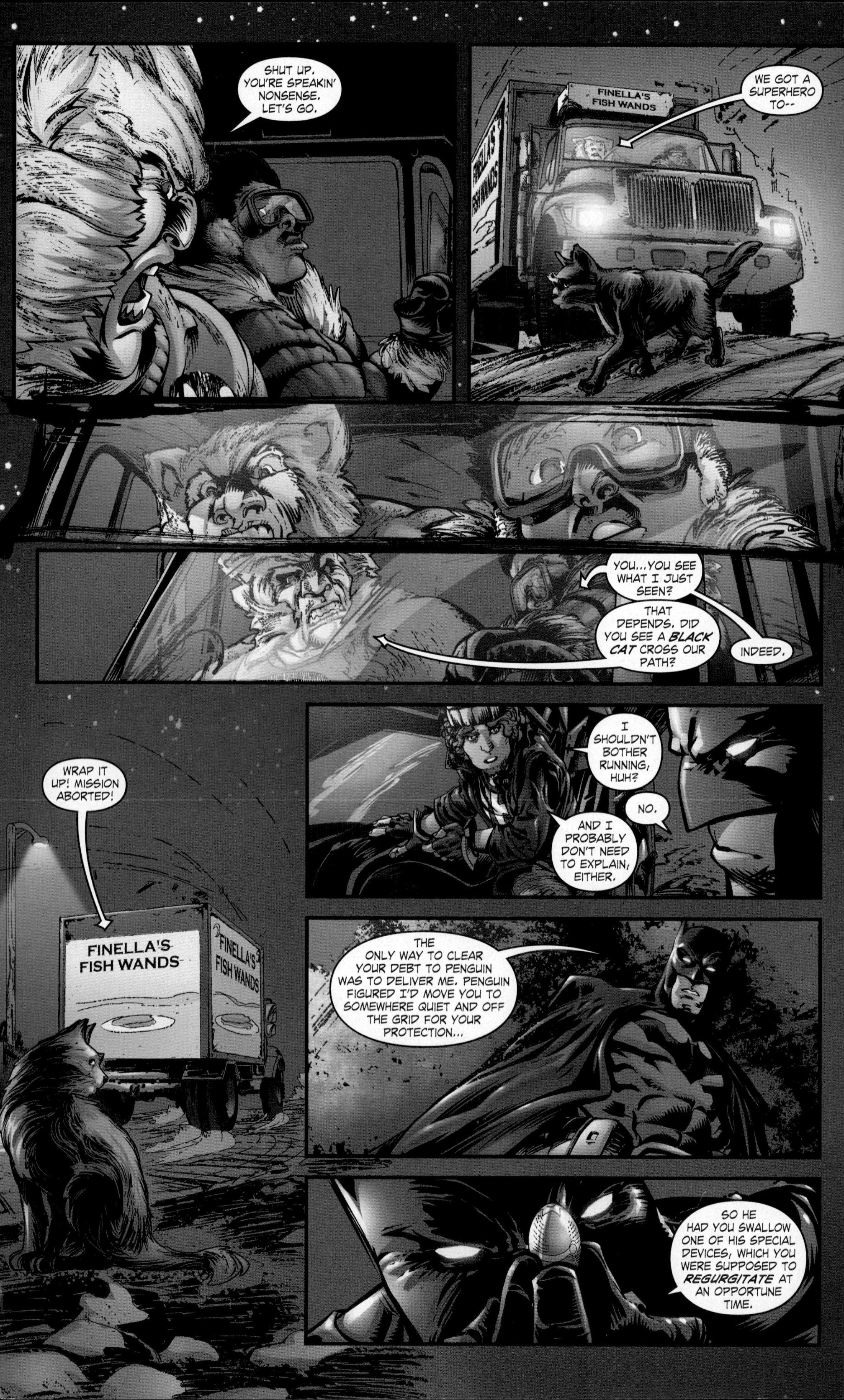
SHUT UP. YOU'RE SPEAKIN' NONSENSE. LET'S GO.
FINELLA'S FISH WANDS
FINELLA'S FISH WANDS
WE GOT A SUPERHERO TO--
YOU...YOU SEE WHAT I JUST SEEN?
THAT DEPENDS. DID YOU SEE A BLACK CAT CROSS OUR PATH?
INDEED.
WRAP IT UP! MISSION ABORTED!
FINELLA'S FISH WANDS
FINELLA'S FISH WANDS
I SHOULDN'T BOTHER RUNNING, HUH?
NO.
AND I PROBABLY DON'T NEED TO EXPLAIN, EITHER.
THE ONLY WAY TO CLEAR YOUR DEBT TO PENGUIN WAS TO DELIVER ME. PENGUIN FIGURED I'D MOVE YOU TO SOMEWHERE QUIET AND OFF THE GRID FOR YOUR PROTECTION...
SO HE HAD YOU SWALLOW ONE OF HIS SPECIAL DEVICES, WHICH YOU WERE SUPPOSED TO REGURGITATE AT AN OPPORTUNE TIME.

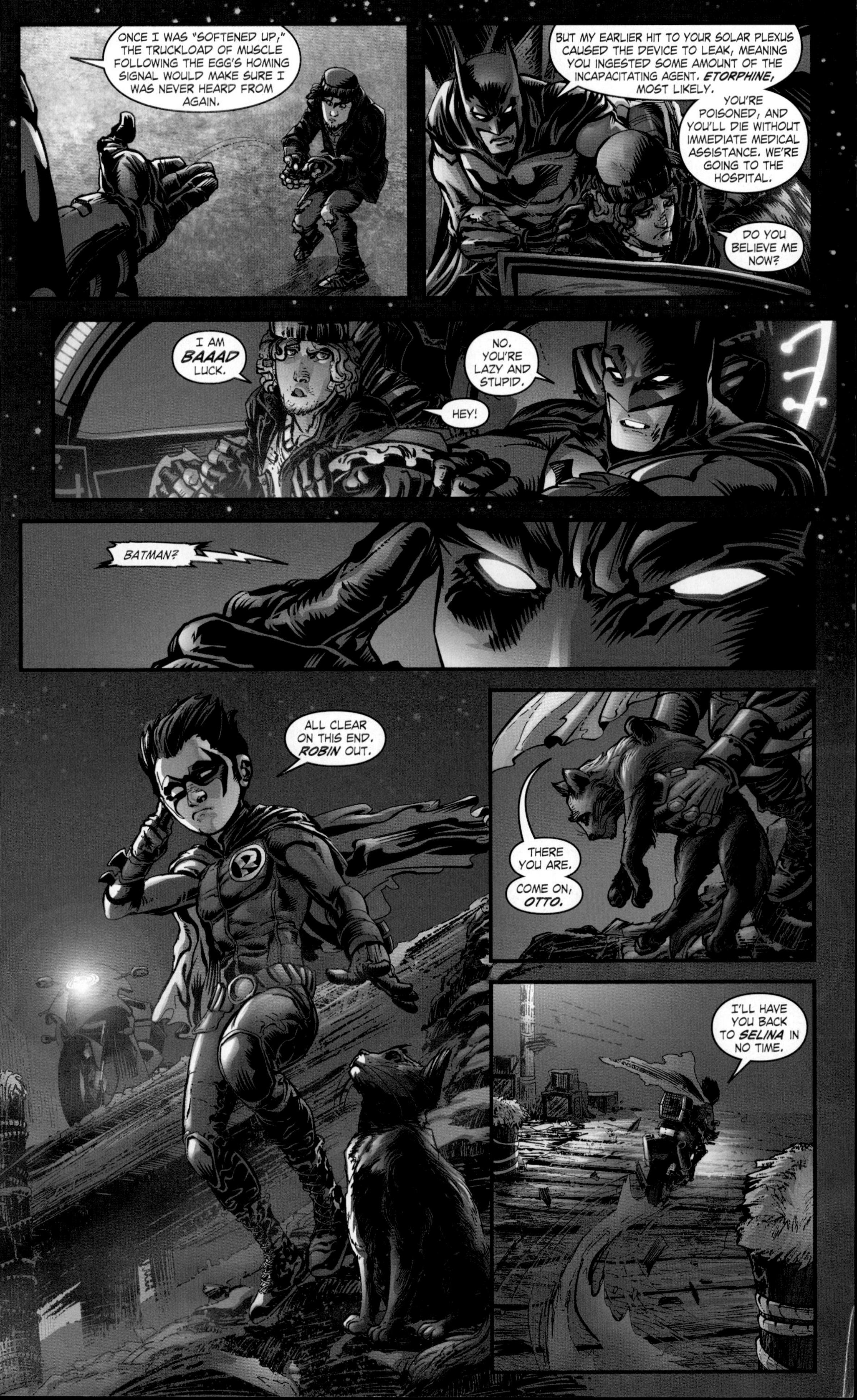
ONCE I WAS "SOFTENED UP," THE TRUCKLOAD OF MUSCLE FOLLOWING THE EGG'S HOMING SIGNAL WOULD MAKE SURE I WAS NEVER HEARD FROM AGAIN.
BUT MY EARLIER HIT TO YOUR SOLAR PLEXUS CAUSED THE DEVICE TO LEAK, MEANING YOU INGESTED SOME AMOUNT OF THE INCAPACITATING AGENT. ETORPHINE, MOST LIKELY.
YOU'RE POISONED, AND YOU'LL DIE WITHOUT IMMEDIATE MEDICAL ASSISTANCE. WE'RE GOING TO THE HOSPITAL.
DO YOU BELIEVE ME NOW?
I AM BAAAD LUCK.
NO. YOU'RE LAZY AND STUPID.
HEY!
BATMAN?
ALL CLEAR ON THIS END. ROBIN OUT.
THERE YOU ARE.
COME ON, OTTO.
I'LL HAVE YOU BACK TO SELINA IN NO TIME.

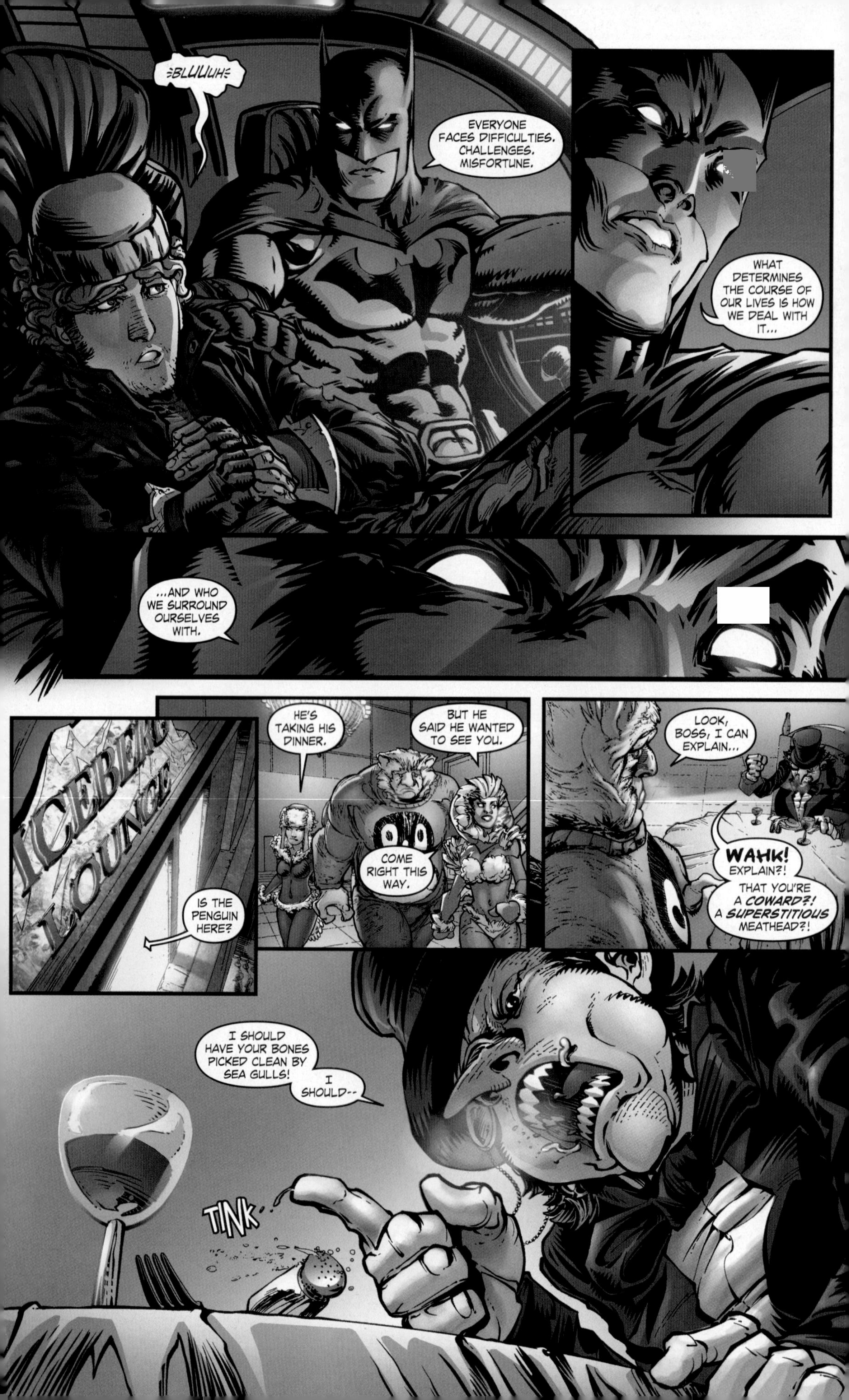

BLUUUH
EVERYONE FACES DIFFICULTIES. CHALLENGES. MISFORTUNE.
WHAT DETERMINES THE COURSE OF OUR LIVES IS HOW WE DEAL WITH IT...
...AND WHO WE SURROUND OURSELVES WITH.
LOUNGE
IS THE PENGUIN HERE?
HE'S TAKING HIS DINNER.
BUT HE SAID HE WANTED TO SEE YOU.
COME RIGHT THIS WAY.
LOOK, BOSS, I CAN EXPLAIN...
WAHK! EXPLAIN?! THAT YOU'RE A *COWARD?!* A *SUPERSTITIOUS* MEATHEAD?!
I SHOULD HAVE YOUR BONES PICKED CLEAN BY SEA GULLS!
I SHOULD--
TINK

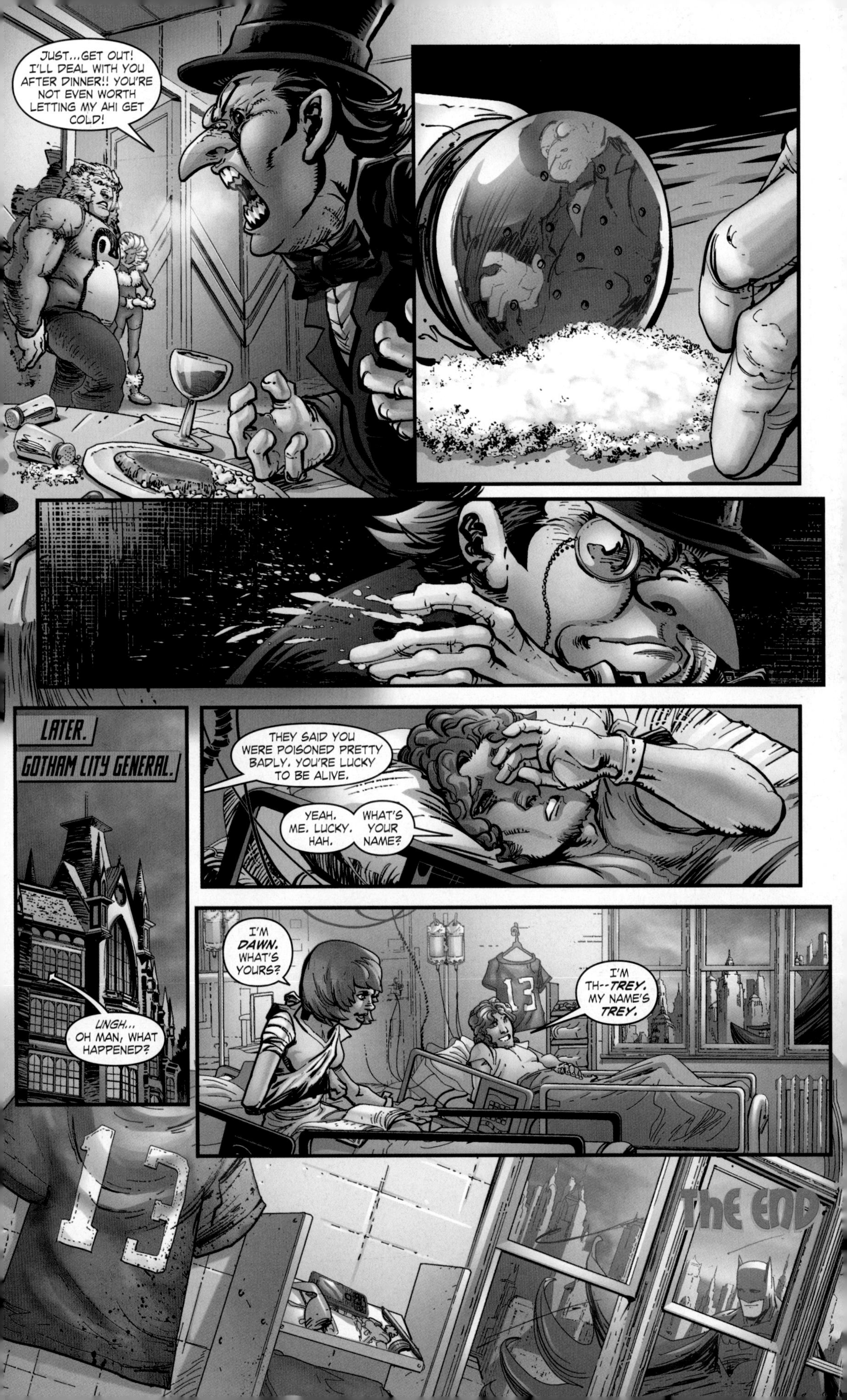
JUST...GET OUT! I'LL DEAL WITH YOU AFTER DINNER!! YOU'RE NOT EVEN WORTH LETTING MY AHI GET COLD!
LATER.
GOTHAM CITY GENERAL.
UNGH... OH MAN, WHAT HAPPENED?
THEY SAID YOU WERE POISONED PRETTY BADLY. YOU'RE LUCKY TO BE ALIVE.
YEAH. ME. LUCKY. HAH.
WHAT'S YOUR NAME?
I'M DAWN. WHAT'S YOURS?
I'M TH--TREY. MY NAME'S TREY.
THE END

WITHOUT SIN

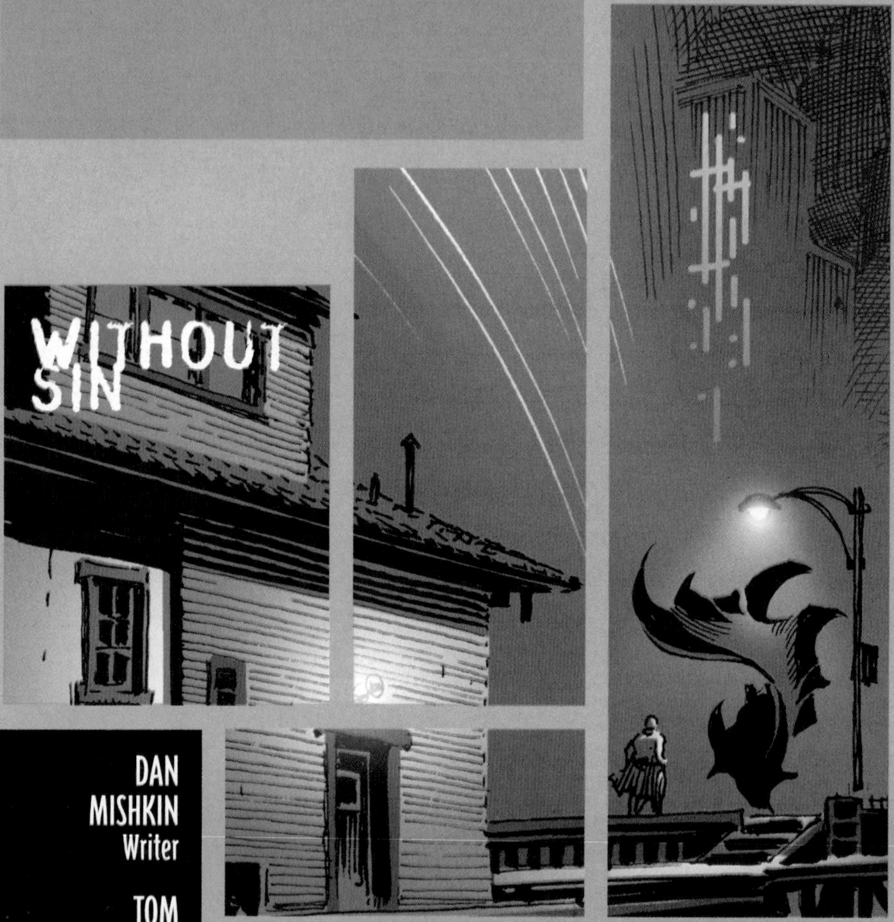

DAN MISHKIN
Writer

TOM MANDRAKE
Artist

WENDY BROOME
Colorist

SAIDA TEMOFONTE
Letterer

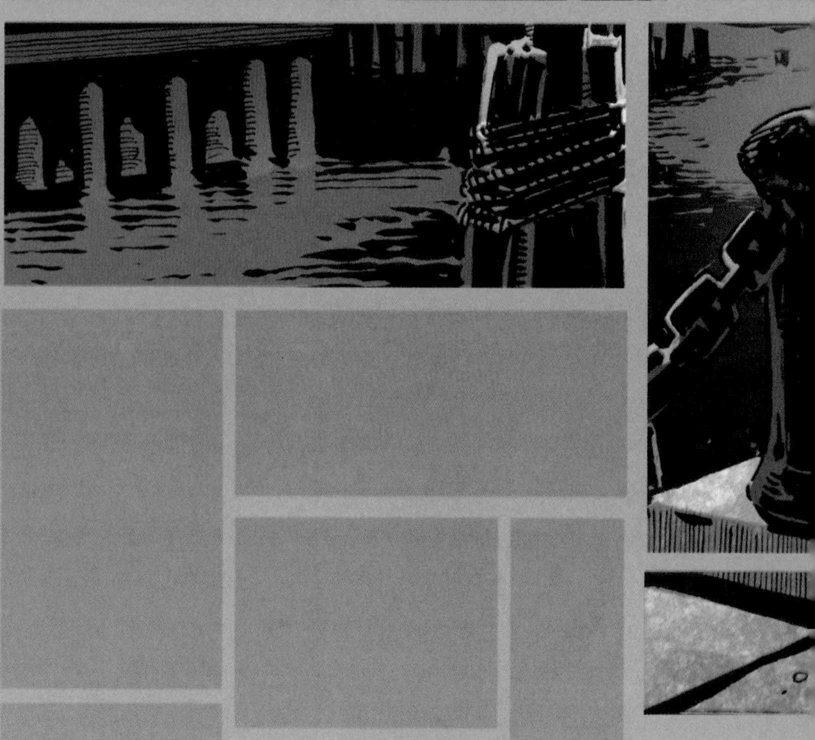

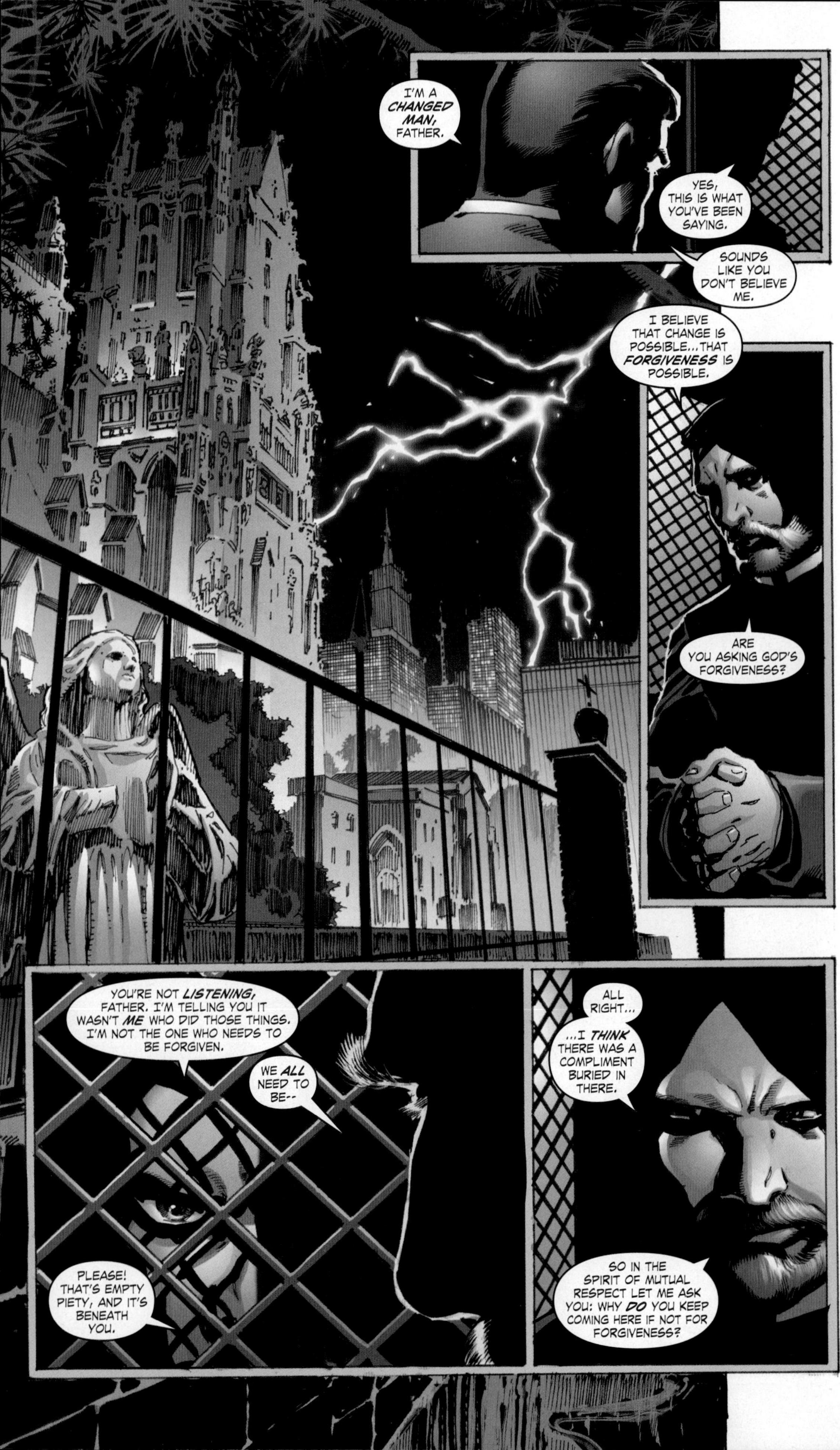
I'M A CHANGED MAN, FATHER.
YES, THIS IS WHAT YOU'VE BEEN SAYING.
SOUNDS LIKE YOU DON'T BELIEVE ME.
I BELIEVE THAT CHANGE IS POSSIBLE...THAT FORGIVENESS IS POSSIBLE.
ARE YOU ASKING GOD'S FORGIVENESS?
YOU'RE NOT LISTENING, FATHER. I'M TELLING YOU IT WASN'T ME WHO DID THOSE THINGS. I'M NOT THE ONE WHO NEEDS TO BE FORGIVEN.
WE ALL NEED TO BE--
PLEASE! THAT'S EMPTY PIETY, AND IT'S BENEATH YOU.
ALL RIGHT...
...I THINK THERE WAS A COMPLIMENT BURIED IN THERE.
SO IN THE SPIRIT OF MUTUAL RESPECT LET ME ASK YOU: WHY DO YOU KEEP COMING HERE IF NOT FOR FORGIVENESS?

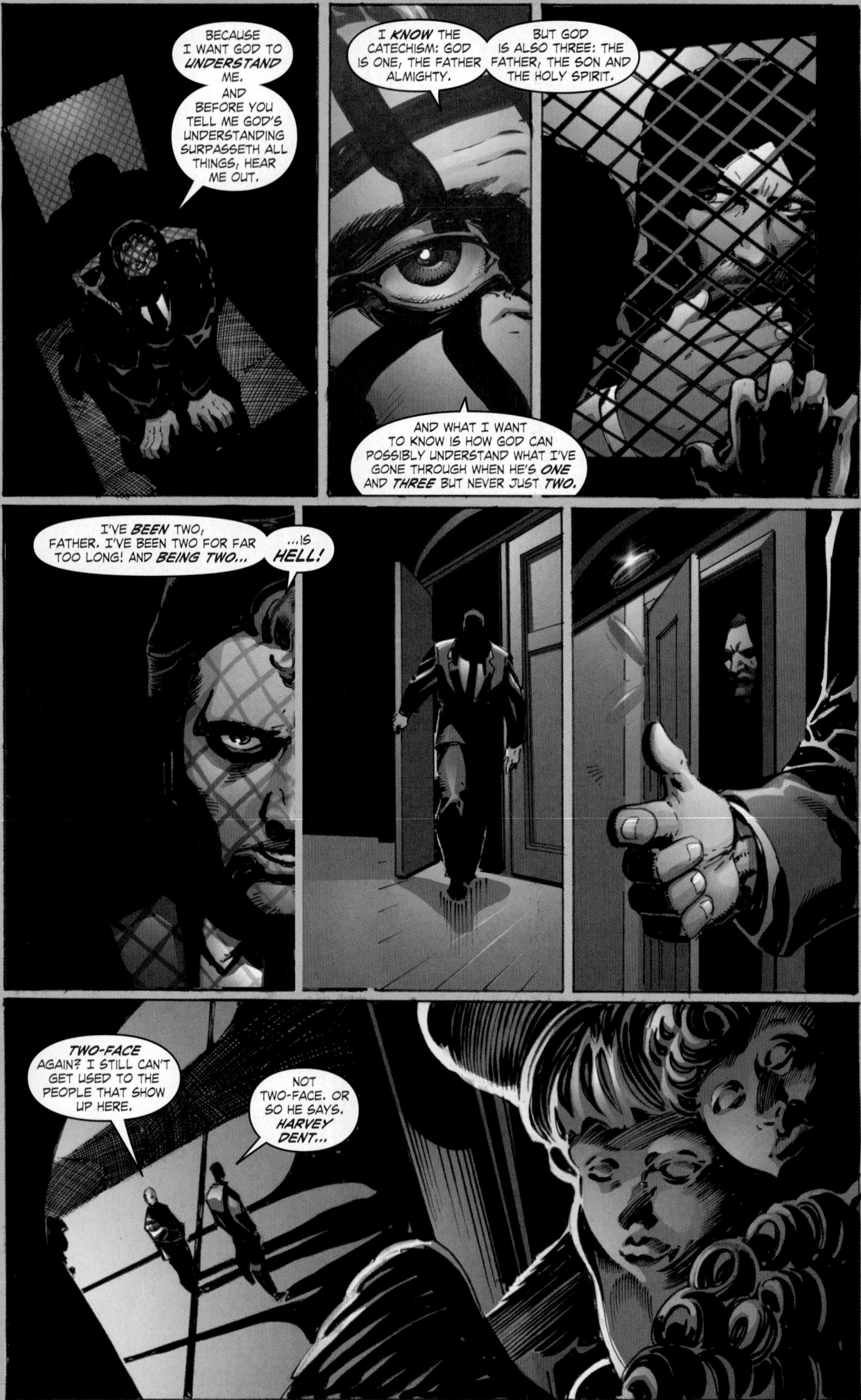

BECAUSE I WANT GOD TO *UNDERSTAND* ME.
AND BEFORE YOU TELL ME GOD'S UNDERSTANDING SURPASSETH ALL THINGS, HEAR ME OUT.
I *KNOW* THE CATECHISM: GOD IS ONE, THE FATHER ALMIGHTY.
BUT GOD IS ALSO THREE: THE FATHER, THE SON AND THE HOLY SPIRIT.
AND WHAT I WANT TO KNOW IS HOW GOD CAN POSSIBLY UNDERSTAND WHAT I'VE GONE THROUGH WHEN HE'S *ONE* AND *THREE* BUT NEVER JUST *TWO.*
I'VE *BEEN* TWO, FATHER. I'VE BEEN TWO FOR FAR TOO LONG! AND *BEING TWO...*
...IS *HELL!*
TWO-FACE AGAIN? I STILL CAN'T GET USED TO THE PEOPLE THAT SHOW UP HERE.
NOT TWO-FACE. OR SO HE SAYS. *HARVEY DENT...*

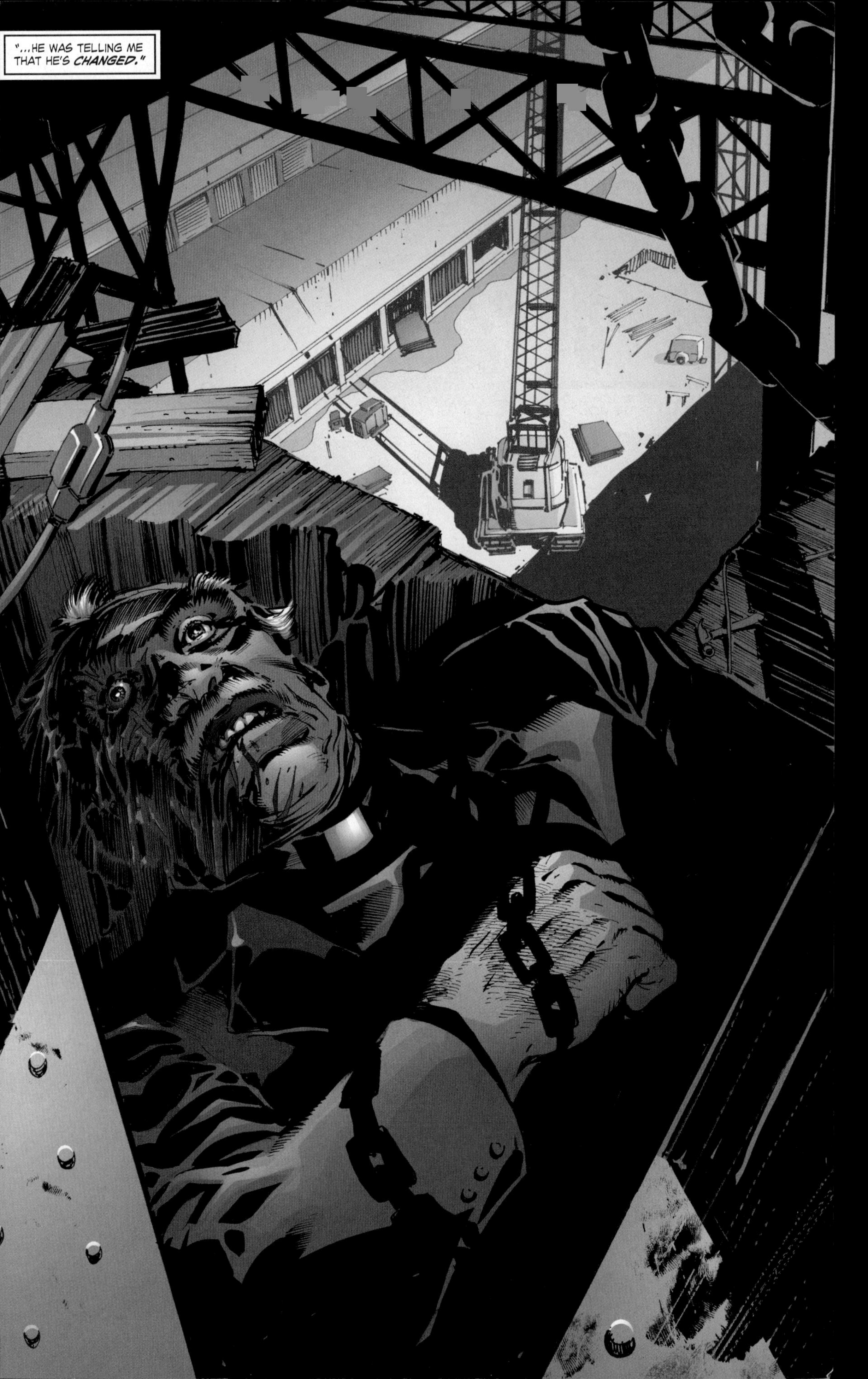
"...HE WAS TELLING ME THAT HE'S *CHANGED.*"

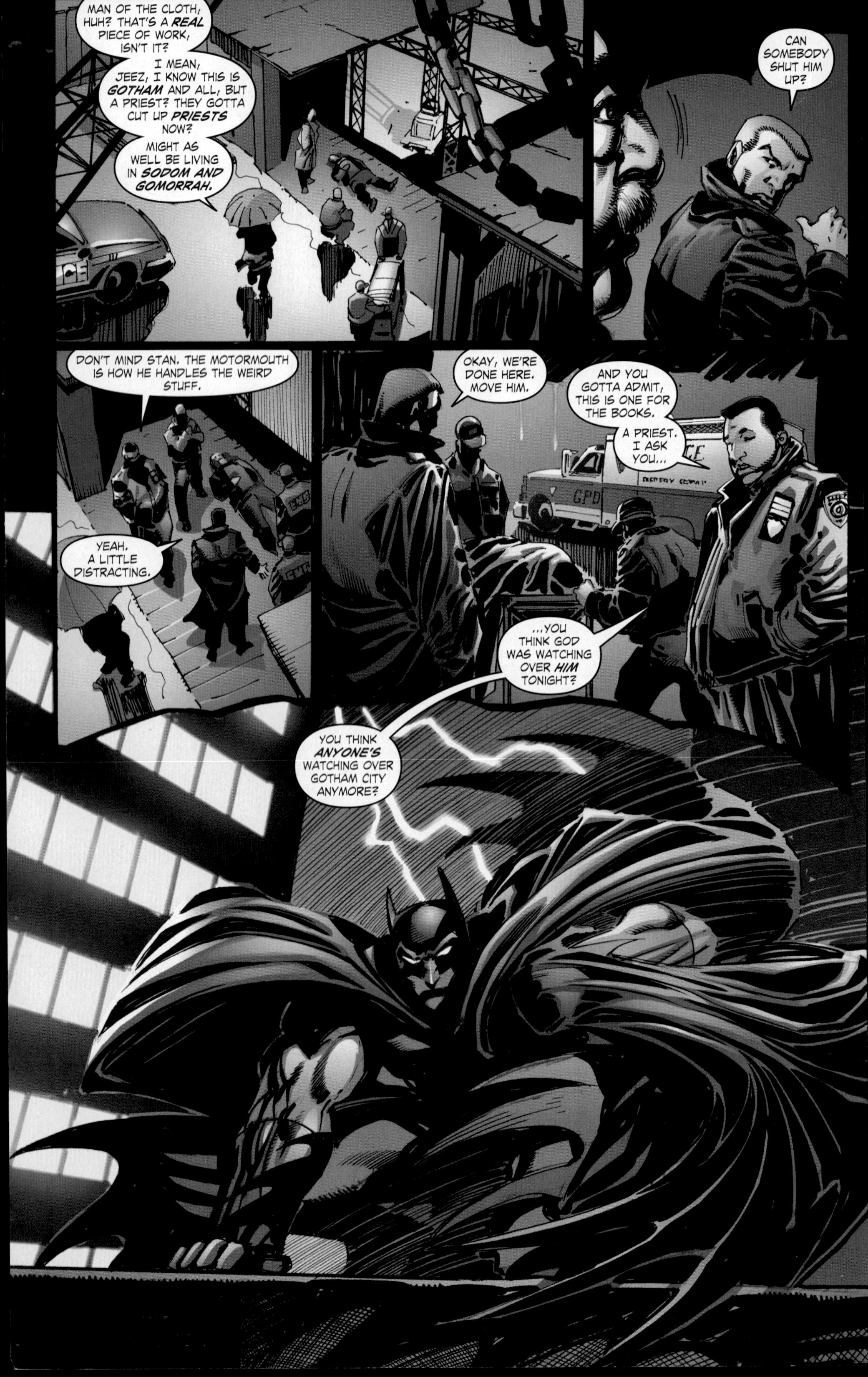
MAN OF THE CLOTH, HUH? THAT'S A REAL PIECE OF WORK, ISN'T IT?
I MEAN, JEEZ, I KNOW THIS IS GOTHAM AND ALL, BUT A PRIEST? THEY GOTTA CUT UP PRIESTS NOW?
MIGHT AS WELL BE LIVING IN SODOM AND GOMORRAH.
CAN SOMEBODY SHUT HIM UP?
DON'T MIND STAN. THE MOTORMOUTH IS HOW HE HANDLES THE WEIRD STUFF.
YEAH. A LITTLE DISTRACTING.
OKAY, WE'RE DONE HERE. MOVE HIM.
AND YOU GOTTA ADMIT, THIS IS ONE FOR THE BOOKS.
A PRIEST. I ASK YOU...
...YOU THINK GOD WAS WATCHING OVER HIM TONIGHT?
YOU THINK ANYONE'S WATCHING OVER GOTHAM CITY ANYMORE?
GPD

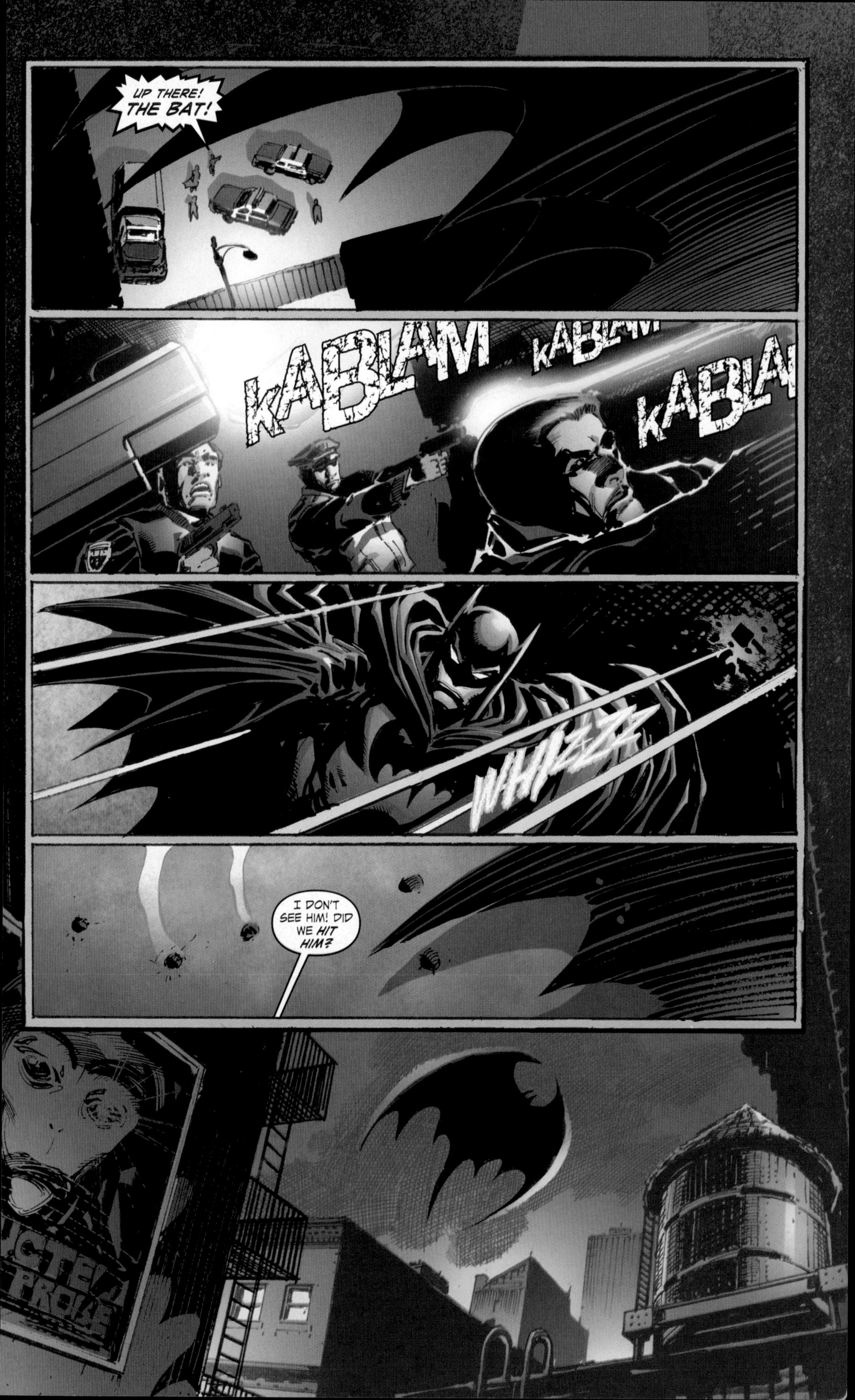

UP THERE! THE BAT!
kABLAM
kABLAM
kABLA
WHIZZZ
I DON'T SEE HIM! DID WE HIT HIM?

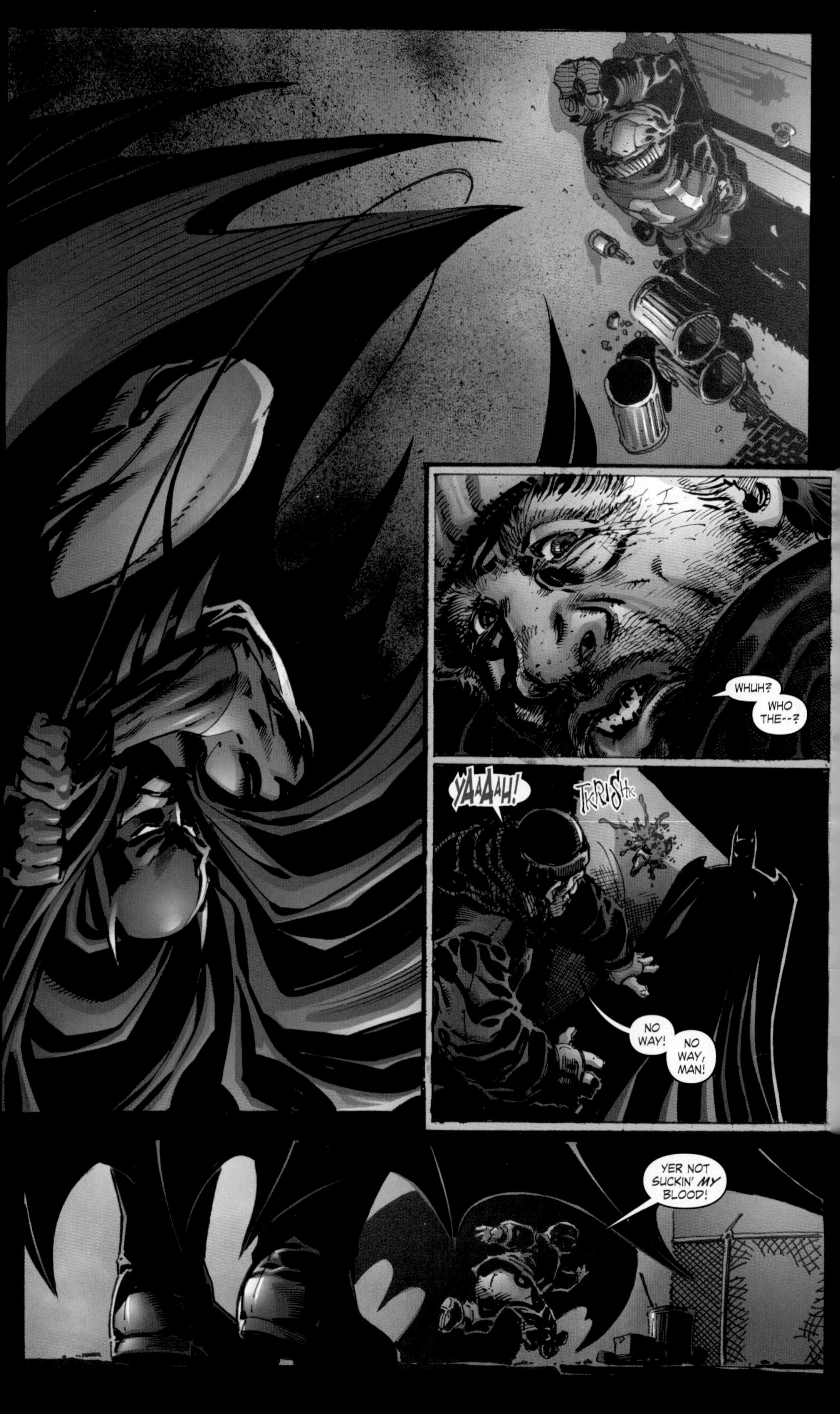
WHUH? WHO THE--?
YAAAAH!
TKRISHK
NO WAY!
NO WAY, MAN!
YER NOT SUCKIN' MY BLOOD!

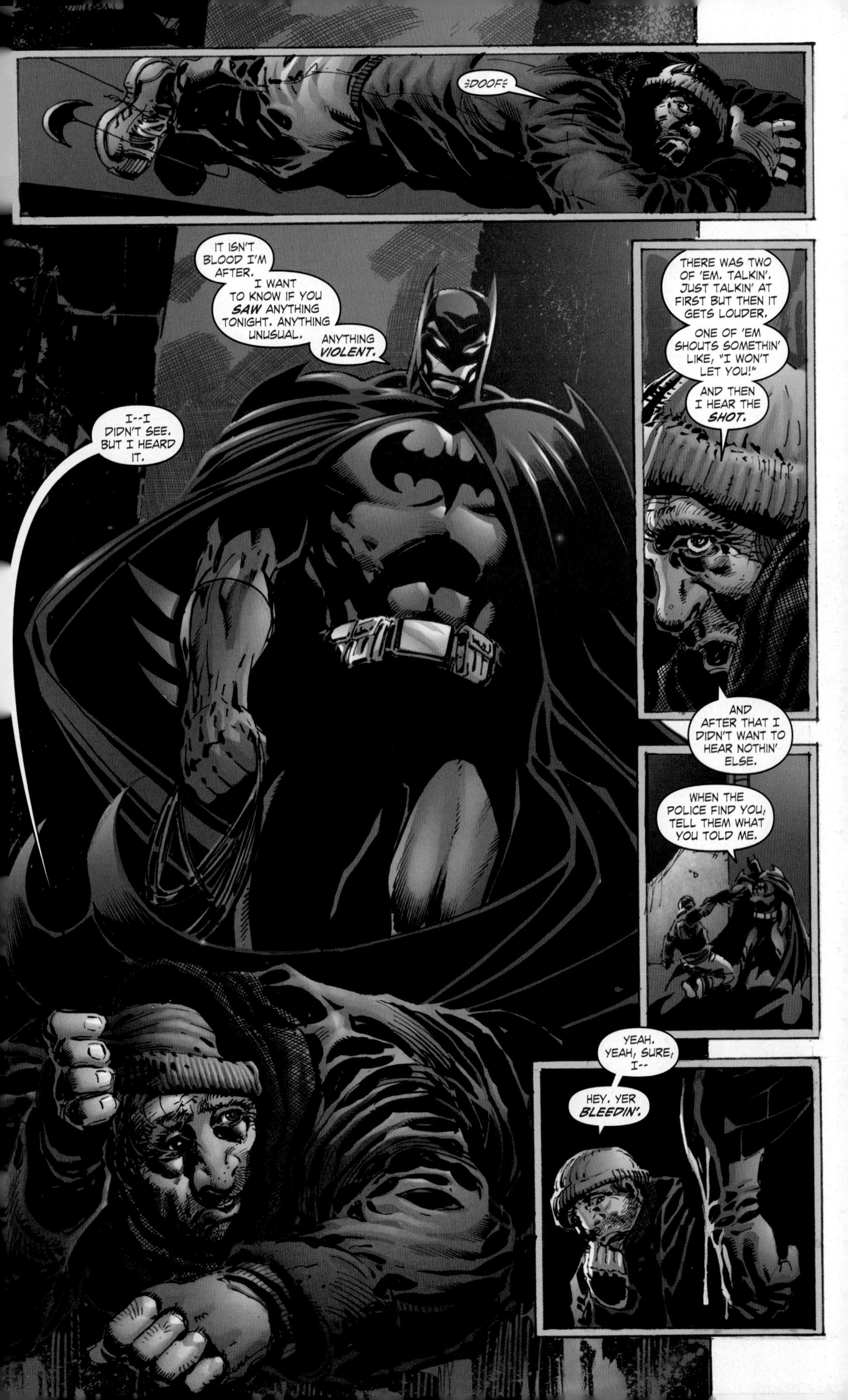

DOOF
IT ISN'T BLOOD I'M AFTER.
I WANT TO KNOW IF YOU SAW ANYTHING TONIGHT. ANYTHING UNUSUAL.
ANYTHING VIOLENT.
I--I DIDN'T SEE. BUT I HEARD IT.
THERE WAS TWO OF 'EM. TALKIN'. JUST TALKIN' AT FIRST BUT THEN IT GETS LOUDER.
ONE OF 'EM SHOUTS SOMETHIN' LIKE, "I WON'T LET YOU!"
AND THEN I HEAR THE SHOT.
AND AFTER THAT I DIDN'T WANT TO HEAR NOTHIN' ELSE.
WHEN THE POLICE FIND YOU, TELL THEM WHAT YOU TOLD ME.
YEAH. YEAH, SURE, I--
HEY. YER BLEEDIN'.

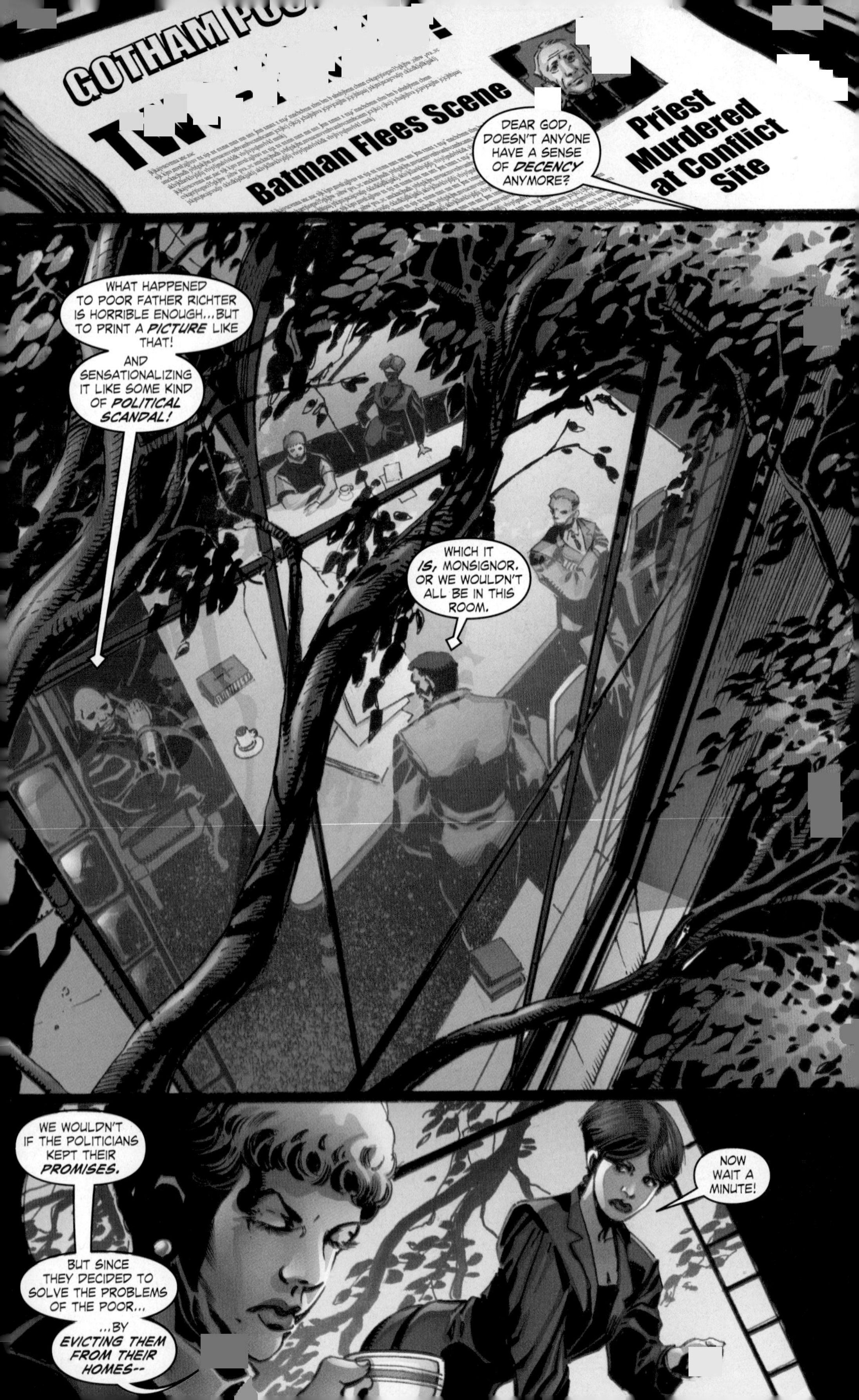
Batman Flees Scene
Priest Murdered at Conflict Site
DEAR GOD, DOESN'T ANYONE HAVE A SENSE OF *DECENCY* ANYMORE?
WHAT HAPPENED TO POOR FATHER RICHTER IS HORRIBLE ENOUGH...BUT TO PRINT A *PICTURE* LIKE THAT!
AND SENSATIONALIZING IT LIKE SOME KIND OF *POLITICAL SCANDAL!*
WHICH IT *IS,* MONSIGNOR. OR WE WOULDN'T ALL BE IN THIS ROOM.
WE WOULDN'T IF THE POLITICIANS KEPT THEIR *PROMISES.*
BUT SINCE THEY DECIDED TO SOLVE THE PROBLEMS OF THE POOR...
...BY *EVICTING THEM FROM THEIR HOMES--*
NOW WAIT A MINUTE!

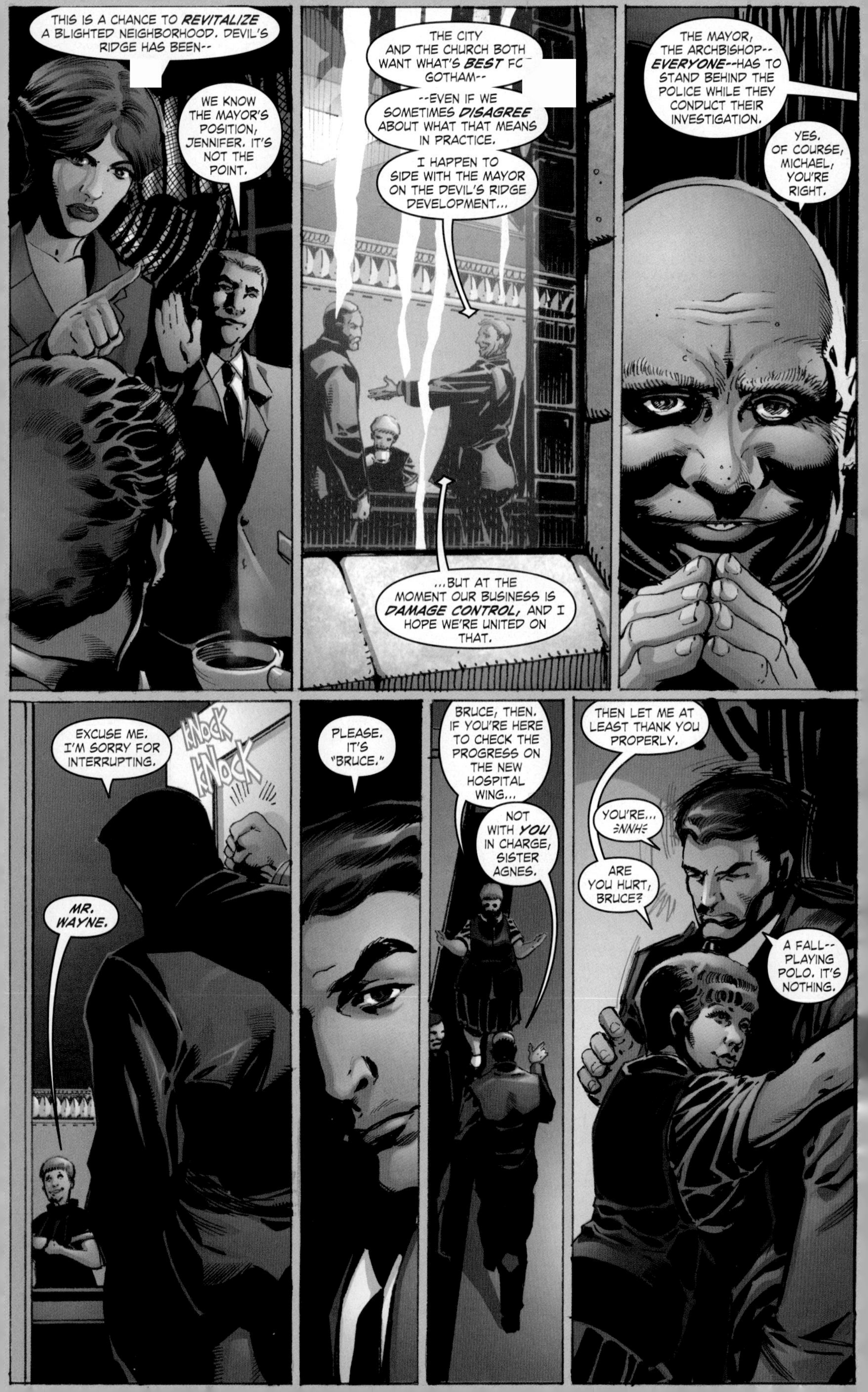

THIS IS A CHANCE TO REVITALIZE A BLIGHTED NEIGHBORHOOD. DEVIL'S RIDGE HAS BEEN--
WE KNOW THE MAYOR'S POSITION, JENNIFER. IT'S NOT THE POINT.
THE CITY AND THE CHURCH BOTH WANT WHAT'S BEST FO
GOTHAM--
--EVEN IF WE SOMETIMES DISAGREE ABOUT WHAT THAT MEANS IN PRACTICE.
I HAPPEN TO SIDE WITH THE MAYOR ON THE DEVIL'S RIDGE DEVELOPMENT...
...BUT AT THE MOMENT OUR BUSINESS IS DAMAGE CONTROL, AND I HOPE WE'RE UNITED ON THAT.
THE MAYOR, THE ARCHBISHOP--EVERYONE--HAS TO STAND BEHIND THE POLICE WHILE THEY CONDUCT THEIR INVESTIGATION.
YES. OF COURSE, MICHAEL, YOU'RE RIGHT.
EXCUSE ME. I'M SORRY FOR INTERRUPTING.
KNOCK KNOCK
MR. WAYNE.
PLEASE. IT'S "BRUCE."
BRUCE, THEN. IF YOU'RE HERE TO CHECK THE PROGRESS ON THE NEW HOSPITAL WING...
NOT WITH YOU IN CHARGE, SISTER AGNES.
THEN LET ME AT LEAST THANK YOU PROPERLY.
YOU'RE... NNH
ARE YOU HURT, BRUCE?
A FALL--PLAYING POLO. IT'S NOTHING.

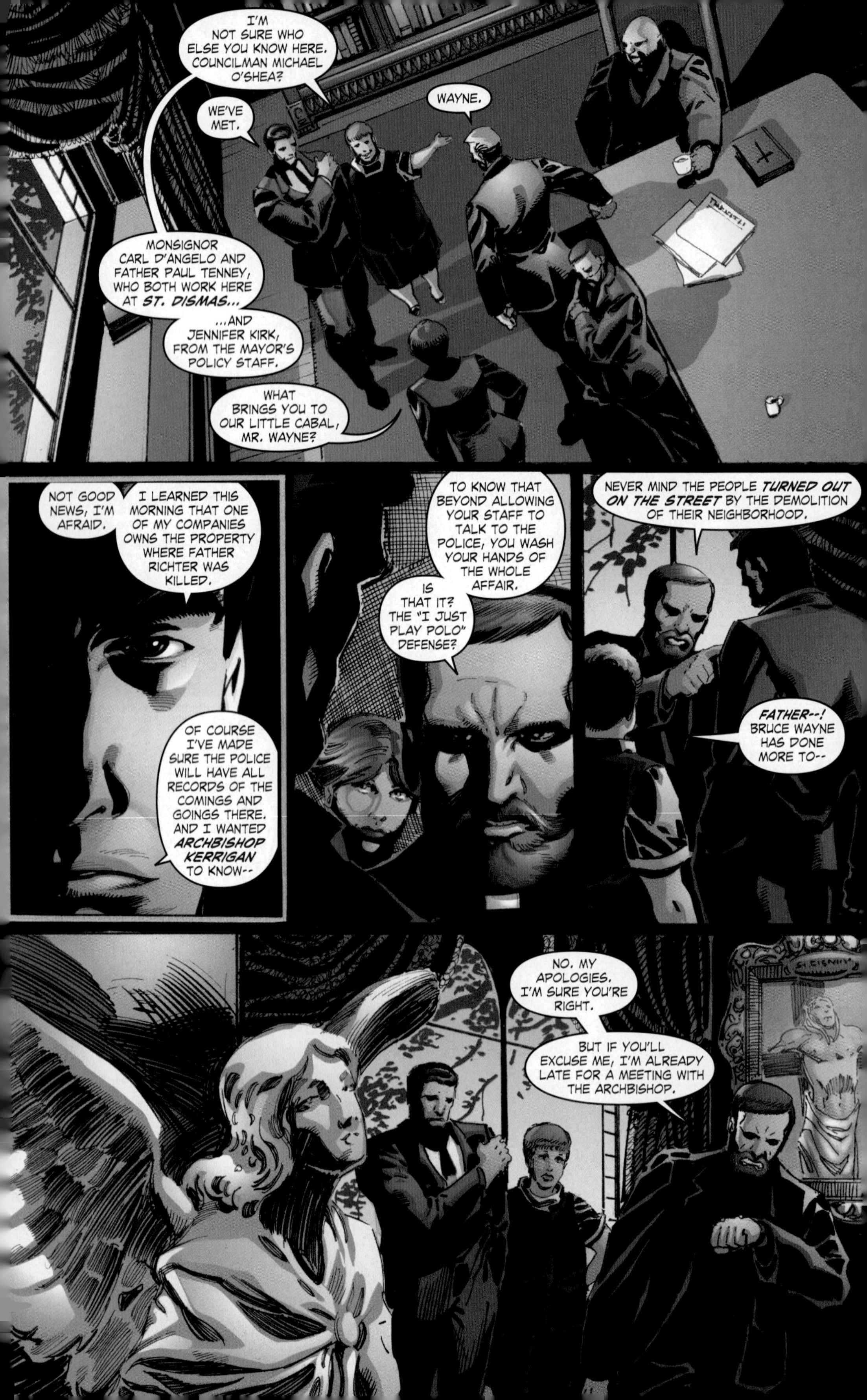
I'M NOT SURE WHO ELSE YOU KNOW HERE. COUNCILMAN MICHAEL O'SHEA?
WE'VE MET.
WAYNE.
MONSIGNOR CARL D'ANGELO AND FATHER PAUL TENNEY, WHO BOTH WORK HERE AT ST. DISMAS...
...AND JENNIFER KIRK, FROM THE MAYOR'S POLICY STAFF.
WHAT BRINGS YOU TO OUR LITTLE CABAL, MR. WAYNE?
NOT GOOD NEWS, I'M AFRAID.
I LEARNED THIS MORNING THAT ONE OF MY COMPANIES OWNS THE PROPERTY WHERE FATHER RICHTER WAS KILLED.
OF COURSE I'VE MADE SURE THE POLICE WILL HAVE ALL RECORDS OF THE COMINGS AND GOINGS THERE. AND I WANTED ARCHBISHOP KERRIGAN TO KNOW--
TO KNOW THAT BEYOND ALLOWING YOUR STAFF TO TALK TO THE POLICE, YOU WASH YOUR HANDS OF THE WHOLE AFFAIR.
IS THAT IT? THE "I JUST PLAY POLO" DEFENSE?
NEVER MIND THE PEOPLE TURNED OUT ON THE STREET BY THE DEMOLITION OF THEIR NEIGHBORHOOD.
FATHER--! BRUCE WAYNE HAS DONE MORE TO--
NO. MY APOLOGIES. I'M SURE YOU'RE RIGHT.
BUT IF YOU'LL EXCUSE ME, I'M ALREADY LATE FOR A MEETING WITH THE ARCHBISHOP.

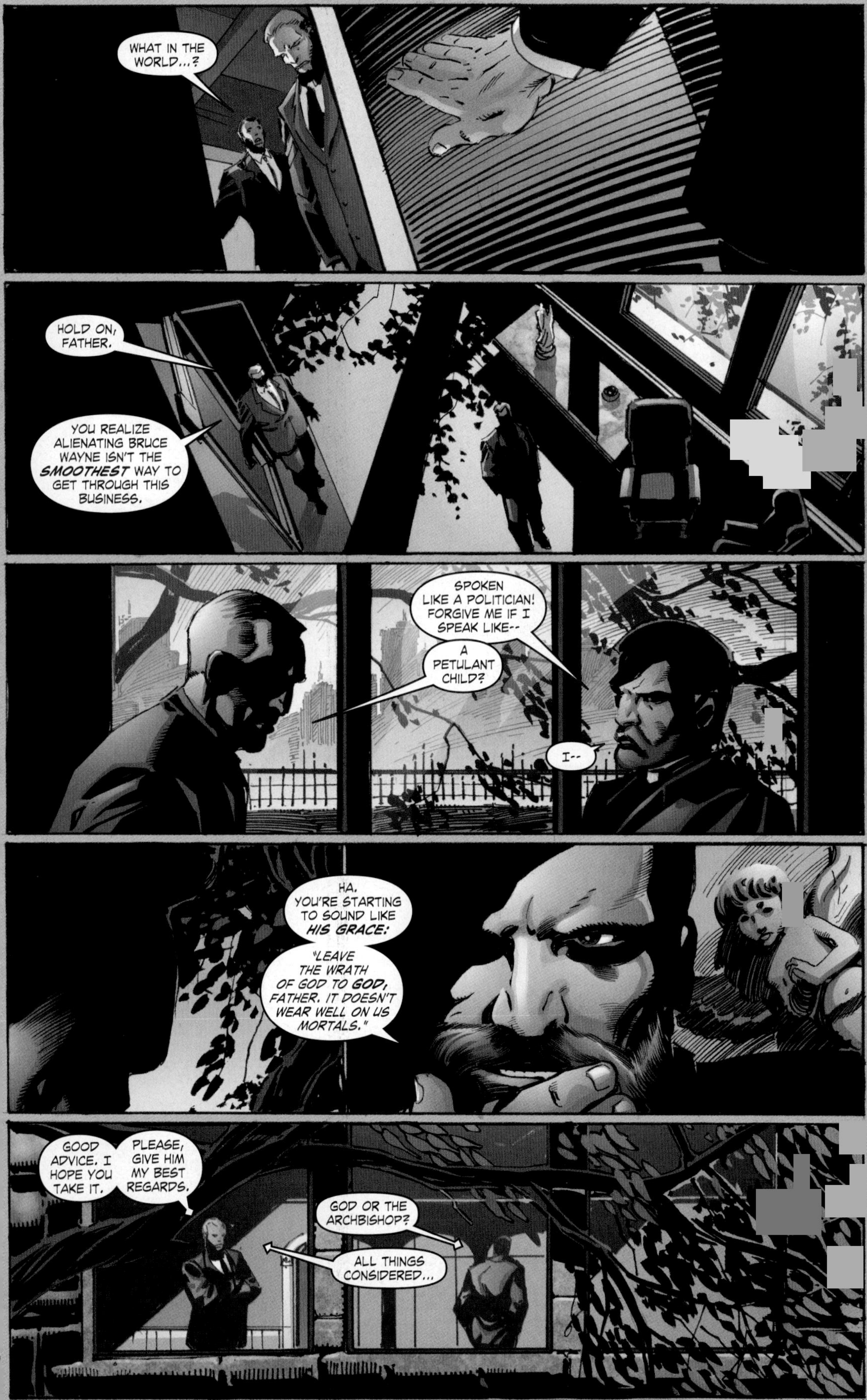
WHAT IN THE WORLD...?
HOLD ON, FATHER.
YOU REALIZE ALIENATING BRUCE WAYNE ISN'T THE **SMOOTHEST** WAY TO GET THROUGH THIS BUSINESS.
SPOKEN LIKE A POLITICIAN! FORGIVE ME IF I SPEAK LIKE--
A PETULANT CHILD?
I--
HA. YOU'RE STARTING TO SOUND LIKE **HIS GRACE:**
"LEAVE THE WRATH OF GOD TO **GOD**, FATHER. IT DOESN'T WEAR WELL ON US MORTALS."
GOOD ADVICE. I HOPE YOU TAKE IT.
PLEASE, GIVE HIM MY BEST REGARDS.
GOD OR THE ARCHBISHOP?
ALL THINGS CONSIDERED...

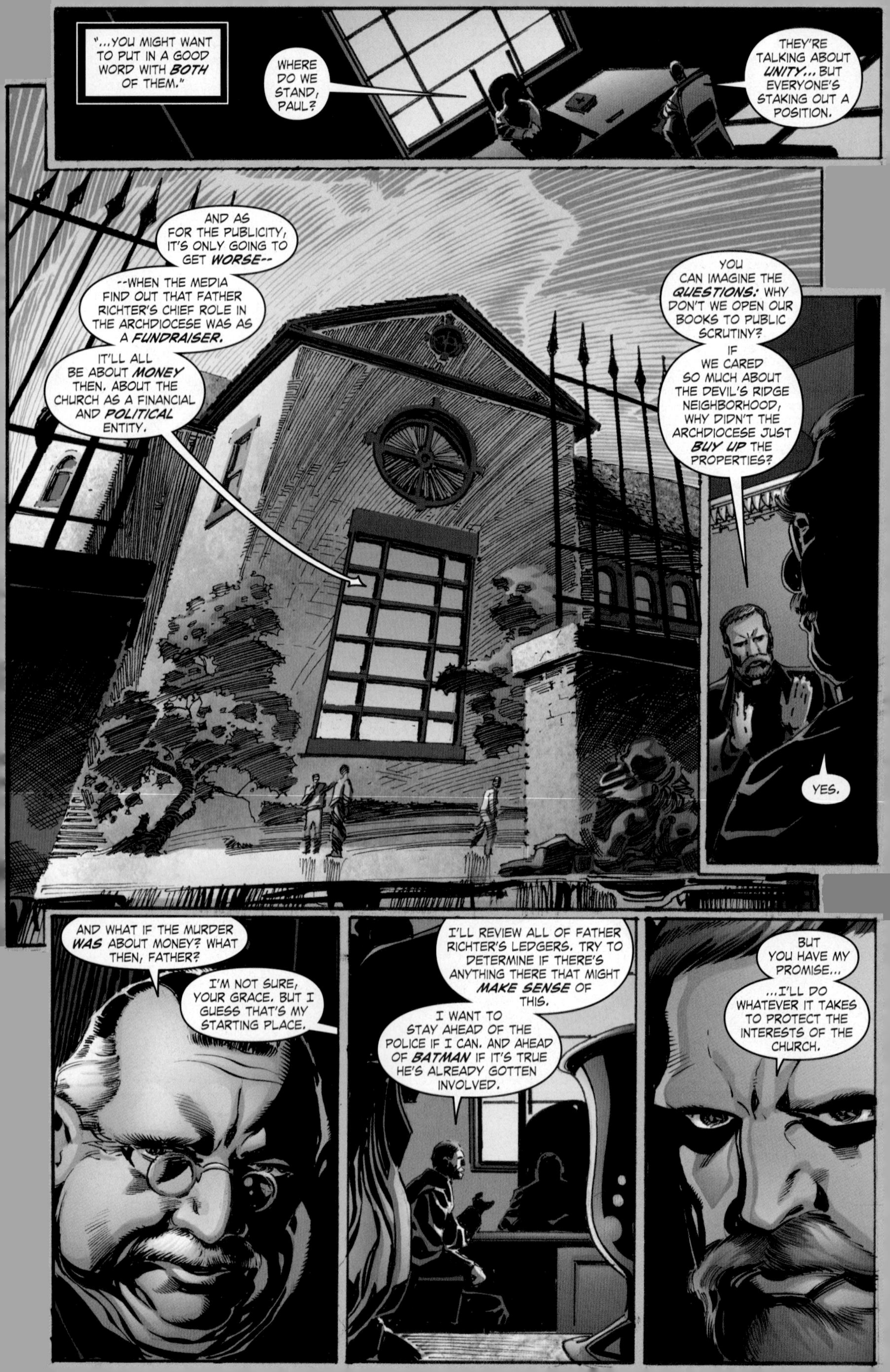

"...YOU MIGHT WANT TO PUT IN A GOOD WORD WITH BOTH OF THEM."
WHERE DO WE STAND, PAUL?
THEY'RE TALKING ABOUT UNITY... BUT EVERYONE'S STAKING OUT A POSITION.
AND AS FOR THE PUBLICITY, IT'S ONLY GOING TO GET WORSE--
--WHEN THE MEDIA FIND OUT THAT FATHER RICHTER'S CHIEF ROLE IN THE ARCHDIOCESE WAS AS A FUNDRAISER.
IT'LL ALL BE ABOUT MONEY THEN. ABOUT THE CHURCH AS A FINANCIAL AND POLITICAL ENTITY.
YOU CAN IMAGINE THE QUESTIONS: WHY DON'T WE OPEN OUR BOOKS TO PUBLIC SCRUTINY?
IF WE CARED SO MUCH ABOUT THE DEVIL'S RIDGE NEIGHBORHOOD, WHY DIDN'T THE ARCHDIOCESE JUST BUY UP THE PROPERTIES?
YES.
AND WHAT IF THE MURDER WAS ABOUT MONEY? WHAT THEN, FATHER?
I'M NOT SURE, YOUR GRACE. BUT I GUESS THAT'S MY STARTING PLACE.
I'LL REVIEW ALL OF FATHER RICHTER'S LEDGERS. TRY TO DETERMINE IF THERE'S ANYTHING THERE THAT MIGHT MAKE SENSE OF THIS.
I WANT TO STAY AHEAD OF THE POLICE IF I CAN. AND AHEAD OF BATMAN IF IT'S TRUE HE'S ALREADY GOTTEN INVOLVED.
BUT YOU HAVE MY PROMISE...
...I'LL DO WHATEVER IT TAKES TO PROTECT THE INTERESTS OF THE CHURCH.

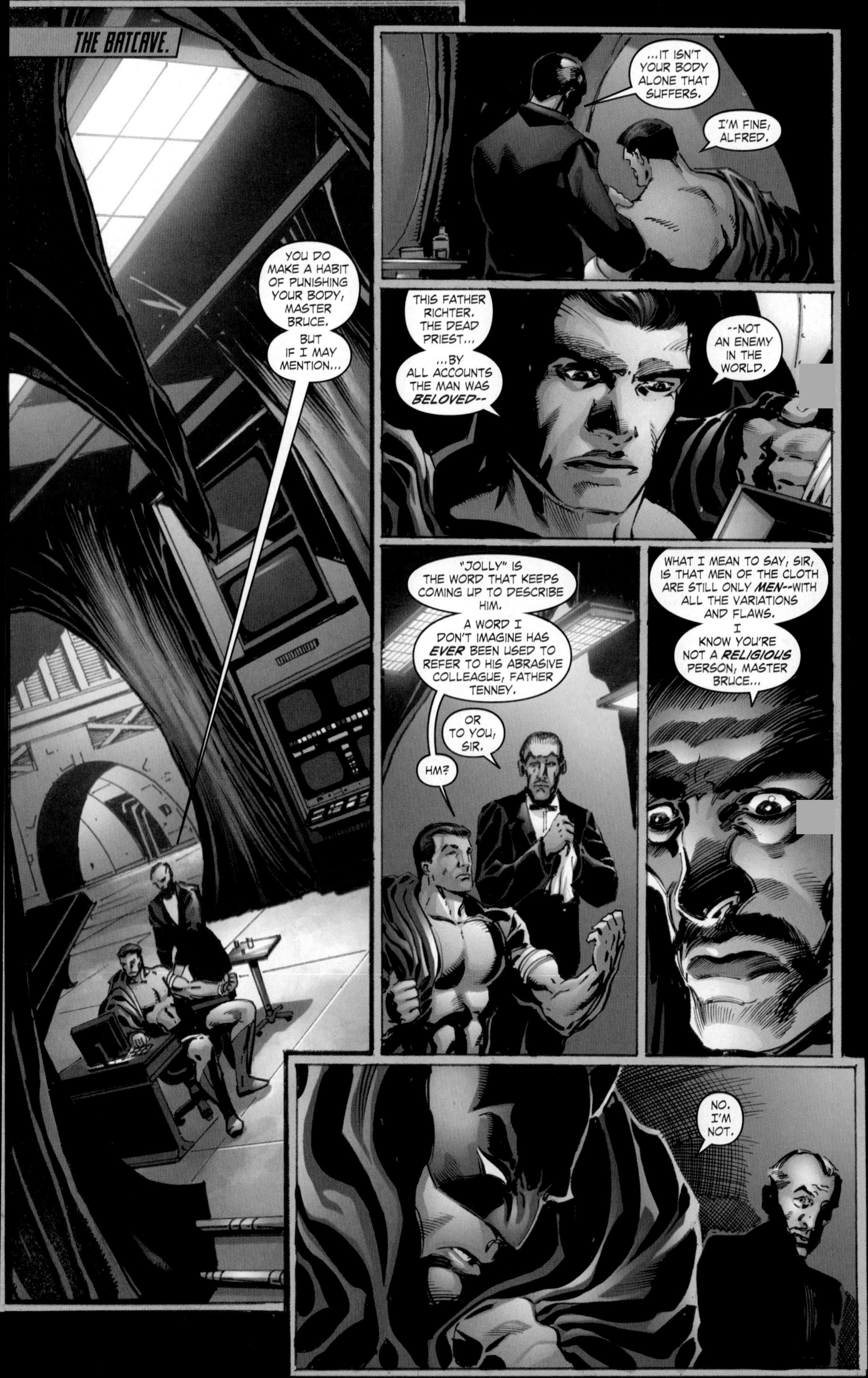
THE BATCAVE.
YOU DO MAKE A HABIT OF PUNISHING YOUR BODY, MASTER BRUCE.
BUT IF I MAY MENTION...
...IT ISN'T YOUR BODY ALONE THAT SUFFERS.
I'M FINE, ALFRED.
THIS FATHER RICHTER. THE DEAD PRIEST...
...BY ALL ACCOUNTS THE MAN WAS BELOVED--
--NOT AN ENEMY IN THE WORLD.
"JOLLY" IS THE WORD THAT KEEPS COMING UP TO DESCRIBE HIM.
A WORD I DON'T IMAGINE HAS EVER BEEN USED TO REFER TO HIS ABRASIVE COLLEAGUE, FATHER TENNEY.
OR TO YOU, SIR.
HM?
WHAT I MEAN TO SAY, SIR, IS THAT MEN OF THE CLOTH ARE STILL ONLY MEN--WITH ALL THE VARIATIONS AND FLAWS.
I KNOW YOU'RE NOT A RELIGIOUS PERSON, MASTER BRUCE...
NO. I'M NOT.

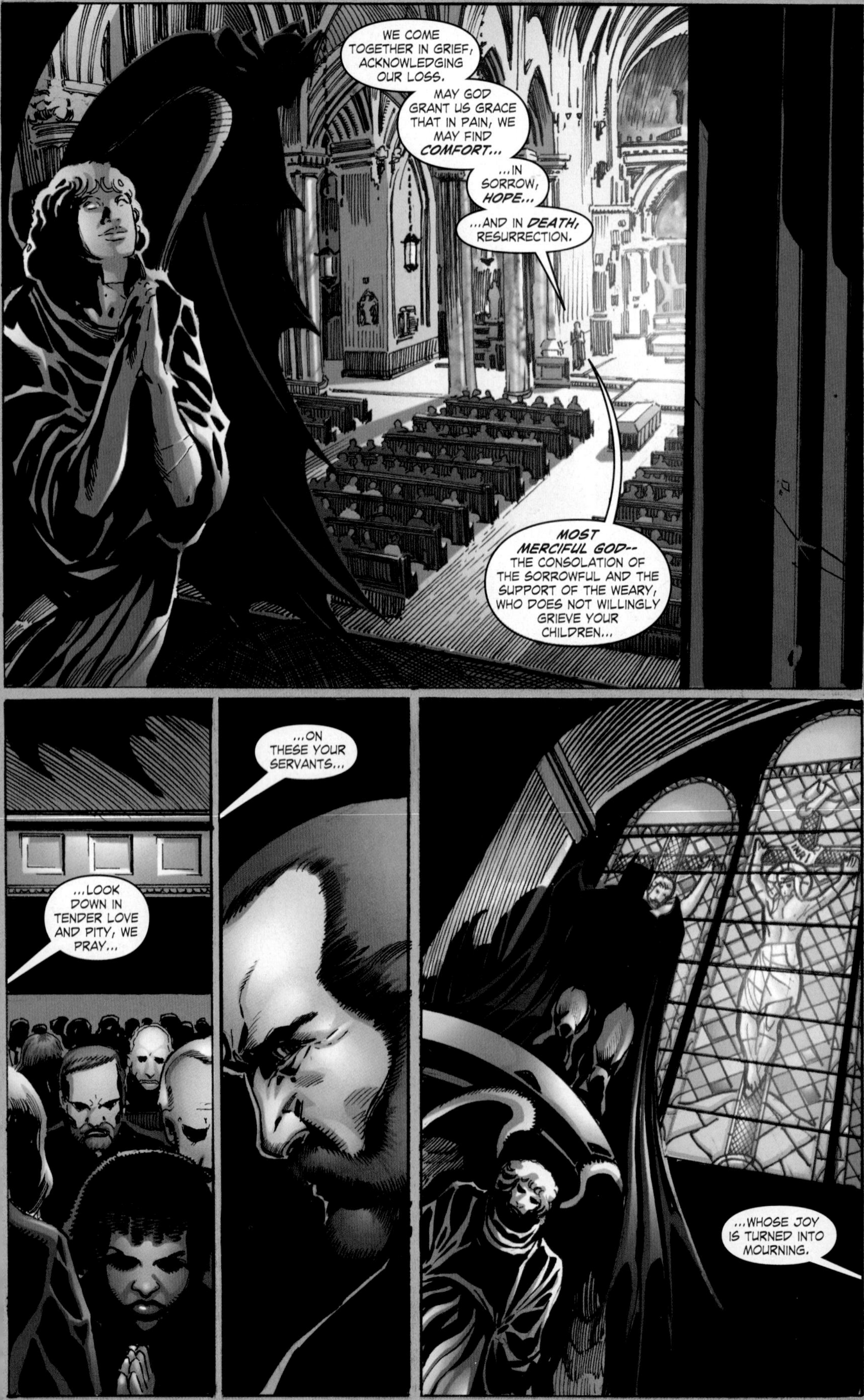
WE COME TOGETHER IN GRIEF, ACKNOWLEDGING OUR LOSS.
MAY GOD GRANT US GRACE THAT IN PAIN, WE MAY FIND COMFORT...
...IN SORROW, HOPE...
...AND IN DEATH, RESURRECTION.
MOST MERCIFUL GOD-- THE CONSOLATION OF THE SORROWFUL AND THE SUPPORT OF THE WEARY, WHO DOES NOT WILLINGLY GRIEVE YOUR CHILDREN...
...LOOK DOWN IN TENDER LOVE AND PITY, WE PRAY...
...ON THESE YOUR SERVANTS...
...WHOSE JOY IS TURNED INTO MOURNING.

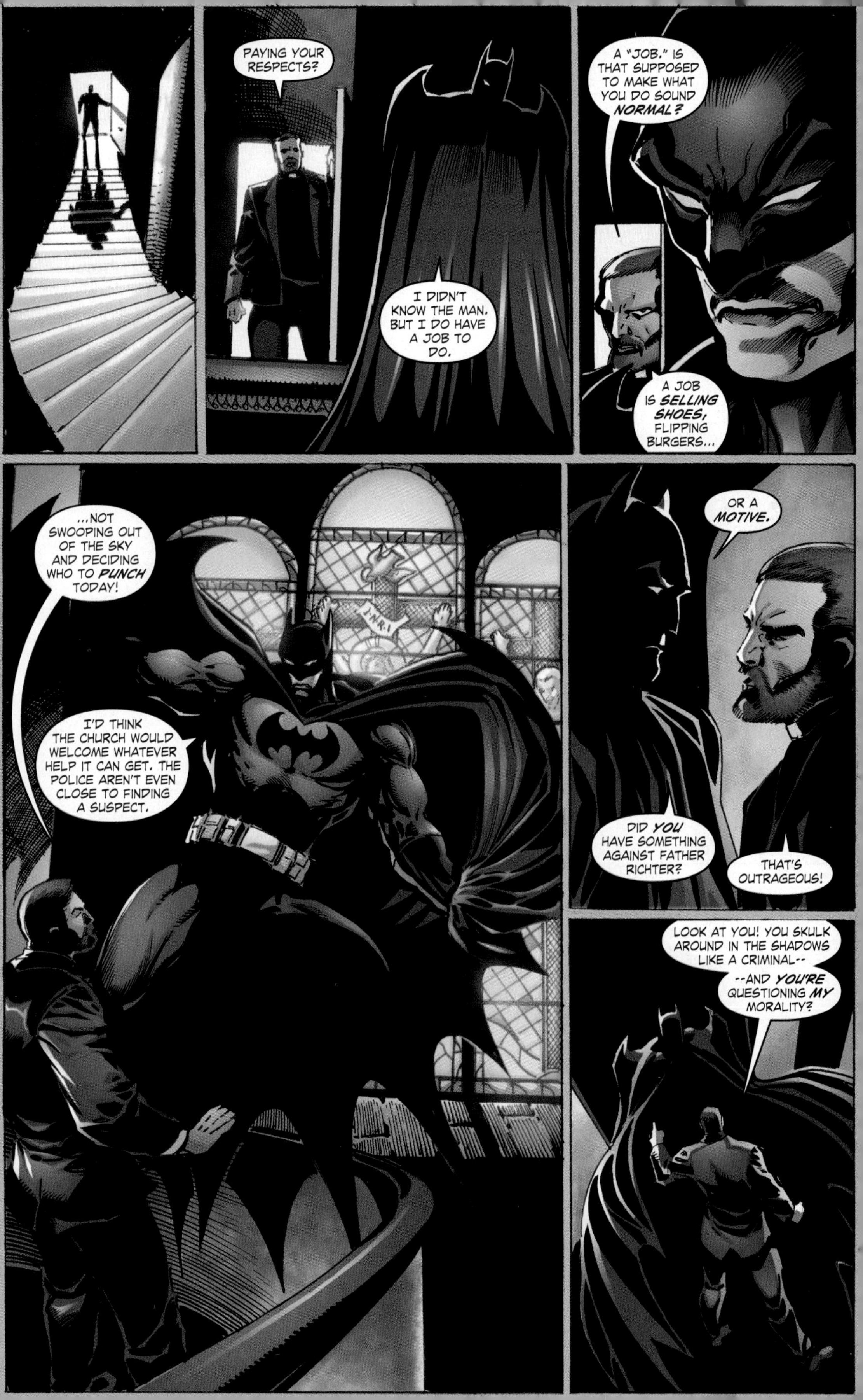
PAYING YOUR RESPECTS?
I DIDN'T KNOW THE MAN. BUT I DO HAVE A JOB TO DO.
A "JOB." IS THAT SUPPOSED TO MAKE WHAT YOU DO SOUND NORMAL?
A JOB IS SELLING SHOES, FLIPPING BURGERS...
...NOT SWOOPING OUT OF THE SKY AND DECIDING WHO TO PUNCH TODAY!
I'D THINK THE CHURCH WOULD WELCOME WHATEVER HELP IT CAN GET. THE POLICE AREN'T EVEN CLOSE TO FINDING A SUSPECT.
OR A MOTIVE.
DID YOU HAVE SOMETHING AGAINST FATHER RICHTER?
THAT'S OUTRAGEOUS!
LOOK AT YOU! YOU SKULK AROUND IN THE SHADOWS LIKE A CRIMINAL--
--AND YOU'RE QUESTIONING MY MORALITY?

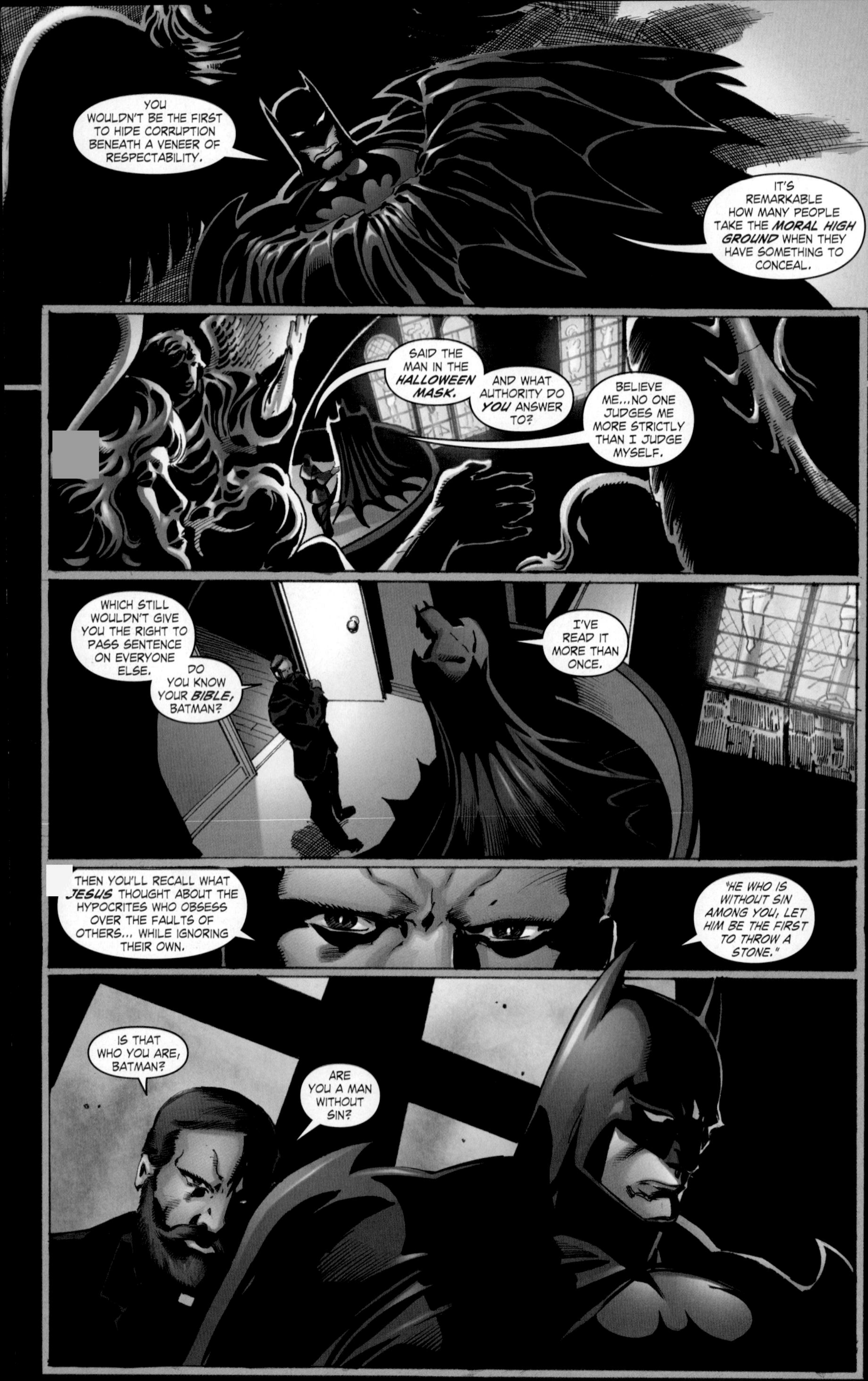
YOU WOULDN'T BE THE FIRST TO HIDE CORRUPTION BENEATH A VENEER OF RESPECTABILITY.
IT'S REMARKABLE HOW MANY PEOPLE TAKE THE MORAL HIGH GROUND WHEN THEY HAVE SOMETHING TO CONCEAL.
SAID THE MAN IN THE HALLOWEEN MASK.
AND WHAT AUTHORITY DO YOU ANSWER TO?
BELIEVE ME...NO ONE JUDGES ME MORE STRICTLY THAN I JUDGE MYSELF.
WHICH STILL WOULDN'T GIVE YOU THE RIGHT TO PASS SENTENCE ON EVERYONE ELSE.
DO YOU KNOW YOUR BIBLE, BATMAN?
I'VE READ IT MORE THAN ONCE.
THEN YOU'LL RECALL WHAT JESUS THOUGHT ABOUT THE HYPOCRITES WHO OBSESS OVER THE FAULTS OF OTHERS... WHILE IGNORING THEIR OWN.
"HE WHO IS WITHOUT SIN AMONG YOU, LET HIM BE THE FIRST TO THROW A STONE."
IS THAT WHO YOU ARE, BATMAN?
ARE YOU A MAN WITHOUT SIN?

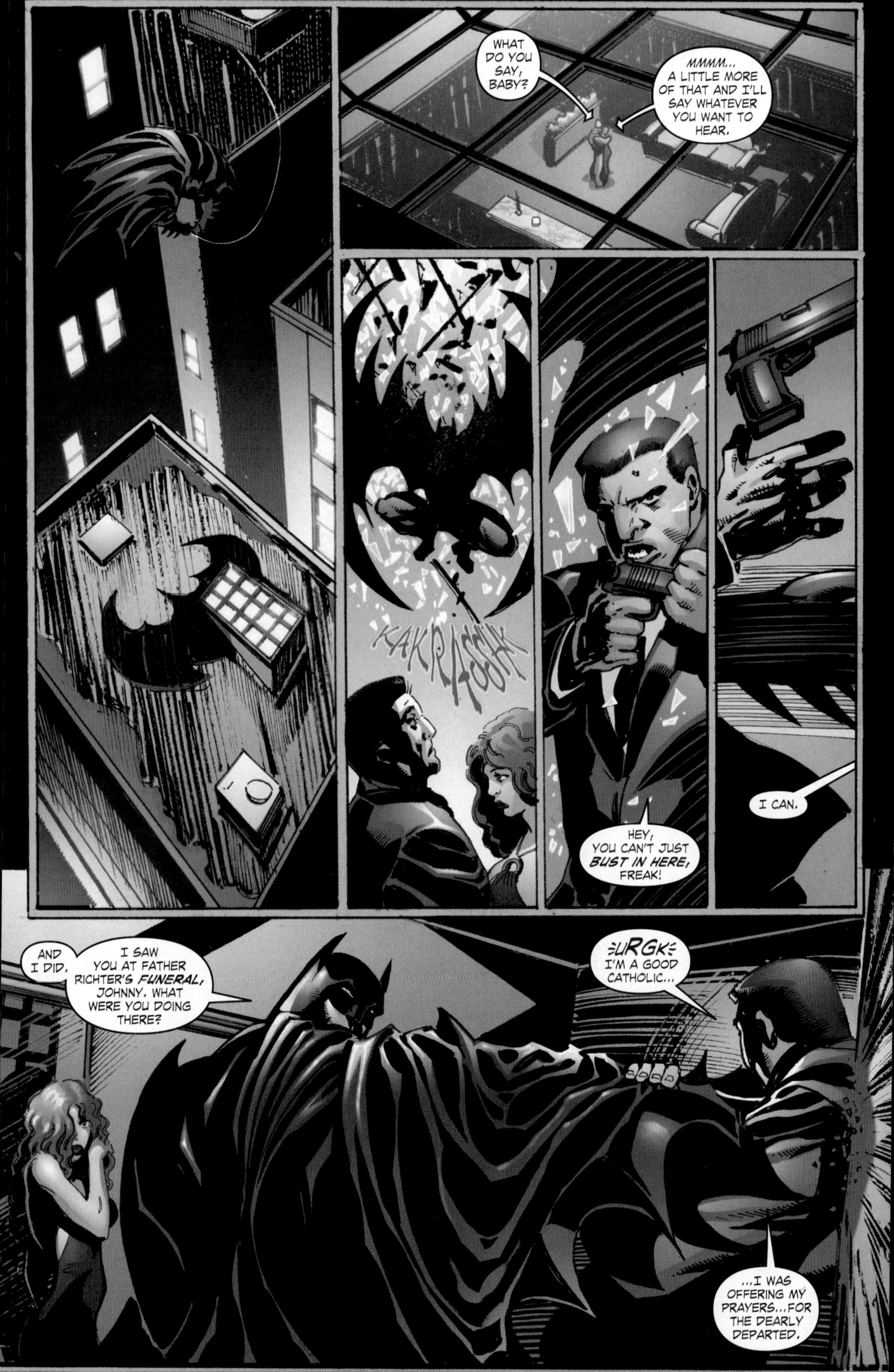
WHAT DO YOU SAY, BABY?
MMMM... A LITTLE MORE OF THAT AND I'LL SAY WHATEVER YOU WANT TO HEAR.
KAKRASSHK
HEY, YOU CAN'T JUST BUST IN HERE, FREAK!
I CAN.
AND I DID.
I SAW YOU AT FATHER RICHTER'S FUNERAL, JOHNNY. WHAT WERE YOU DOING THERE?
URGK
I'M A GOOD CATHOLIC...
...I WAS OFFERING MY PRAYERS...FOR THE DEARLY DEPARTED.

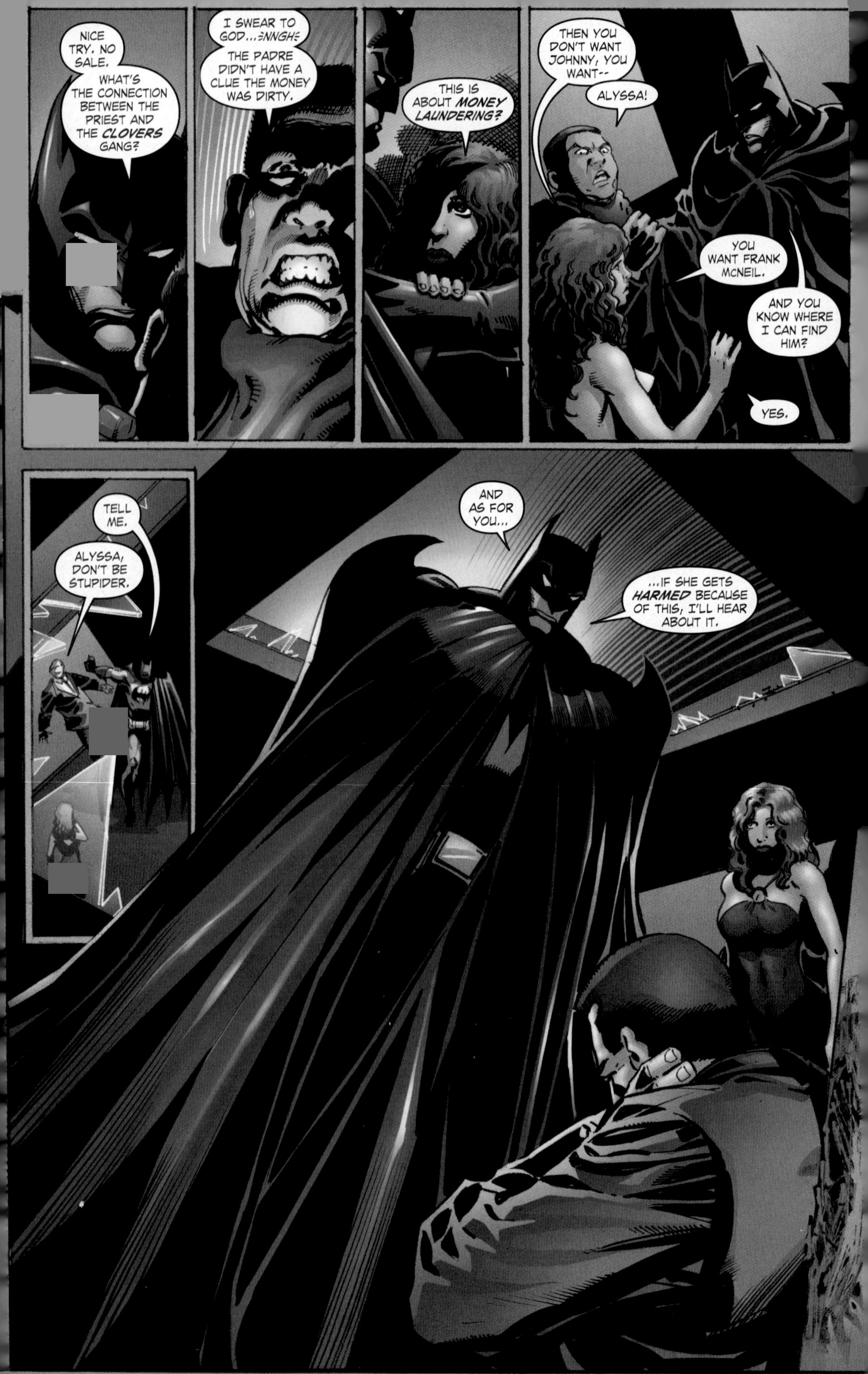
NICE TRY. NO SALE.
WHAT'S THE CONNECTION BETWEEN THE PRIEST AND THE *CLOVERS* GANG?
I SWEAR TO GOD...ENNGH!
THE PADRE DIDN'T HAVE A CLUE THE MONEY WAS DIRTY.
THIS IS ABOUT *MONEY LAUNDERING?*
THEN YOU DON'T WANT JOHNNY, YOU WANT--
ALYSSA!
YOU WANT FRANK McNEIL.
AND YOU KNOW WHERE I CAN FIND HIM?
YES.
TELL ME.
ALYSSA, DON'T BE STUPIDER.
AND AS FOR YOU...
...IF SHE GETS *HARMED* BECAUSE OF THIS, I'LL HEAR ABOUT IT.

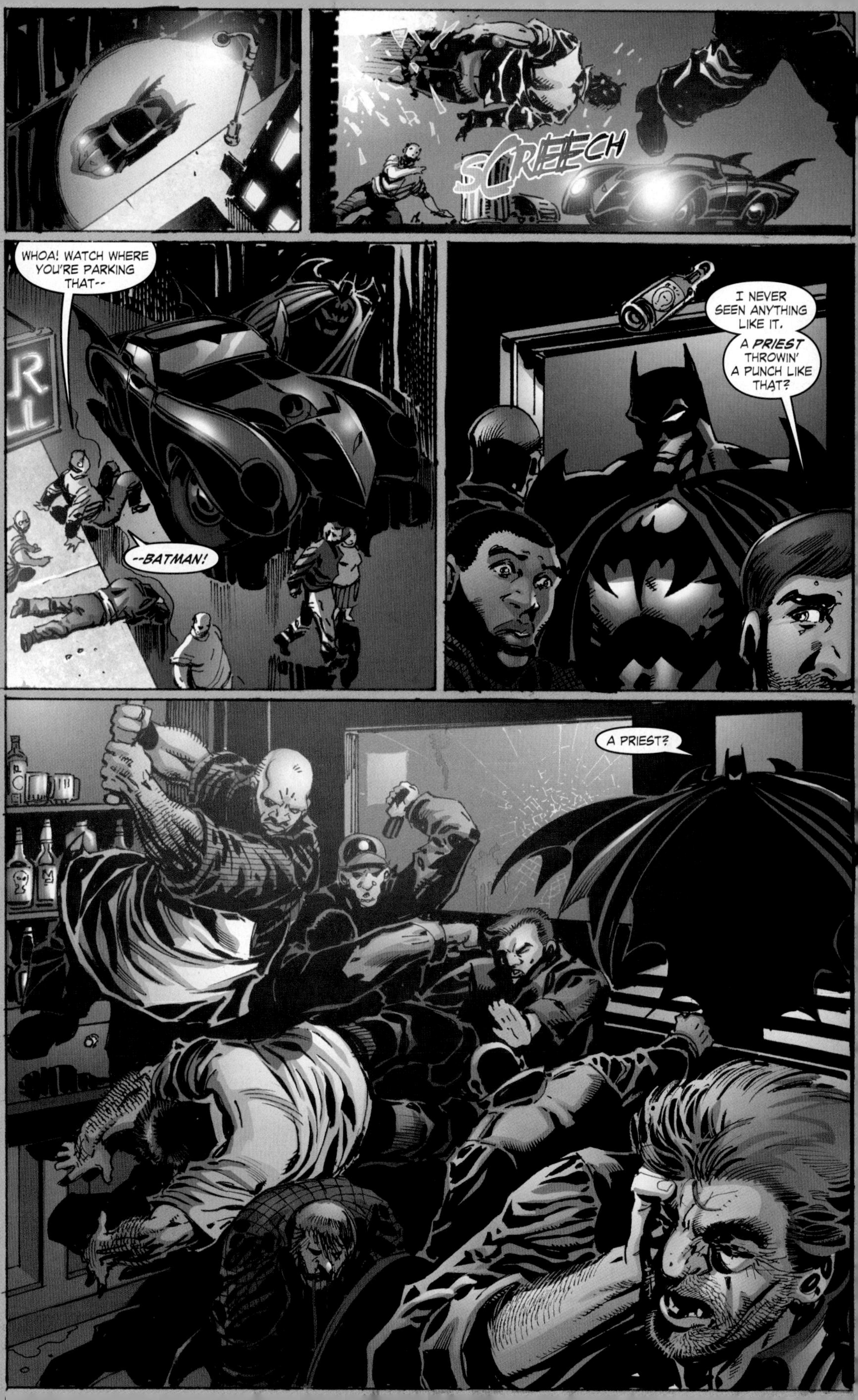
SCREEECH
WHOA! WATCH WHERE YOU'RE PARKING THAT--
--BATMAN!
I NEVER SEEN ANYTHING LIKE IT.
A PRIEST THROWIN' A PUNCH LIKE THAT?
A PRIEST?

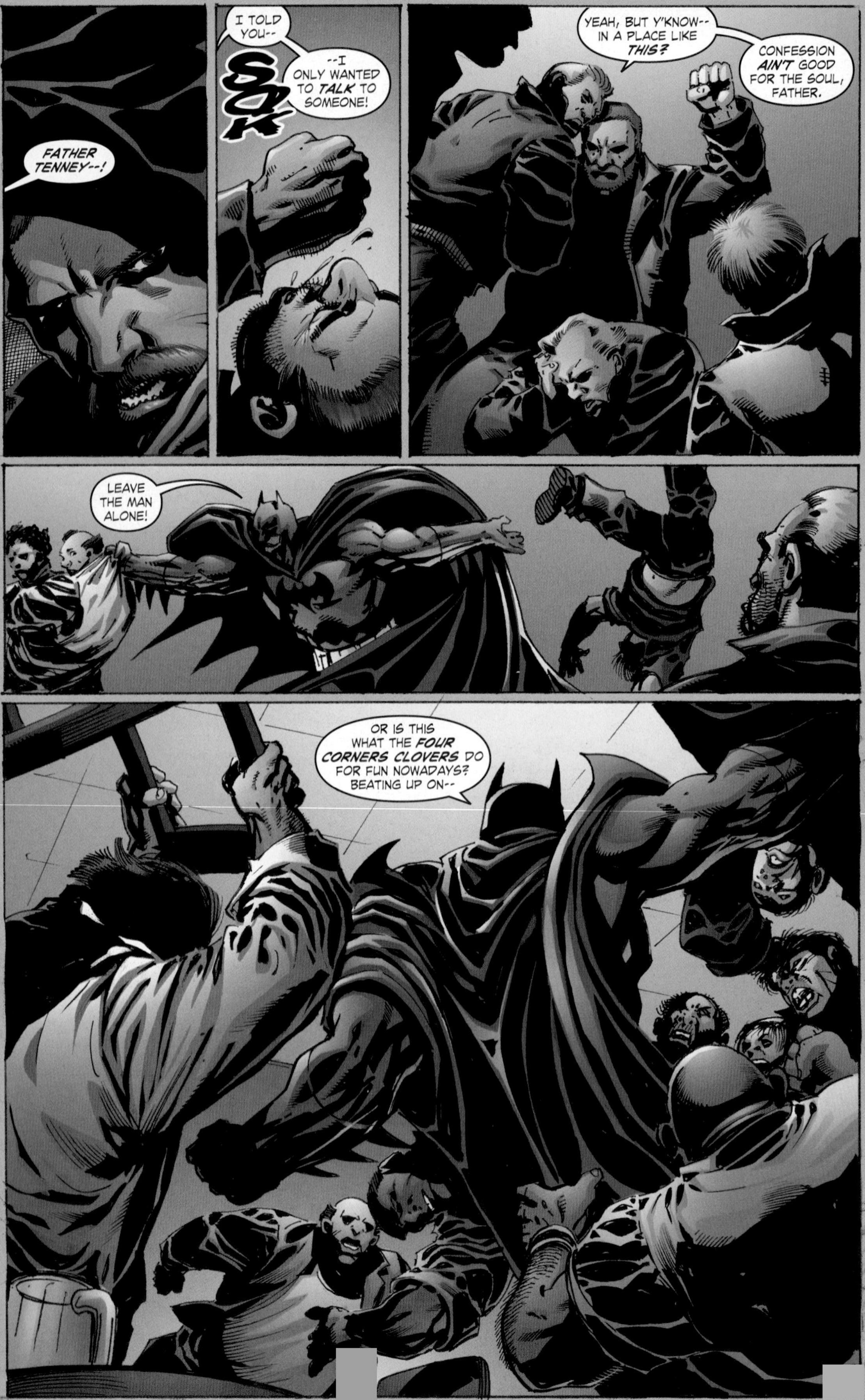
FATHER TENNEY--!
I TOLD YOU--
SOK
--I ONLY WANTED TO *TALK* TO SOMEONE!
YEAH, BUT Y'KNOW-- IN A PLACE LIKE *THIS?*
CONFESSION *AIN'T* GOOD FOR THE SOUL, FATHER.
LEAVE THE MAN ALONE!
OR IS THIS WHAT THE *FOUR CORNERS CLOVERS* DO FOR FUN NOWADAYS? BEATING UP ON--

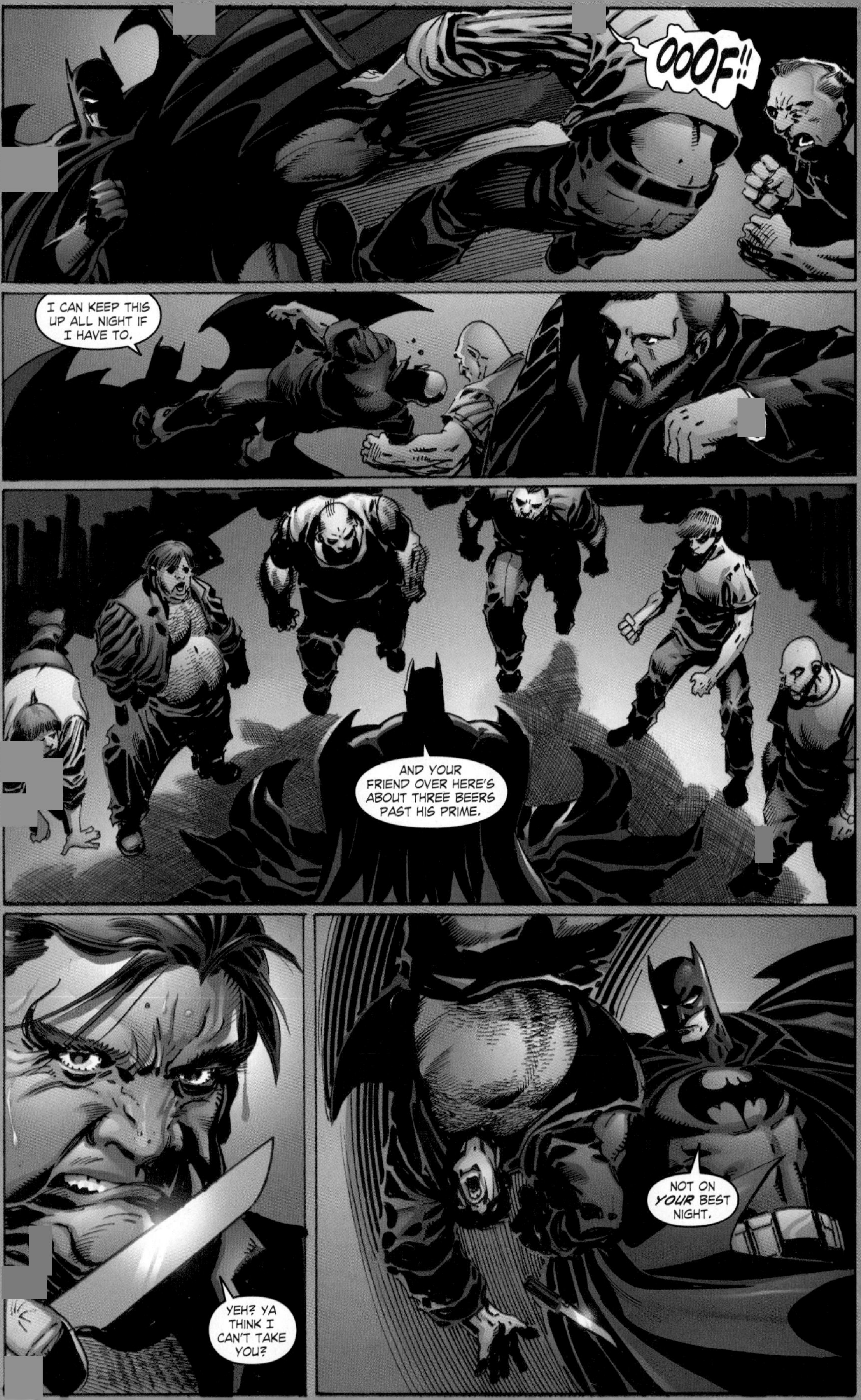
OOOF!!
I CAN KEEP THIS UP ALL NIGHT IF I HAVE TO.
AND YOUR FRIEND OVER HERE'S ABOUT THREE BEERS PAST HIS PRIME.
YEH? YA THINK I CAN'T TAKE YOU?
NOT ON *YOUR* BEST NIGHT.

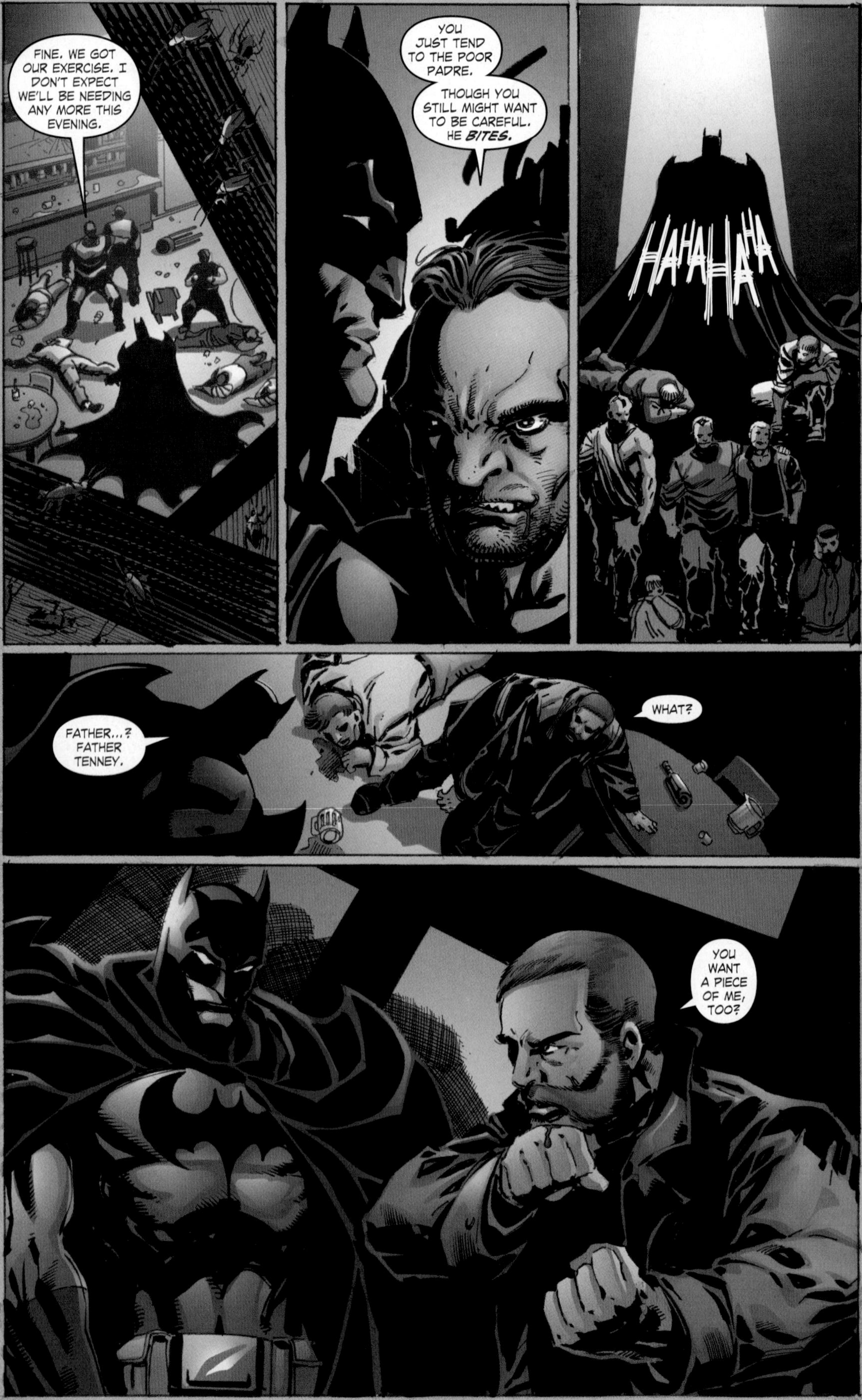
FINE. WE GOT OUR EXERCISE. I DON'T EXPECT WE'LL BE NEEDING ANY MORE THIS EVENING.
YOU JUST TEND TO THE POOR PADRE.
THOUGH YOU STILL MIGHT WANT TO BE CAREFUL. HE *BITES.*
HAHAHAHAHA
FATHER...? FATHER TENNEY.
WHAT?
YOU WANT A PIECE OF ME, TOO?

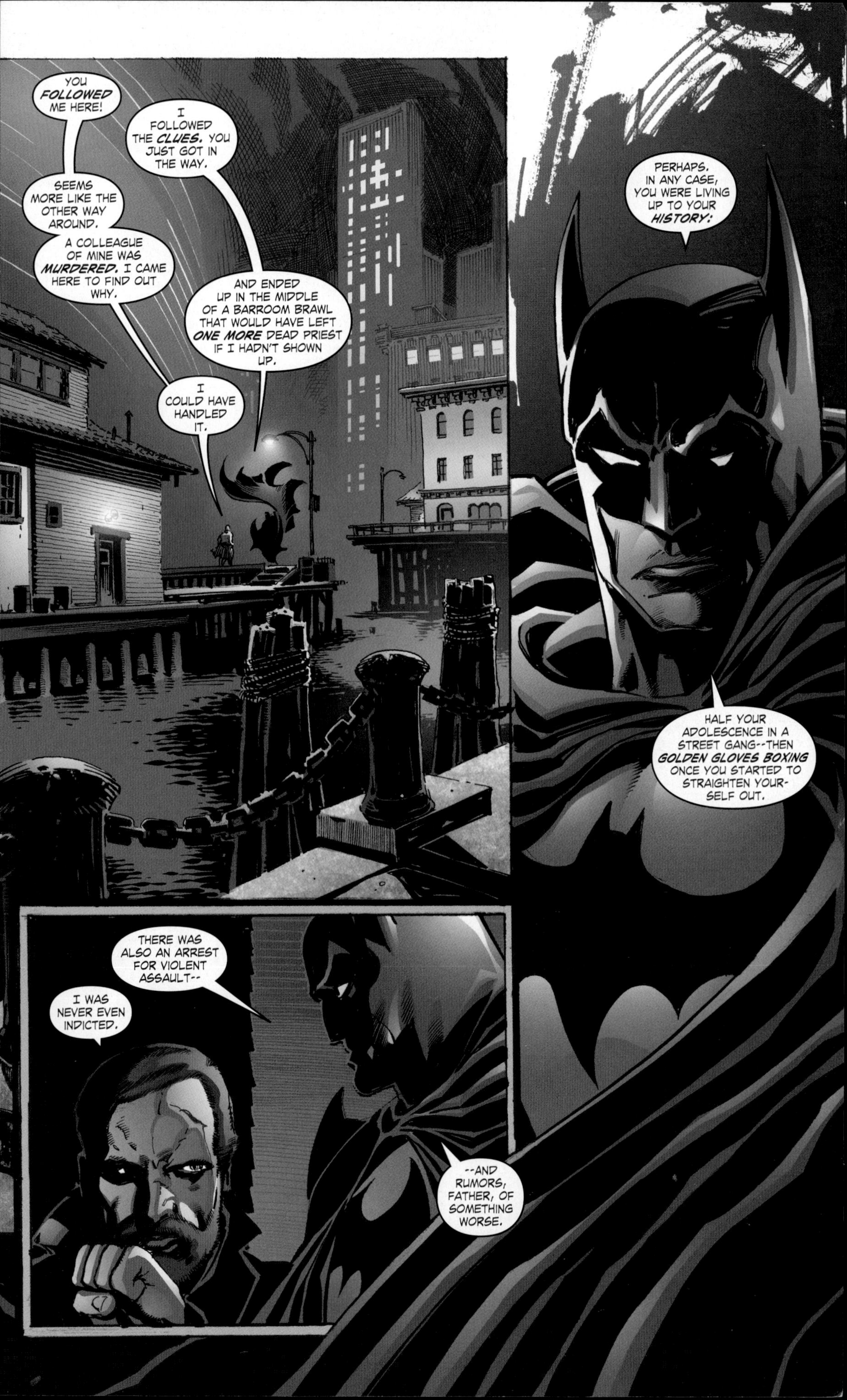

YOU *FOLLOWED* ME HERE!
I FOLLOWED THE *CLUES.* YOU JUST GOT IN THE WAY.
SEEMS MORE LIKE THE OTHER WAY AROUND.
A COLLEAGUE OF MINE WAS *MURDERED.* I CAME HERE TO FIND OUT WHY.
AND ENDED UP IN THE MIDDLE OF A BARROOM BRAWL THAT WOULD HAVE LEFT *ONE MORE* DEAD PRIEST IF I HADN'T SHOWN UP.
I COULD HAVE HANDLED IT.
PERHAPS. IN ANY CASE, YOU WERE LIVING UP TO YOUR *HISTORY:*
HALF YOUR ADOLESCENCE IN A STREET GANG--THEN *GOLDEN GLOVES BOXING* ONCE YOU STARTED TO STRAIGHTEN YOUR-SELF OUT.
THERE WAS ALSO AN ARREST FOR VIOLENT ASSAULT--
I WAS NEVER EVEN INDICTED.
--AND RUMORS, FATHER, OF SOMETHING WORSE.

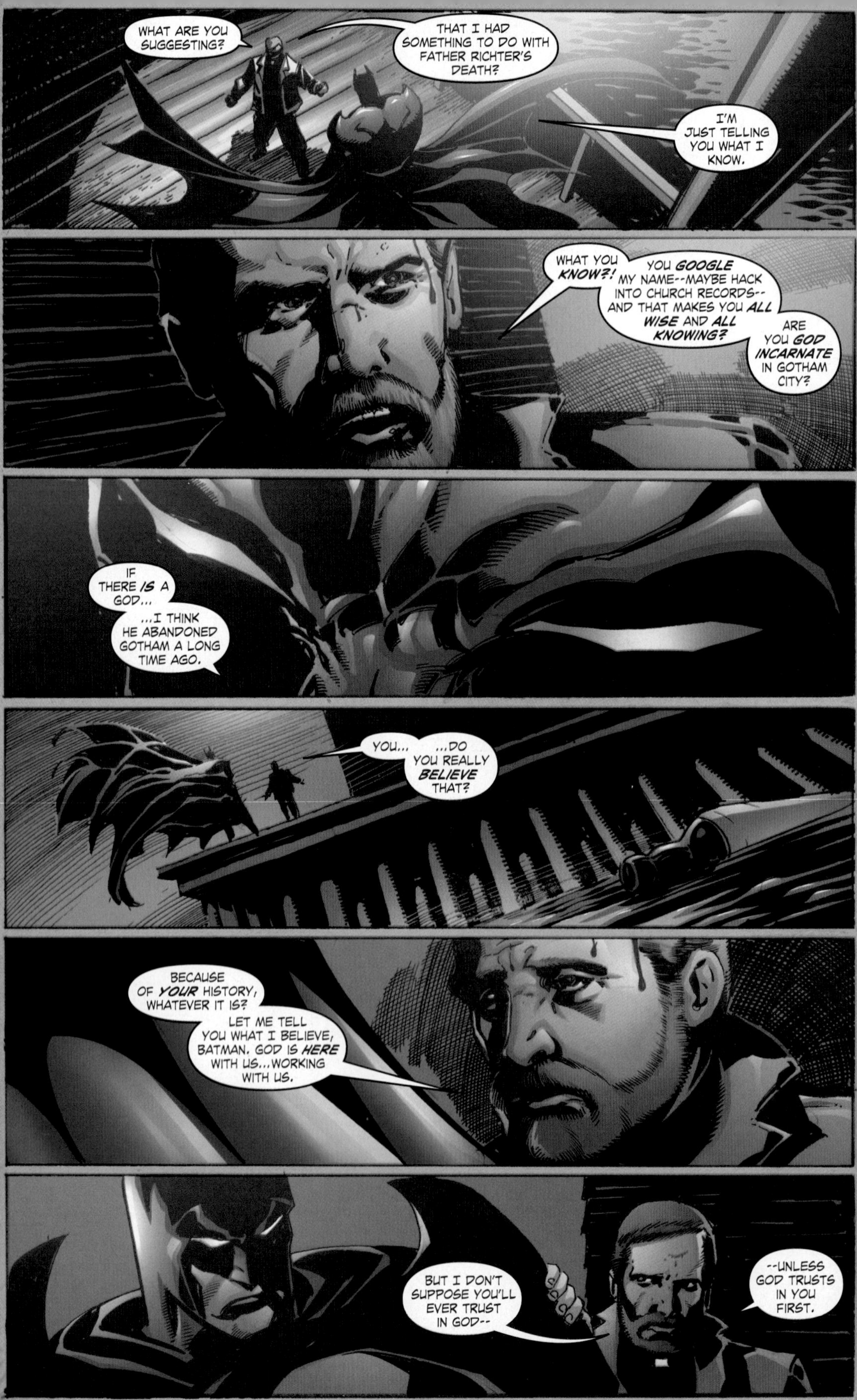
WHAT ARE YOU SUGGESTING?
THAT I HAD SOMETHING TO DO WITH FATHER RICHTER'S DEATH?
I'M JUST TELLING YOU WHAT I KNOW.
WHAT YOU KNOW?!
YOU GOOGLE MY NAME--MAYBE HACK INTO CHURCH RECORDS--AND THAT MAKES YOU ALL WISE AND ALL KNOWING?
ARE YOU GOD INCARNATE IN GOTHAM CITY?
IF THERE IS A GOD...
...I THINK HE ABANDONED GOTHAM A LONG TIME AGO.
YOU...
...DO YOU REALLY BELIEVE THAT?
BECAUSE OF YOUR HISTORY, WHATEVER IT IS?
LET ME TELL YOU WHAT I BELIEVE, BATMAN. GOD IS HERE WITH US...WORKING WITH US.
BUT I DON'T SUPPOSE YOU'LL EVER TRUST IN GOD--
--UNLESS GOD TRUSTS IN YOU FIRST.

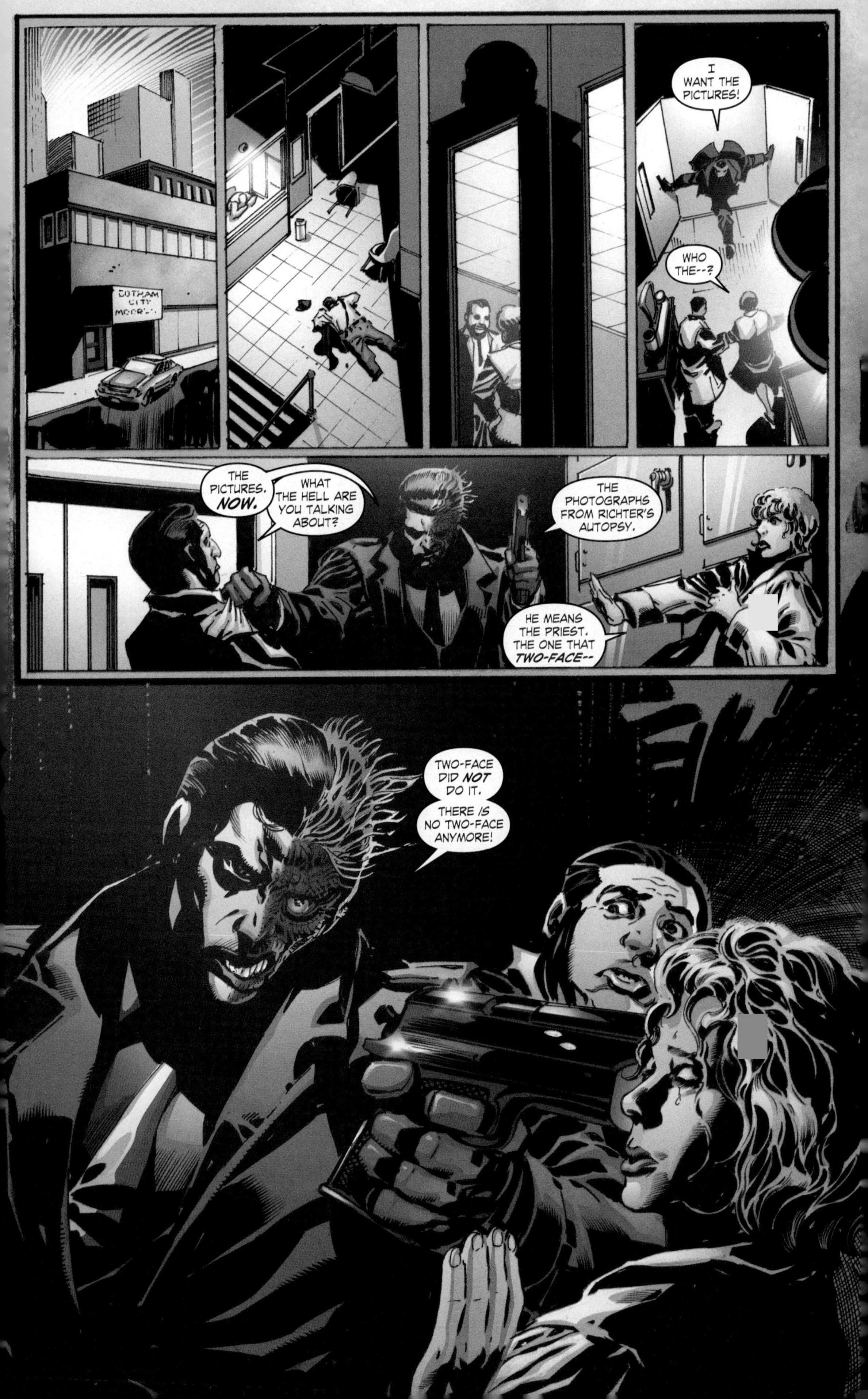
GOTHAM CITY MORGUE
I WANT THE PICTURES!
WHO THE--?
THE PICTURES. NOW.
WHAT THE HELL ARE YOU TALKING ABOUT?
THE PHOTOGRAPHS FROM RICHTER'S AUTOPSY.
HE MEANS THE PRIEST. THE ONE THAT TWO-FACE--
TWO-FACE DID NOT DO IT.
THERE IS NO TWO-FACE ANYMORE!

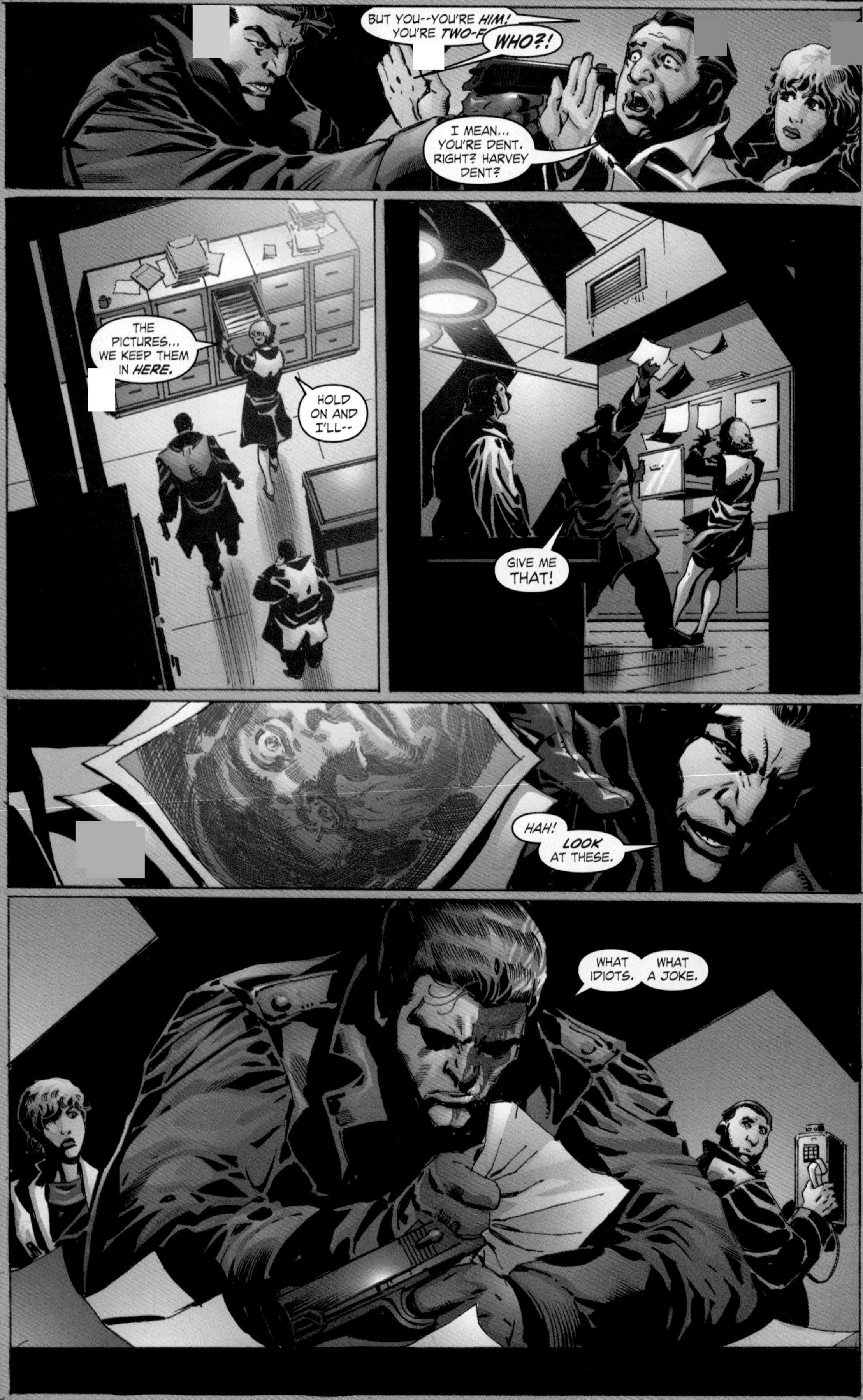
BUT YOU--YOU'RE HIM! YOU'RE TWO-F
WHO?!
I MEAN... YOU'RE DENT. RIGHT? HARVEY DENT?
THE PICTURES... WE KEEP THEM IN HERE.
HOLD ON AND I'LL--
GIVE ME THAT!
HAH! LOOK AT THESE.
WHAT IDIOTS.
WHAT A JOKE.

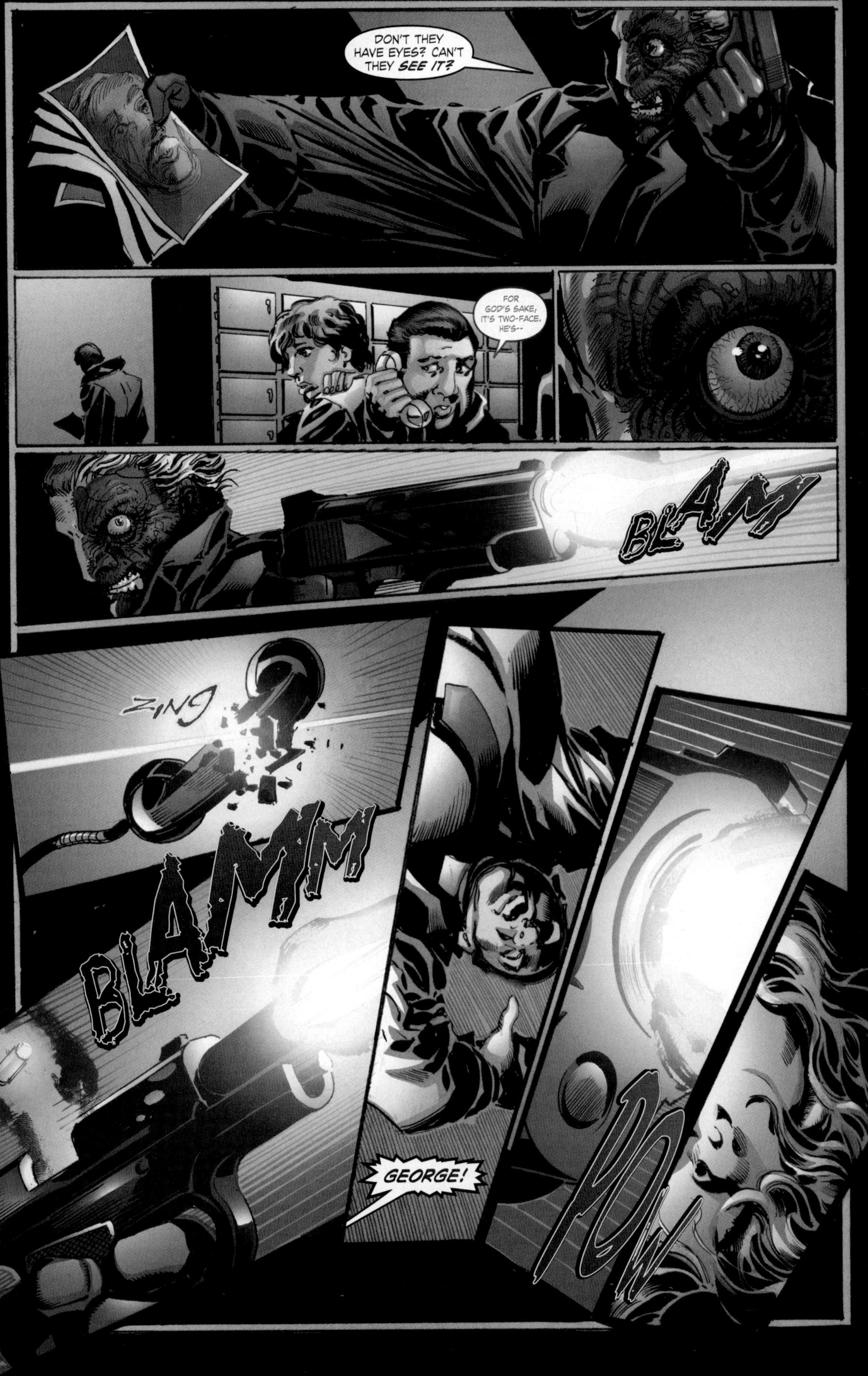
DON'T THEY HAVE EYES? CAN'T THEY SEE IT?
FOR GOD'S SAKE, IT'S TWO-FACE. HE'S--
BLAM
ZING
BLAMM
GEORGE!
POW

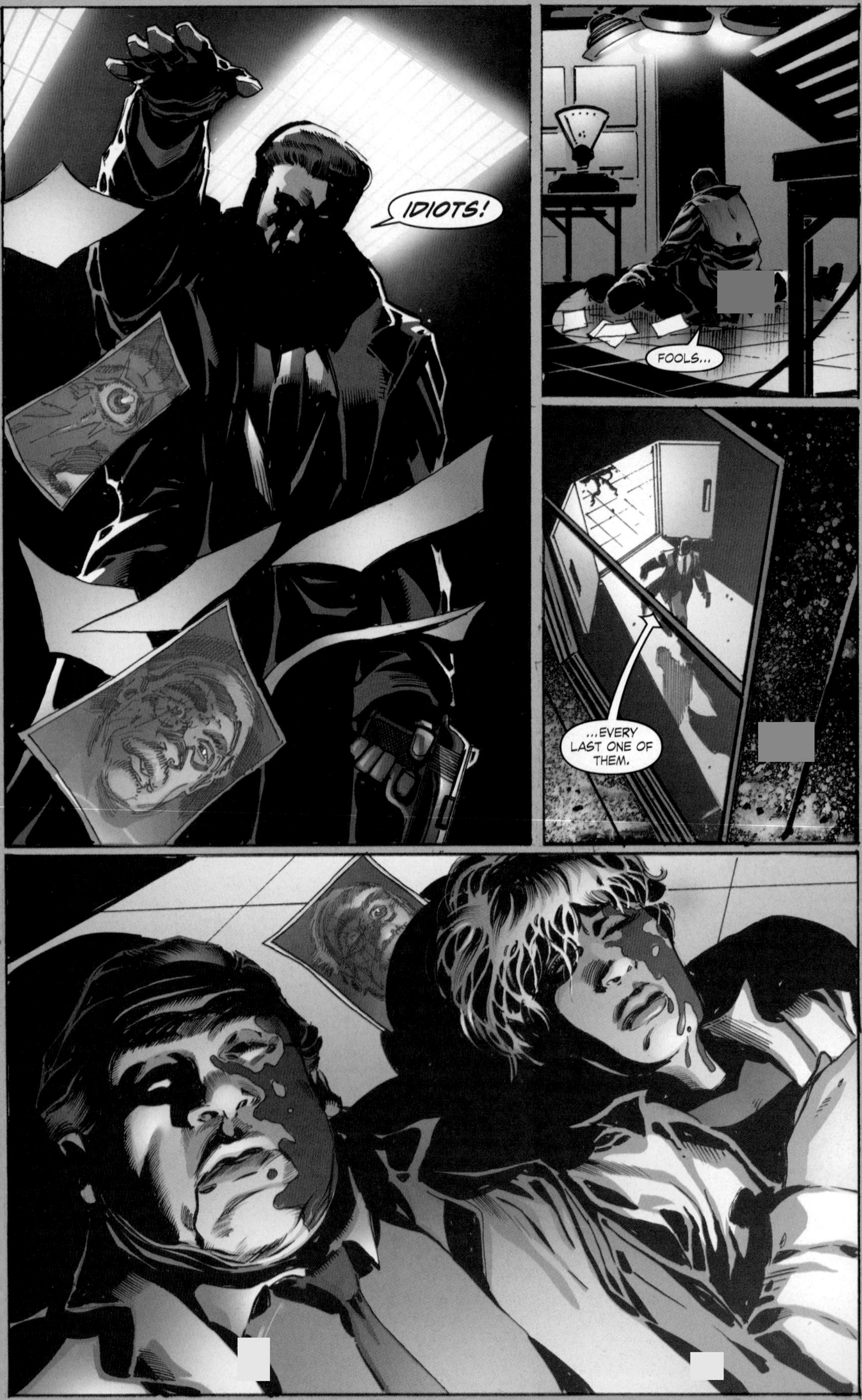
IDIOTS!
FOOLS...
...EVERY LAST ONE OF THEM.

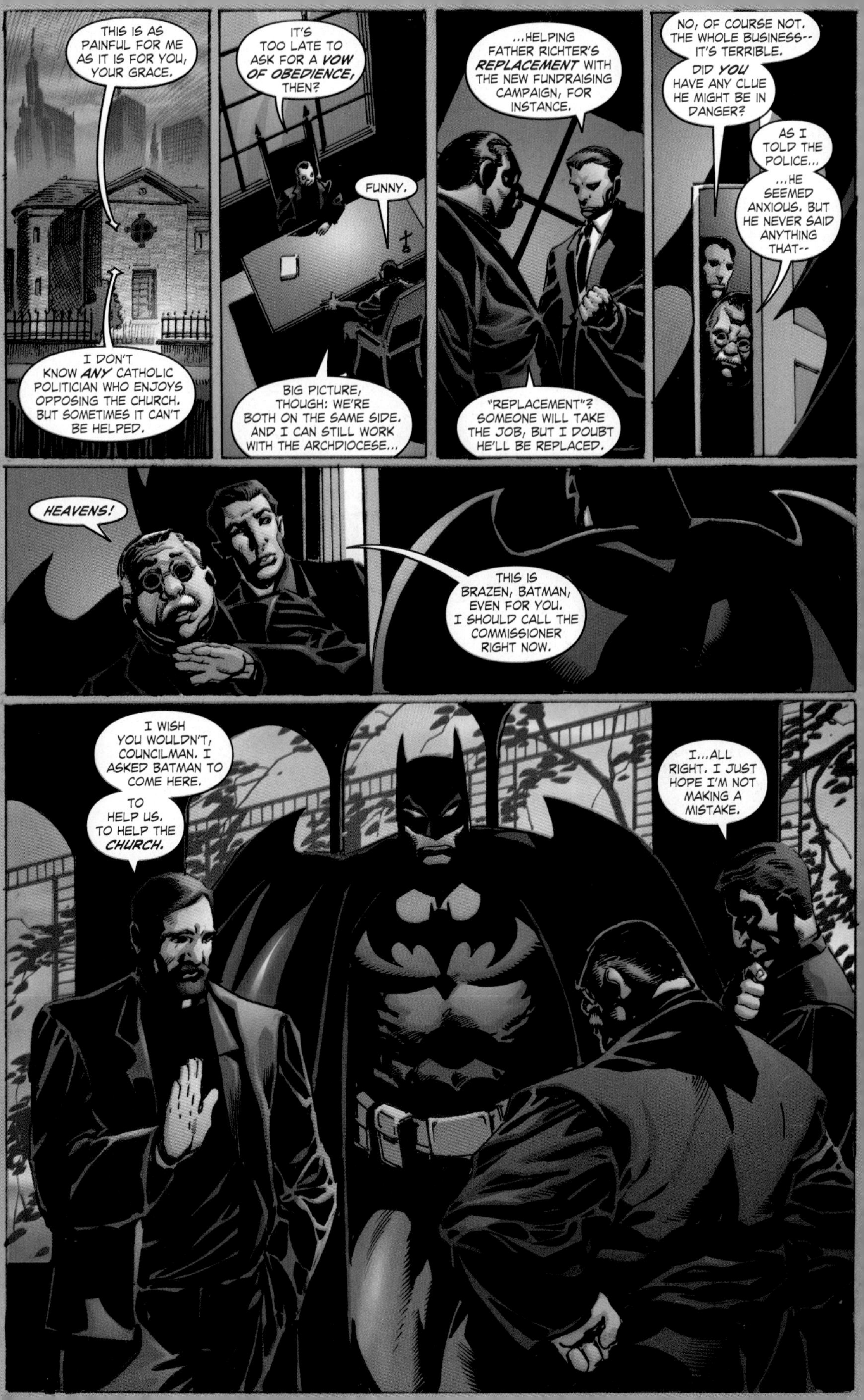
THIS IS AS PAINFUL FOR ME AS IT IS FOR YOU, YOUR GRACE.
I DON'T KNOW ANY CATHOLIC POLITICIAN WHO ENJOYS OPPOSING THE CHURCH. BUT SOMETIMES IT CAN'T BE HELPED.
IT'S TOO LATE TO ASK FOR A VOW OF OBEDIENCE, THEN?
FUNNY.
BIG PICTURE, THOUGH: WE'RE BOTH ON THE SAME SIDE. AND I CAN STILL WORK WITH THE ARCHDIOCESE...
...HELPING FATHER RICHTER'S REPLACEMENT WITH THE NEW FUNDRAISING CAMPAIGN, FOR INSTANCE.
"REPLACEMENT"? SOMEONE WILL TAKE THE JOB, BUT I DOUBT HE'LL BE REPLACED.
NO, OF COURSE NOT. THE WHOLE BUSINESS-- IT'S TERRIBLE.
DID YOU HAVE ANY CLUE HE MIGHT BE IN DANGER?
AS I TOLD THE POLICE...
...HE SEEMED ANXIOUS. BUT HE NEVER SAID ANYTHING THAT--
HEAVENS!
THIS IS BRAZEN, BATMAN, EVEN FOR YOU. I SHOULD CALL THE COMMISSIONER RIGHT NOW.
I WISH YOU WOULDN'T, COUNCILMAN. I ASKED BATMAN TO COME HERE.
TO HELP US. TO HELP THE CHURCH.
I...ALL RIGHT. I JUST HOPE I'M NOT MAKING A MISTAKE.

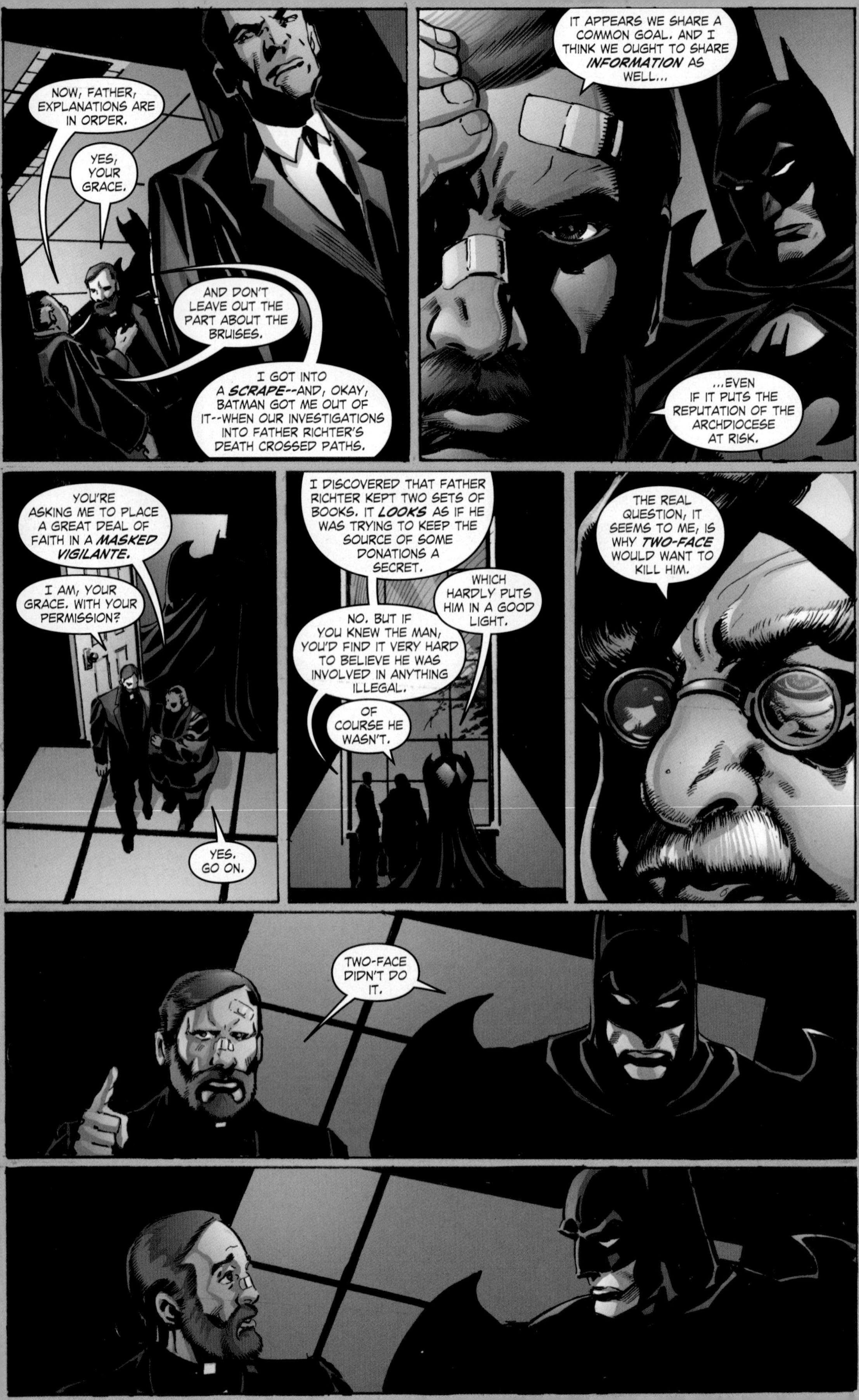
NOW, FATHER, EXPLANATIONS ARE IN ORDER.
YES, YOUR GRACE.
AND DON'T LEAVE OUT THE PART ABOUT THE BRUISES.
I GOT INTO A *SCRAPE*--AND, OKAY, BATMAN GOT ME OUT OF IT--WHEN OUR INVESTIGATIONS INTO FATHER RICHTER'S DEATH CROSSED PATHS.
IT APPEARS WE SHARE A COMMON GOAL. AND I THINK WE OUGHT TO SHARE *INFORMATION* AS WELL...
...EVEN IF IT PUTS THE REPUTATION OF THE ARCHDIOCESE AT RISK.
YOU'RE ASKING ME TO PLACE A GREAT DEAL OF FAITH IN A *MASKED VIGILANTE.*
I AM, YOUR GRACE. WITH YOUR PERMISSION?
YES. GO ON.
I DISCOVERED THAT FATHER RICHTER KEPT TWO SETS OF BOOKS. IT *LOOKS* AS IF HE WAS TRYING TO KEEP THE SOURCE OF SOME DONATIONS A SECRET.
WHICH HARDLY PUTS HIM IN A GOOD LIGHT.
NO. BUT IF YOU KNEW THE MAN, YOU'D FIND IT VERY HARD TO BELIEVE HE WAS INVOLVED IN ANYTHING ILLEGAL.
OF COURSE HE WASN'T.
THE REAL QUESTION, IT SEEMS TO ME, IS WHY *TWO-FACE* WOULD WANT TO KILL HIM.
TWO-FACE DIDN'T DO IT.

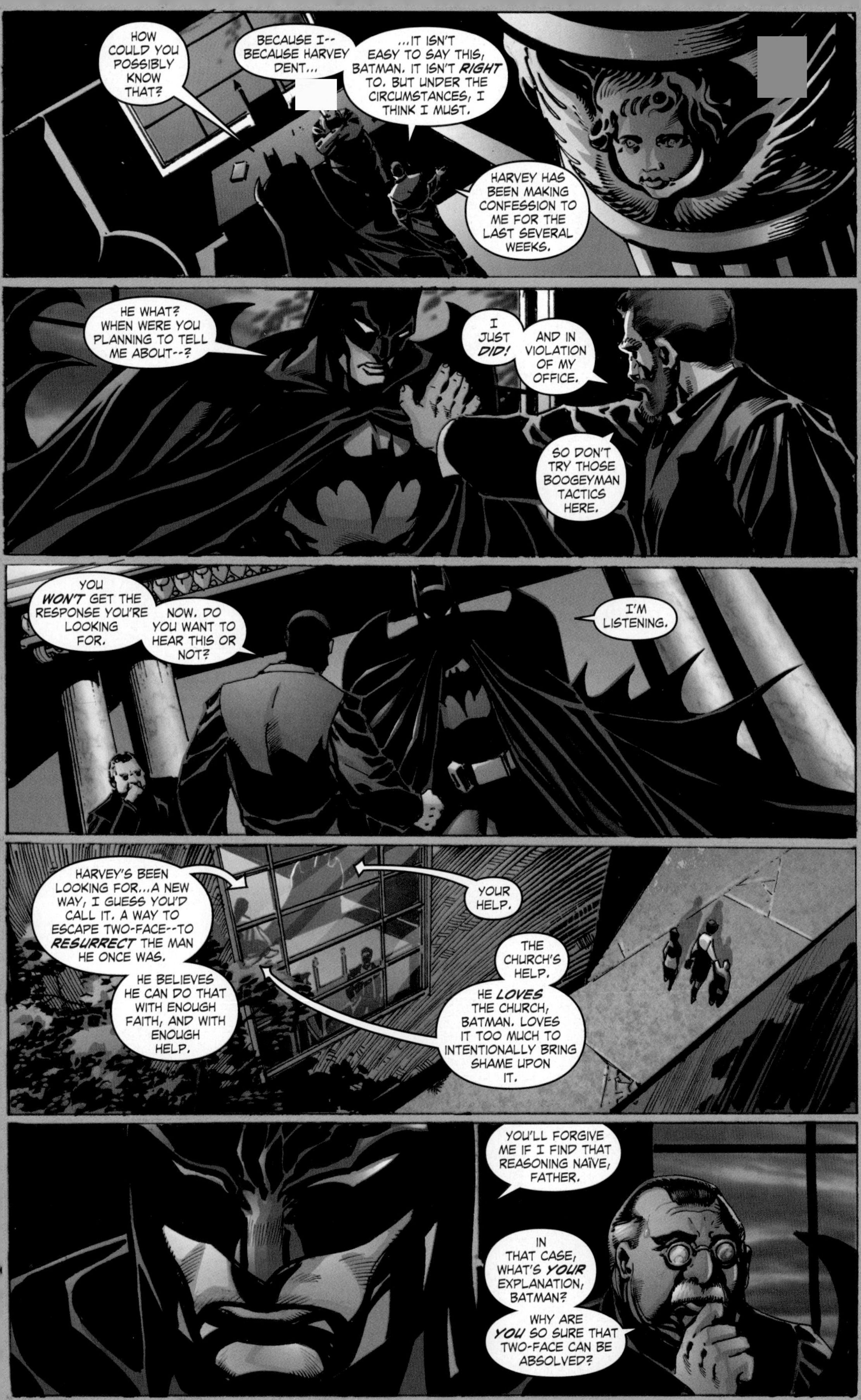
HOW COULD YOU POSSIBLY KNOW THAT?
BECAUSE I-- BECAUSE HARVEY DENT...
...IT ISN'T EASY TO SAY THIS, BATMAN. IT ISN'T RIGHT TO. BUT UNDER THE CIRCUMSTANCES, I THINK I MUST.
HARVEY HAS BEEN MAKING CONFESSION TO ME FOR THE LAST SEVERAL WEEKS.
HE WHAT? WHEN WERE YOU PLANNING TO TELL ME ABOUT--?
I JUST DID!
AND IN VIOLATION OF MY OFFICE.
SO DON'T TRY THOSE BOOGEYMAN TACTICS HERE.
YOU WON'T GET THE RESPONSE YOU'RE LOOKING FOR.
NOW. DO YOU WANT TO HEAR THIS OR NOT?
I'M LISTENING.
HARVEY'S BEEN LOOKING FOR...A NEW WAY, I GUESS YOU'D CALL IT. A WAY TO ESCAPE TWO-FACE--TO RESURRECT THE MAN HE ONCE WAS.
YOUR HELP.
HE BELIEVES HE CAN DO THAT WITH ENOUGH FAITH, AND WITH ENOUGH HELP.
THE CHURCH'S HELP.
HE LOVES THE CHURCH, BATMAN. LOVES IT TOO MUCH TO INTENTIONALLY BRING SHAME UPON IT.
YOU'LL FORGIVE ME IF I FIND THAT REASONING NAÏVE, FATHER.
IN THAT CASE, WHAT'S YOUR EXPLANATION, BATMAN?
WHY ARE YOU SO SURE THAT TWO-FACE CAN BE ABSOLVED?

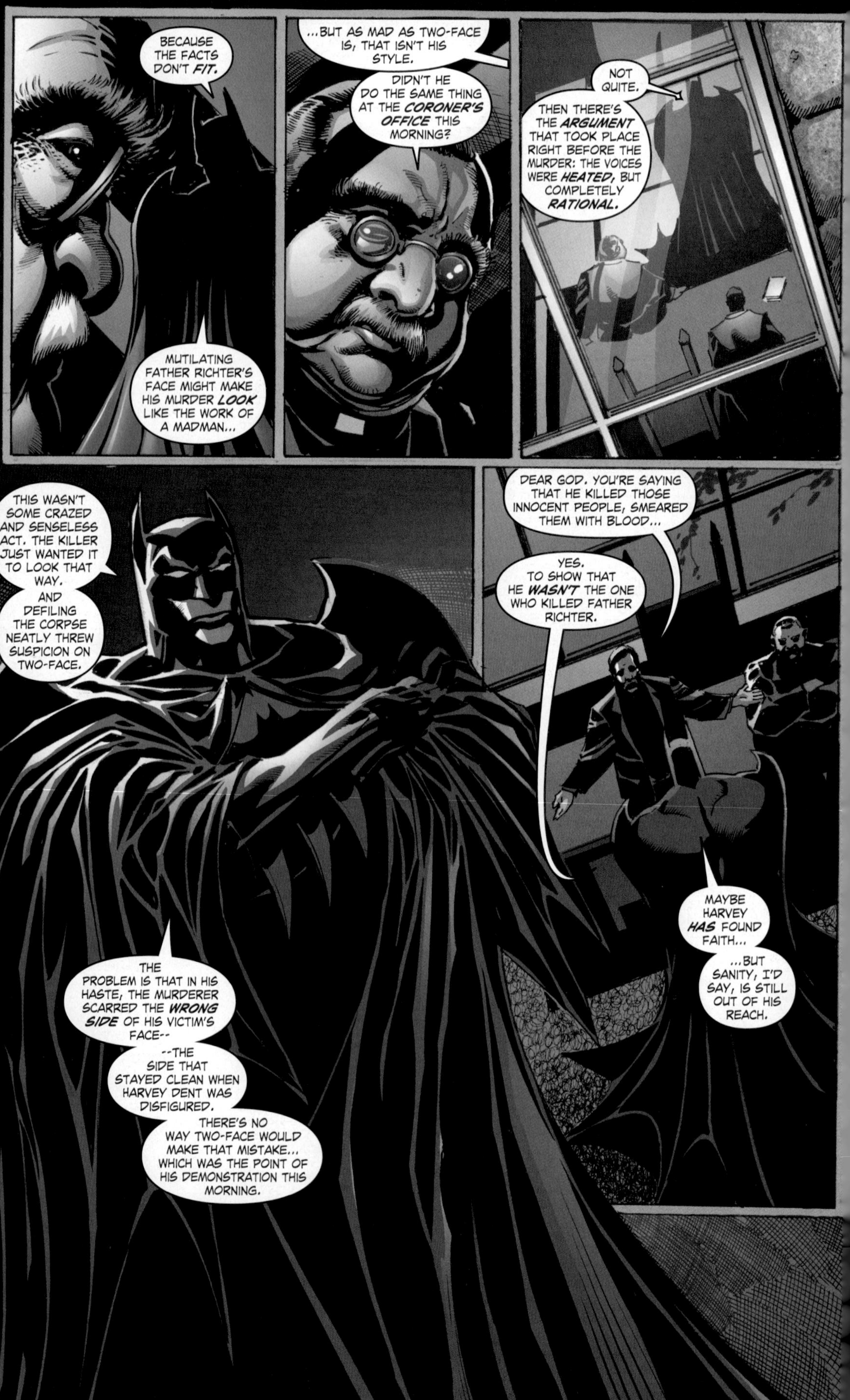
BECAUSE THE FACTS DON'T *FIT*.
MUTILATING FATHER RICHTER'S FACE MIGHT MAKE HIS MURDER *LOOK* LIKE THE WORK OF A MADMAN...
...BUT AS MAD AS TWO-FACE IS, THAT ISN'T HIS STYLE.
DIDN'T HE DO THE SAME THING AT THE *CORONER'S OFFICE* THIS MORNING?
NOT QUITE.
THEN THERE'S THE *ARGUMENT* THAT TOOK PLACE RIGHT BEFORE THE MURDER: THE VOICES WERE *HEATED*, BUT COMPLETELY *RATIONAL*.
THIS WASN'T SOME CRAZED AND SENSELESS ACT. THE KILLER JUST WANTED IT TO LOOK THAT WAY.
AND DEFILING THE CORPSE NEATLY THREW SUSPICION ON TWO-FACE.
THE PROBLEM IS THAT IN HIS HASTE, THE MURDERER SCARRED THE *WRONG SIDE* OF HIS VICTIM'S FACE--
--THE SIDE THAT STAYED CLEAN WHEN HARVEY DENT WAS DISFIGURED.
THERE'S NO WAY TWO-FACE WOULD MAKE THAT MISTAKE... WHICH WAS THE POINT OF HIS DEMONSTRATION THIS MORNING.
DEAR GOD. YOU'RE SAYING THAT HE KILLED THOSE INNOCENT PEOPLE, SMEARED THEM WITH BLOOD...
YES. TO SHOW THAT HE *WASN'T* THE ONE WHO KILLED FATHER RICHTER.
MAYBE HARVEY *HAS* FOUND FAITH...
...BUT SANITY, I'D SAY, IS STILL OUT OF HIS REACH.

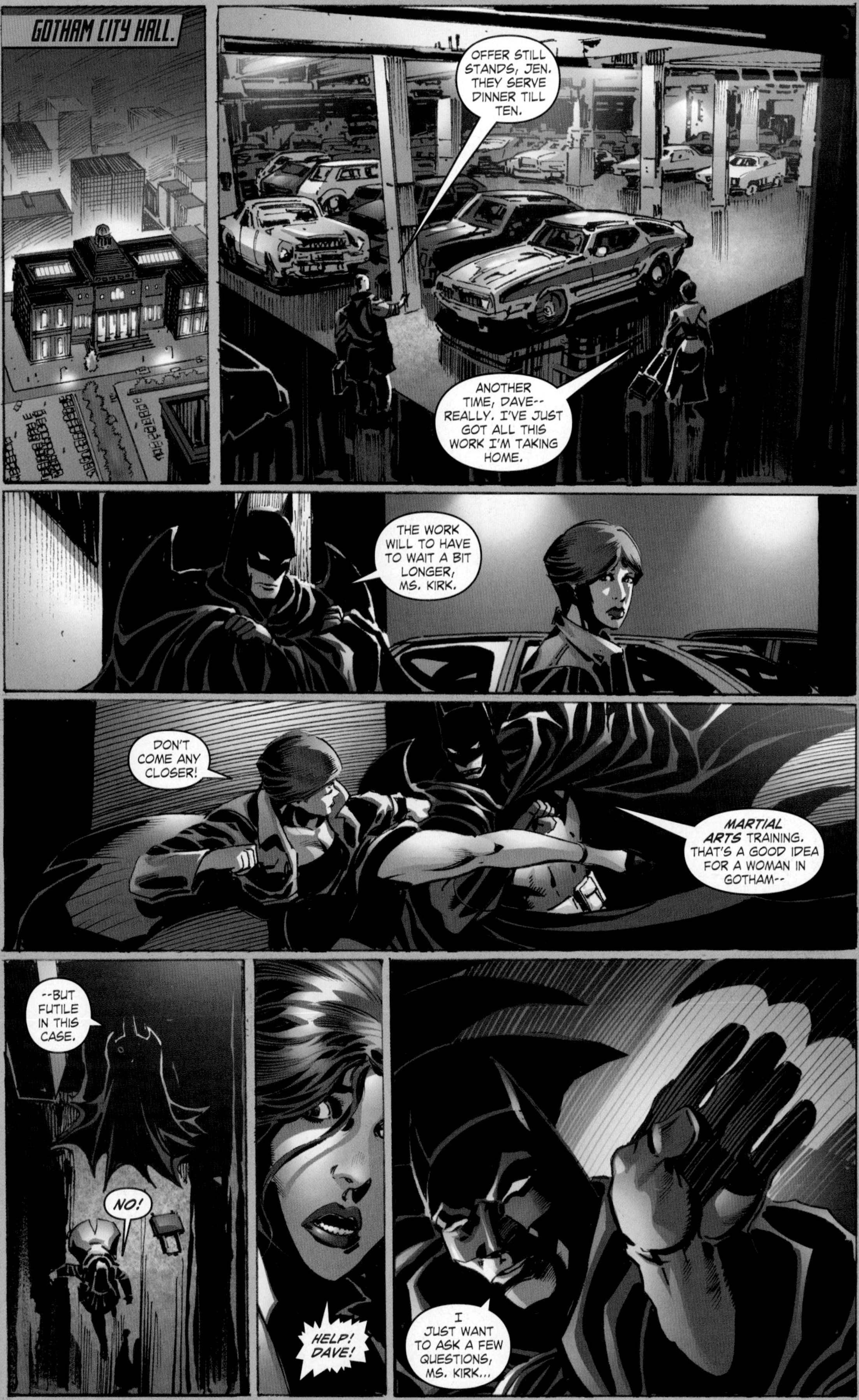
GOTHAM CITY HALL.
OFFER STILL STANDS, JEN. THEY SERVE DINNER TILL TEN.
ANOTHER TIME, DAVE--REALLY. I'VE JUST GOT ALL THIS WORK I'M TAKING HOME.
THE WORK WILL TO HAVE TO WAIT A BIT LONGER, MS. KIRK.
DON'T COME ANY CLOSER!
MARTIAL ARTS TRAINING. THAT'S A GOOD IDEA FOR A WOMAN IN GOTHAM--
--BUT FUTILE IN THIS CASE.
NO!
HELP! DAVE!
I JUST WANT TO ASK A FEW QUESTIONS, MS. KIRK...

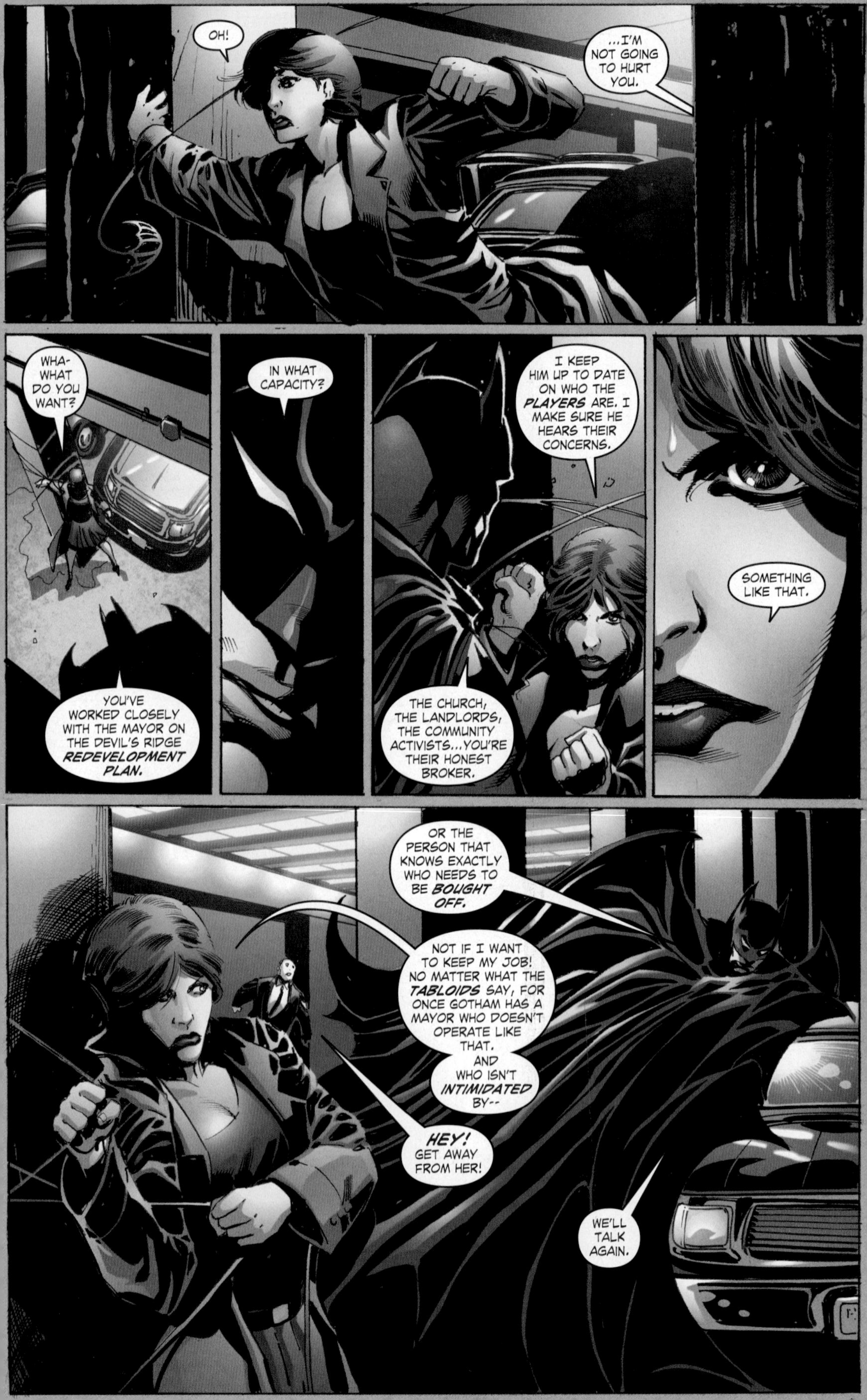

OH!
...I'M NOT GOING TO HURT YOU.
WHA-WHAT DO YOU WANT?
YOU'VE WORKED CLOSELY WITH THE MAYOR ON THE DEVIL'S RIDGE REDEVELOPMENT PLAN.
IN WHAT CAPACITY?
I KEEP HIM UP TO DATE ON WHO THE PLAYERS ARE. I MAKE SURE HE HEARS THEIR CONCERNS.
THE CHURCH, THE LANDLORDS, THE COMMUNITY ACTIVISTS...YOU'RE THEIR HONEST BROKER.
SOMETHING LIKE THAT.
OR THE PERSON THAT KNOWS EXACTLY WHO NEEDS TO BE BOUGHT OFF.
NOT IF I WANT TO KEEP MY JOB! NO MATTER WHAT THE TABLOIDS SAY, FOR ONCE GOTHAM HAS A MAYOR WHO DOESN'T OPERATE LIKE THAT.
AND WHO ISN'T INTIMIDATED BY--
HEY! GET AWAY FROM HER!
WE'LL TALK AGAIN.

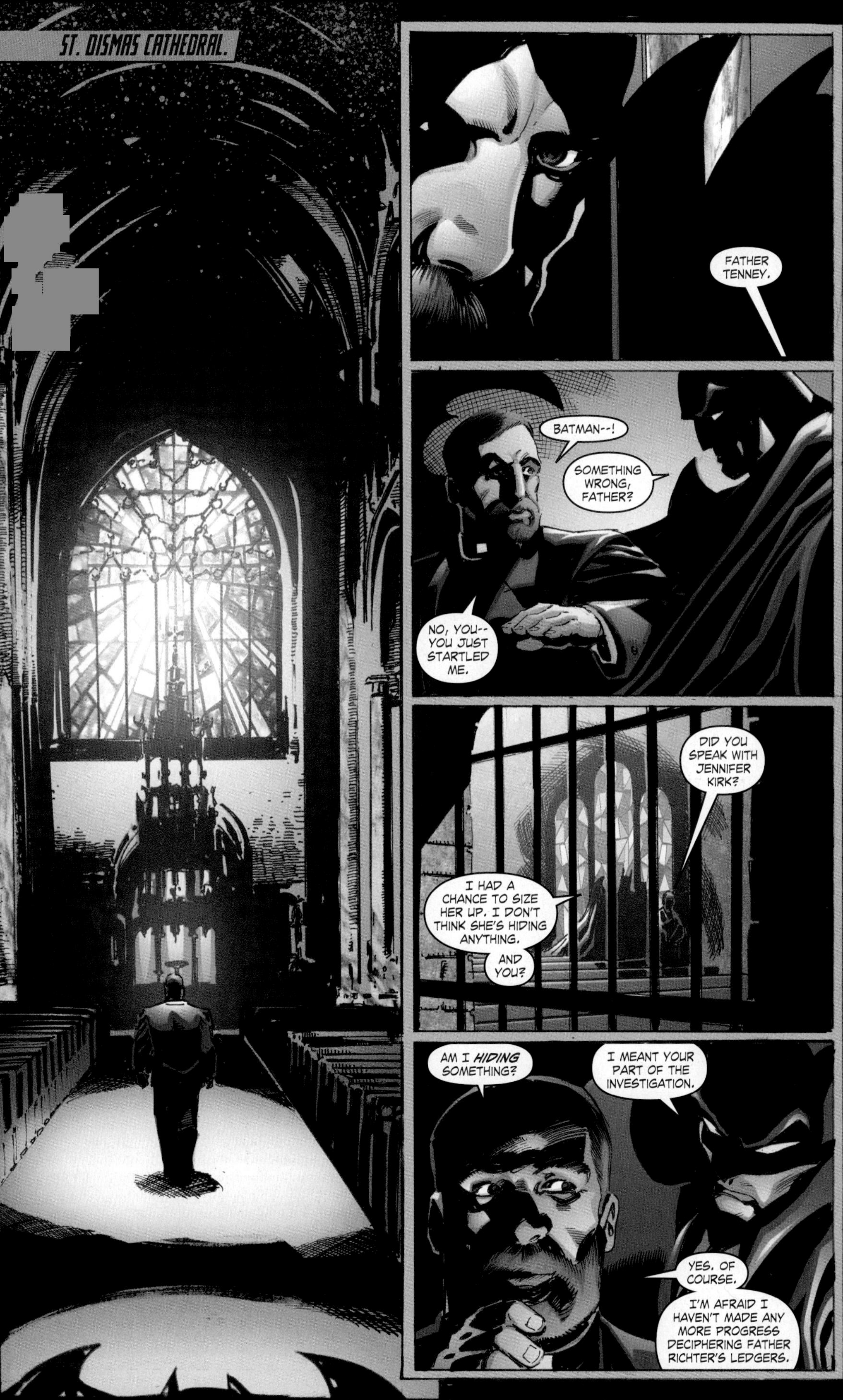
ST. DISMAS CATHEDRAL.
FATHER TENNEY.
BATMAN--!
SOMETHING WRONG, FATHER?
NO, YOU-- YOU JUST STARTLED ME.
DID YOU SPEAK WITH JENNIFER KIRK?
I HAD A CHANCE TO SIZE HER UP. I DON'T THINK SHE'S HIDING ANYTHING.
AND YOU?
AM I *HIDING* SOMETHING?
I MEANT YOUR PART OF THE INVESTIGATION.
YES. OF COURSE.
I'M AFRAID I HAVEN'T MADE ANY MORE PROGRESS DECIPHERING FATHER RICHTER'S LEDGERS.

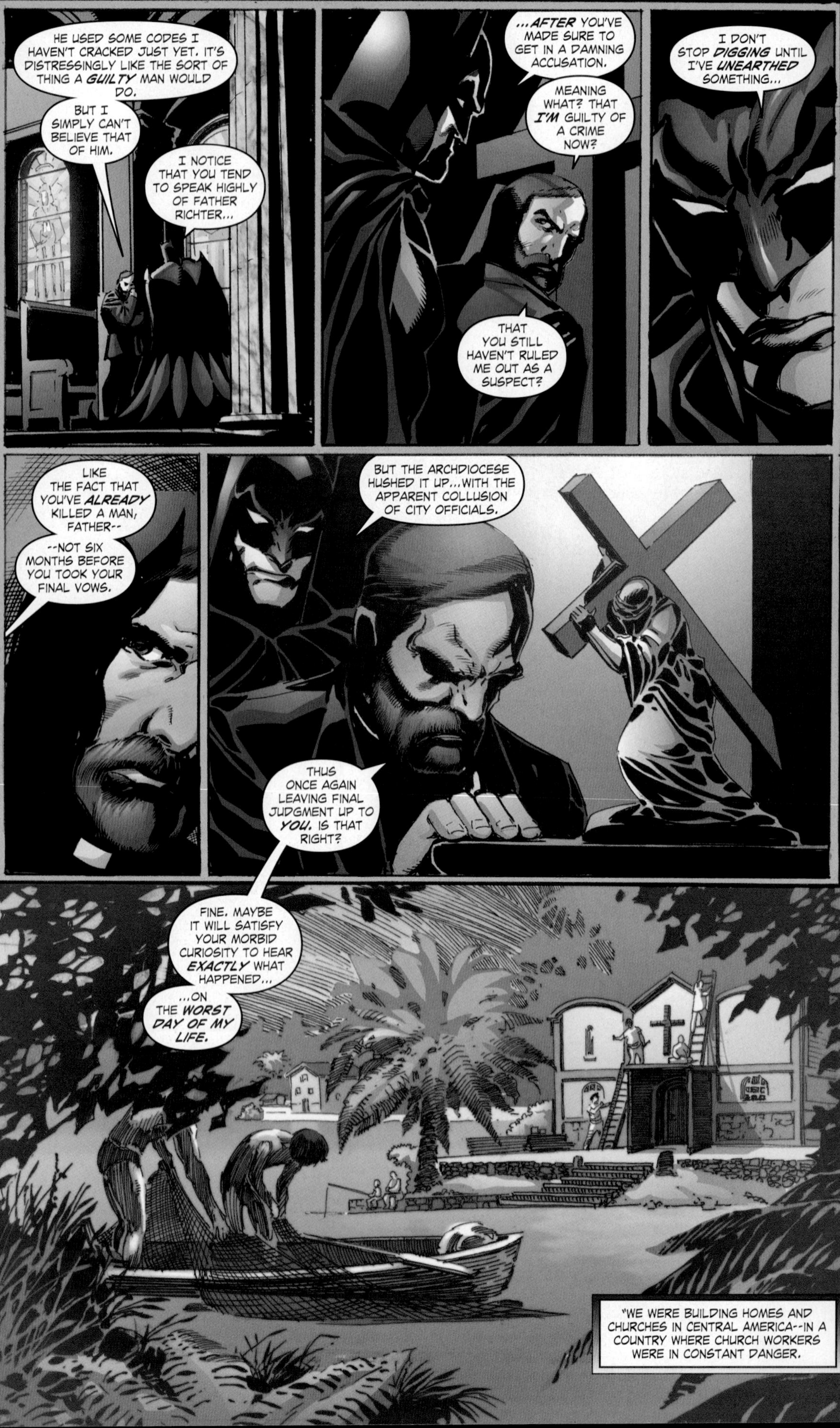
HE USED SOME CODES I HAVEN'T CRACKED JUST YET. IT'S DISTRESSINGLY LIKE THE SORT OF THING A GUILTY MAN WOULD DO.
BUT I SIMPLY CAN'T BELIEVE THAT OF HIM.
I NOTICE THAT YOU TEND TO SPEAK HIGHLY OF FATHER RICHTER...
...AFTER YOU'VE MADE SURE TO GET IN A DAMNING ACCUSATION.
MEANING WHAT? THAT I'M GUILTY OF A CRIME NOW?
THAT YOU STILL HAVEN'T RULED ME OUT AS A SUSPECT?
I DON'T STOP DIGGING UNTIL I'VE UNEARTHED SOMETHING...
LIKE THE FACT THAT YOU'VE ALREADY KILLED A MAN, FATHER--
--NOT SIX MONTHS BEFORE YOU TOOK YOUR FINAL VOWS.
BUT THE ARCHDIOCESE HUSHED IT UP...WITH THE APPARENT COLLUSION OF CITY OFFICIALS.
THUS ONCE AGAIN LEAVING FINAL JUDGMENT UP TO YOU. IS THAT RIGHT?
FINE. MAYBE IT WILL SATISFY YOUR MORBID CURIOSITY TO HEAR EXACTLY WHAT HAPPENED...
...ON THE WORST DAY OF MY LIFE.
"WE WERE BUILDING HOMES AND CHURCHES IN CENTRAL AMERICA--IN A COUNTRY WHERE CHURCH WORKERS WERE IN CONSTANT DANGER.

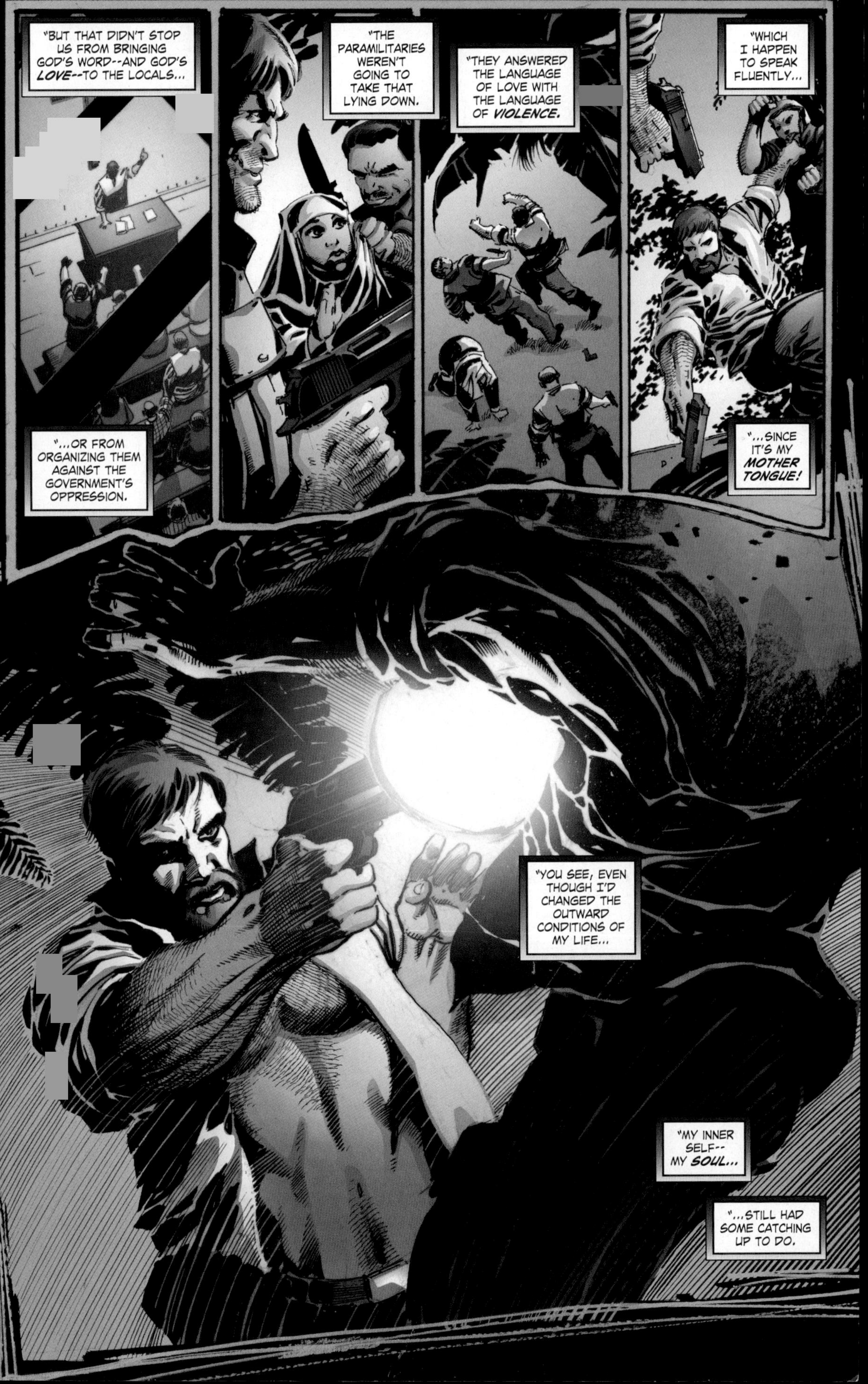
"BUT THAT DIDN'T STOP US FROM BRINGING GOD'S WORD--AND GOD'S LOVE--TO THE LOCALS...
"...OR FROM ORGANIZING THEM AGAINST THE GOVERNMENT'S OPPRESSION.
"THE PARAMILITARIES WEREN'T GOING TO TAKE THAT LYING DOWN.
"THEY ANSWERED THE LANGUAGE OF LOVE WITH THE LANGUAGE OF VIOLENCE.
"WHICH I HAPPEN TO SPEAK FLUENTLY...
"...SINCE IT'S MY MOTHER TONGUE!
"YOU SEE, EVEN THOUGH I'D CHANGED THE OUTWARD CONDITIONS OF MY LIFE...
"MY INNER SELF-- MY SOUL...
"...STILL HAD SOME CATCHING UP TO DO.

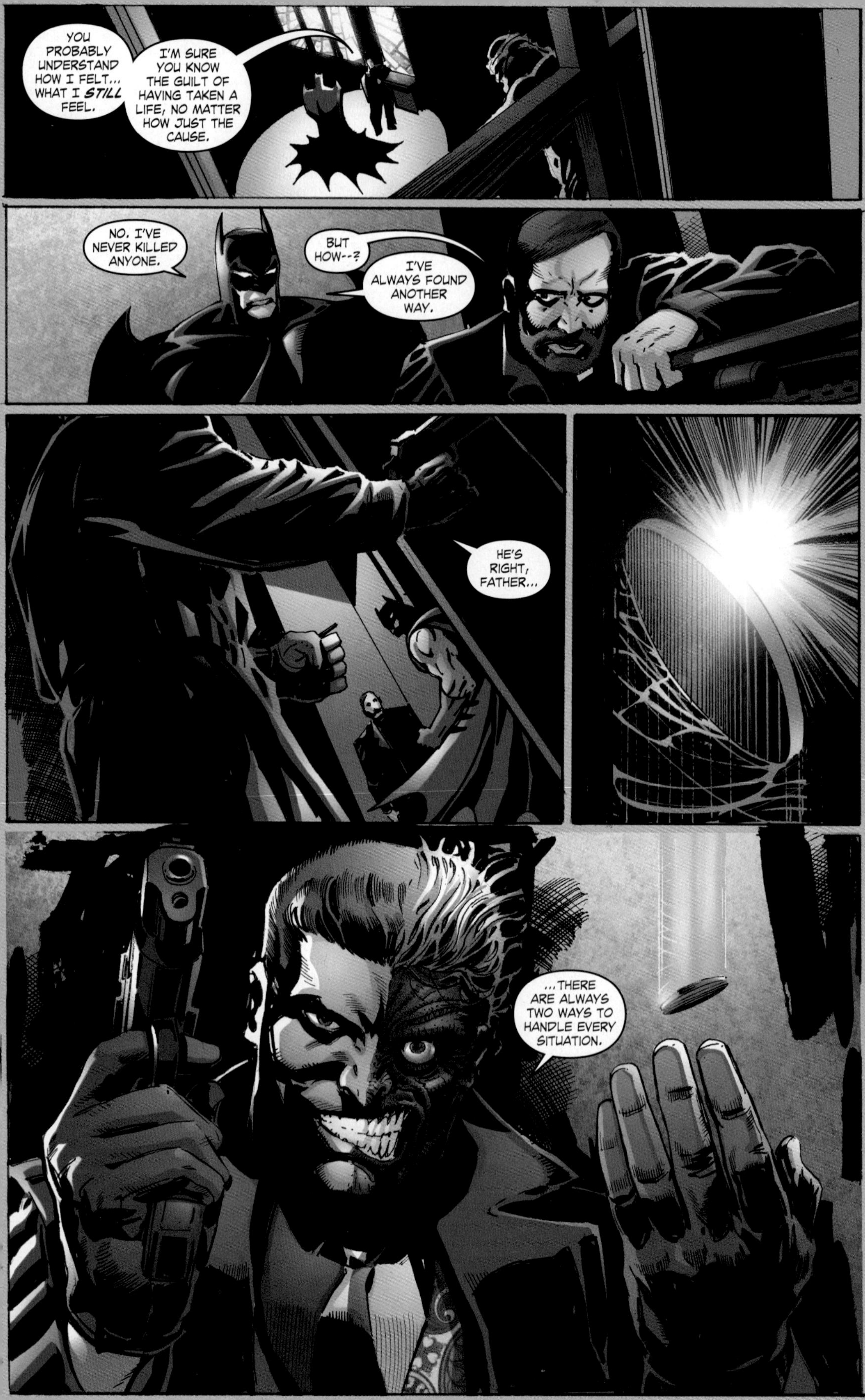
YOU PROBABLY UNDERSTAND HOW I FELT... WHAT I STILL FEEL.
I'M SURE YOU KNOW THE GUILT OF HAVING TAKEN A LIFE, NO MATTER HOW JUST THE CAUSE.
NO. I'VE NEVER KILLED ANYONE.
BUT HOW--?
I'VE ALWAYS FOUND ANOTHER WAY.
HE'S RIGHT, FATHER...
...THERE ARE ALWAYS TWO WAYS TO HANDLE EVERY SITUATION.

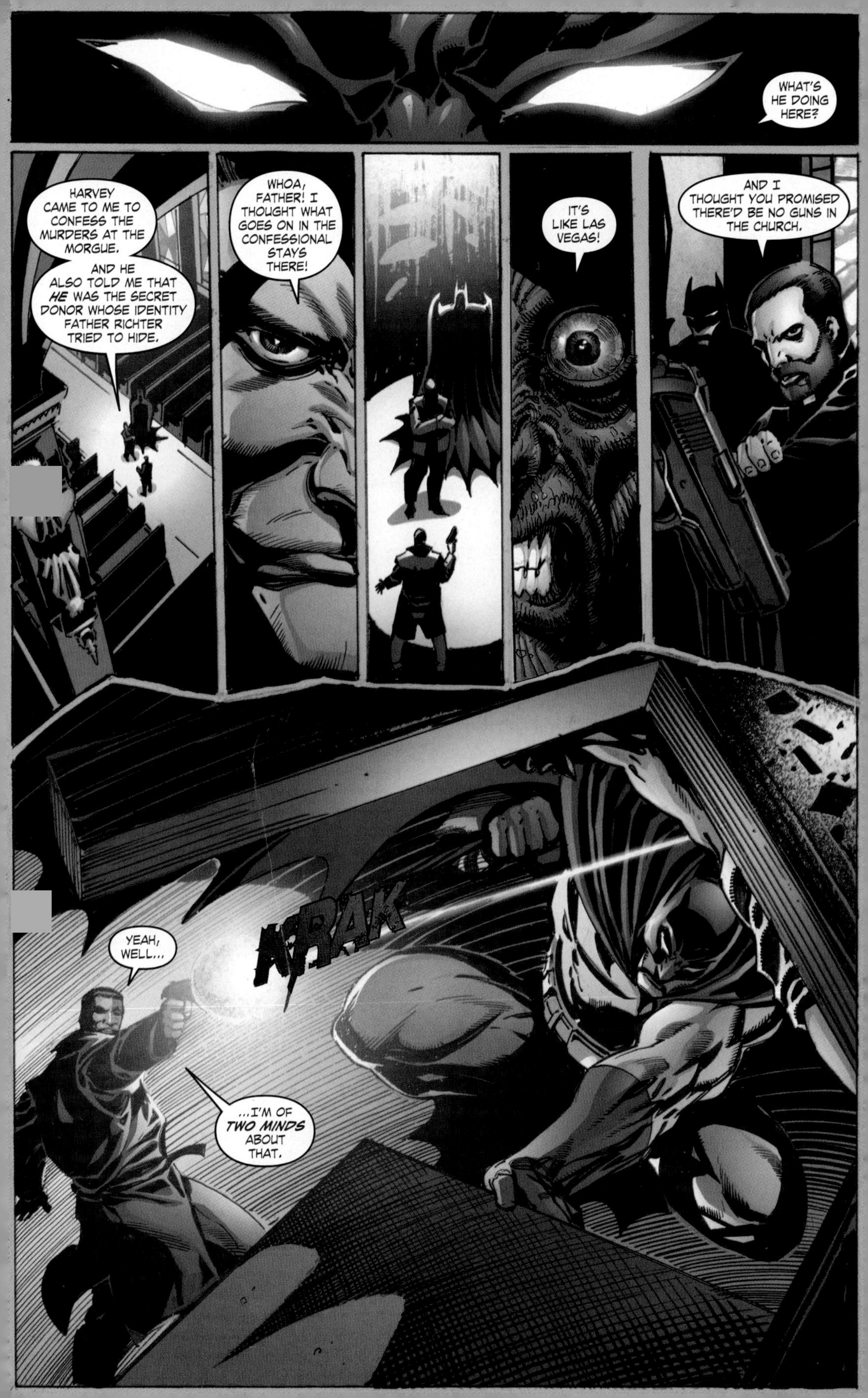
WHAT'S HE DOING HERE?
HARVEY CAME TO ME TO CONFESS THE MURDERS AT THE MORGUE.
AND HE ALSO TOLD ME THAT *HE* WAS THE SECRET DONOR WHOSE IDENTITY FATHER RICHTER TRIED TO HIDE.
WHOA, FATHER! I THOUGHT WHAT GOES ON IN THE CONFESSIONAL STAYS THERE!
IT'S LIKE LAS VEGAS!
AND I THOUGHT YOU PROMISED THERE'D BE NO GUNS IN THE CHURCH.
KRAK
YEAH, WELL...
...I'M OF *TWO MINDS* ABOUT THAT.

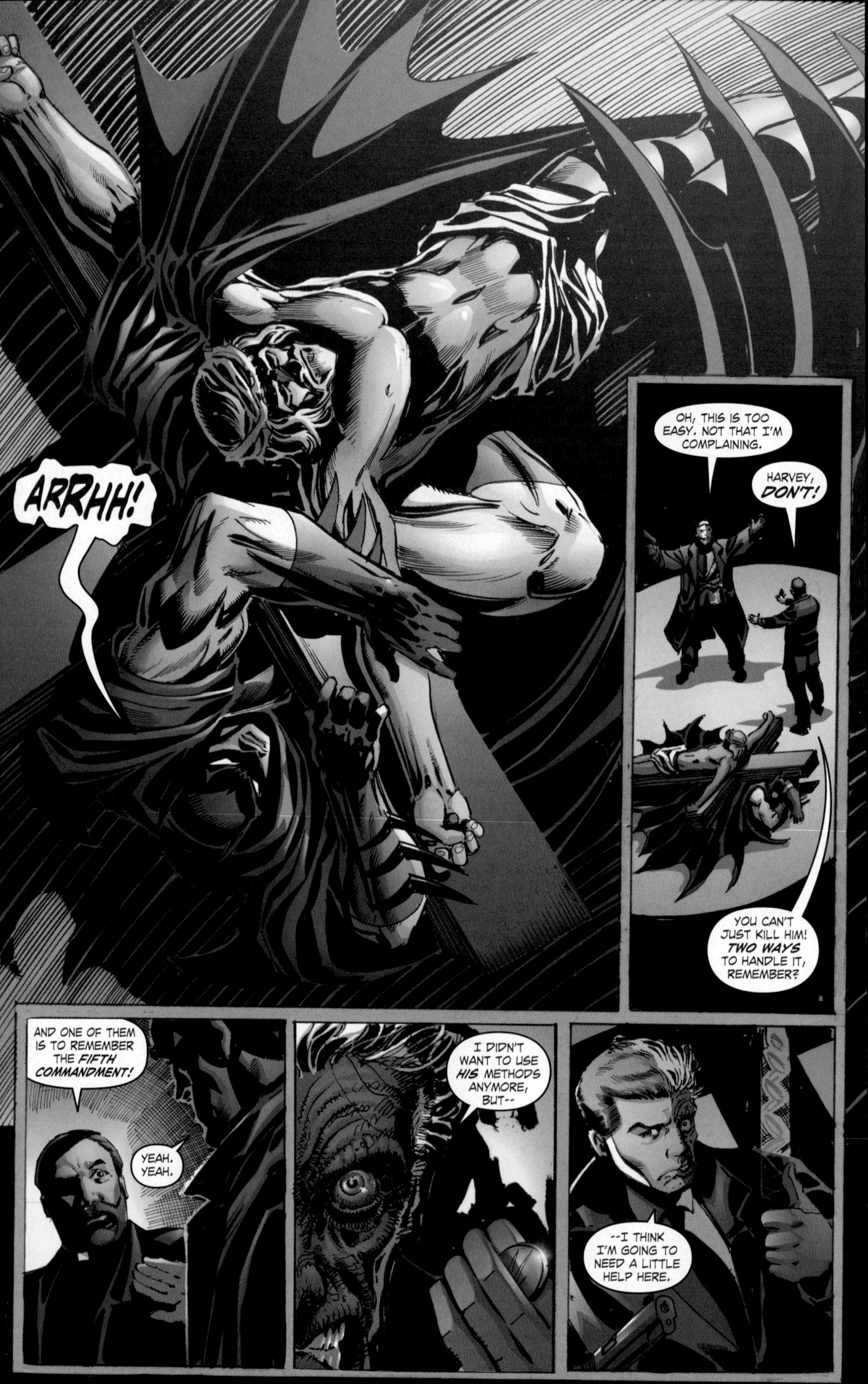
ARRHH!
OH, THIS IS TOO EASY. NOT THAT I'M COMPLAINING.
HARVEY, DON'T!
YOU CAN'T JUST KILL HIM! TWO WAYS TO HANDLE IT, REMEMBER?
AND ONE OF THEM IS TO REMEMBER THE FIFTH COMMANDMENT!
YEAH. YEAH.
I DIDN'T WANT TO USE HIS METHODS ANYMORE, BUT--
--I THINK I'M GOING TO NEED A LITTLE HELP HERE.

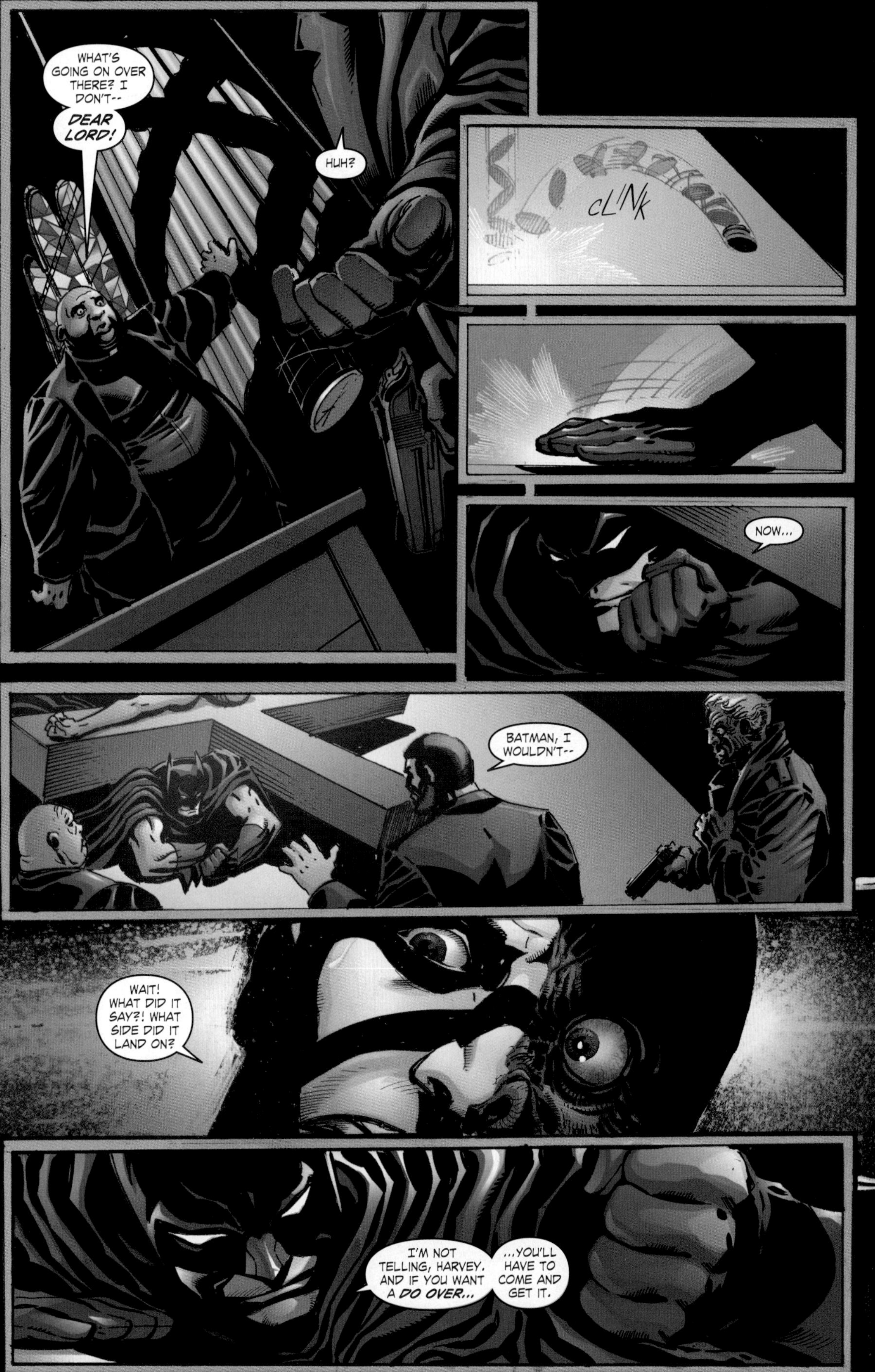
WHAT'S GOING ON OVER THERE? I DON'T--
DEAR LORD!
HUH?
CLINK
NOW...
BATMAN, I WOULDN'T--
WAIT! WHAT DID IT SAY?! WHAT SIDE DID IT LAND ON?
I'M NOT TELLING, HARVEY. AND IF YOU WANT A DO OVER...
...YOU'LL HAVE TO COME AND GET IT.

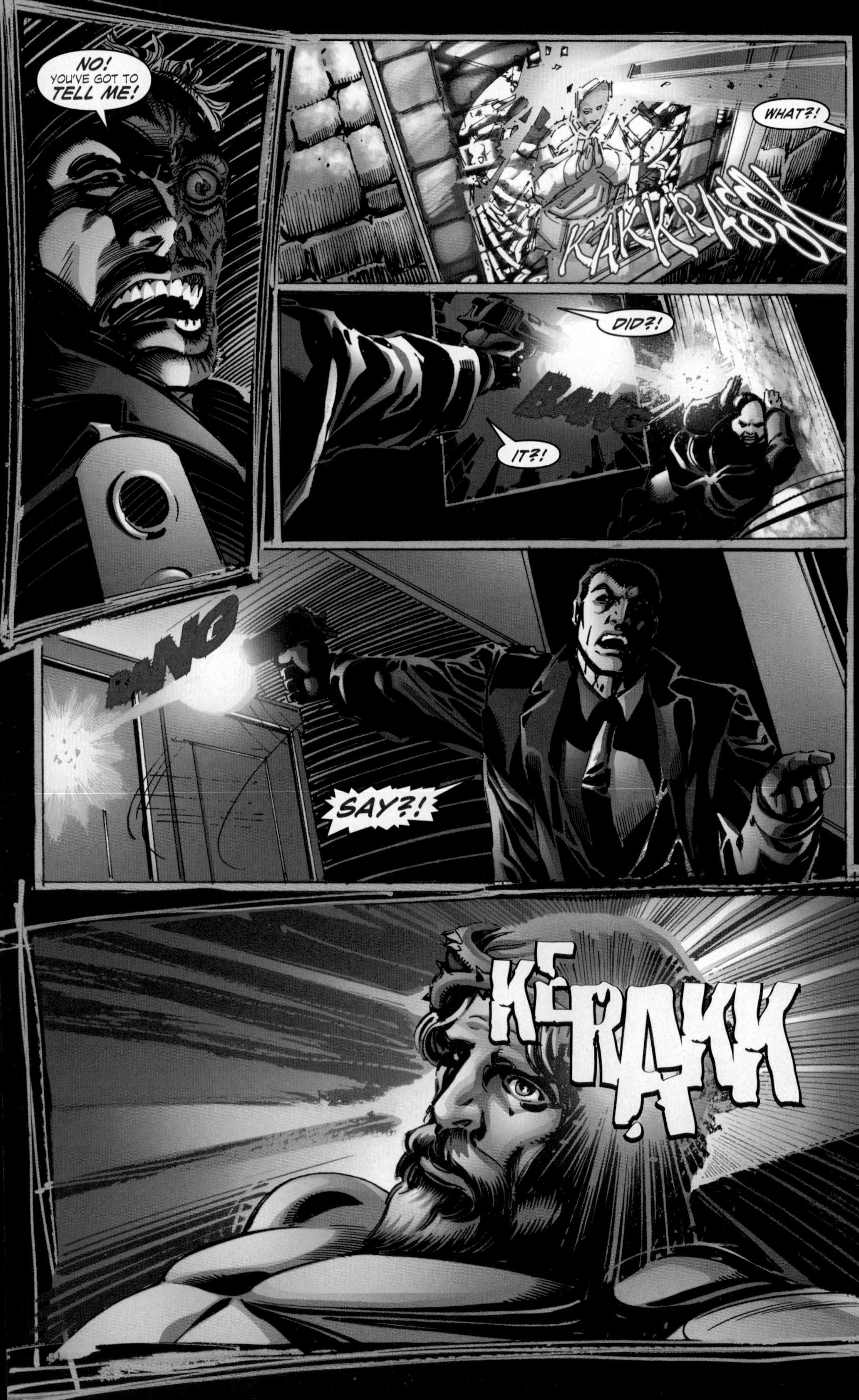

NO! YOU'VE GOT TO TELL ME!
WHAT?!
KAKKRASH
DID?!
BANG
IT?!
BANG
SAY?!
KERAKK

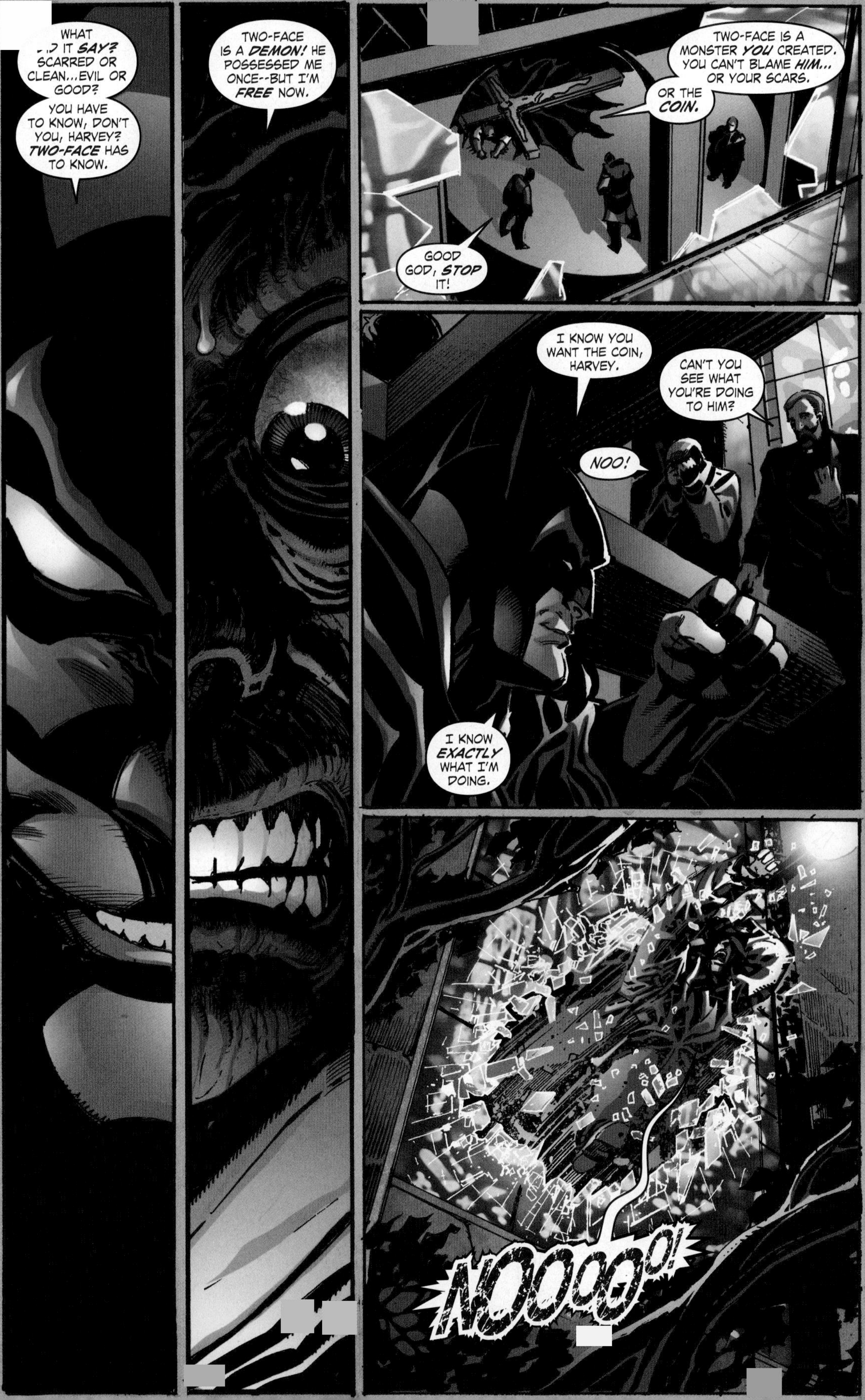
WHAT ID IT SAY? SCARRED OR CLEAN...EVIL OR GOOD?
YOU HAVE TO KNOW, DON'T YOU, HARVEY? TWO-FACE HAS TO KNOW.
TWO-FACE IS A DEMON! HE POSSESSED ME ONCE--BUT I'M FREE NOW.
TWO-FACE IS A MONSTER YOU CREATED. YOU CAN'T BLAME HIM... OR YOUR SCARS.
OR THE COIN.
GOOD GOD, STOP IT!
I KNOW YOU WANT THE COIN, HARVEY.
CAN'T YOU SEE WHAT YOU'RE DOING TO HIM?
NOO!
I KNOW EXACTLY WHAT I'M DOING.
NOOOOO!

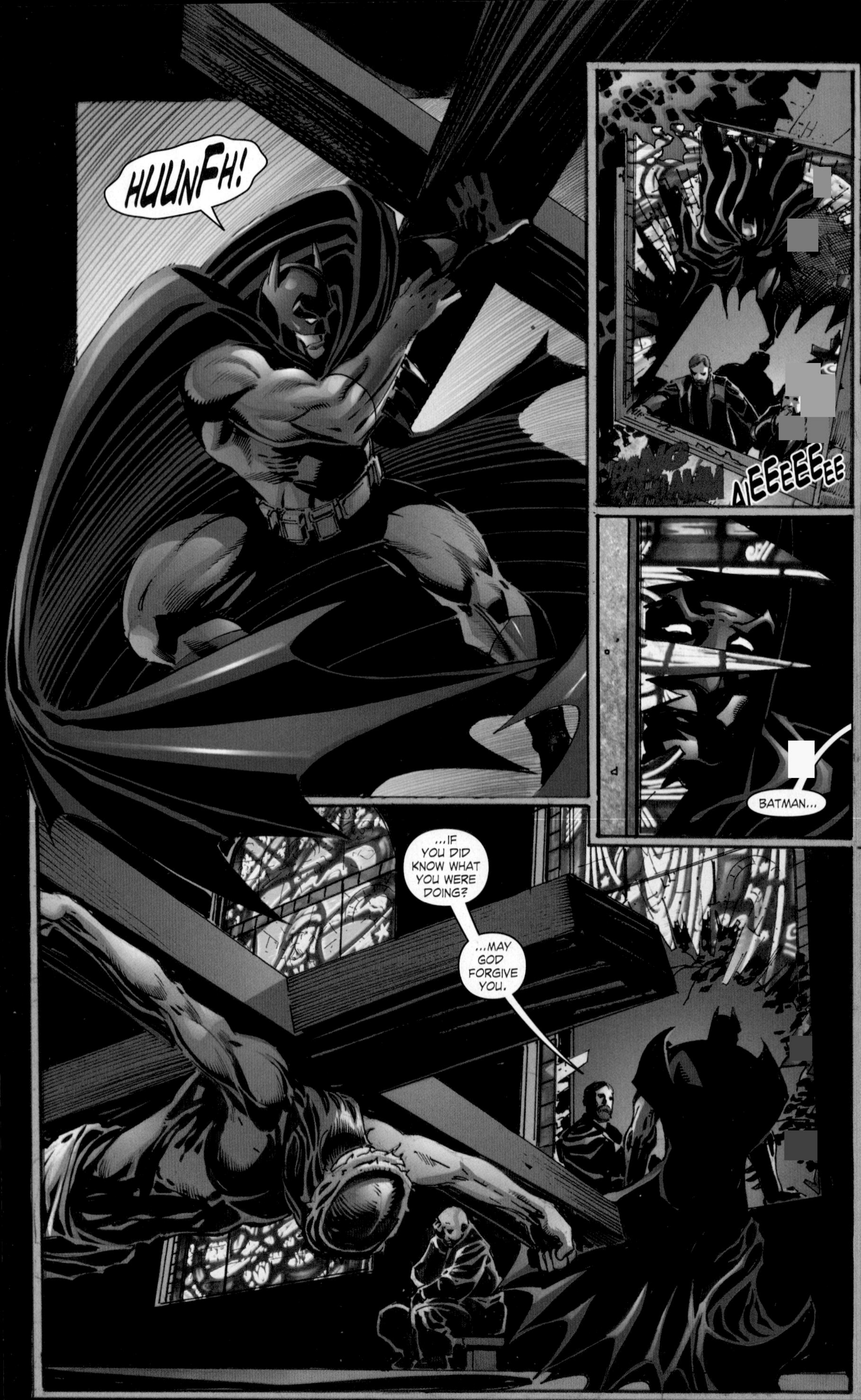
HUUNFH!
AIEEEEEEE
BATMAN...
...IF YOU DID KNOW WHAT YOU WERE DOING?
...MAY GOD FORGIVE YOU.

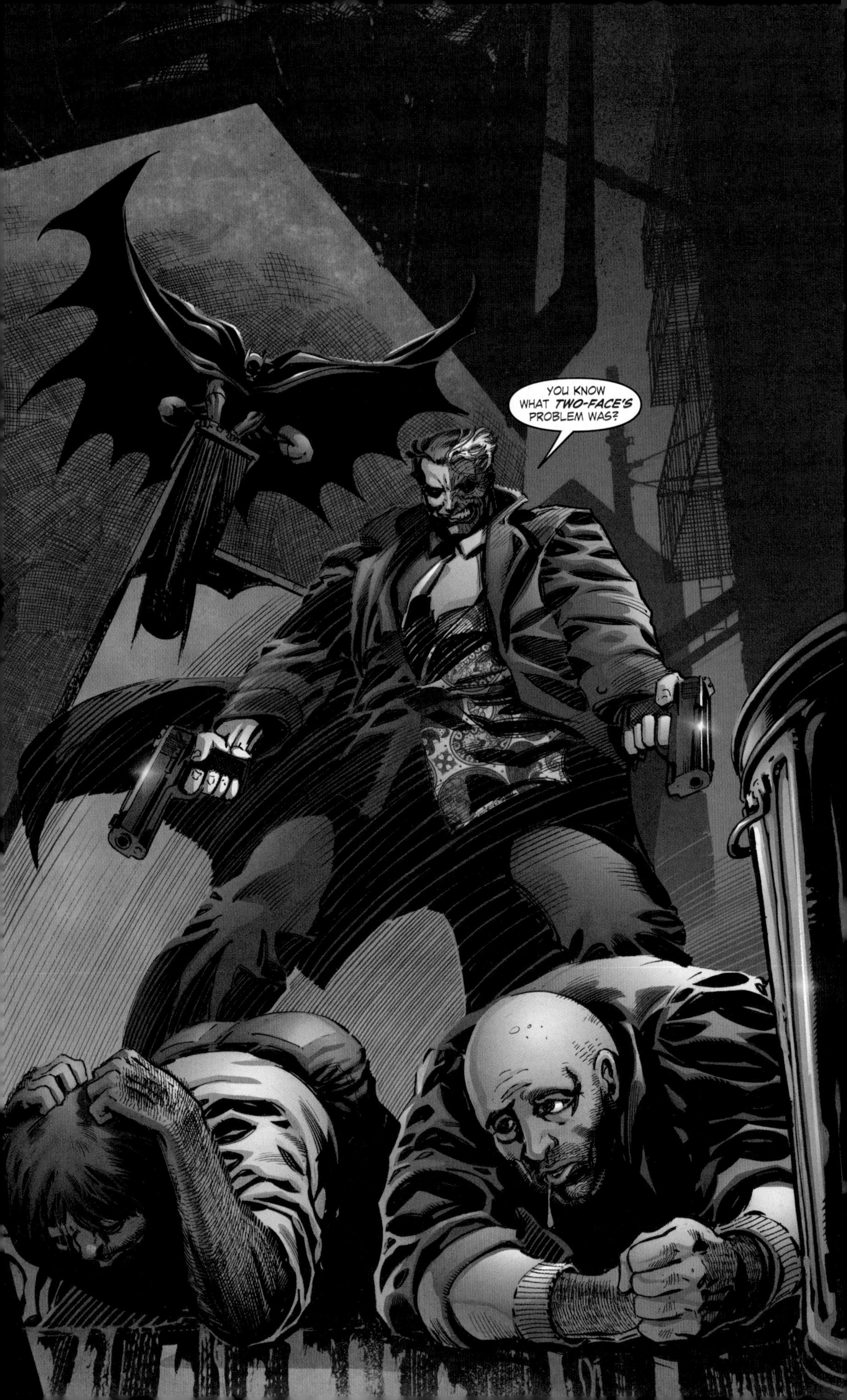
YOU KNOW WHAT TWO-FACE'S PROBLEM WAS?

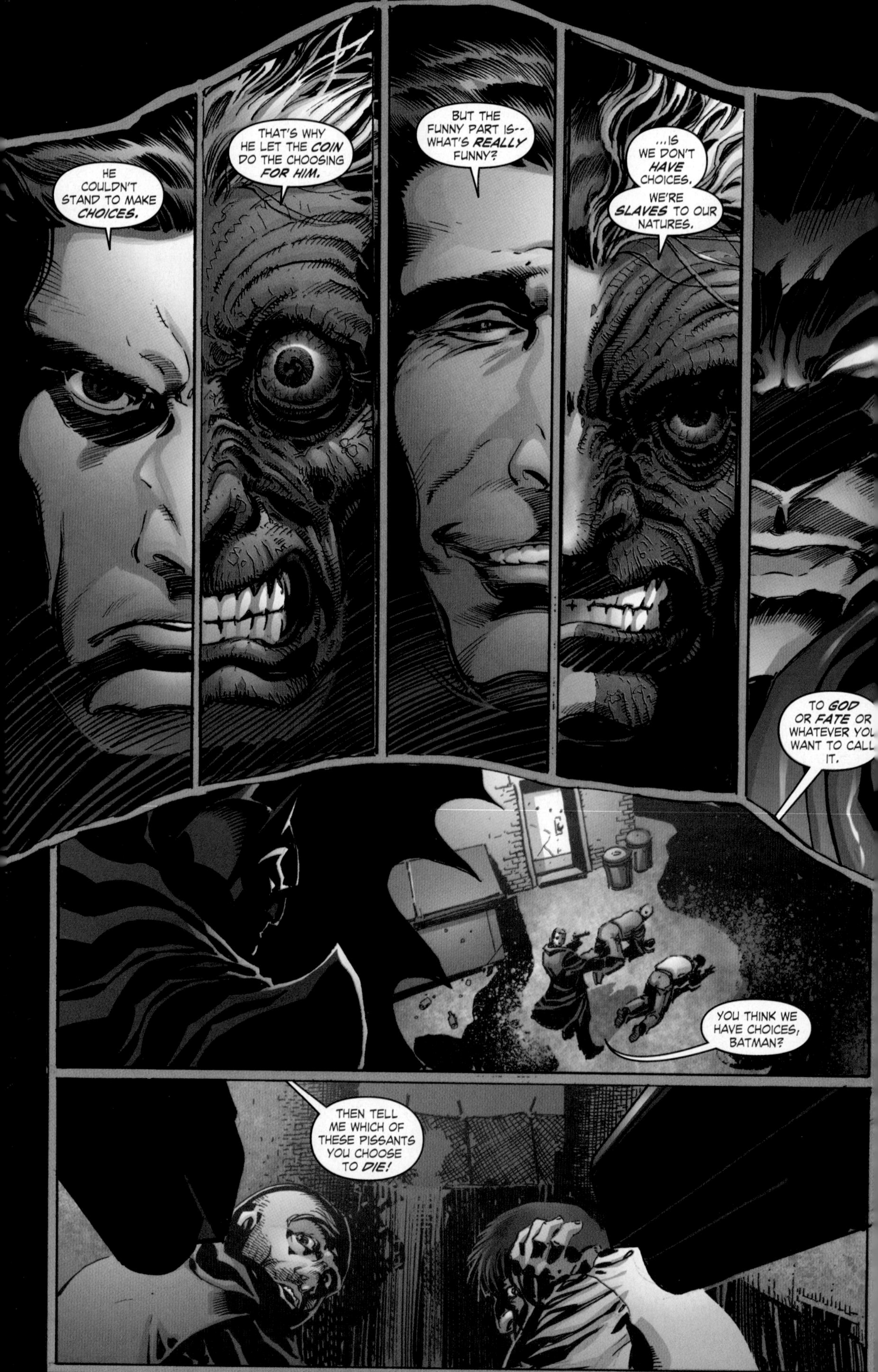

HE COULDN'T STAND TO MAKE *CHOICES.*
THAT'S WHY HE LET THE *COIN* DO THE CHOOSING *FOR HIM.*
BUT THE FUNNY PART IS-- WHAT'S *REALLY* FUNNY?
...IS WE DON'T *HAVE* CHOICES.
WE'RE *SLAVES* TO OUR NATURES.
TO *GOD* OR *FATE* OR WHATEVER YOU WANT TO CALL IT.
YOU THINK WE HAVE CHOICES, BATMAN?
THEN TELL ME WHICH OF THESE PISSANTS YOU CHOOSE TO *DIE!*

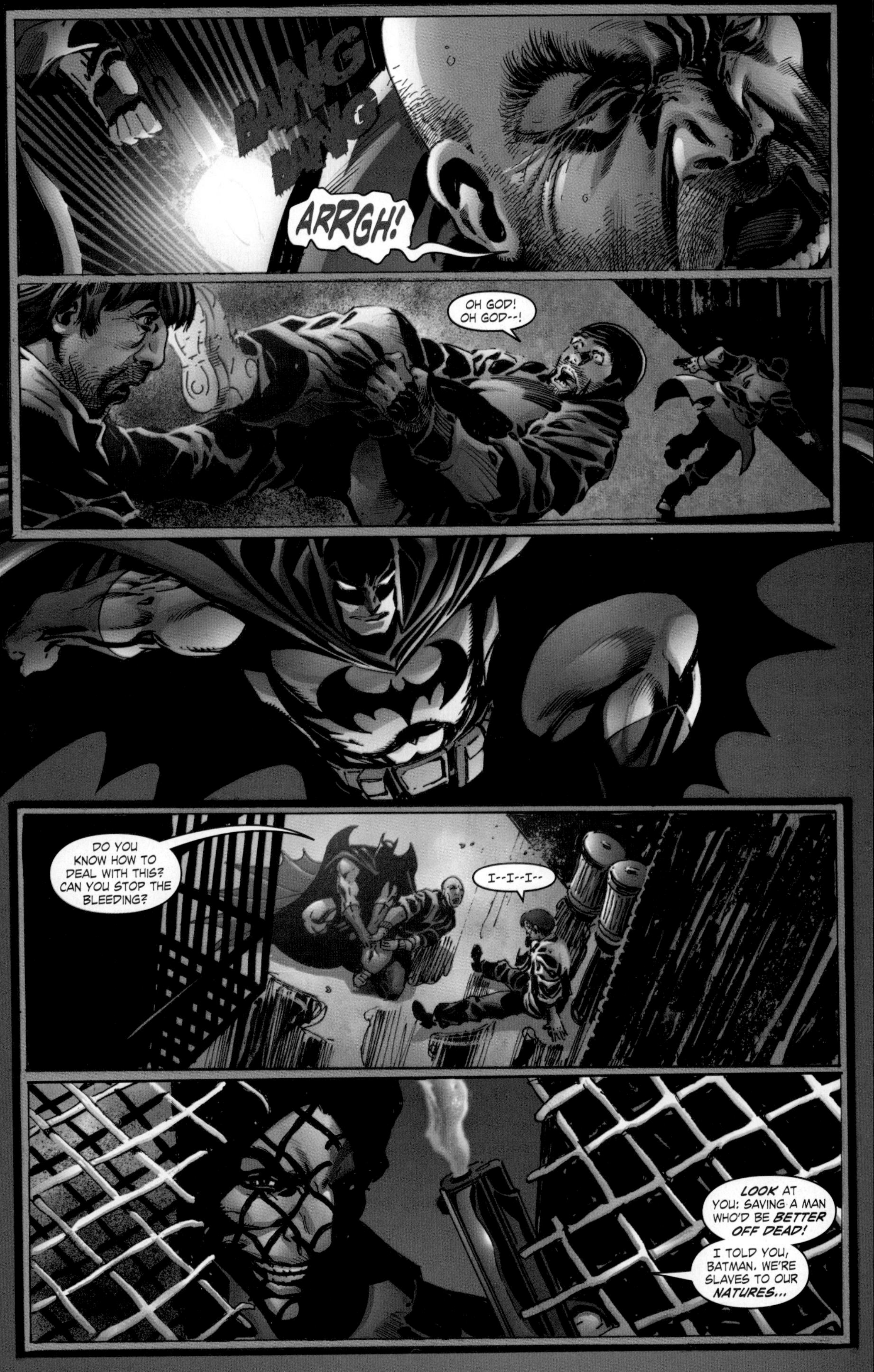
BANG
BANG
ARRGH!
OH GOD! OH GOD--!
DO YOU KNOW HOW TO DEAL WITH THIS? CAN YOU STOP THE BLEEDING?
I--I--I--
LOOK AT YOU: SAVING A MAN WHO'D BE BETTER OFF DEAD!
I TOLD YOU, BATMAN. WE'RE SLAVES TO OUR NATURES...

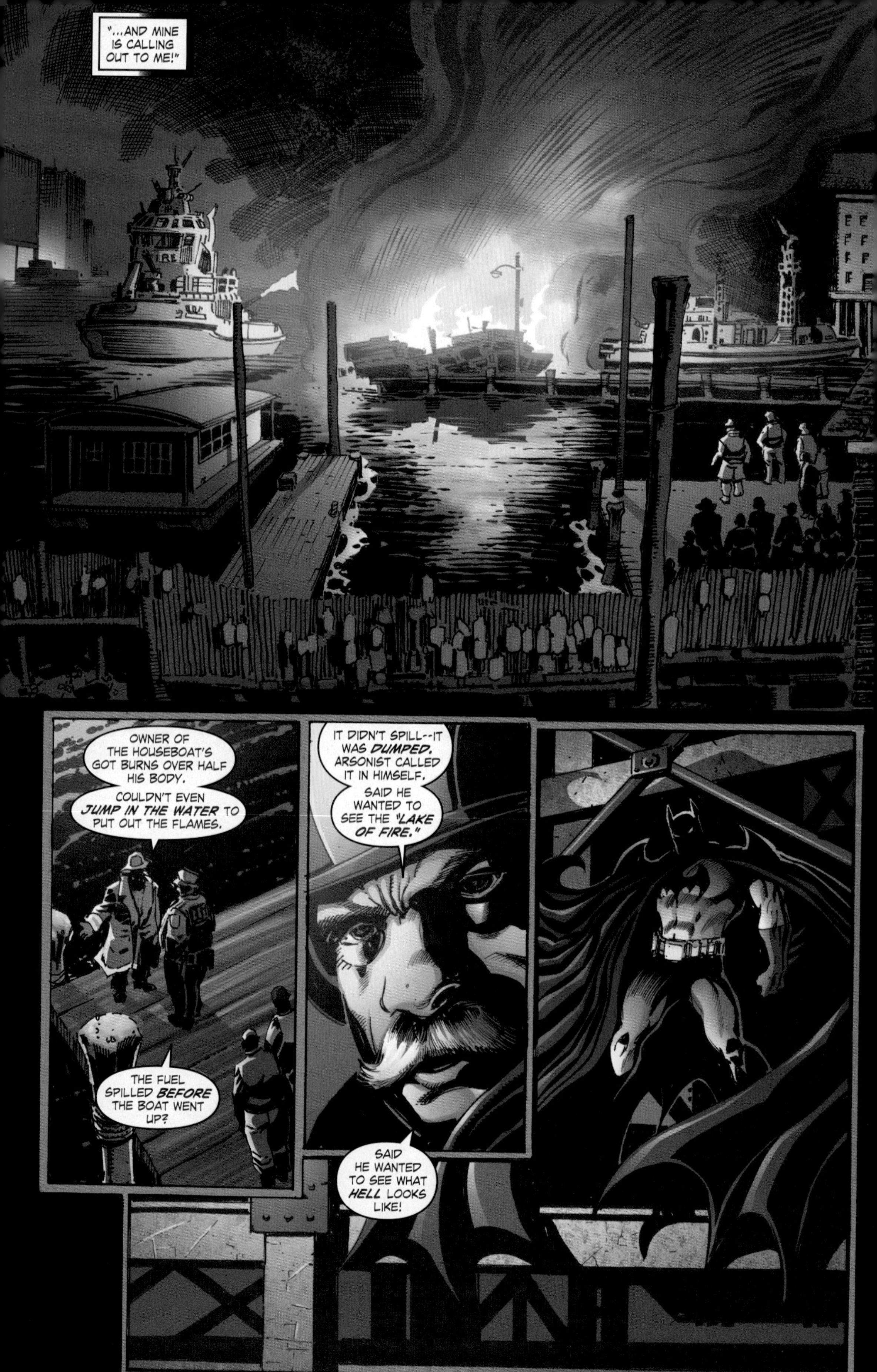
"...AND MINE IS CALLING OUT TO ME!"
OWNER OF THE HOUSEBOAT'S GOT BURNS OVER HALF HIS BODY.
COULDN'T EVEN *JUMP IN THE WATER* TO PUT OUT THE FLAMES.
THE FUEL SPILLED *BEFORE* THE BOAT WENT UP?
IT DIDN'T SPILL--IT WAS *DUMPED.* ARSONIST CALLED IT IN HIMSELF.
SAID HE WANTED TO SEE THE *"LAKE OF FIRE."*
SAID HE WANTED TO SEE WHAT *HELL* LOOKS LIKE!

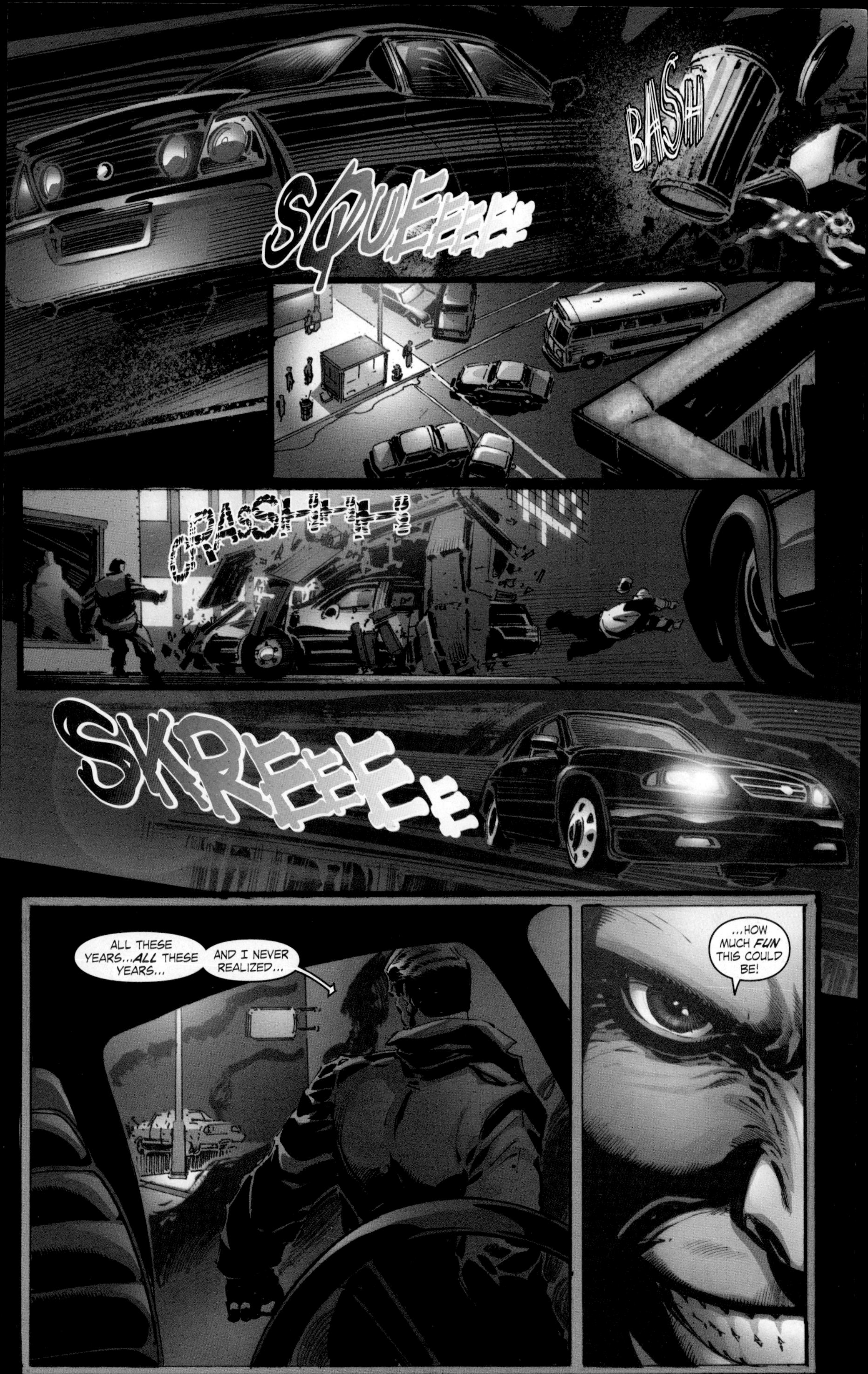
BASH
SQUEEEE
CRASH!!
SKREEEE
ALL THESE YEARS...ALL THESE YEARS...
AND I NEVER REALIZED...
...HOW MUCH FUN THIS COULD BE!

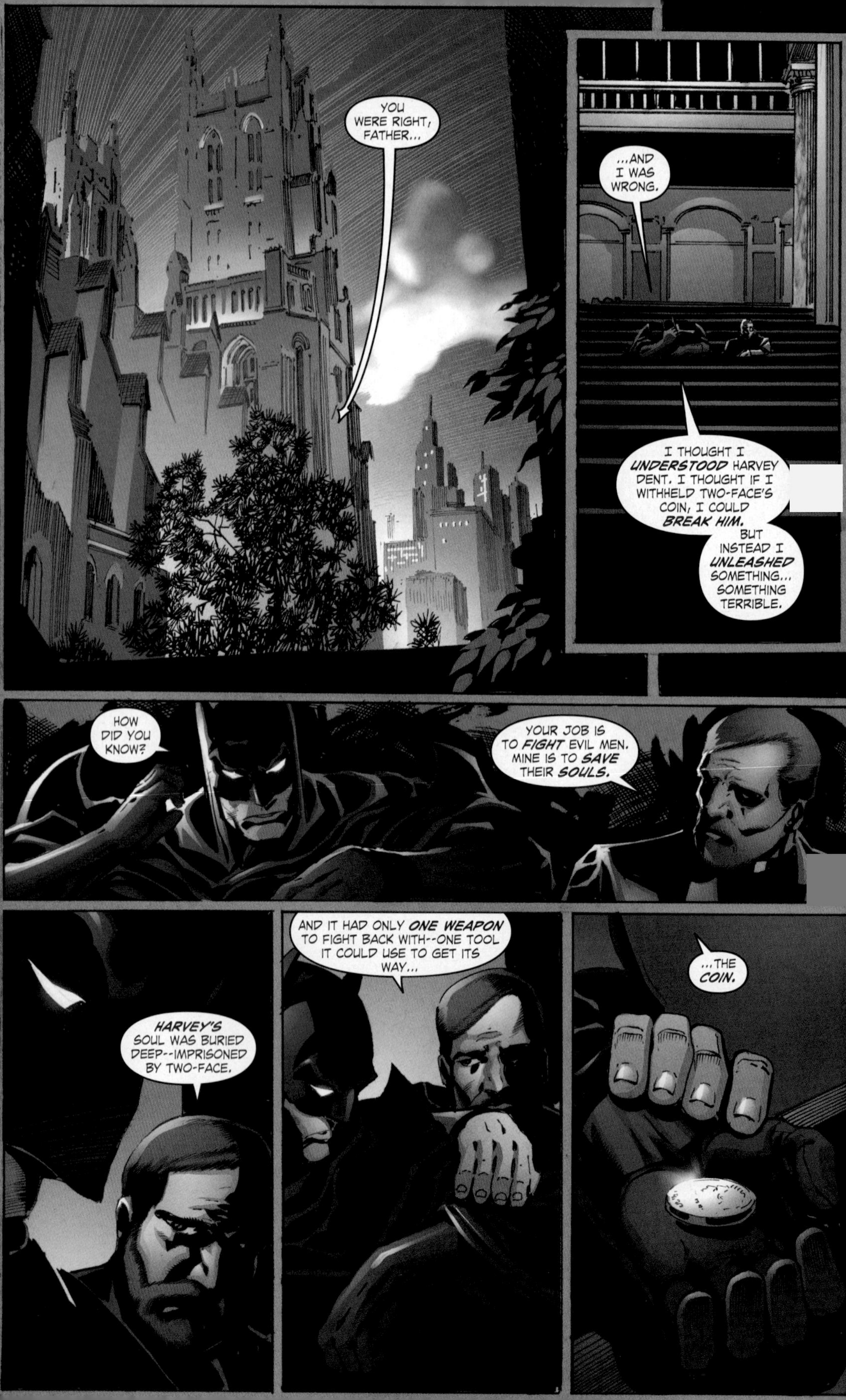
YOU WERE RIGHT, FATHER...
...AND I WAS WRONG.
I THOUGHT I UNDERSTOOD HARVEY DENT. I THOUGHT IF I WITHHELD TWO-FACE'S COIN, I COULD BREAK HIM.
BUT INSTEAD I UNLEASHED SOMETHING... SOMETHING TERRIBLE.
HOW DID YOU KNOW?
YOUR JOB IS TO FIGHT EVIL MEN. MINE IS TO SAVE THEIR SOULS.
HARVEY'S SOUL WAS BURIED DEEP--IMPRISONED BY TWO-FACE.
AND IT HAD ONLY ONE WEAPON TO FIGHT BACK WITH--ONE TOOL IT COULD USE TO GET ITS WAY...
...THE COIN.

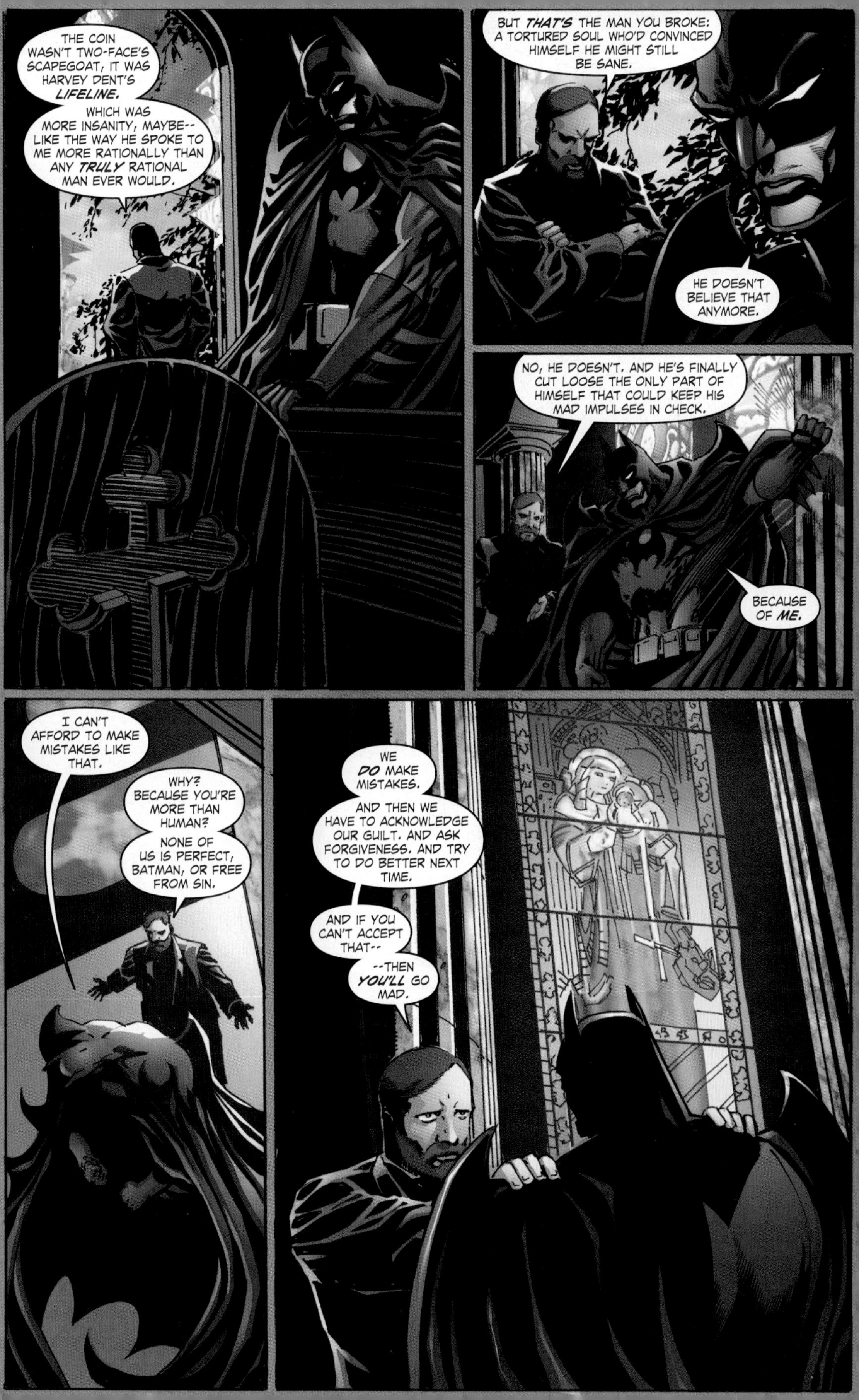

THE COIN WASN'T TWO-FACE'S SCAPEGOAT, IT WAS HARVEY DENT'S *LIFELINE.*
WHICH WAS MORE INSANITY, MAYBE-- LIKE THE WAY HE SPOKE TO ME MORE RATIONALLY THAN ANY *TRULY* RATIONAL MAN EVER WOULD.
BUT *THAT'S* THE MAN YOU BROKE: A TORTURED SOUL WHO'D CONVINCED HIMSELF HE MIGHT STILL BE SANE.
HE DOESN'T BELIEVE THAT ANYMORE.
NO, HE DOESN'T. AND HE'S FINALLY CUT LOOSE THE ONLY PART OF HIMSELF THAT COULD KEEP HIS MAD IMPULSES IN CHECK.
BECAUSE OF *ME.*
I CAN'T AFFORD TO MAKE MISTAKES LIKE THAT.
WHY? BECAUSE YOU'RE MORE THAN HUMAN?
NONE OF US IS PERFECT, BATMAN, OR FREE FROM SIN.
WE *DO* MAKE MISTAKES.
AND THEN WE HAVE TO ACKNOWLEDGE OUR GUILT. AND ASK FORGIVENESS. AND TRY TO DO BETTER NEXT TIME.
AND IF YOU CAN'T ACCEPT THAT--
--THEN *YOU'LL* GO MAD.

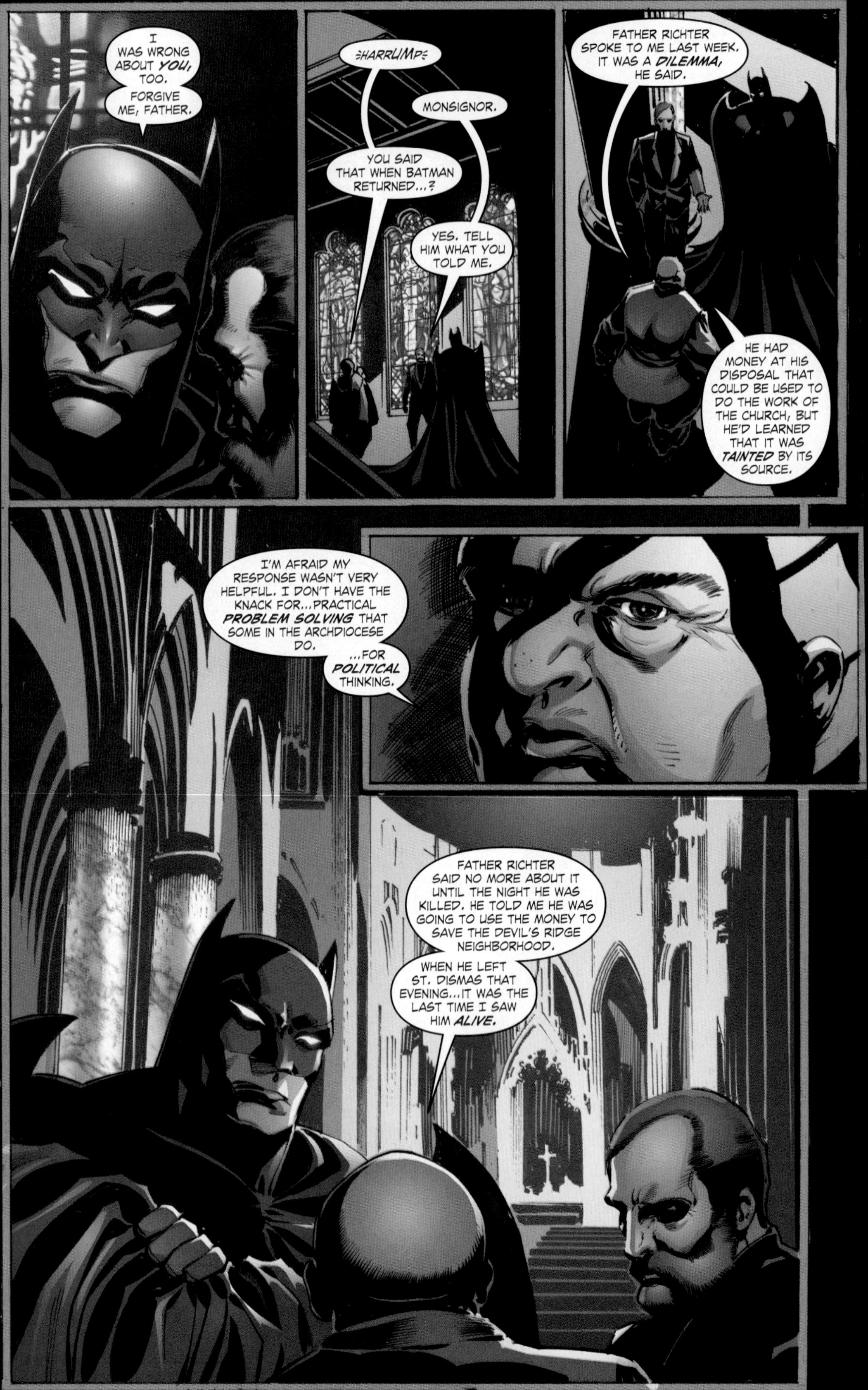
I WAS WRONG ABOUT YOU, TOO.
FORGIVE ME, FATHER.
HARRUMPH
MONSIGNOR.
YOU SAID THAT WHEN BATMAN RETURNED...?
YES. TELL HIM WHAT YOU TOLD ME.
FATHER RICHTER SPOKE TO ME LAST WEEK. IT WAS A DILEMMA, HE SAID.
HE HAD MONEY AT HIS DISPOSAL THAT COULD BE USED TO DO THE WORK OF THE CHURCH, BUT HE'D LEARNED THAT IT WAS TAINTED BY ITS SOURCE.
I'M AFRAID MY RESPONSE WASN'T VERY HELPFUL. I DON'T HAVE THE KNACK FOR...PRACTICAL PROBLEM SOLVING THAT SOME IN THE ARCHDIOCESE DO.
...FOR POLITICAL THINKING.
FATHER RICHTER SAID NO MORE ABOUT IT UNTIL THE NIGHT HE WAS KILLED. HE TOLD ME HE WAS GOING TO USE THE MONEY TO SAVE THE DEVIL'S RIDGE NEIGHBORHOOD.
WHEN HE LEFT ST. DISMAS THAT EVENING...IT WAS THE LAST TIME I SAW HIM ALIVE.

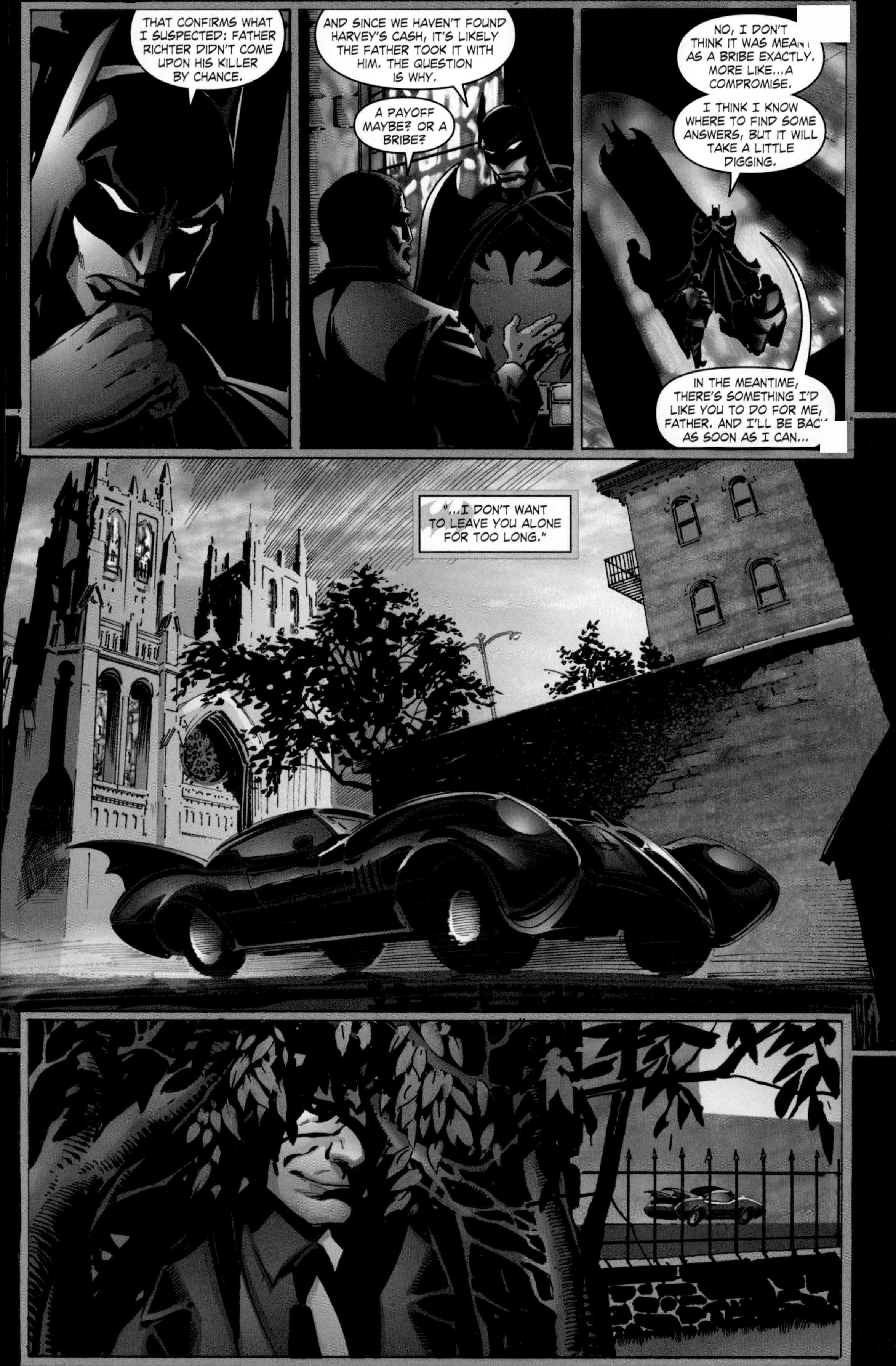
THAT CONFIRMS WHAT I SUSPECTED: FATHER RICHTER DIDN'T COME UPON HIS KILLER BY CHANCE.
AND SINCE WE HAVEN'T FOUND HARVEY'S CASH, IT'S LIKELY THE FATHER TOOK IT WITH HIM. THE QUESTION IS WHY.
A PAYOFF MAYBE? OR A BRIBE?
NO, I DON'T THINK IT WAS MEAN AS A BRIBE EXACTLY. MORE LIKE...A COMPROMISE.
I THINK I KNOW WHERE TO FIND SOME ANSWERS, BUT IT WILL TAKE A LITTLE DIGGING.
IN THE MEANTIME, THERE'S SOMETHING I'D LIKE YOU TO DO FOR ME, FATHER. AND I'LL BE BAC AS SOON AS I CAN...
"...I DON'T WANT TO LEAVE YOU ALONE FOR TOO LONG."

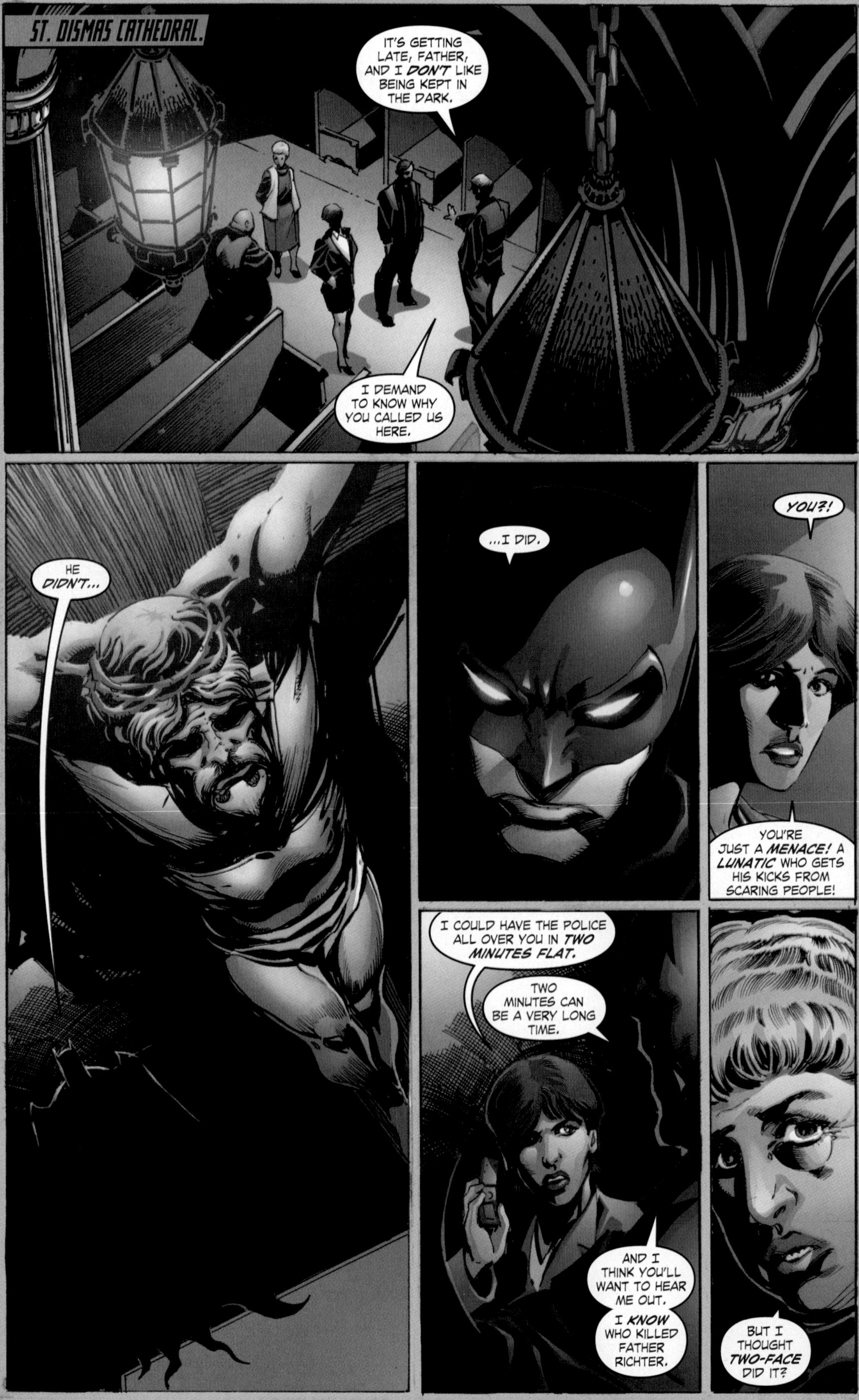
ST. DISMAS CATHEDRAL.
IT'S GETTING LATE, FATHER, AND I DON'T LIKE BEING KEPT IN THE DARK.
I DEMAND TO KNOW WHY YOU CALLED US HERE.
HE DIDN'T...
...I DID.
YOU?!
YOU'RE JUST A MENACE! A LUNATIC WHO GETS HIS KICKS FROM SCARING PEOPLE!
I COULD HAVE THE POLICE ALL OVER YOU IN TWO MINUTES FLAT.
TWO MINUTES CAN BE A VERY LONG TIME.
AND I THINK YOU'LL WANT TO HEAR ME OUT.
I KNOW WHO KILLED FATHER RICHTER.
BUT I THOUGHT TWO-FACE DID IT?

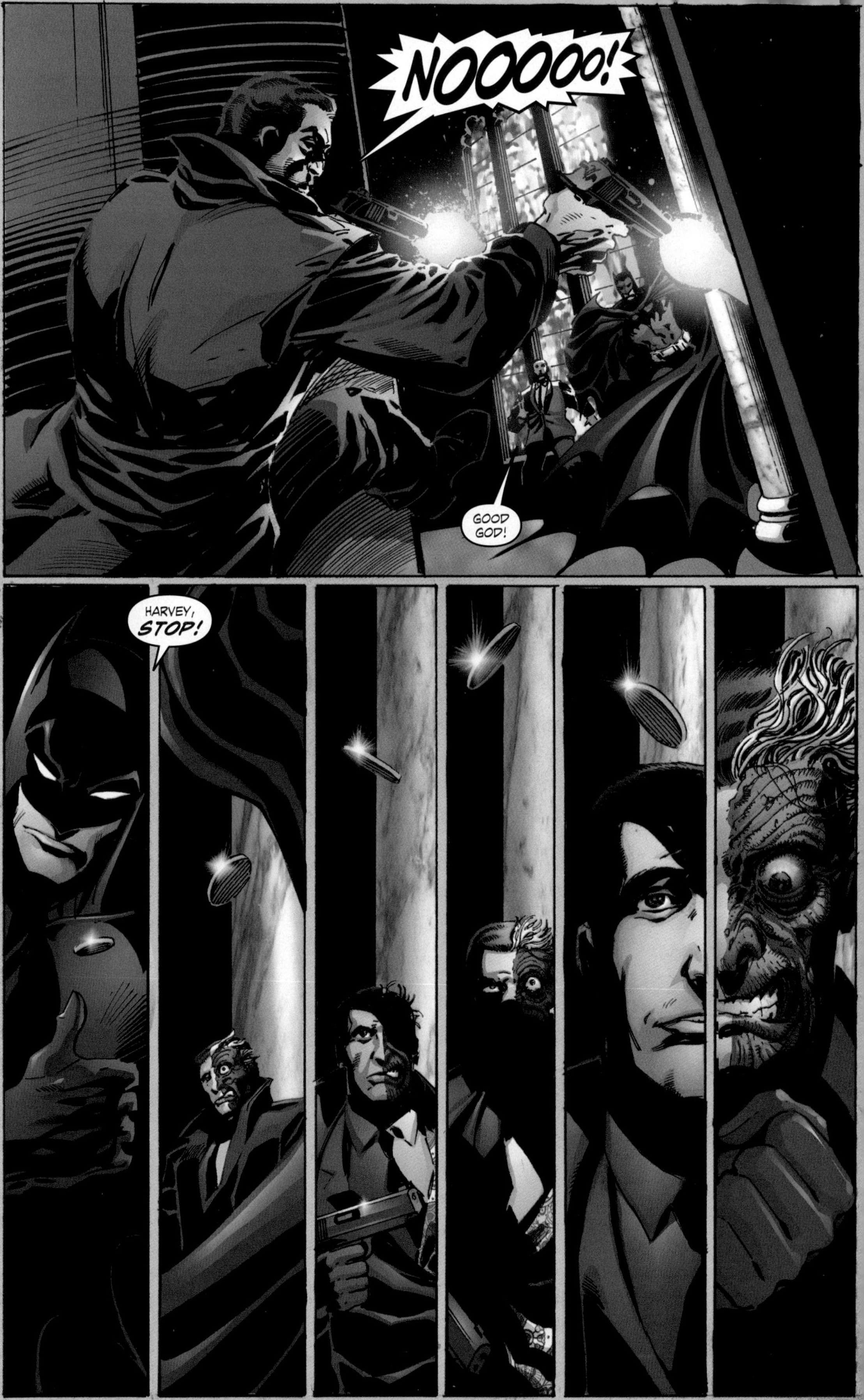
NOOOOO!
GOOD GOD!
HARVEY, STOP!

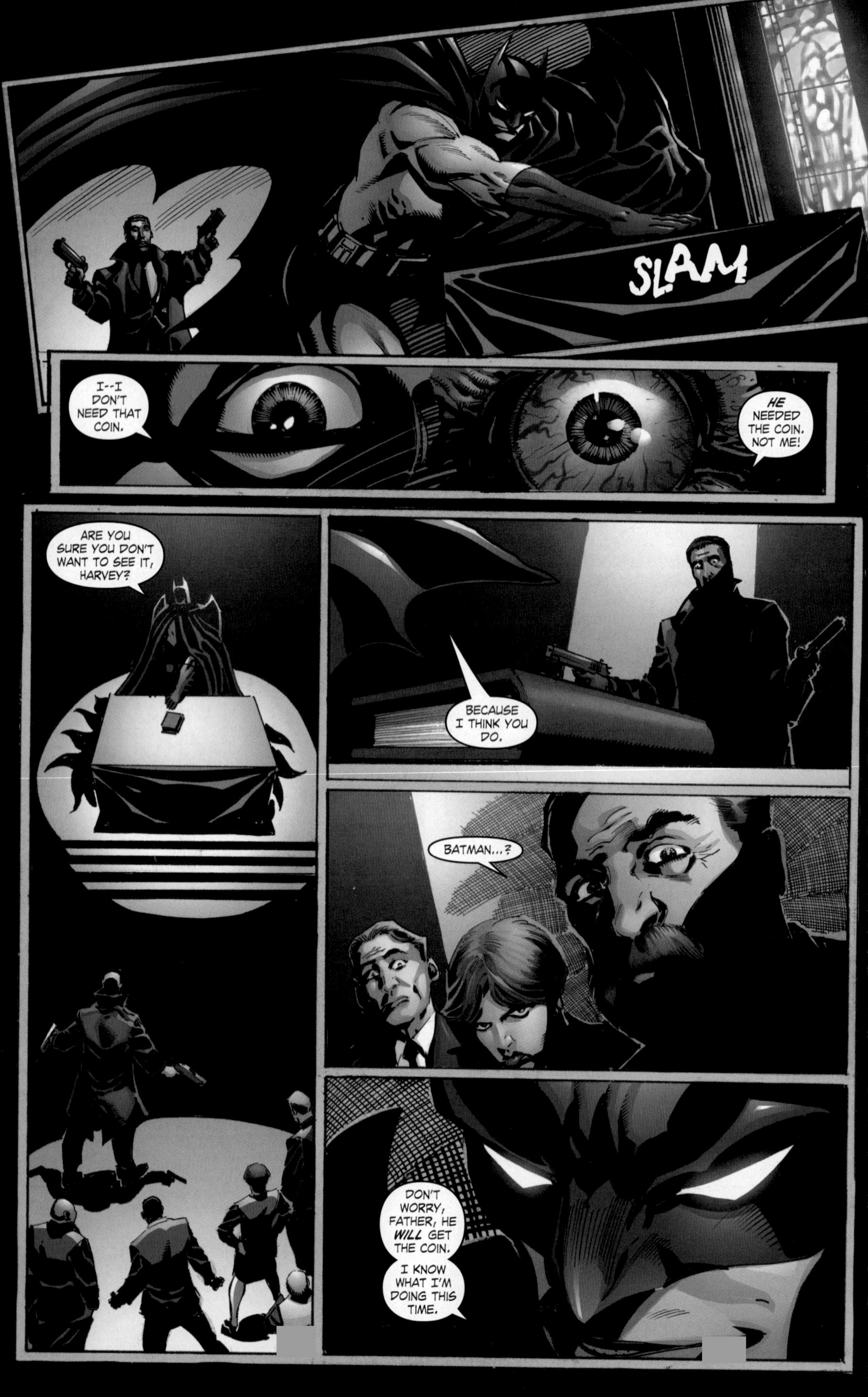
SLAM
I--I DON'T NEED THAT COIN.
HE NEEDED THE COIN. NOT ME!
ARE YOU SURE YOU DON'T WANT TO SEE IT, HARVEY?
BECAUSE I THINK YOU DO.
BATMAN...?
DON'T WORRY, FATHER, HE WILL GET THE COIN.
I KNOW WHAT I'M DOING THIS TIME.

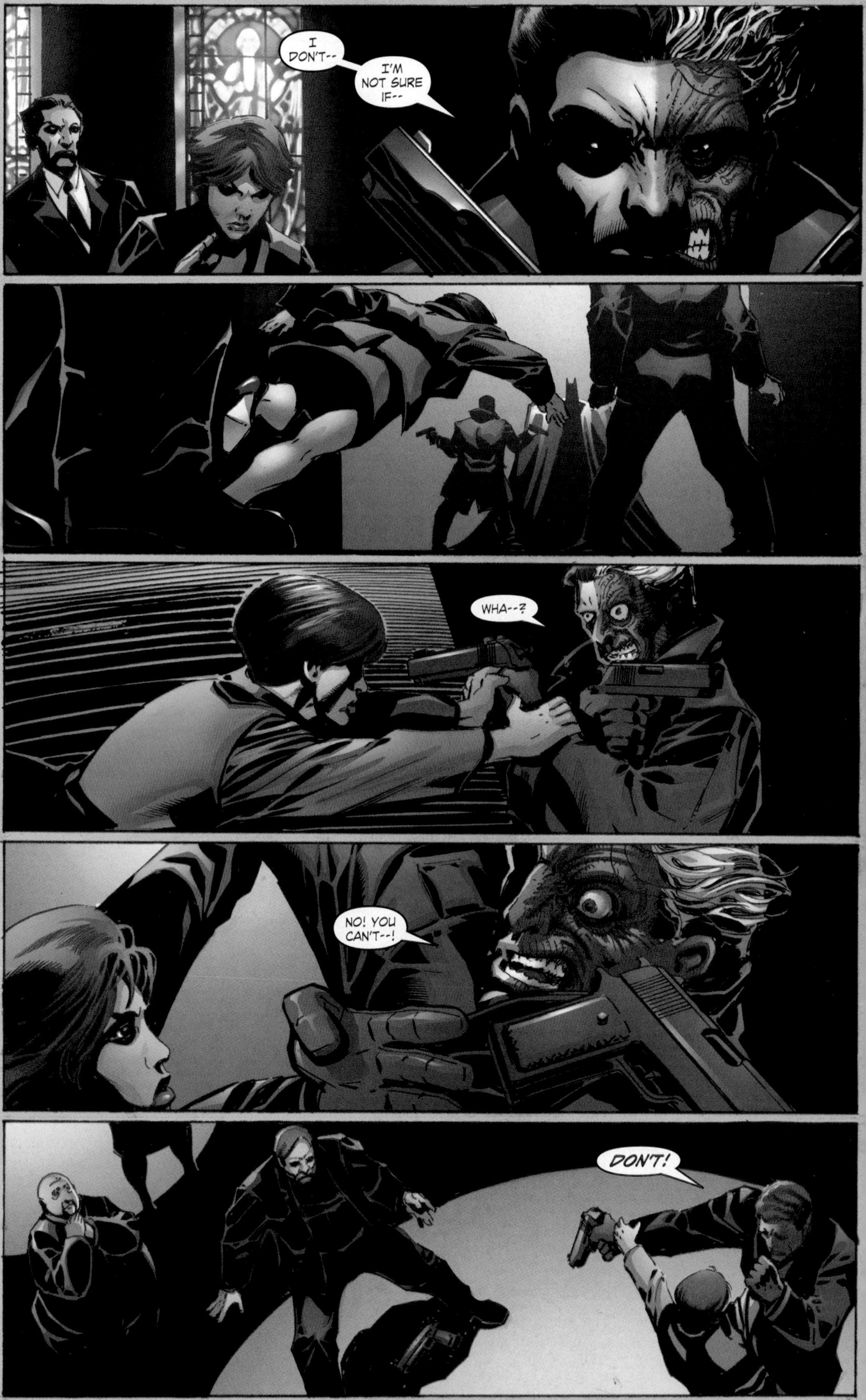
I DON'T--
I'M NOT SURE IF--
WHA--?
NO! YOU CAN'T--!
DON'T!

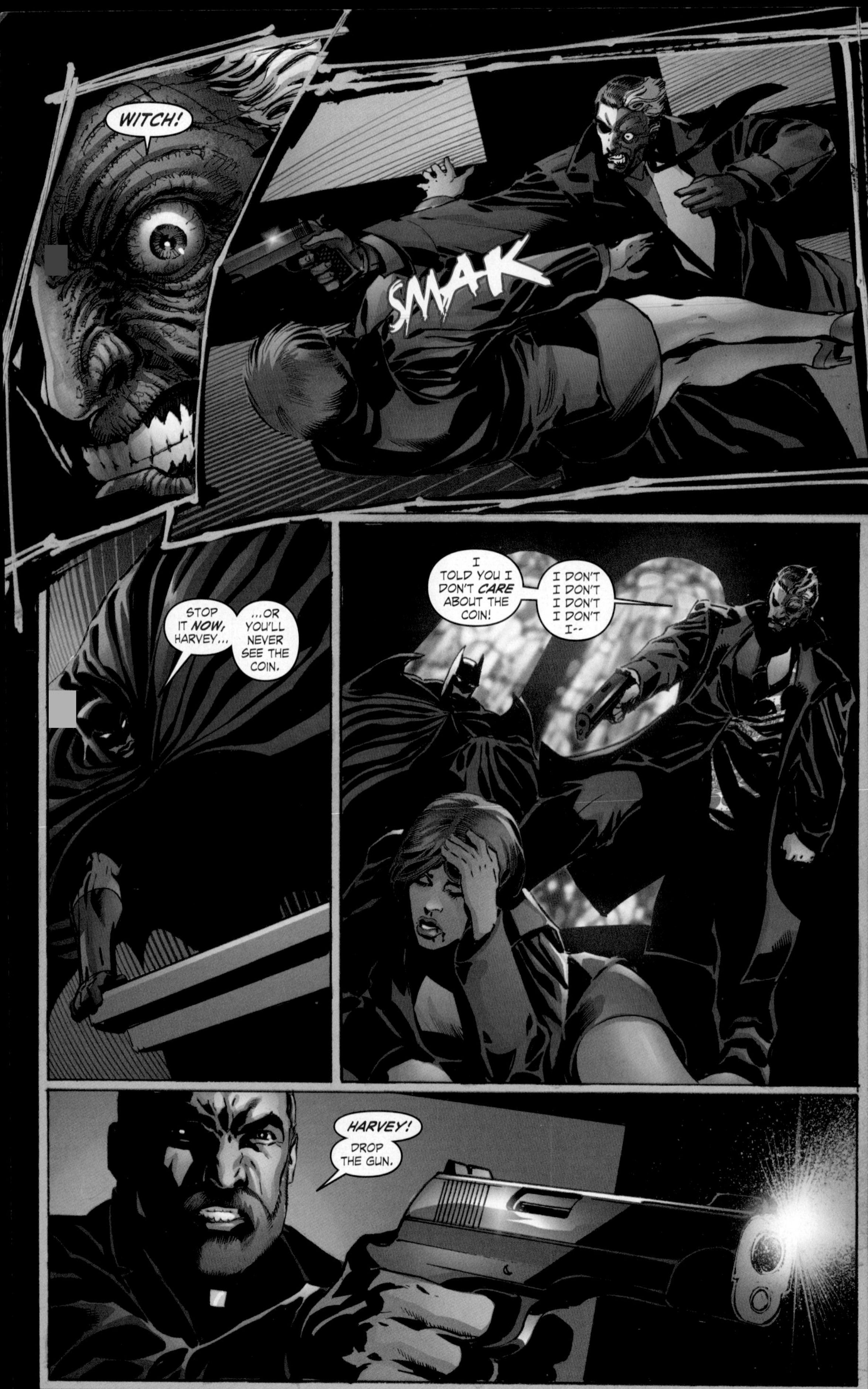
WITCH!
SMAK
STOP IT NOW, HARVEY...
...OR YOU'LL NEVER SEE THE COIN.
I TOLD YOU I DON'T CARE ABOUT THE COIN!
I DON'T I DON'T I DON'T I DON'T I--
HARVEY!
DROP THE GUN.

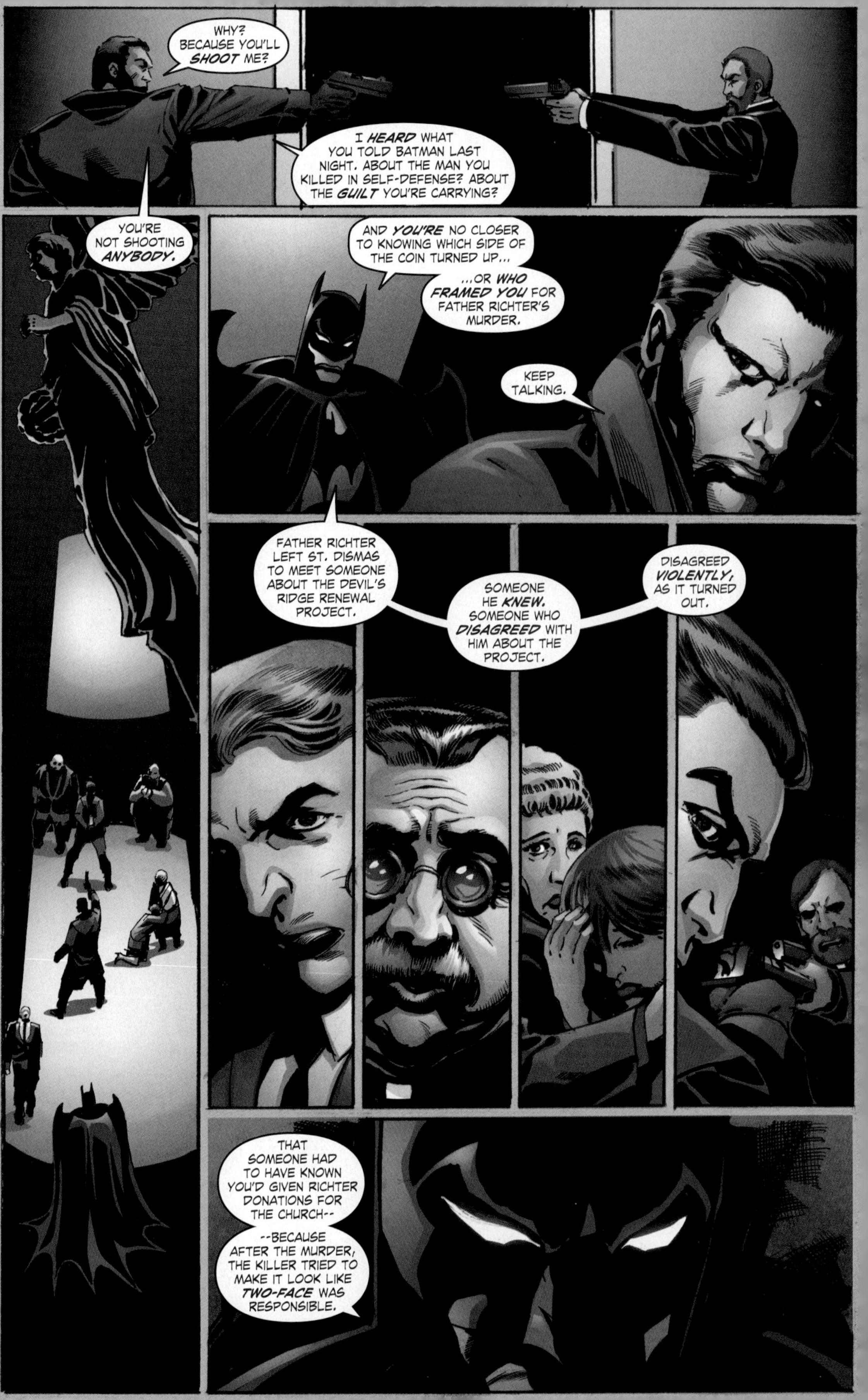
WHY? BECAUSE YOU'LL SHOOT ME?
I HEARD WHAT YOU TOLD BATMAN LAST NIGHT. ABOUT THE MAN YOU KILLED IN SELF-DEFENSE? ABOUT THE GUILT YOU'RE CARRYING?
YOU'RE NOT SHOOTING ANYBODY.
AND YOU'RE NO CLOSER TO KNOWING WHICH SIDE OF THE COIN TURNED UP...
...OR WHO FRAMED YOU FOR FATHER RICHTER'S MURDER.
KEEP TALKING.
FATHER RICHTER LEFT ST. DISMAS TO MEET SOMEONE ABOUT THE DEVIL'S RIDGE RENEWAL PROJECT.
SOMEONE HE KNEW. SOMEONE WHO DISAGREED WITH HIM ABOUT THE PROJECT.
DISAGREED VIOLENTLY, AS IT TURNED OUT.
THAT SOMEONE HAD TO HAVE KNOWN YOU'D GIVEN RICHTER DONATIONS FOR THE CHURCH--
--BECAUSE AFTER THE MURDER, THE KILLER TRIED TO MAKE IT LOOK LIKE TWO-FACE WAS RESPONSIBLE.

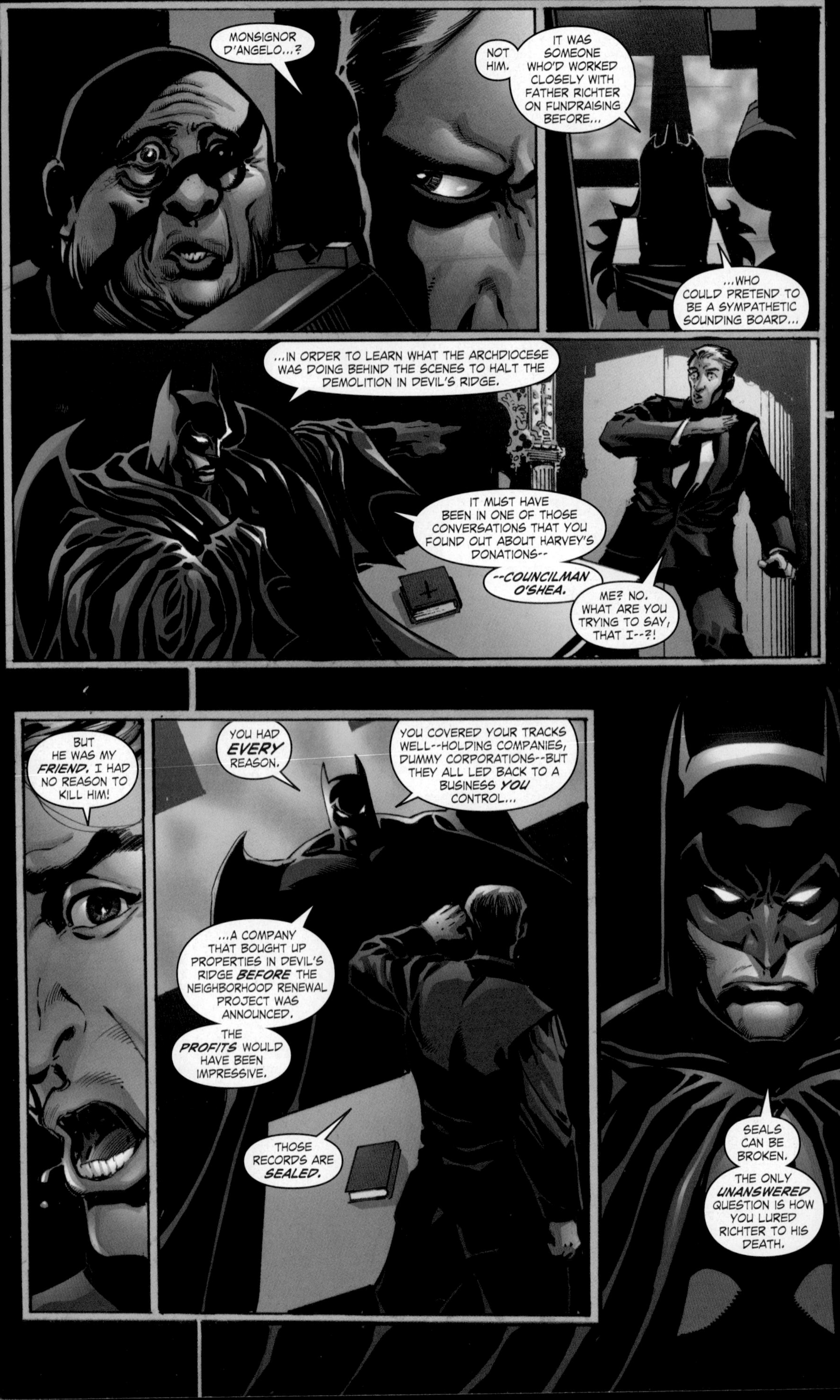
MONSIGNOR D'ANGELO...?
NOT HIM.
IT WAS SOMEONE WHO'D WORKED CLOSELY WITH FATHER RICHTER ON FUNDRAISING BEFORE...
...WHO COULD PRETEND TO BE A SYMPATHETIC SOUNDING BOARD...
...IN ORDER TO LEARN WHAT THE ARCHDIOCESE WAS DOING BEHIND THE SCENES TO HALT THE DEMOLITION IN DEVIL'S RIDGE.
IT MUST HAVE BEEN IN ONE OF THOSE CONVERSATIONS THAT YOU FOUND OUT ABOUT HARVEY'S DONATIONS--
--COUNCILMAN O'SHEA.
ME? NO. WHAT ARE YOU TRYING TO SAY, THAT I--?!
BUT HE WAS MY FRIEND. I HAD NO REASON TO KILL HIM!
YOU HAD EVERY REASON.
YOU COVERED YOUR TRACKS WELL--HOLDING COMPANIES, DUMMY CORPORATIONS--BUT THEY ALL LED BACK TO A BUSINESS YOU CONTROL...
...A COMPANY THAT BOUGHT UP PROPERTIES IN DEVIL'S RIDGE BEFORE THE NEIGHBORHOOD RENEWAL PROJECT WAS ANNOUNCED.
THE PROFITS WOULD HAVE BEEN IMPRESSIVE.
THOSE RECORDS ARE SEALED.
SEALS CAN BE BROKEN.
THE ONLY UNANSWERED QUESTION IS HOW YOU LURED RICHTER TO HIS DEATH.

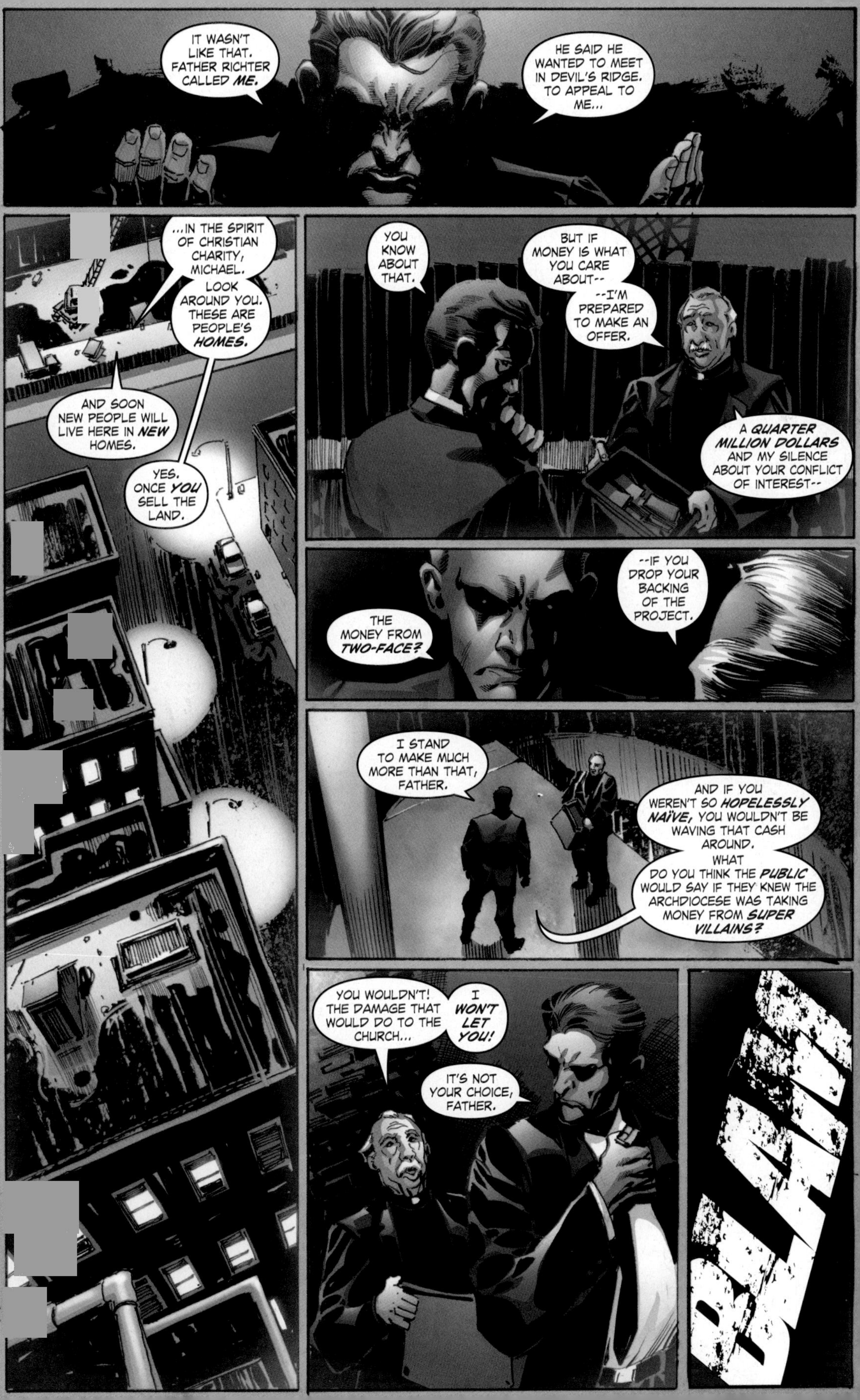

IT WASN'T LIKE THAT. FATHER RICHTER CALLED *ME.*
HE SAID HE WANTED TO MEET IN DEVIL'S RIDGE. TO APPEAL TO ME...
...IN THE SPIRIT OF CHRISTIAN CHARITY, MICHAEL.
LOOK AROUND YOU. THESE ARE PEOPLE'S *HOMES.*
AND SOON NEW PEOPLE WILL LIVE HERE IN *NEW* HOMES.
YES. ONCE *YOU* SELL THE LAND.
YOU KNOW ABOUT THAT.
BUT IF MONEY IS WHAT YOU CARE ABOUT--
--I'M PREPARED TO MAKE AN OFFER.
A *QUARTER MILLION DOLLARS* AND MY SILENCE ABOUT YOUR CONFLICT OF INTEREST--
--IF YOU DROP YOUR BACKING OF THE PROJECT.
THE MONEY FROM *TWO-FACE?*
I STAND TO MAKE MUCH MORE THAN THAT, FATHER.
AND IF YOU WEREN'T SO *HOPELESSLY NAÏVE,* YOU WOULDN'T BE WAVING THAT CASH AROUND.
WHAT DO YOU THINK THE *PUBLIC* WOULD SAY IF THEY KNEW THE ARCHDIOCESE WAS TAKING MONEY FROM *SUPER VILLAINS?*
YOU WOULDN'T! THE DAMAGE THAT WOULD DO TO THE CHURCH...
I *WON'T LET YOU!*
IT'S NOT YOUR CHOICE, FATHER.

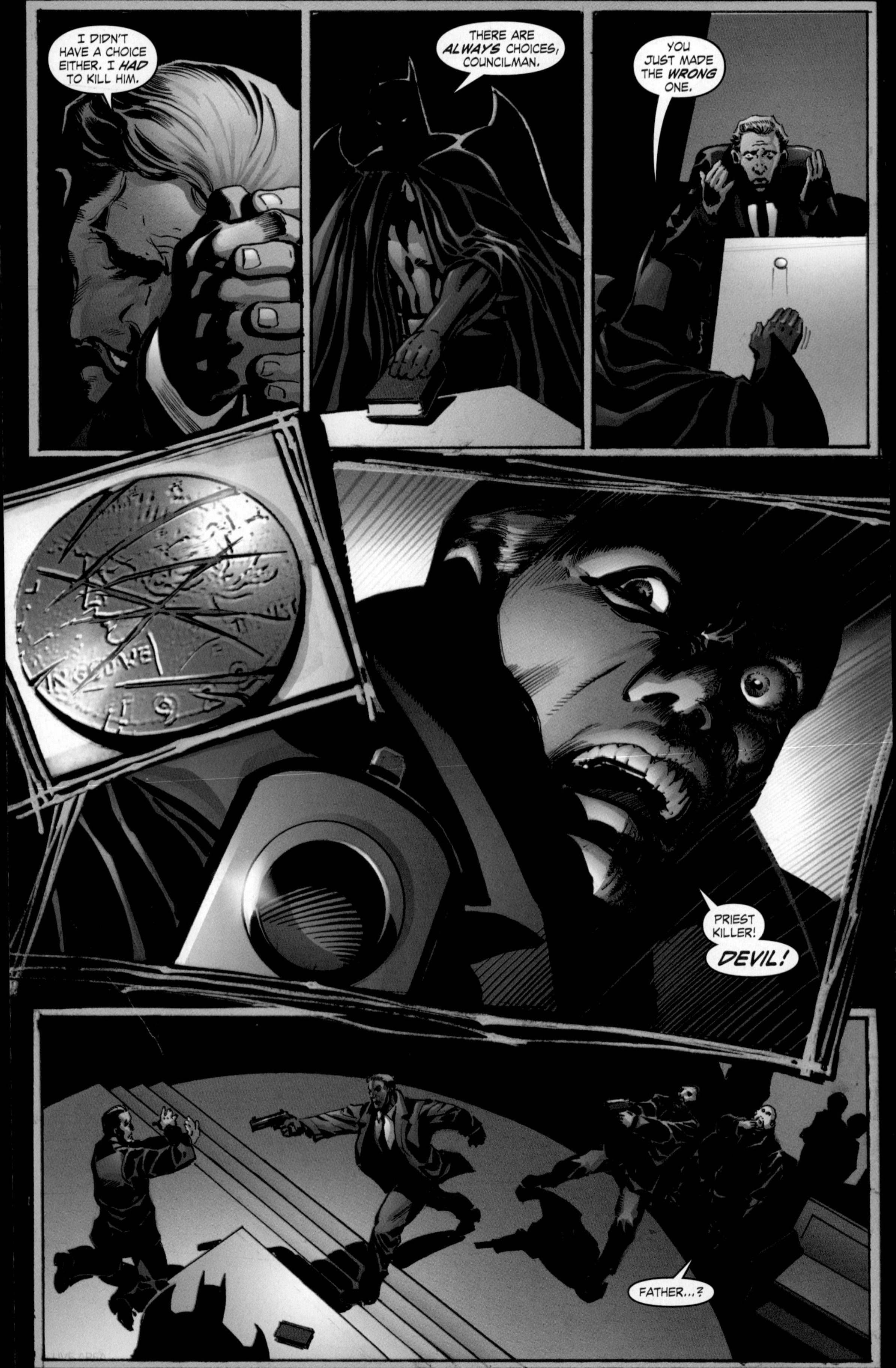
I DIDN'T HAVE A CHOICE EITHER. I HAD TO KILL HIM.
THERE ARE ALWAYS CHOICES, COUNCILMAN.
YOU JUST MADE THE WRONG ONE.
PRIEST KILLER!
DEVIL!
FATHER...?

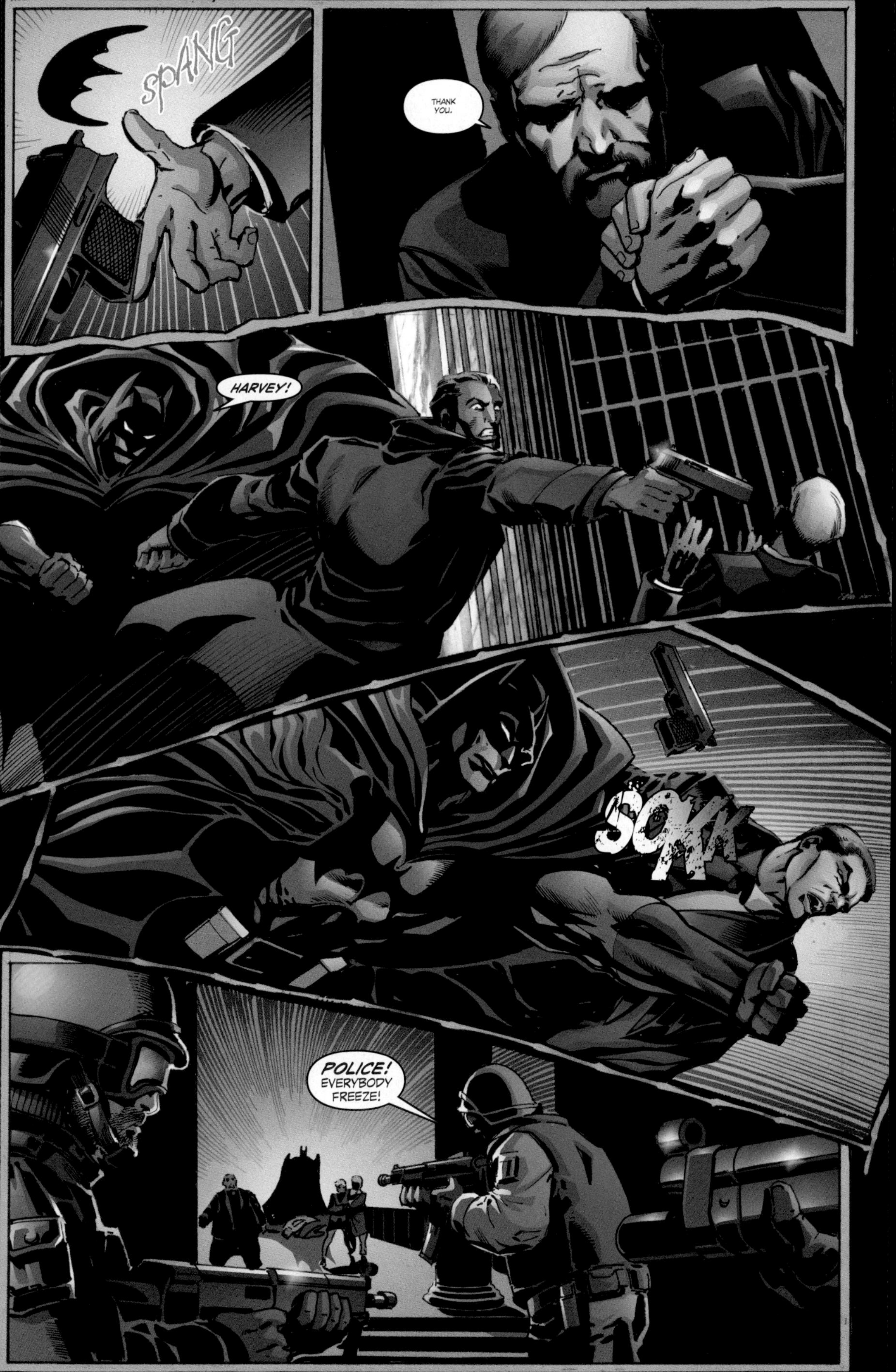
SPANG
THANK YOU.
HARVEY!
SOKK
POLICE! EVERYBODY FREEZE!

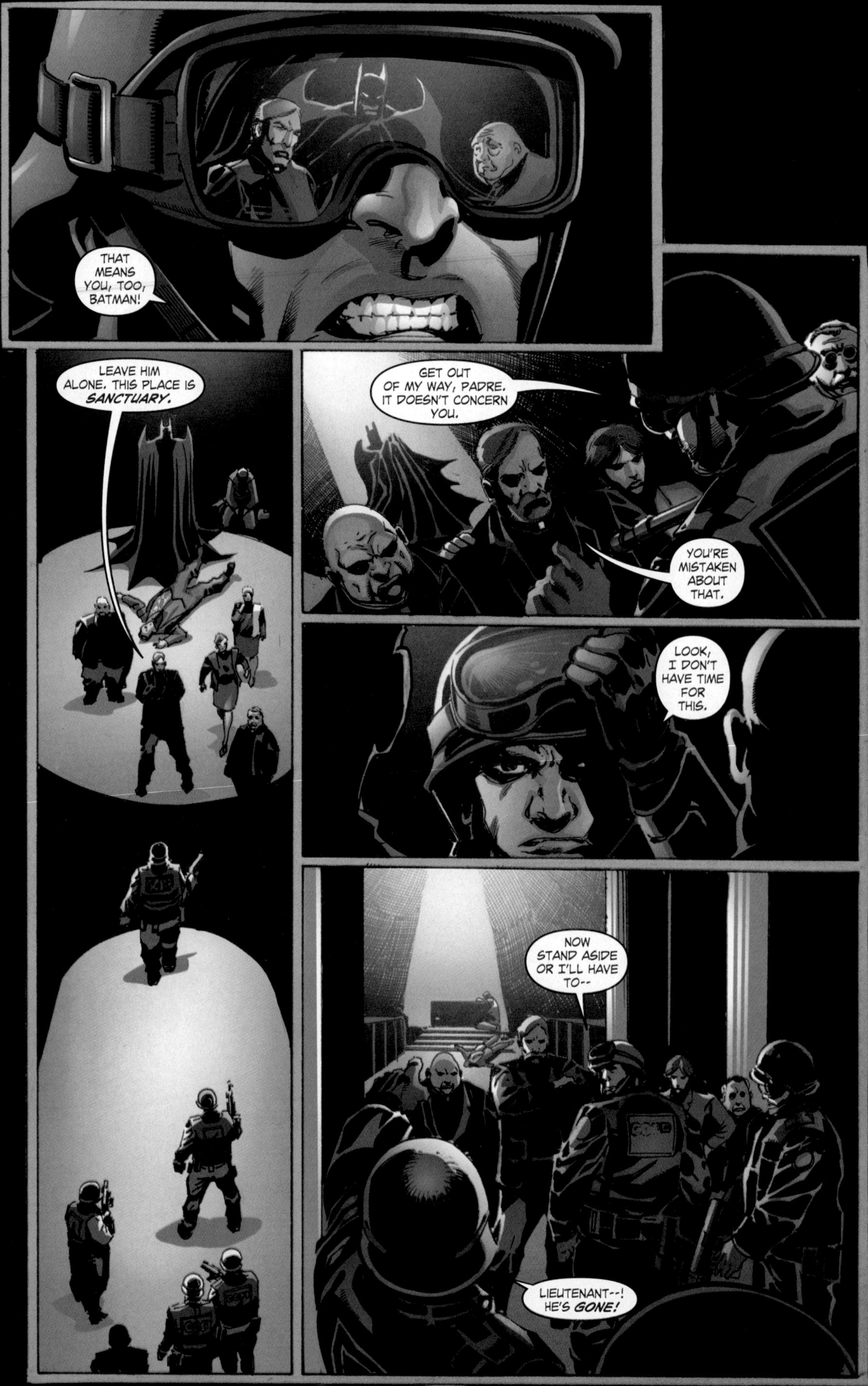
THAT MEANS YOU, TOO, BATMAN!
LEAVE HIM ALONE. THIS PLACE IS *SANCTUARY.*
GET OUT OF MY WAY, PADRE. IT DOESN'T CONCERN YOU.
YOU'RE MISTAKEN ABOUT THAT.
LOOK, I DON'T HAVE TIME FOR THIS.
NOW STAND ASIDE OR I'LL HAVE TO--
LIEUTENANT--! HE'S *GONE!*

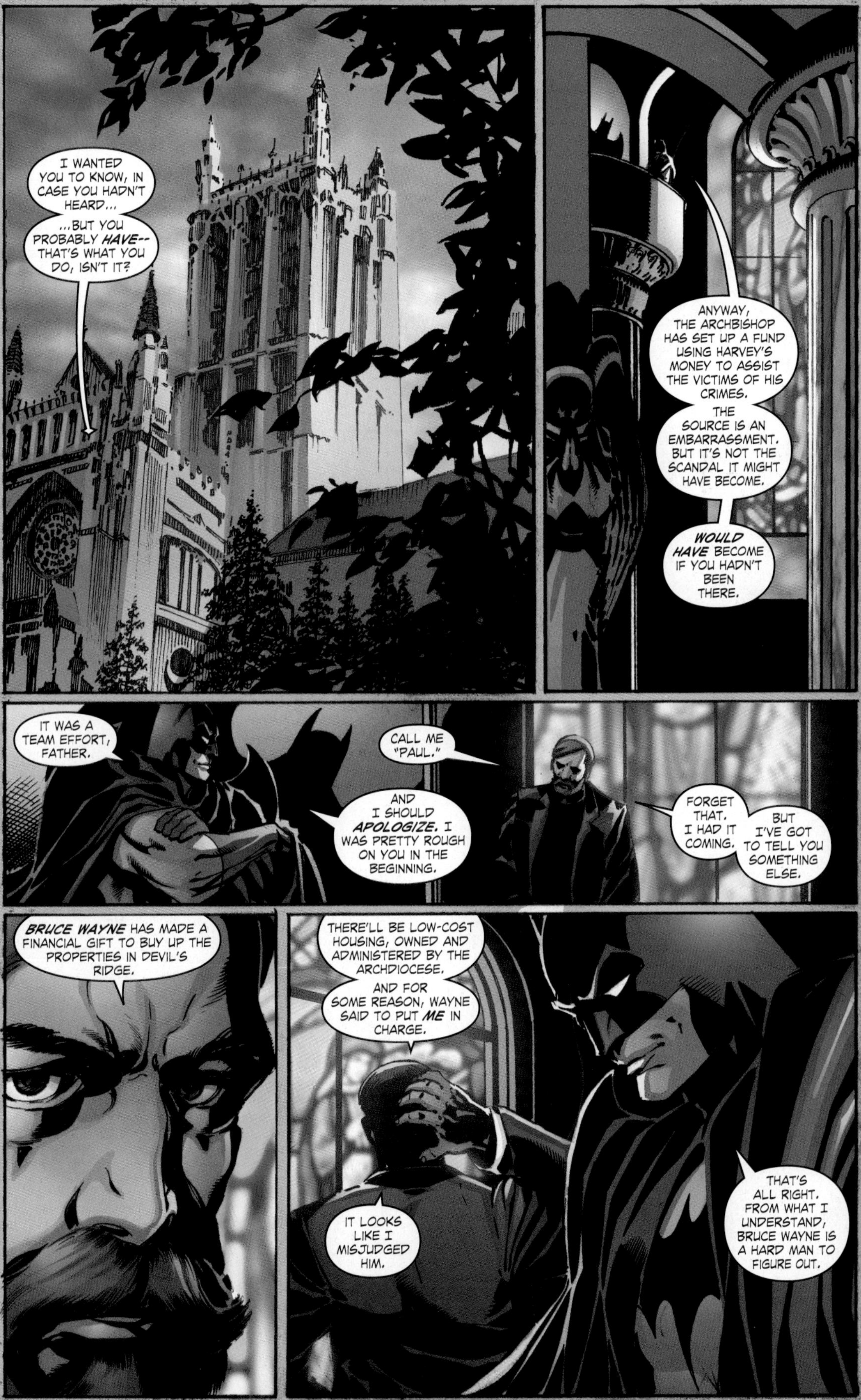
I WANTED YOU TO KNOW, IN CASE YOU HADN'T HEARD...
...BUT YOU PROBABLY **HAVE**-- THAT'S WHAT YOU DO, ISN'T IT?
ANYWAY, THE ARCHBISHOP HAS SET UP A FUND USING HARVEY'S MONEY TO ASSIST THE VICTIMS OF HIS CRIMES.
THE SOURCE IS AN EMBARRASSMENT. BUT IT'S NOT THE SCANDAL IT MIGHT HAVE BECOME.
WOULD HAVE BECOME IF YOU HADN'T BEEN THERE.
IT WAS A TEAM EFFORT, FATHER.
CALL ME "PAUL."
AND I SHOULD **APOLOGIZE.** I WAS PRETTY ROUGH ON YOU IN THE BEGINNING.
FORGET THAT. I HAD IT COMING.
BUT I'VE GOT TO TELL YOU SOMETHING ELSE.
BRUCE WAYNE HAS MADE A FINANCIAL GIFT TO BUY UP THE PROPERTIES IN DEVIL'S RIDGE.
THERE'LL BE LOW-COST HOUSING, OWNED AND ADMINISTERED BY THE ARCHDIOCESE.
AND FOR SOME REASON, WAYNE SAID TO PUT **ME** IN CHARGE.
IT LOOKS LIKE I MISJUDGED HIM.
THAT'S ALL RIGHT. FROM WHAT I UNDERSTAND, BRUCE WAYNE IS A HARD MAN TO FIGURE OUT.

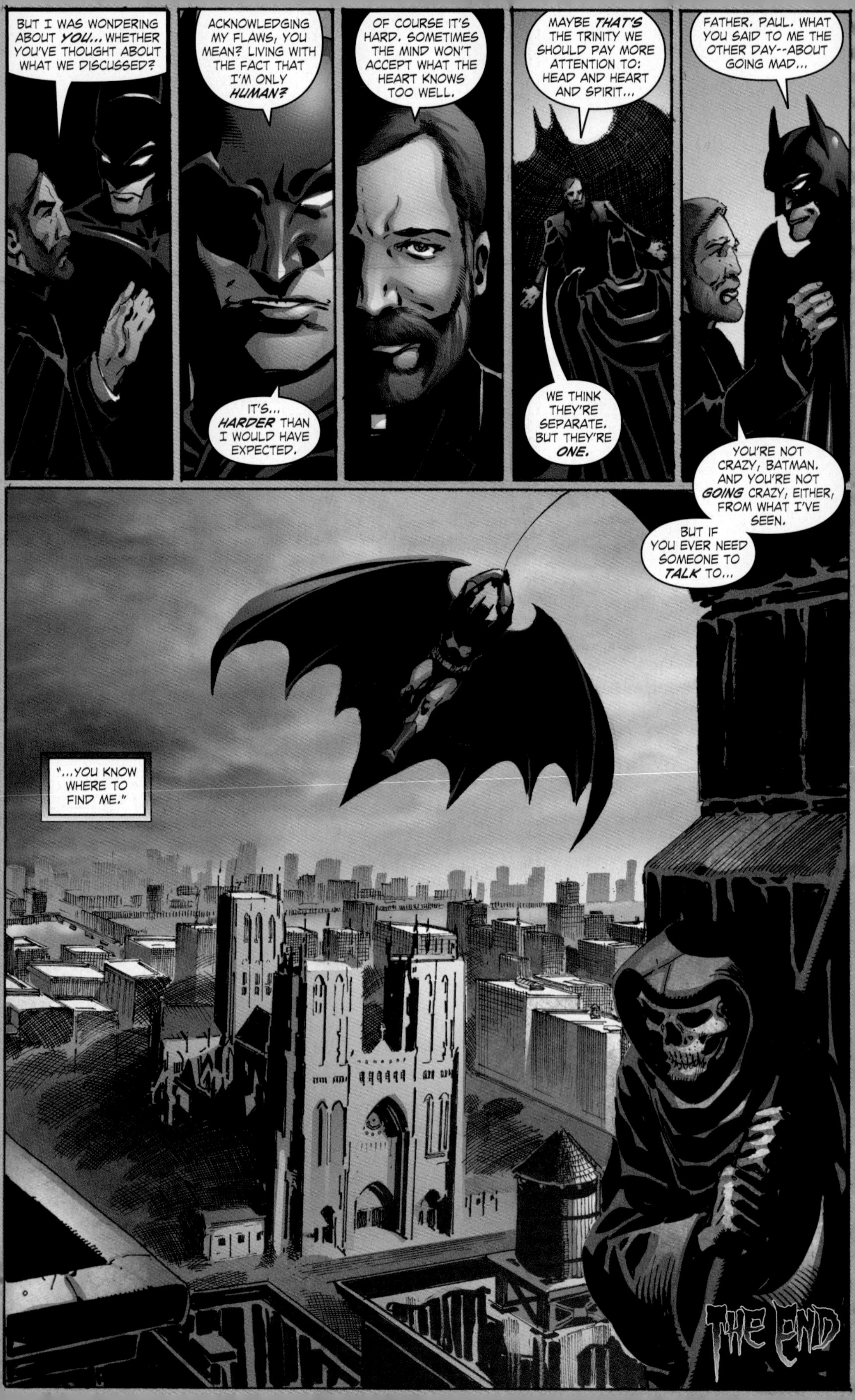
BUT I WAS WONDERING ABOUT YOU... WHETHER YOU'VE THOUGHT ABOUT WHAT WE DISCUSSED?
ACKNOWLEDGING MY FLAWS, YOU MEAN? LIVING WITH THE FACT THAT I'M ONLY HUMAN?
IT'S... HARDER THAN I WOULD HAVE EXPECTED.
OF COURSE IT'S HARD. SOMETIMES THE MIND WON'T ACCEPT WHAT THE HEART KNOWS TOO WELL.
MAYBE THAT'S THE TRINITY WE SHOULD PAY MORE ATTENTION TO: HEAD AND HEART AND SPIRIT...
WE THINK THEY'RE SEPARATE. BUT THEY'RE ONE.
FATHER. PAUL. WHAT YOU SAID TO ME THE OTHER DAY--ABOUT GOING MAD...
YOU'RE NOT CRAZY, BATMAN. AND YOU'RE NOT GOING CRAZY, EITHER, FROM WHAT I'VE SEEN.
BUT IF YOU EVER NEED SOMEONE TO TALK TO...
"...YOU KNOW WHERE TO FIND ME."
THE END

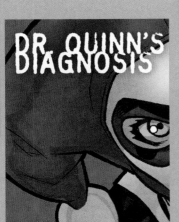

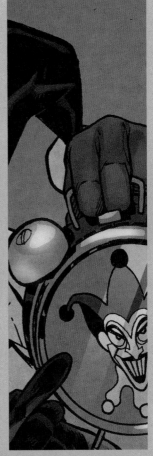

DR. QUINN'S DIAGNOSIS

JIM ZUBKAVICH
Writer

NEIL GOOGE
Artist

KATHRYN LAYNO
Colorist

SAIDA TEMOFONTE
Letterer

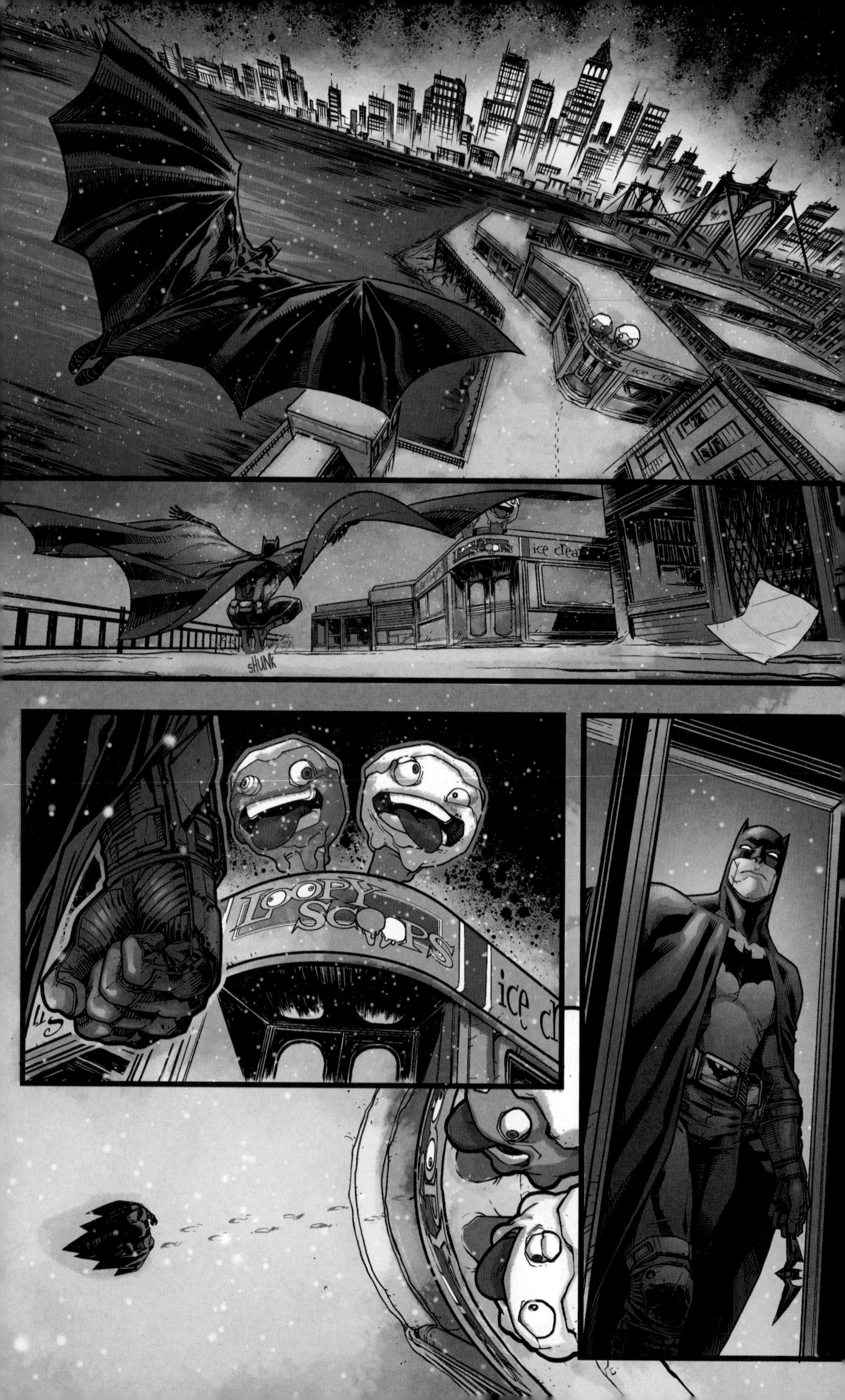
sHUNK
LOOPY SCOOPS

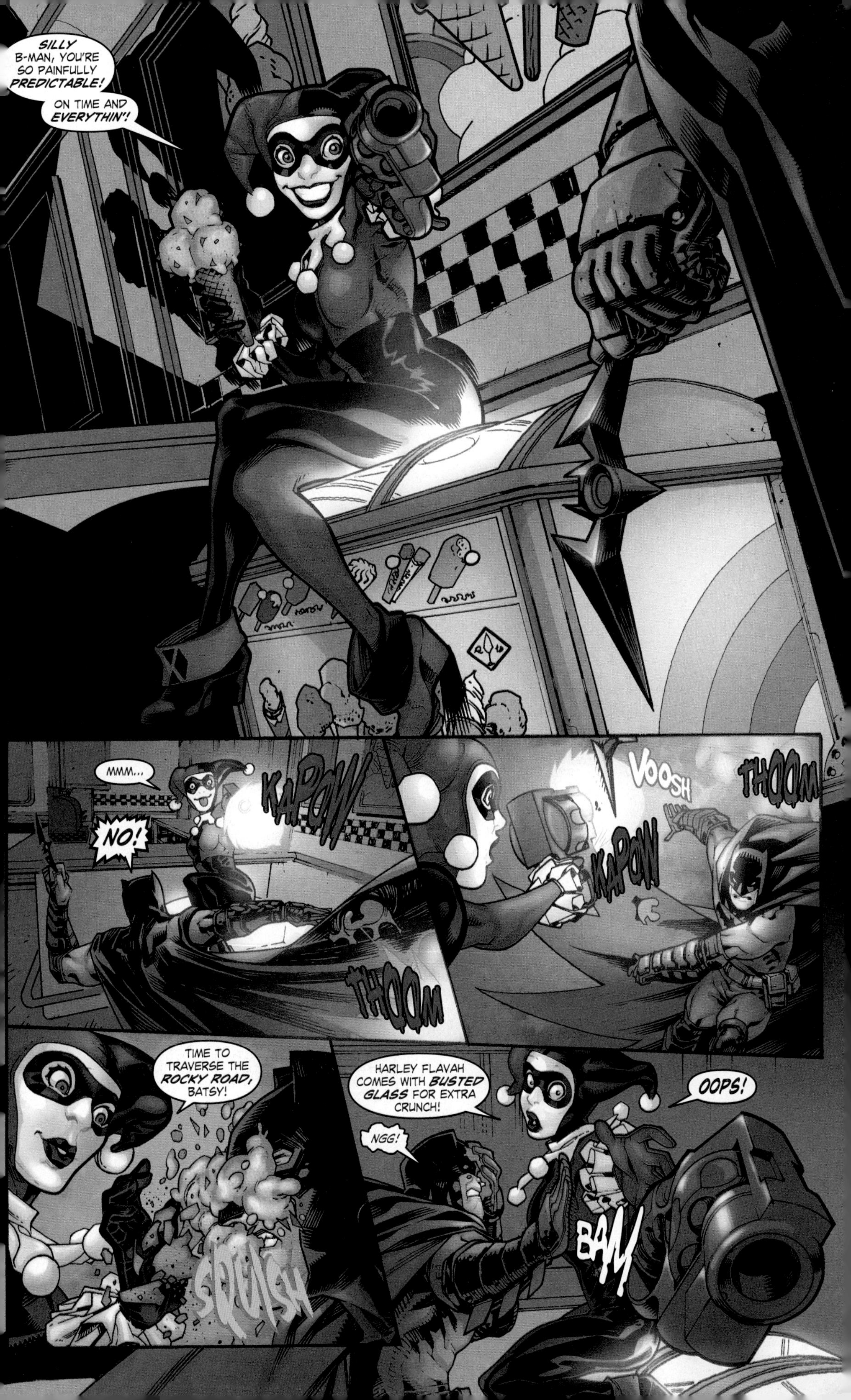
SILLY B-MAN, YOU'RE SO PAINFULLY PREDICTABLE!
ON TIME AND EVERYTHIN'!
MMM...
KAPOW
NO!
VOOSH
THOOM
KAPOW
THOOM
TIME TO TRAVERSE THE ROCKY ROAD, BATSY!
SQUISH
HARLEY FLAVAH COMES WITH BUSTED GLASS FOR EXTRA CRUNCH!
OOPS!
NGG!
BAM

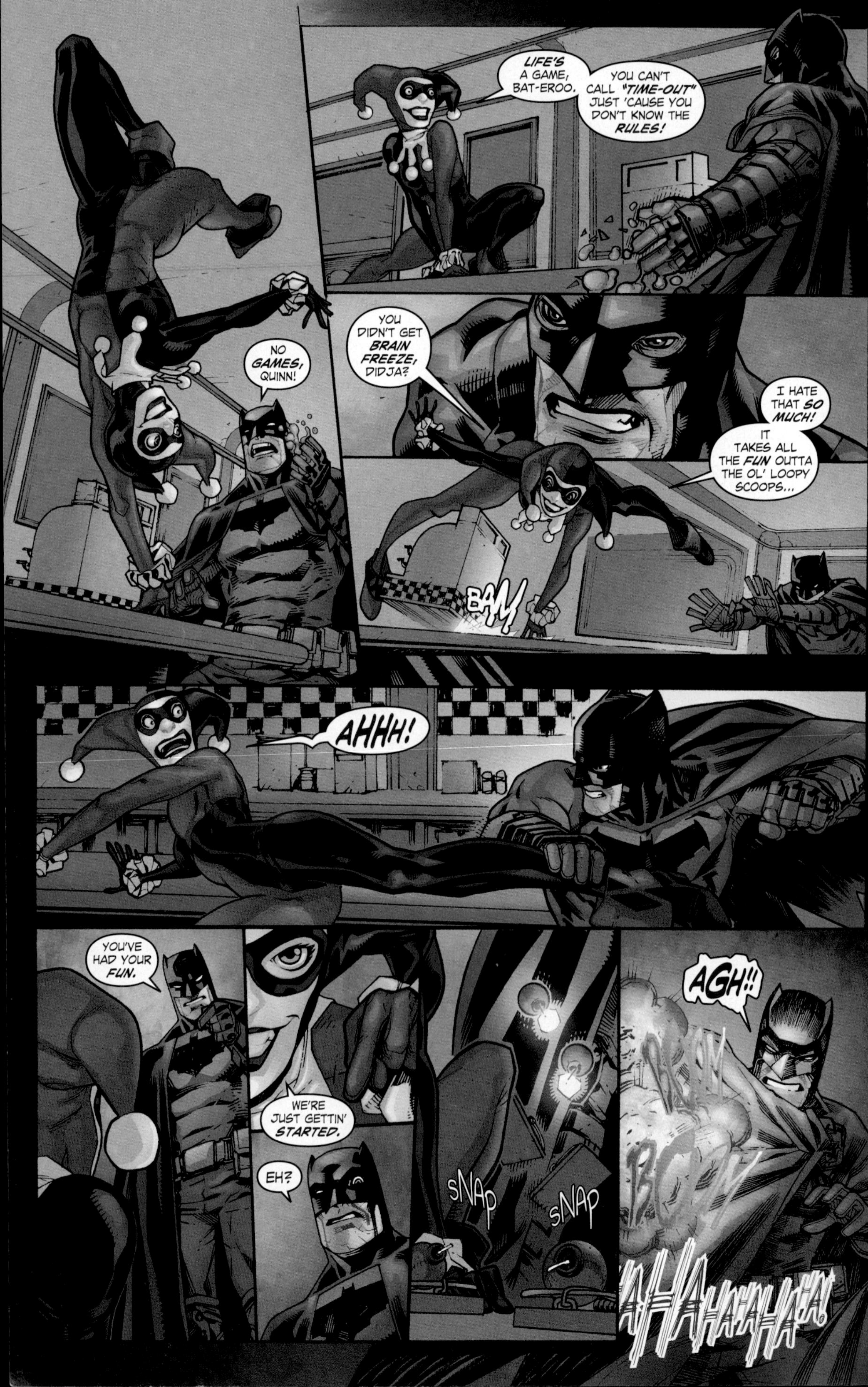
LIFE'S A GAME, BAT-EROO.
YOU CAN'T CALL "TIME-OUT" JUST 'CAUSE YOU DON'T KNOW THE RULES!
NO GAMES, QUINN!
YOU DIDN'T GET BRAIN FREEZE, DIDJA?
I HATE THAT SO MUCH!
IT TAKES ALL THE FUN OUTTA THE OL' LOOPY SCOOPS...
BAM
AHHH!
YOU'VE HAD YOUR FUN.
WE'RE JUST GETTIN' STARTED.
EH?
SNAP
SNAP
AGH!!
BOOM
BOOM
HAHAHAHAHA!

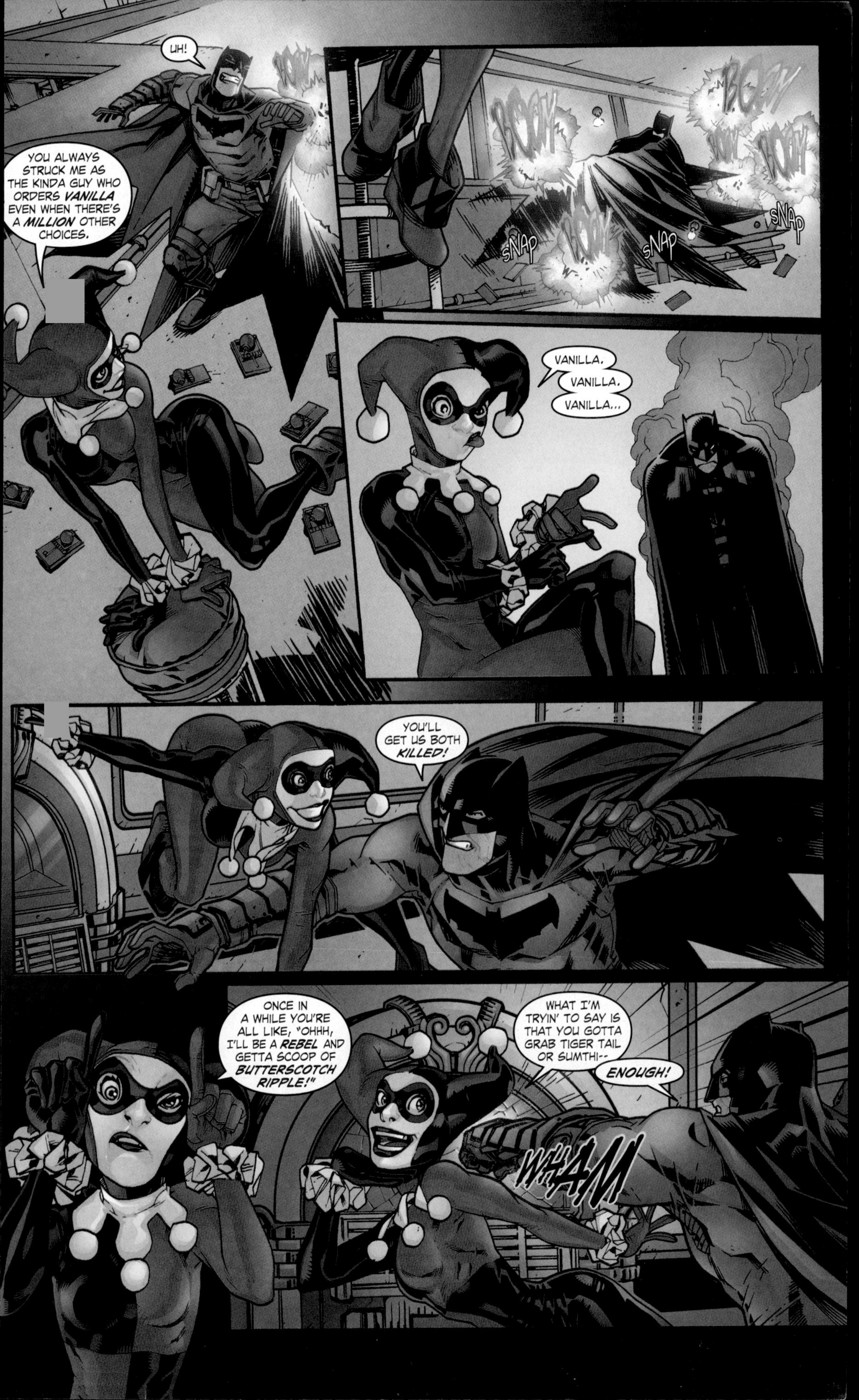

UH!
YOU ALWAYS STRUCK ME AS THE KINDA GUY WHO ORDERS VANILLA EVEN WHEN THERE'S A MILLION OTHER CHOICES.
BOOM
BOOM
BOOM
BOOM
BOOM
BOOM
SNAP
SNAP
SNAP
VANILLA.
VANILLA.
VANILLA...
YOU'LL GET US BOTH KILLED!
ONCE IN A WHILE YOU'RE ALL LIKE, "OHHH, I'LL BE A REBEL AND GETTA SCOOP OF BUTTERSCOTCH RIPPLE!"
WHAT I'M TRYIN' TO SAY IS THAT YOU GOTTA GRAB TIGER TAIL OR SUMTHI--
ENOUGH!
WHAM

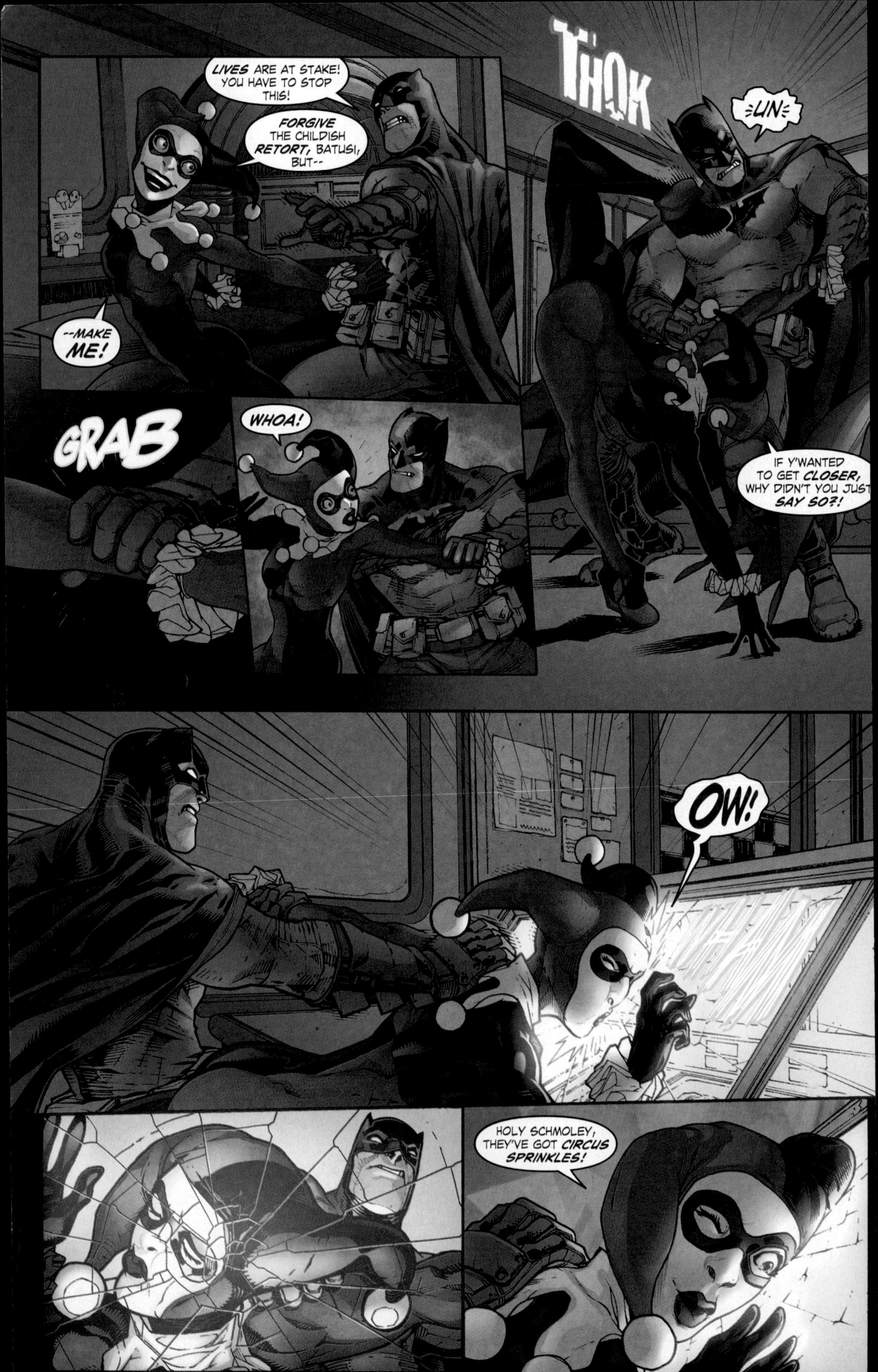
LIVES ARE AT STAKE! YOU HAVE TO STOP THIS!
FORGIVE THE CHILDISH RETORT, BATUSI, BUT--
--MAKE ME!
THOK
UN
GRAB
WHOA!
IF Y'WANTED TO GET CLOSER, WHY DIDN'T YOU JUST SAY SO?!
OW!
HOLY SCHMOLEY, THEY'VE GOT CIRCUS SPRINKLES!

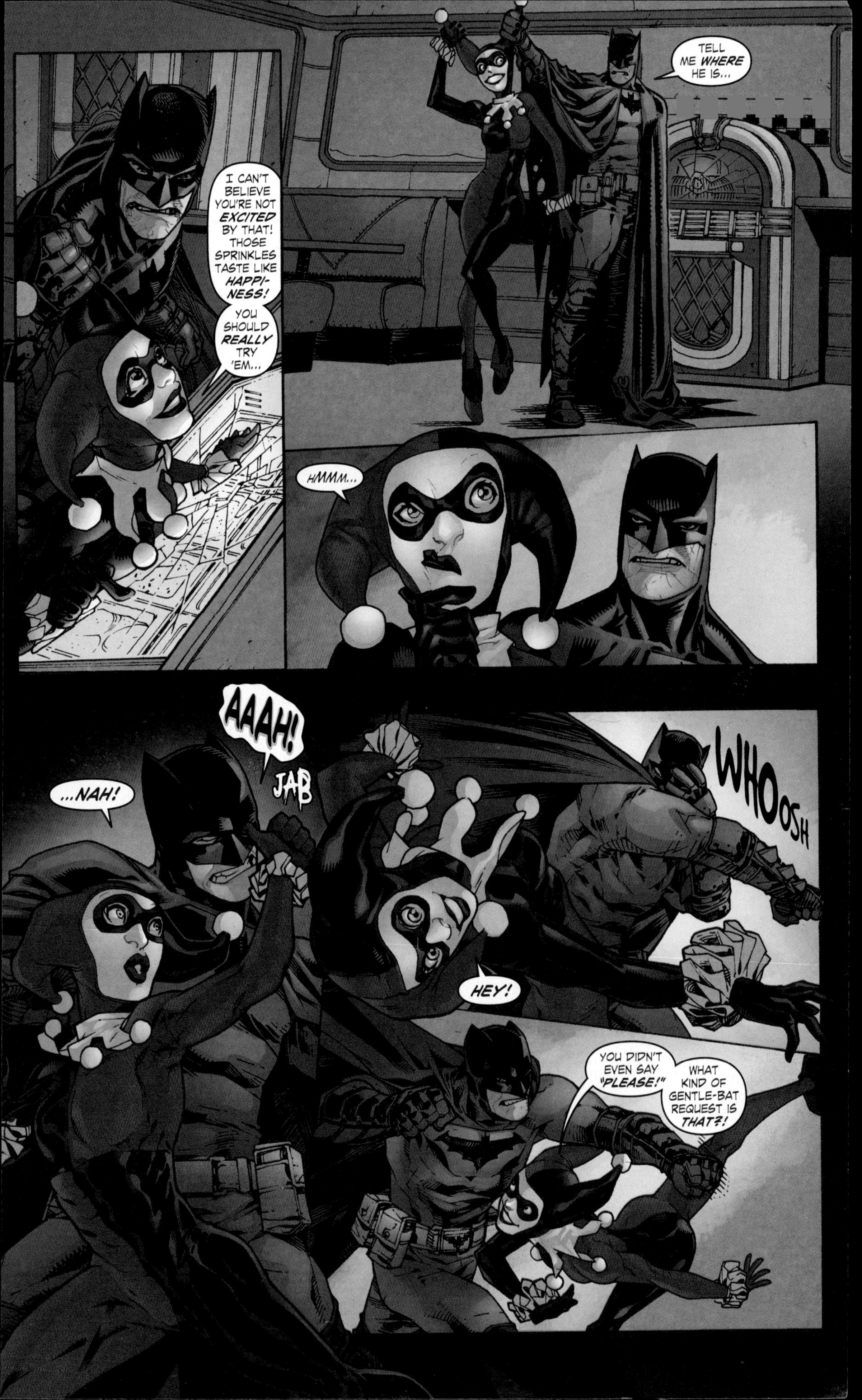
I CAN'T BELIEVE YOU'RE NOT EXCITED BY THAT! THOSE SPRINKLES TASTE LIKE HAPPI-NESS!
YOU SHOULD REALLY TRY 'EM...
TELL ME WHERE HE IS...
HMMM...
...NAH!
AAAH!
JAB
WHOOSH
HEY!
YOU DIDN'T EVEN SAY "PLEASE!"
WHAT KIND OF GENTLE-BAT REQUEST IS THAT?!

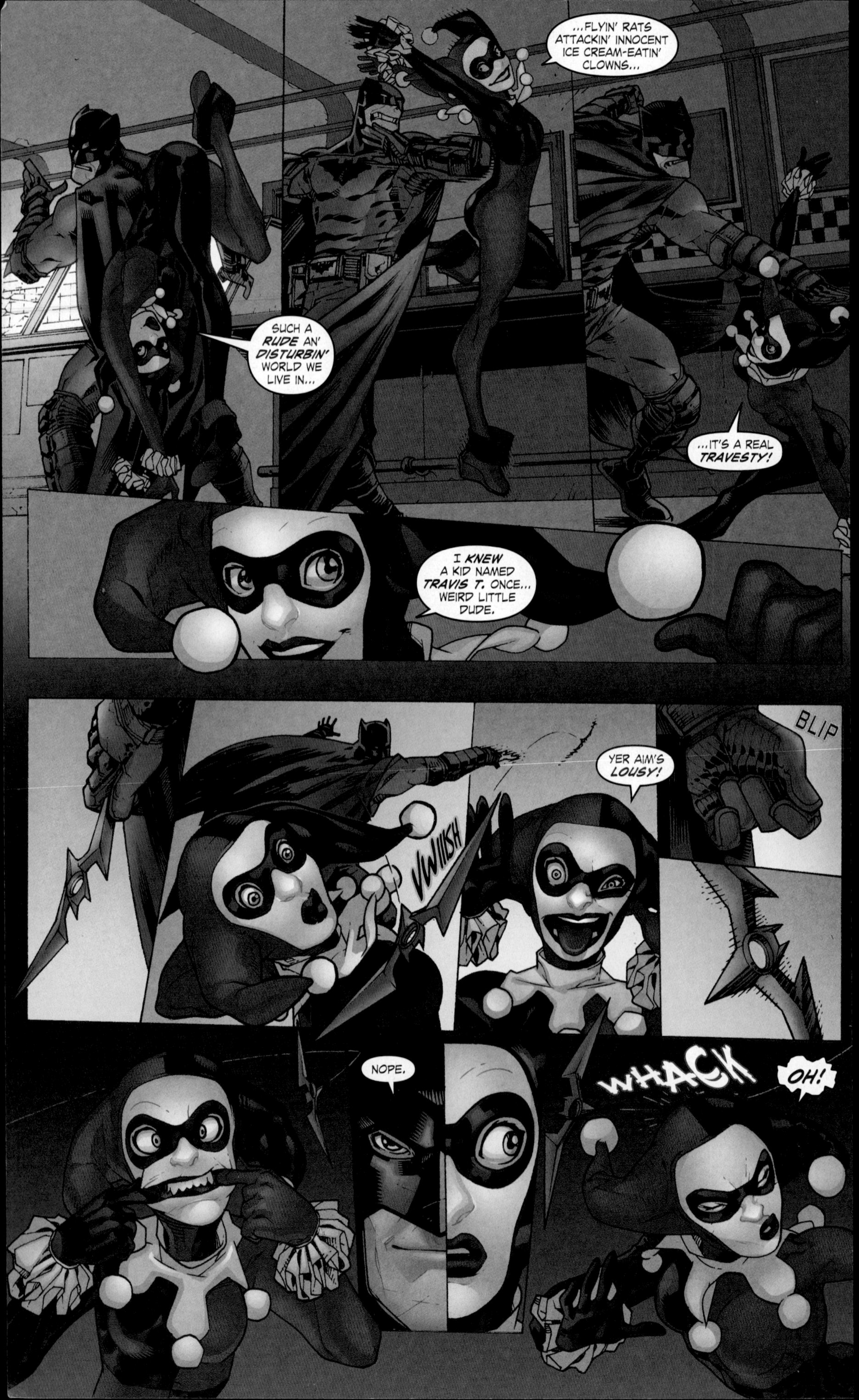
SUCH A RUDE AN' DISTURBIN' WORLD WE LIVE IN...
...FLYIN' RATS ATTACKIN' INNOCENT ICE CREAM-EATIN' CLOWNS...
...IT'S A REAL TRAVESTY!
I KNEW A KID NAMED TRAVIS T. ONCE... WEIRD LITTLE DUDE.
VWIIISH
YER AIM'S LOUSY!
BLIP
NOPE.
WHACK
OH!

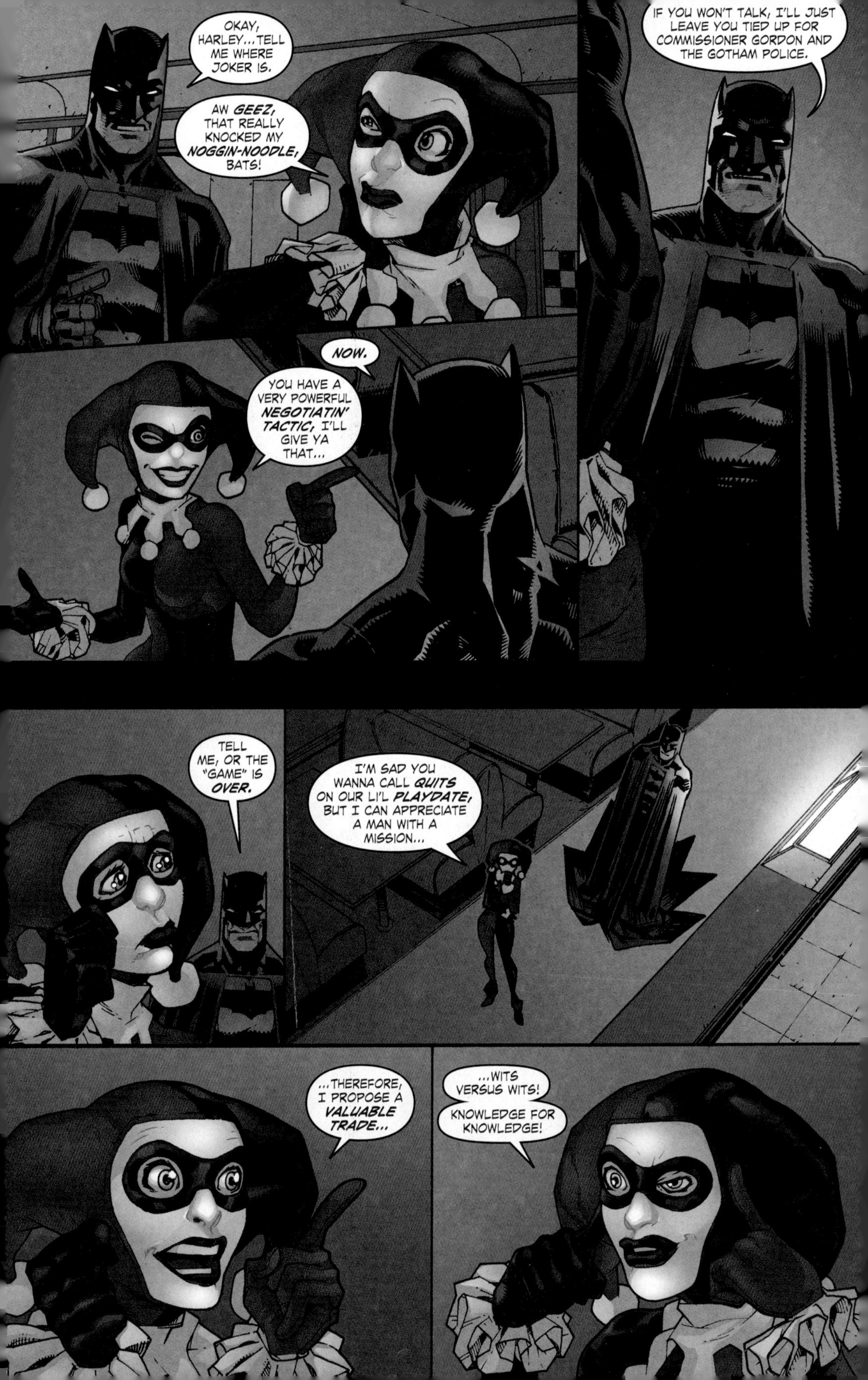
OKAY, HARLEY...TELL ME WHERE JOKER IS.
AW GEEZ, THAT REALLY KNOCKED MY NOGGIN-NOODLE, BATS!
IF YOU WON'T TALK, I'LL JUST LEAVE YOU TIED UP FOR COMMISSIONER GORDON AND THE GOTHAM POLICE.
NOW.
YOU HAVE A VERY POWERFUL NEGOTIATIN' TACTIC, I'LL GIVE YA THAT...
TELL ME, OR THE "GAME" IS OVER.
I'M SAD YOU WANNA CALL QUITS ON OUR LI'L PLAYDATE, BUT I CAN APPRECIATE A MAN WITH A MISSION...
...THEREFORE, I PROPOSE A VALUABLE TRADE...
...WITS VERSUS WITS!
KNOWLEDGE FOR KNOWLEDGE!

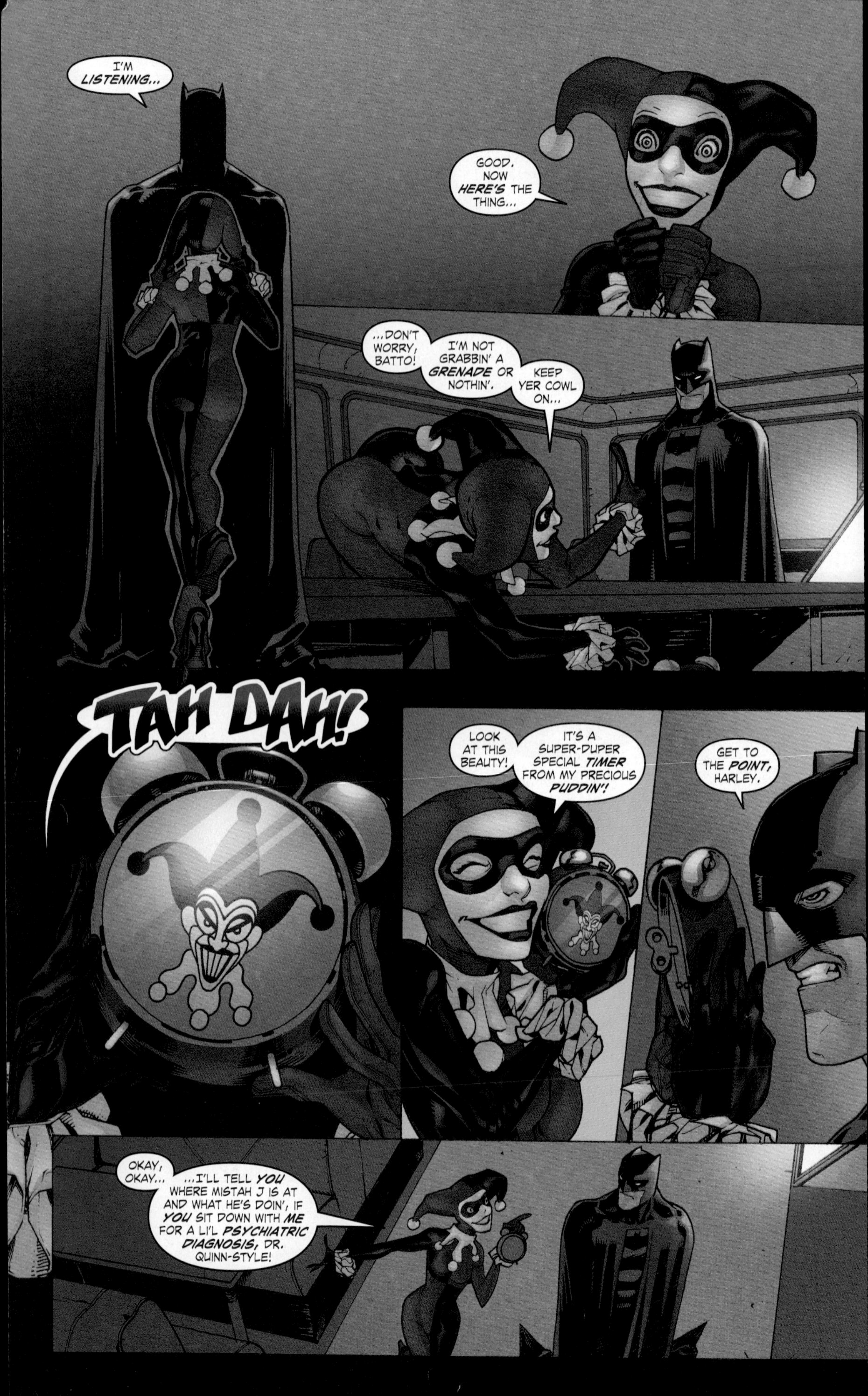
I'M LISTENING...
GOOD. NOW HERE'S THE THING...
...DON'T WORRY, BATTO!
I'M NOT GRABBIN' A GRENADE OR NOTHIN'.
KEEP YER COWL ON...
TAH DAH!
LOOK AT THIS BEAUTY!
IT'S A SUPER-DUPER SPECIAL TIMER FROM MY PRECIOUS PUDDIN'!
GET TO THE POINT, HARLEY.
OKAY, OKAY...
...I'LL TELL YOU WHERE MISTAH J IS AT AND WHAT HE'S DOIN', IF YOU SIT DOWN WITH ME FOR A LI'L PSYCHIATRIC DIAGNOSIS, DR. QUINN-STYLE!

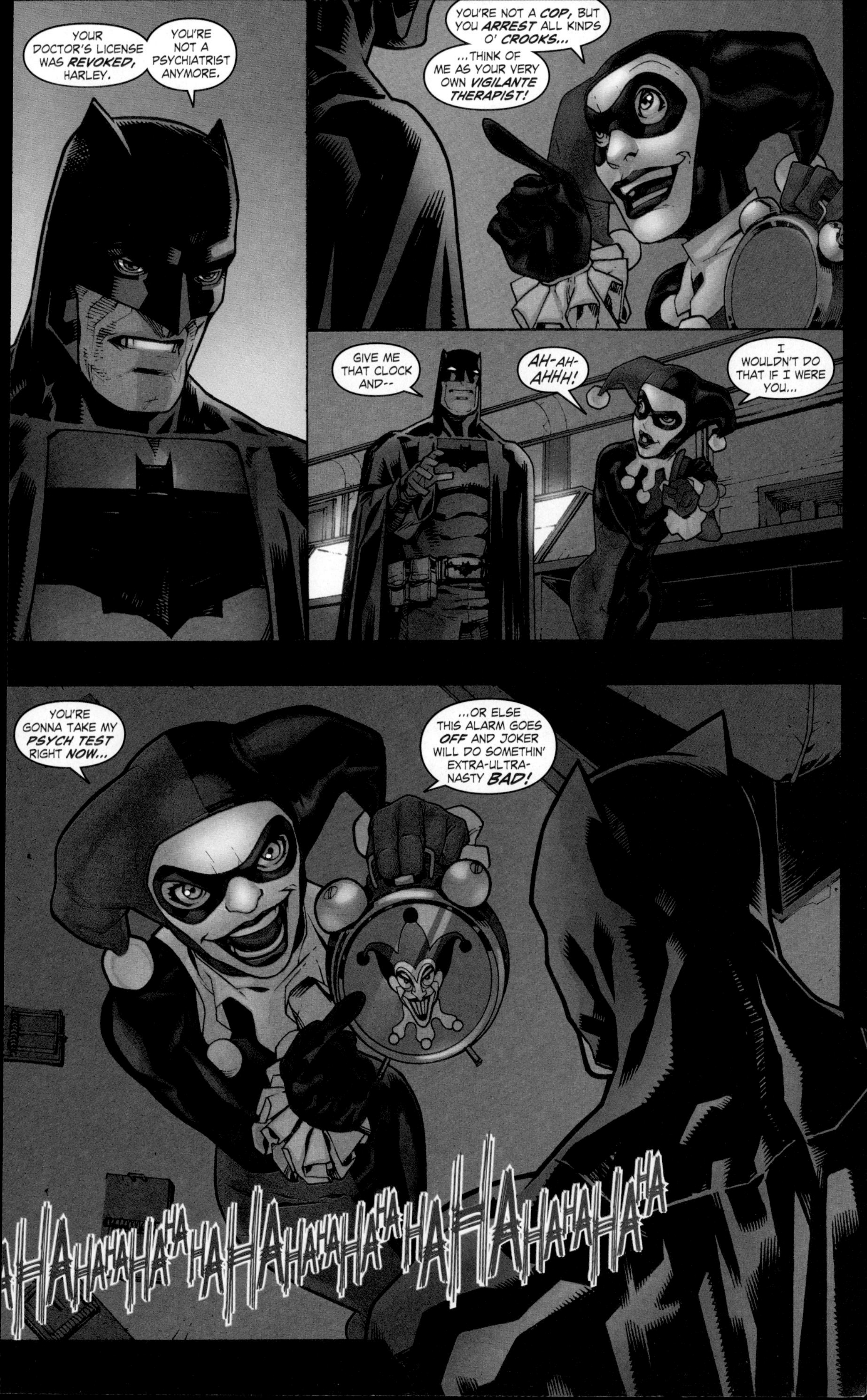
YOUR DOCTOR'S LICENSE WAS REVOKED, HARLEY.
YOU'RE NOT A PSYCHIATRIST ANYMORE.
YOU'RE NOT A COP, BUT YOU ARREST ALL KINDS O' CROOKS...
...THINK OF ME AS YOUR VERY OWN VIGILANTE THERAPIST!
GIVE ME THAT CLOCK AND--
AH-AH-AHHH!
I WOULDN'T DO THAT IF I WERE YOU...
YOU'RE GONNA TAKE MY PSYCH TEST RIGHT NOW...
...OR ELSE THIS ALARM GOES OFF AND JOKER WILL DO SOMETHIN' EXTRA-ULTRA-NASTY BAD!
HAHAHAHAHA HAHAHAHAHAHA HAHAHAHAHAHA

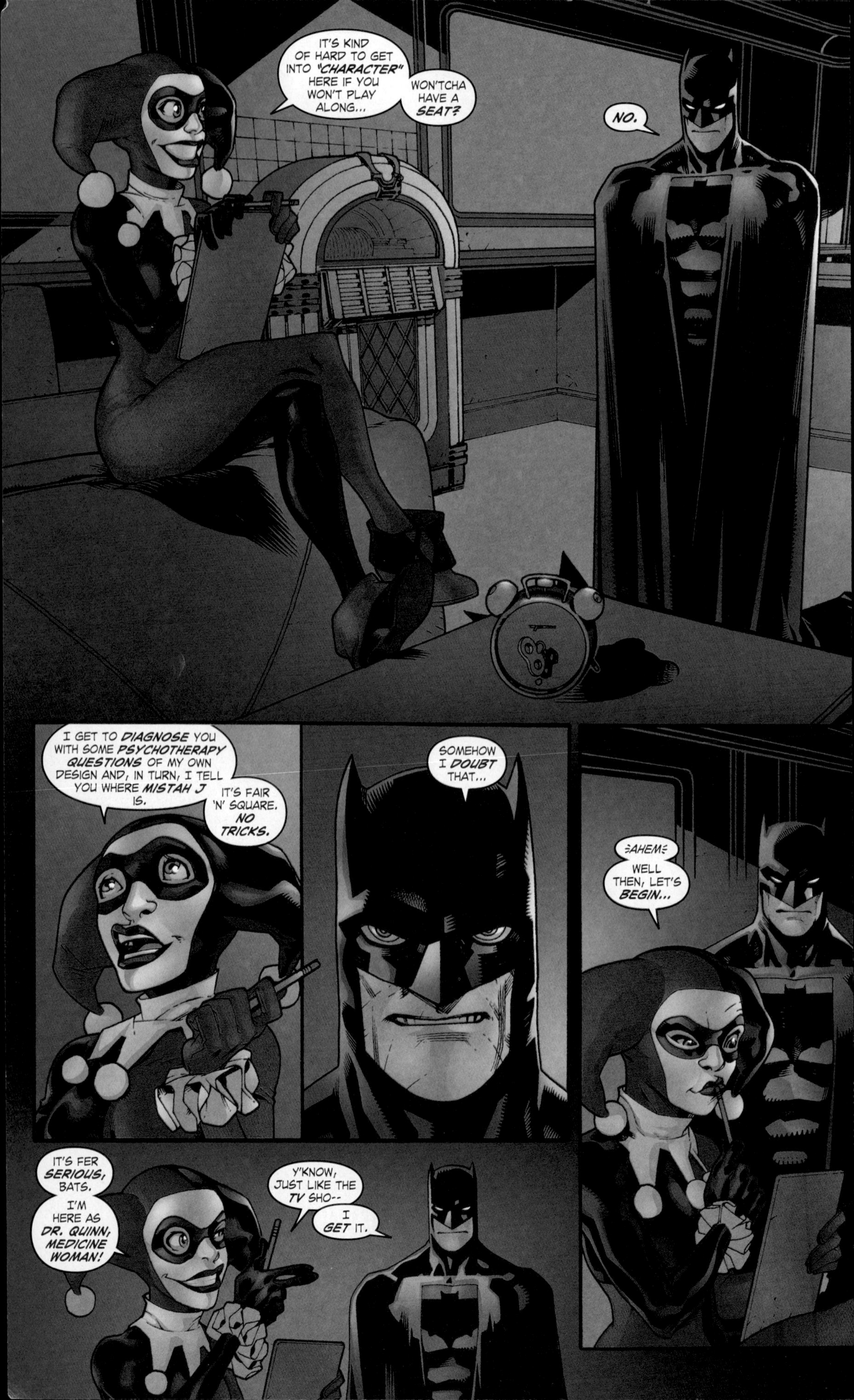
IT'S KIND OF HARD TO GET INTO "CHARACTER" HERE IF YOU WON'T PLAY ALONG...
WON'TCHA HAVE A SEAT?
NO.
I GET TO DIAGNOSE YOU WITH SOME PSYCHOTHERAPY QUESTIONS OF MY OWN DESIGN AND, IN TURN, I TELL YOU WHERE MISTAH J IS.
IT'S FAIR 'N' SQUARE. NO TRICKS.
SOMEHOW I DOUBT THAT...
IT'S FER SERIOUS, BATS.
I'M HERE AS DR. QUINN, MEDICINE WOMAN!
Y'KNOW, JUST LIKE THE TV SHO--
I GET IT.
AHEM
WELL THEN, LET'S BEGIN...

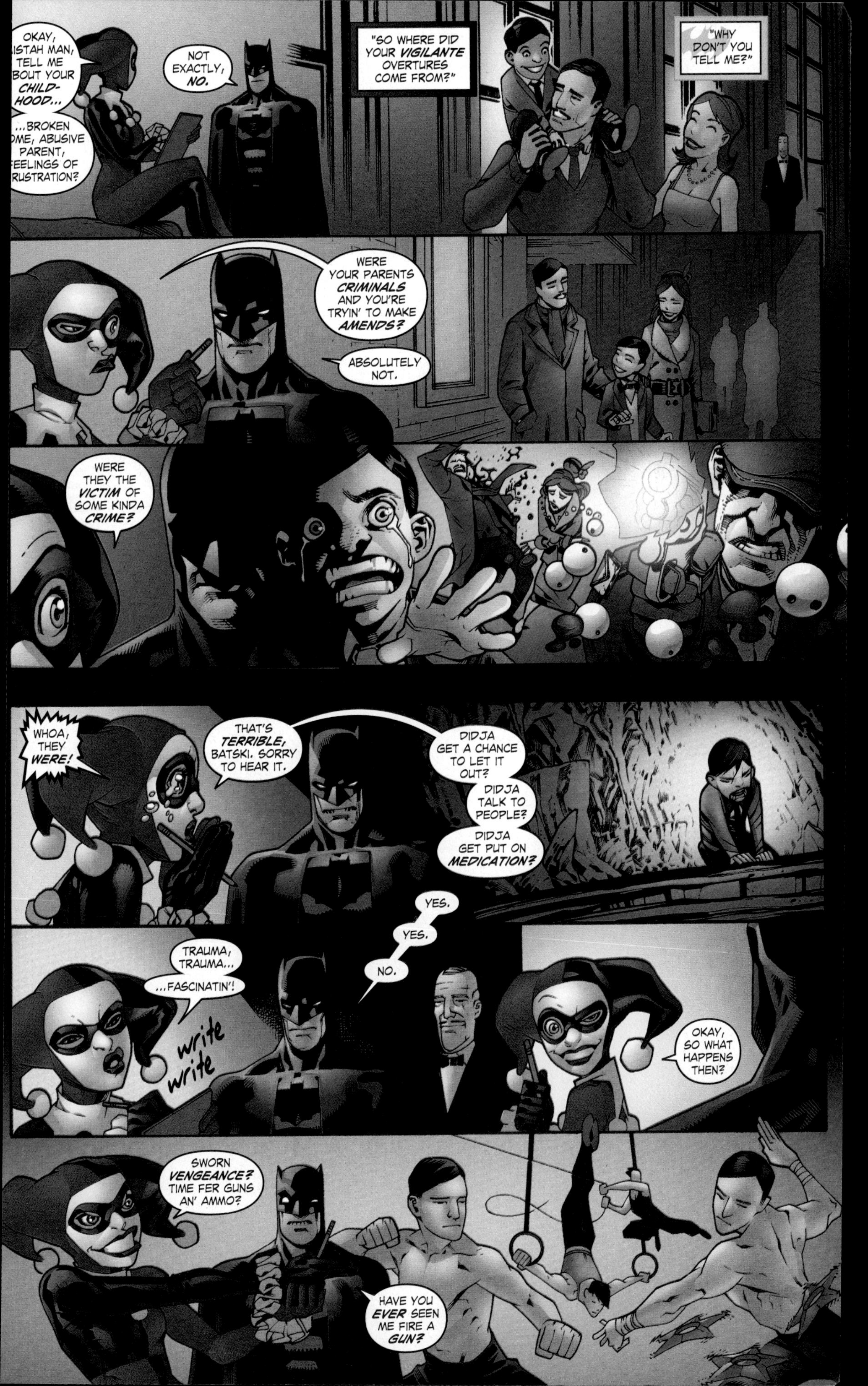

OKAY, MISTAH MAN, TELL ME ABOUT YOUR CHILD-HOOD...
...BROKEN HOME, ABUSIVE PARENT, FEELINGS OF FRUSTRATION?
NOT EXACTLY, NO.
"SO WHERE DID YOUR VIGILANTE OVERTURES COME FROM?"
"WHY DON'T YOU TELL ME?"
WERE YOUR PARENTS CRIMINALS AND YOU'RE TRYIN' TO MAKE AMENDS?
ABSOLUTELY NOT.
WERE THEY THE VICTIM OF SOME KINDA CRIME?
WHOA, THEY WERE!
THAT'S TERRIBLE, BATSKI. SORRY TO HEAR IT.
DIDJA GET A CHANCE TO LET IT OUT?
DIDJA TALK TO PEOPLE?
DIDJA GET PUT ON MEDICATION?
YES.
YES.
NO.
TRAUMA, TRAUMA...
...FASCINATIN'!
write write
OKAY, SO WHAT HAPPENS THEN?
SWORN VENGEANCE? TIME FER GUNS AN' AMMO?
HAVE YOU EVER SEEN ME FIRE A GUN?

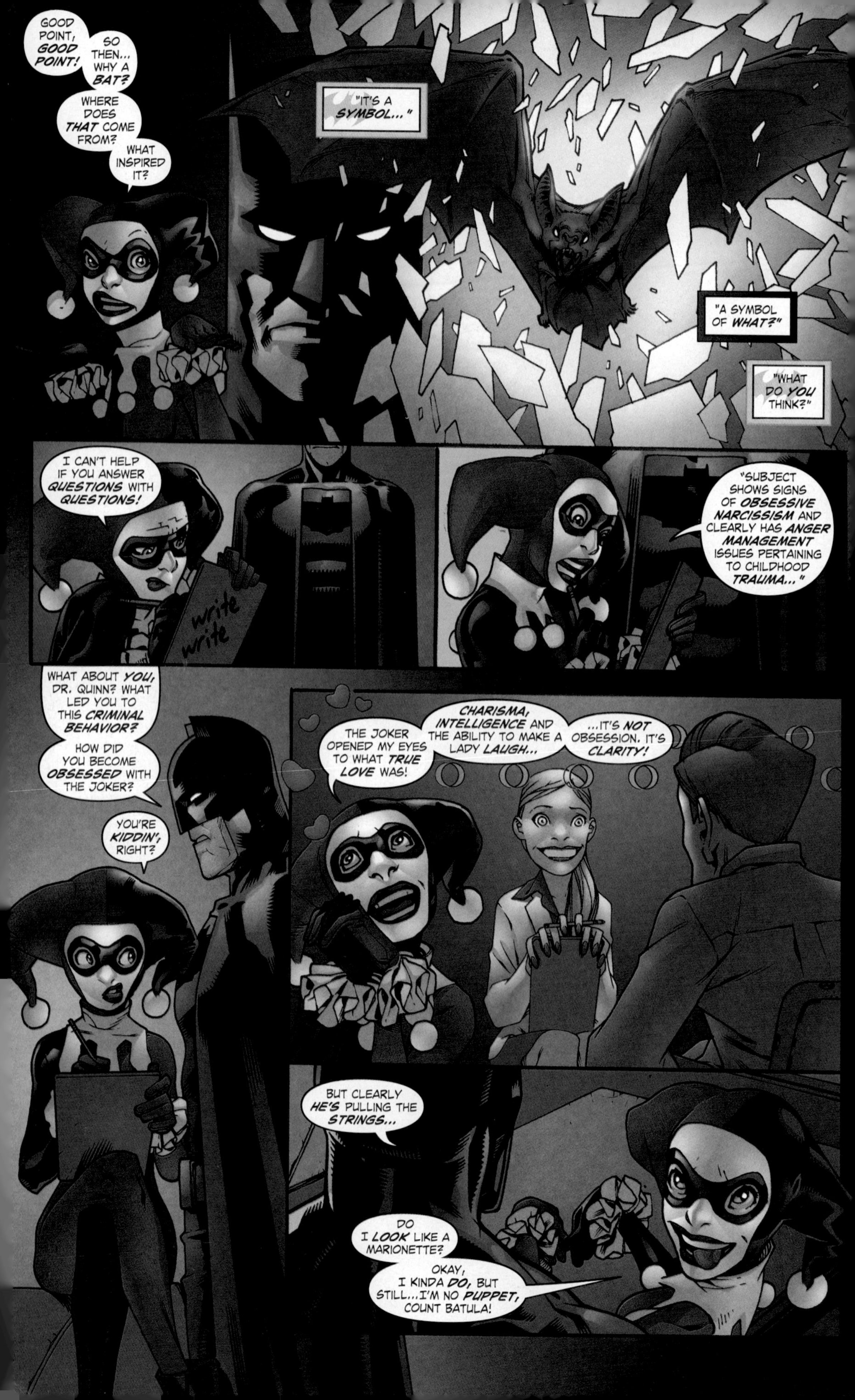
GOOD POINT, GOOD POINT!
SO THEN... WHY A BAT?
WHERE DOES THAT COME FROM?
WHAT INSPIRED IT?
"IT'S A SYMBOL..."
"A SYMBOL OF WHAT?"
"WHAT DO YOU THINK?"
I CAN'T HELP IF YOU ANSWER QUESTIONS WITH QUESTIONS!
write write
"SUBJECT SHOWS SIGNS OF OBSESSIVE NARCISSISM AND CLEARLY HAS ANGER MANAGEMENT ISSUES PERTAINING TO CHILDHOOD TRAUMA..."
WHAT ABOUT YOU, DR. QUINN? WHAT LED YOU TO THIS CRIMINAL BEHAVIOR?
HOW DID YOU BECOME OBSESSED WITH THE JOKER?
YOU'RE KIDDIN', RIGHT?
THE JOKER OPENED MY EYES TO WHAT TRUE LOVE WAS!
CHARISMA, INTELLIGENCE AND THE ABILITY TO MAKE A LADY LAUGH...
...IT'S NOT OBSESSION. IT'S CLARITY!
BUT CLEARLY HE'S PULLING THE STRINGS...
DO I LOOK LIKE A MARIONETTE?
OKAY, I KINDA DO, BUT STILL...I'M NO PUPPET, COUNT BATULA!

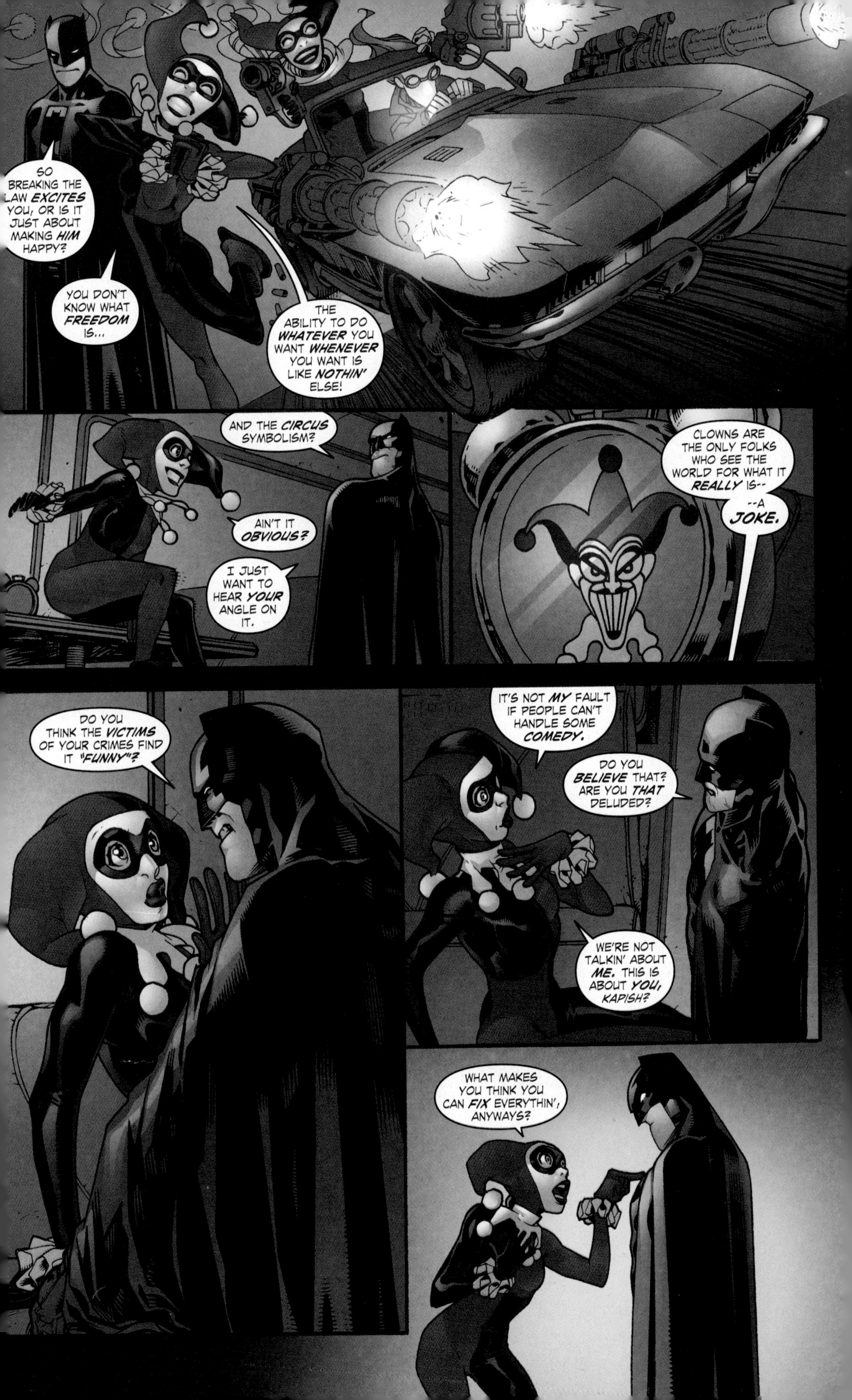
SO BREAKING THE LAW EXCITES YOU, OR IS IT JUST ABOUT MAKING HIM HAPPY?
YOU DON'T KNOW WHAT FREEDOM IS...
THE ABILITY TO DO WHATEVER YOU WANT WHENEVER YOU WANT IS LIKE NOTHIN' ELSE!
AND THE CIRCUS SYMBOLISM?
AIN'T IT OBVIOUS?
I JUST WANT TO HEAR YOUR ANGLE ON IT.
CLOWNS ARE THE ONLY FOLKS WHO SEE THE WORLD FOR WHAT IT REALLY IS--
--A JOKE.
DO YOU THINK THE VICTIMS OF YOUR CRIMES FIND IT "FUNNY"?
IT'S NOT MY FAULT IF PEOPLE CAN'T HANDLE SOME COMEDY.
DO YOU BELIEVE THAT? ARE YOU THAT DELUDED?
WE'RE NOT TALKIN' ABOUT ME. THIS IS ABOUT YOU, KAPISH?
WHAT MAKES YOU THINK YOU CAN FIX EVERYTHIN', ANYWAYS?

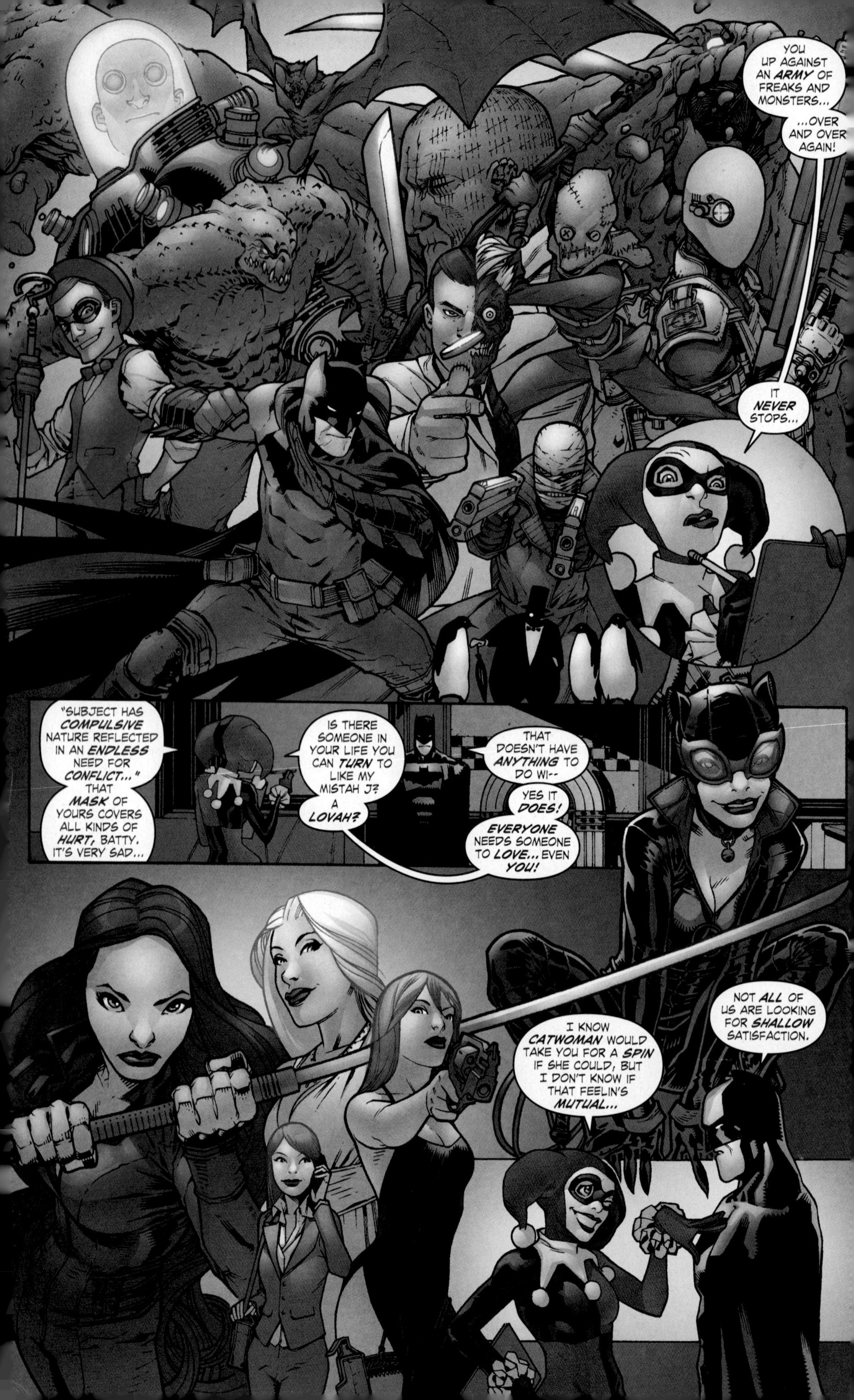
YOU UP AGAINST AN ARMY OF FREAKS AND MONSTERS...
...OVER AND OVER AGAIN!
IT NEVER STOPS...
"SUBJECT HAS COMPULSIVE NATURE REFLECTED IN AN ENDLESS NEED FOR CONFLICT..." THAT MASK OF YOURS COVERS ALL KINDS OF HURT, BATTY. IT'S VERY SAD...
IS THERE SOMEONE IN YOUR LIFE YOU CAN TURN TO LIKE MY MISTAH J? A LOVAH?
THAT DOESN'T HAVE ANYTHING TO DO WI--
YES IT DOES!
EVERYONE NEEDS SOMEONE TO LOVE... EVEN YOU!
I KNOW CATWOMAN WOULD TAKE YOU FOR A SPIN IF SHE COULD, BUT I DON'T KNOW IF THAT FEELIN'S MUTUAL...
NOT ALL OF US ARE LOOKING FOR SHALLOW SATISFACTION.

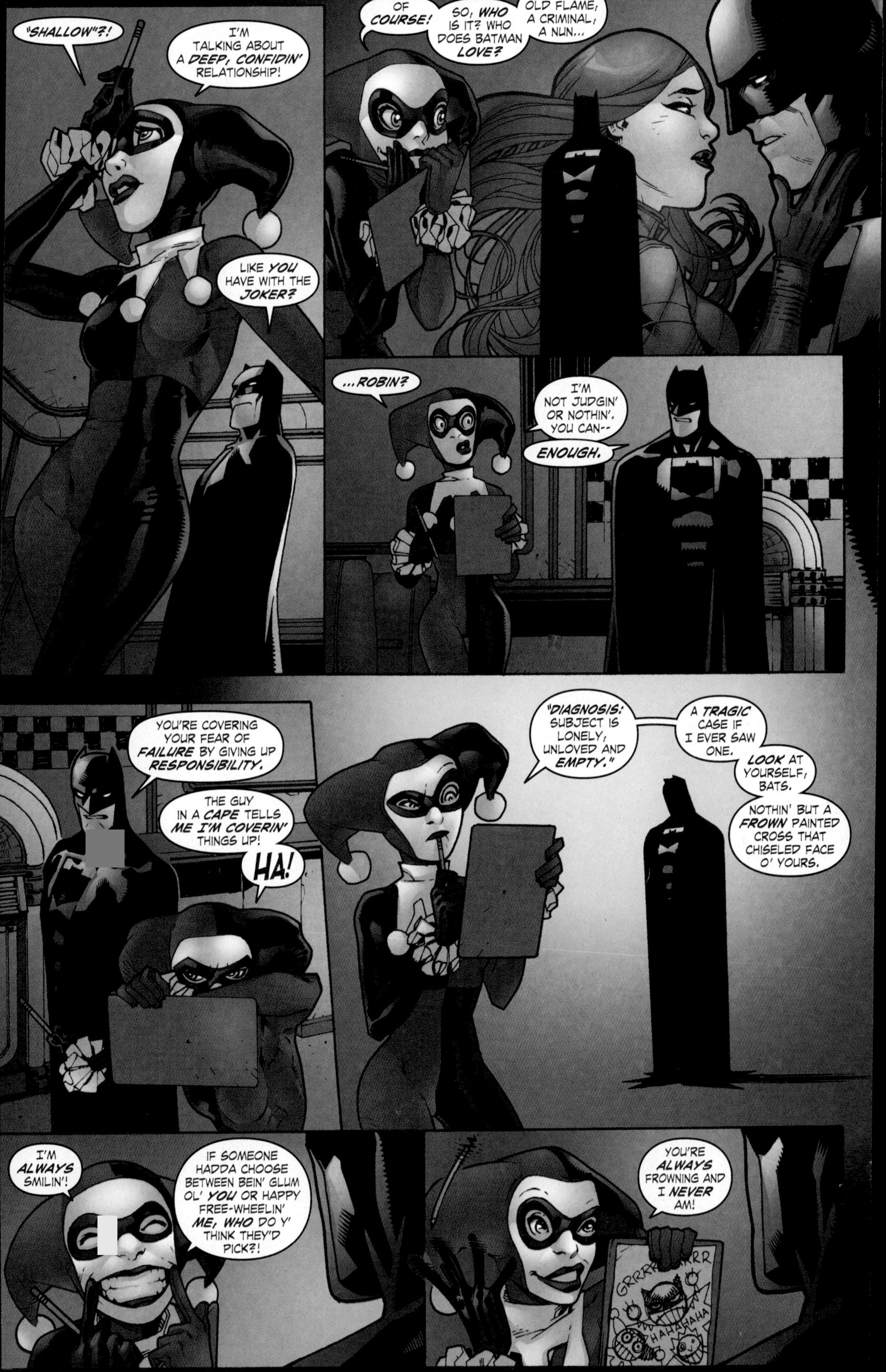
"SHALLOW"?!
I'M TALKING ABOUT A DEEP, CONFIDIN' RELATIONSHIP!
LIKE YOU HAVE WITH THE JOKER?
OF COURSE!
SO, WHO IS IT? WHO DOES BATMAN LOVE?
AN OLD FLAME, A CRIMINAL, A NUN...
...ROBIN?
I'M NOT JUDGIN' OR NOTHIN'. YOU CAN--
ENOUGH.
YOU'RE COVERING YOUR FEAR OF FAILURE BY GIVING UP RESPONSIBILITY.
THE GUY IN A CAPE TELLS ME I'M COVERIN' THINGS UP!
HA!
"DIAGNOSIS: SUBJECT IS LONELY, UNLOVED AND EMPTY."
A TRAGIC CASE IF I EVER SAW ONE.
LOOK AT YOURSELF, BATS.
NOTHIN' BUT A FROWN PAINTED CROSS THAT CHISELED FACE O' YOURS.
I'M ALWAYS SMILIN'!
IF SOMEONE HADDA CHOOSE BETWEEN BEIN' GLUM OL' YOU OR HAPPY FREE-WHEELIN' ME, WHO DO Y' THINK THEY'D PICK?!
YOU'RE ALWAYS FROWNING AND I NEVER AM!

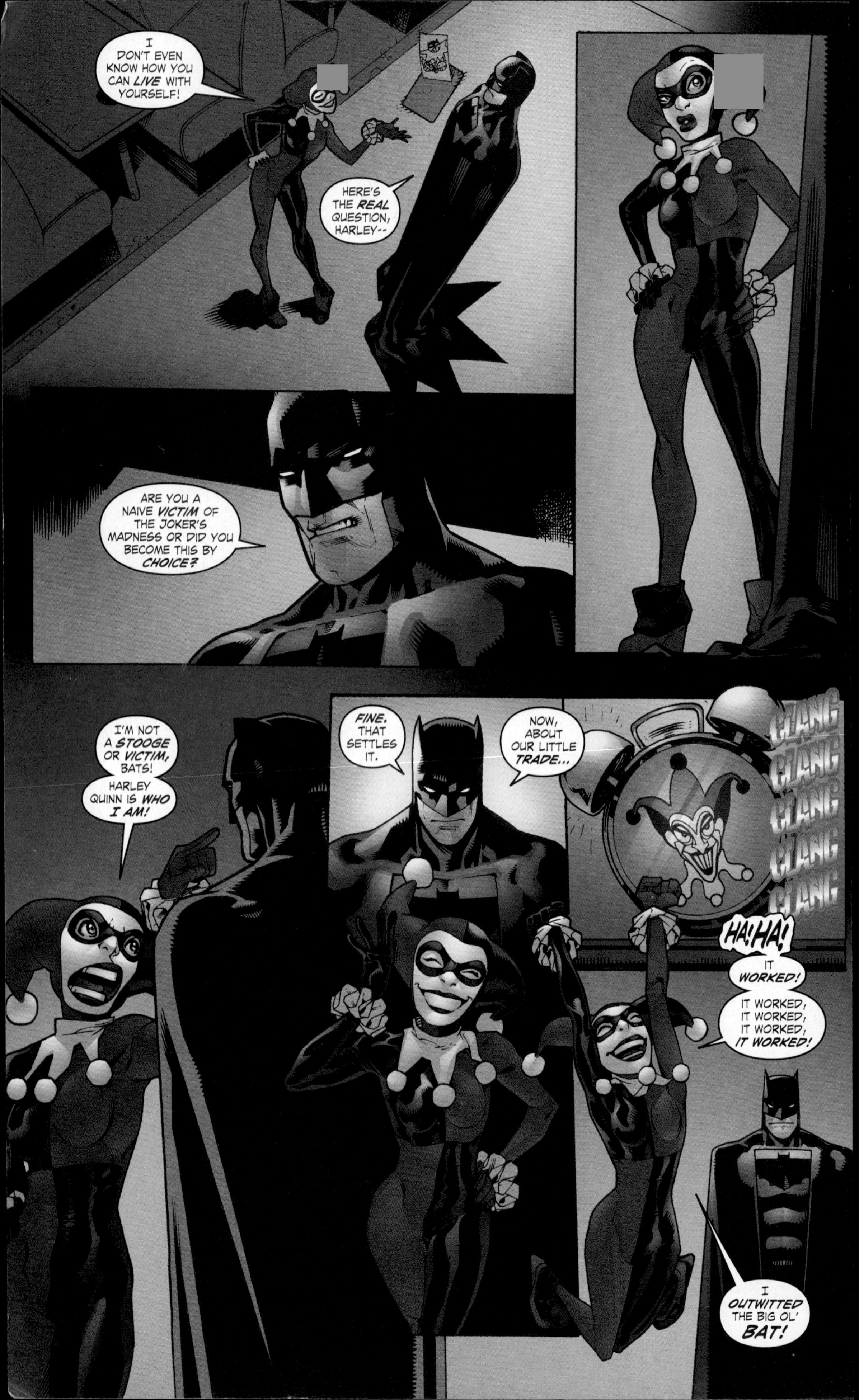
I DON'T EVEN KNOW HOW YOU CAN LIVE WITH YOURSELF!
HERE'S THE REAL QUESTION, HARLEY--
ARE YOU A NAIVE VICTIM OF THE JOKER'S MADNESS OR DID YOU BECOME THIS BY CHOICE?
I'M NOT A STOOGE OR VICTIM, BATS! HARLEY QUINN IS WHO I AM!
FINE. THAT SETTLES IT.
NOW, ABOUT OUR LITTLE TRADE...
CLANG CLANG CLANG CLANG CLANG
HA! HA!
IT WORKED!
IT WORKED, IT WORKED, IT WORKED, IT WORKED!
I OUTWITTED THE BIG OL' BAT!

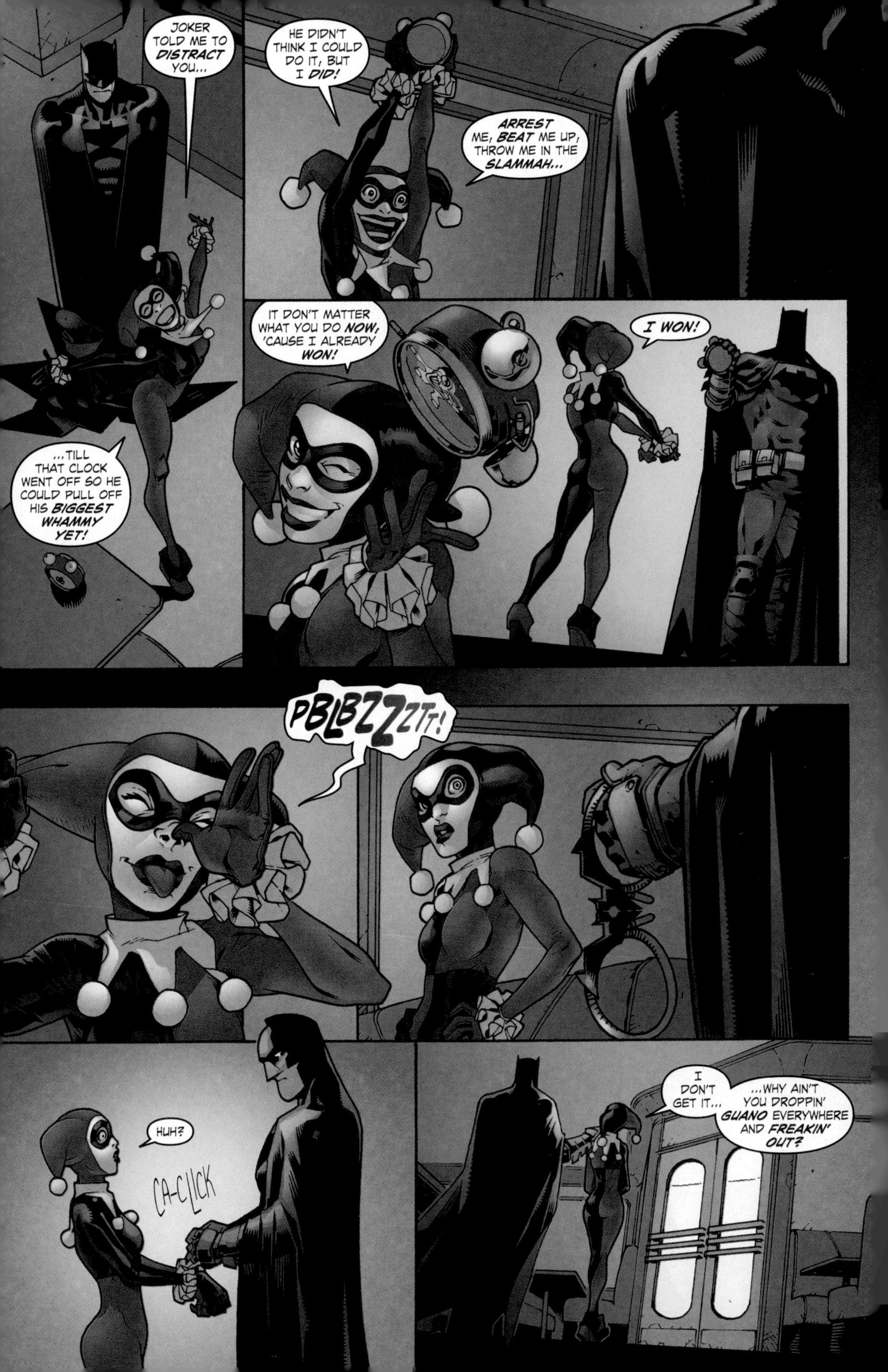
JOKER TOLD ME TO DISTRACT YOU...
...TILL THAT CLOCK WENT OFF SO HE COULD PULL OFF HIS BIGGEST WHAMMY YET!
HE DIDN'T THINK I COULD DO IT, BUT I DID!
ARREST ME, BEAT ME UP, THROW ME IN THE SLAMMAH...
IT DON'T MATTER WHAT YOU DO NOW, 'CAUSE I ALREADY WON!
I WON!
PBLBZZZTT!
HUH?
CA-CLICK
I DON'T GET IT...
...WHY AIN'T YOU DROPPIN' GUANO EVERYWHERE AND FREAKIN' OUT?

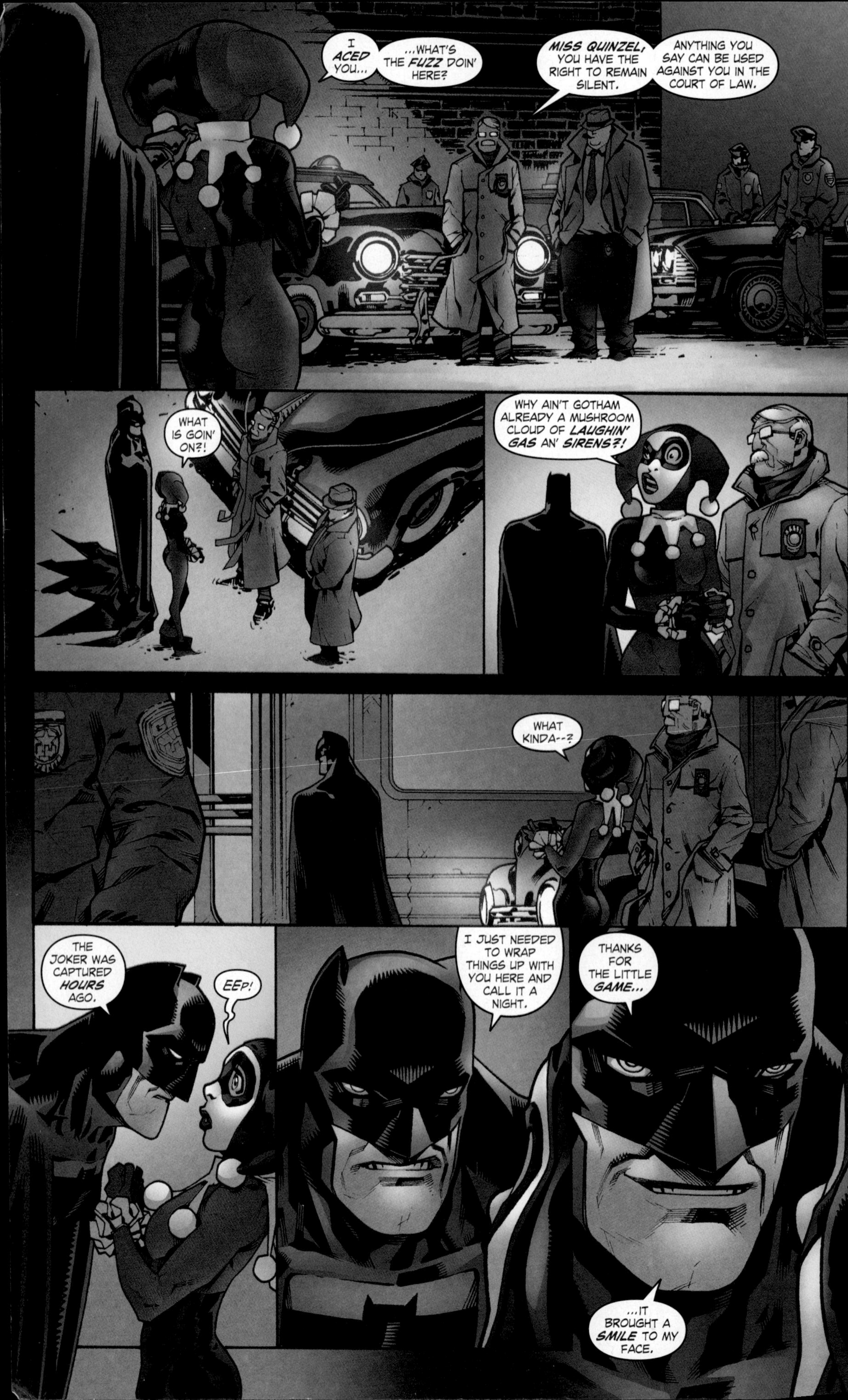

I ACED YOU...
...WHAT'S THE FUZZ DOIN' HERE?
MISS QUINZEL, YOU HAVE THE RIGHT TO REMAIN SILENT.
ANYTHING YOU SAY CAN BE USED AGAINST YOU IN THE COURT OF LAW.
WHAT IS GOIN' ON?!
WHY AIN'T GOTHAM ALREADY A MUSHROOM CLOUD OF LAUGHIN' GAS AN' SIRENS?!
WHAT KINDA--?
THE JOKER WAS CAPTURED HOURS AGO.
EEP!
I JUST NEEDED TO WRAP THINGS UP WITH YOU HERE AND CALL IT A NIGHT.
THANKS FOR THE LITTLE GAME...
...IT BROUGHT A SMILE TO MY FACE.

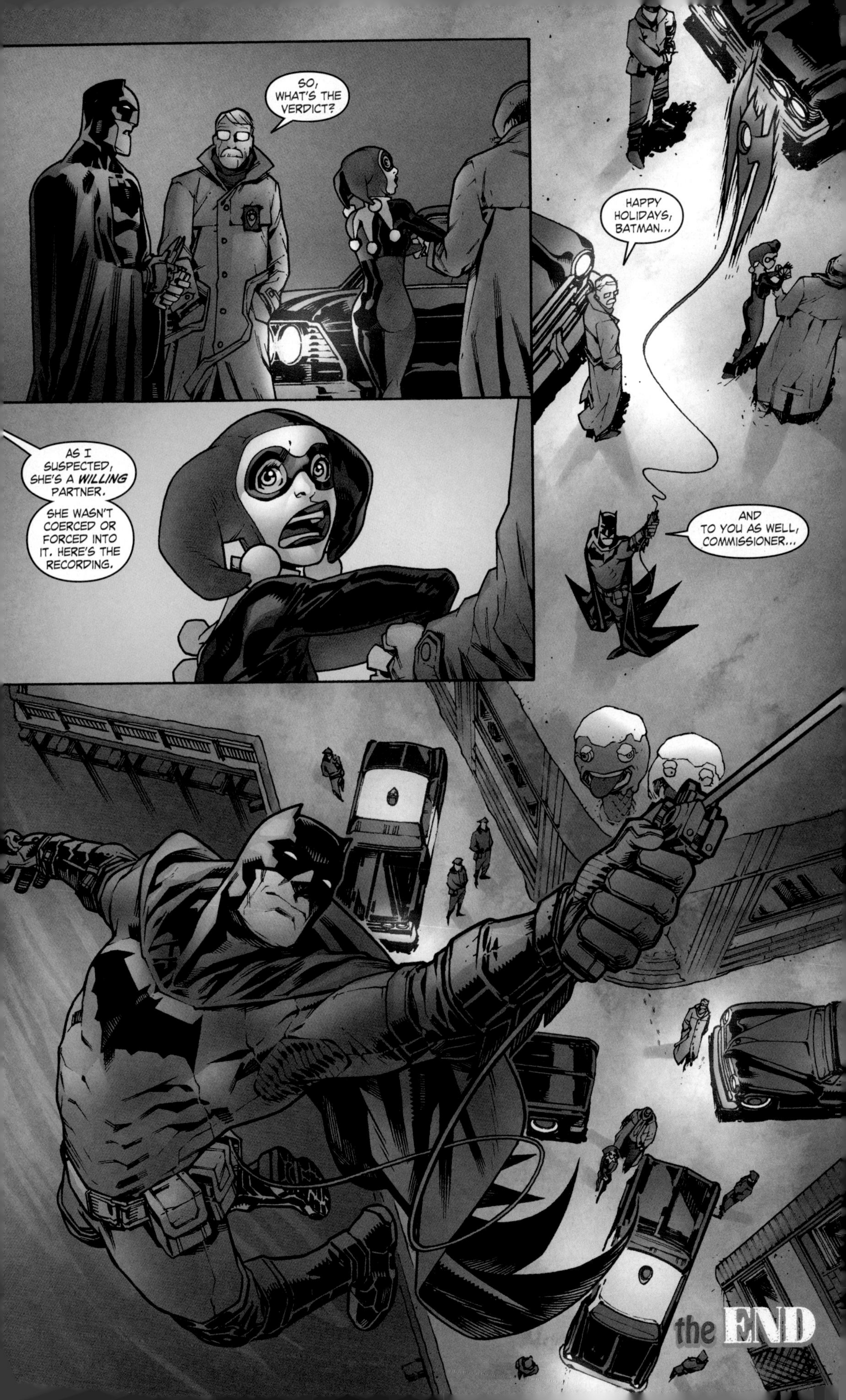
SO, WHAT'S THE VERDICT?
AS I SUSPECTED, SHE'S A WILLING PARTNER.
SHE WASN'T COERCED OR FORCED INTO IT. HERE'S THE RECORDING.
HAPPY HOLIDAYS, BATMAN...
AND TO YOU AS WELL, COMMISSIONER...
the END

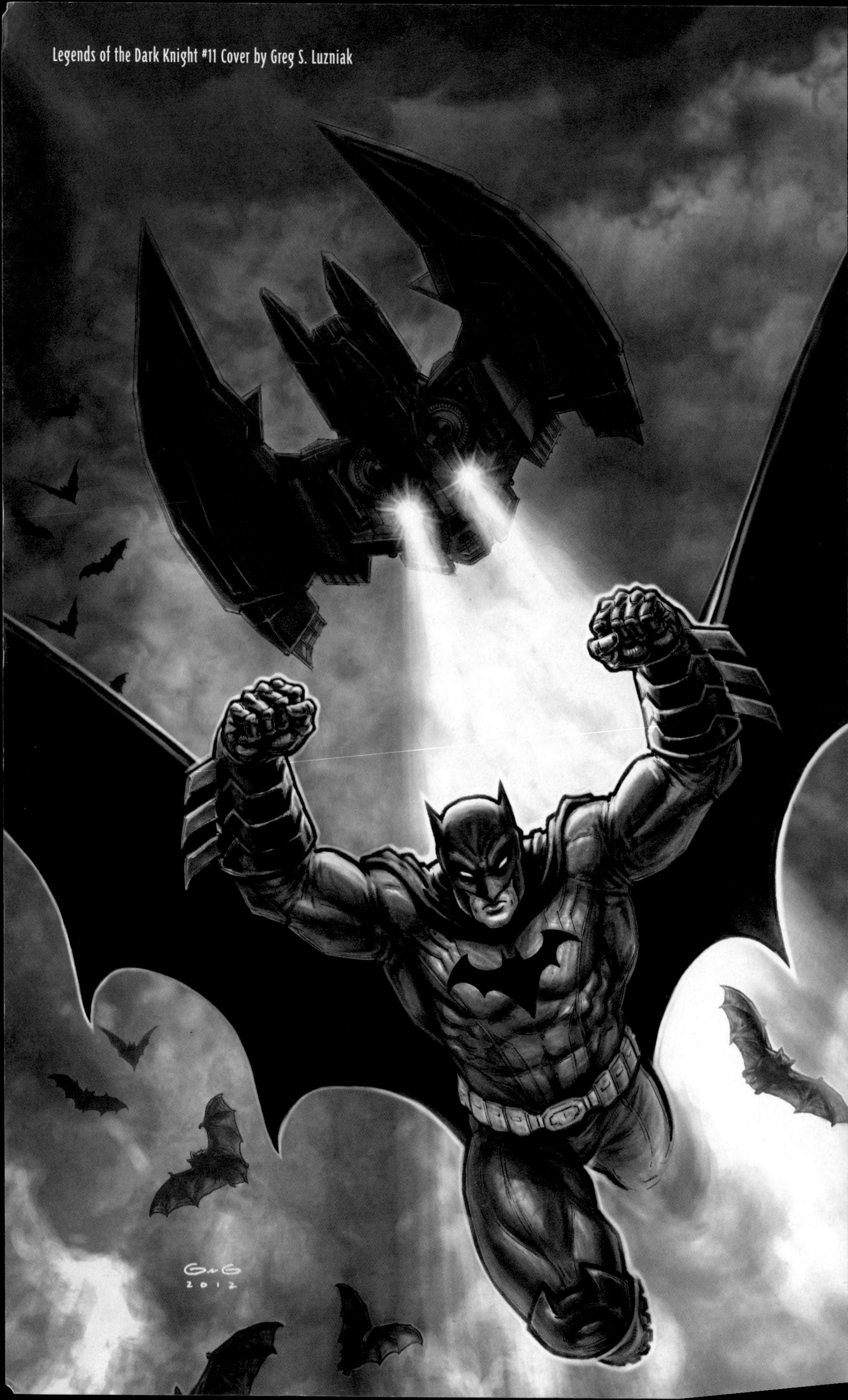

Legends of the Dark Knight #11 Cover by Greg S. Luzniak

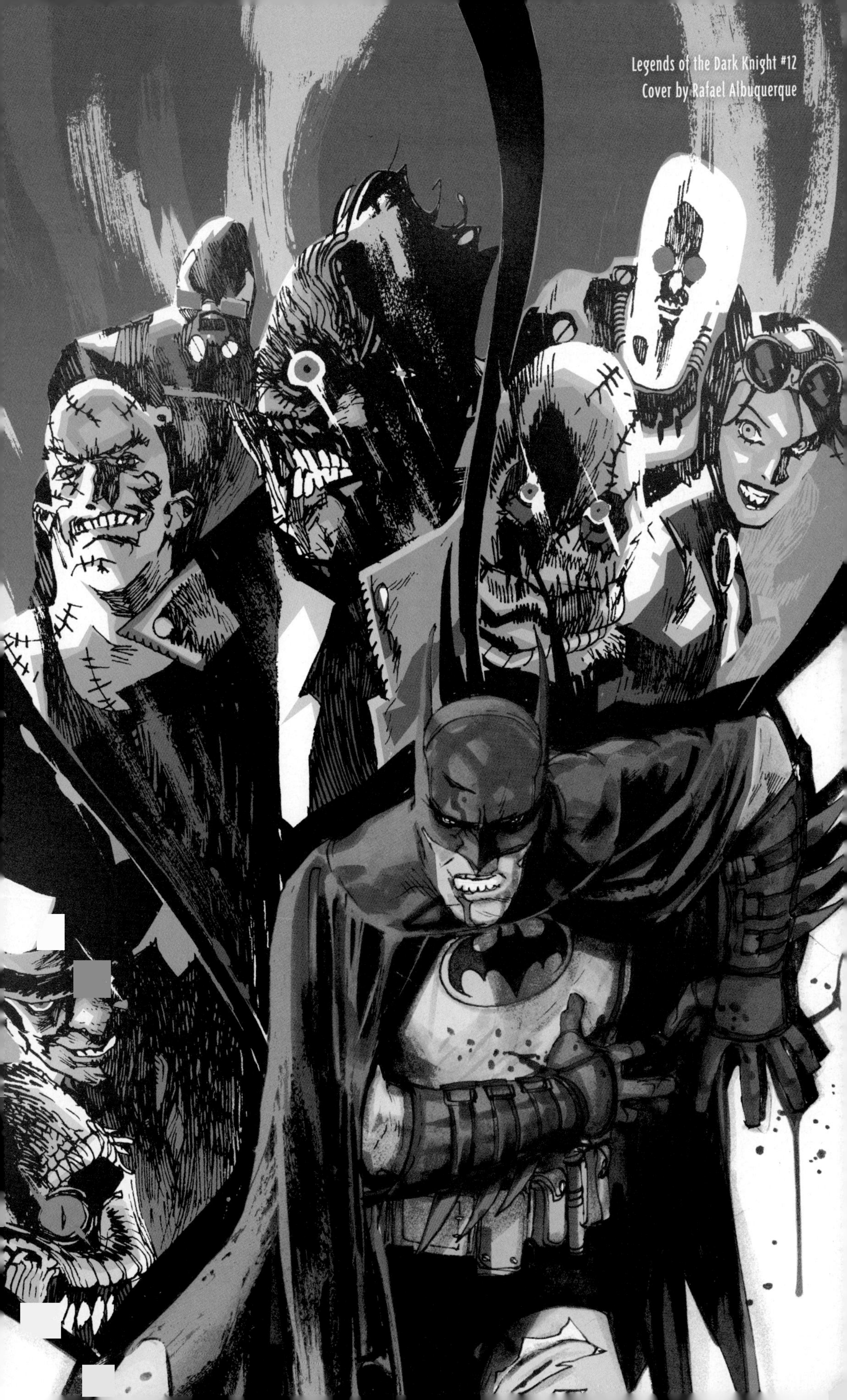

Legends of the Dark Knight #12
Cover by Rafael Albuquerque

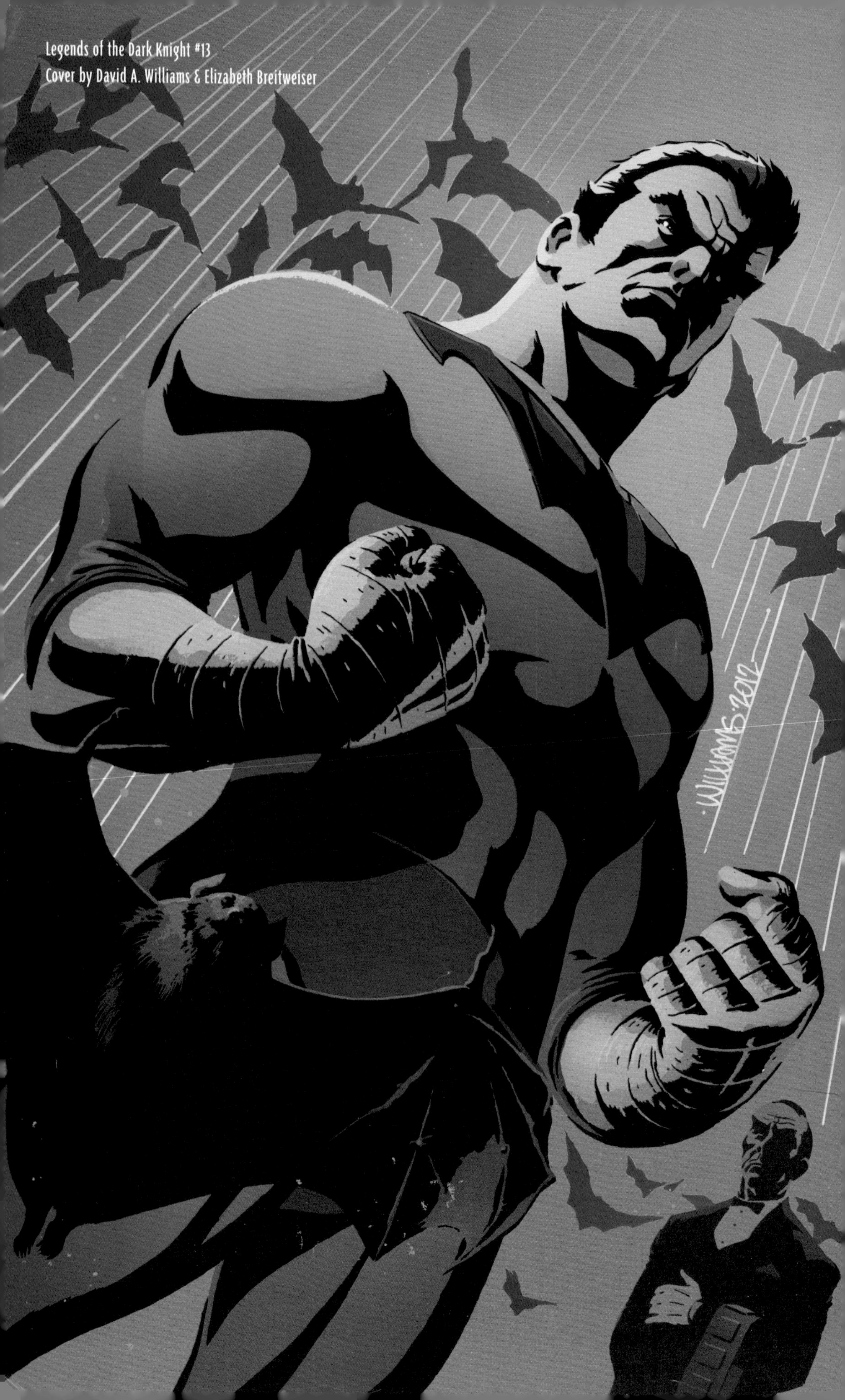
WILLIAMS·2012
Legends of the Dark Knight #13
Cover by David A. Williams & Elizabeth Breitweiser

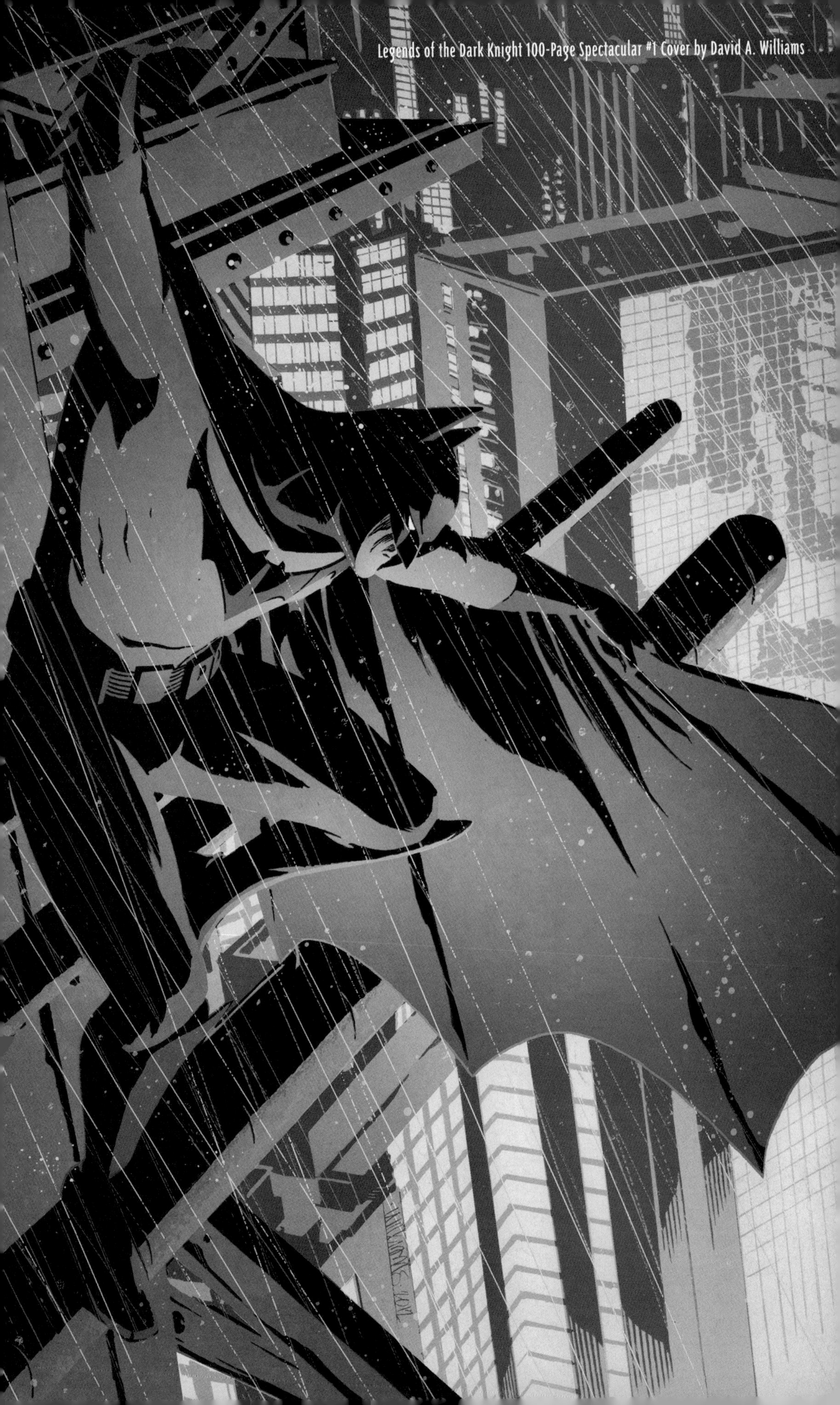

Legends of the Dark Knight 100-Page Spectacular #1 Cover by David A. Williams

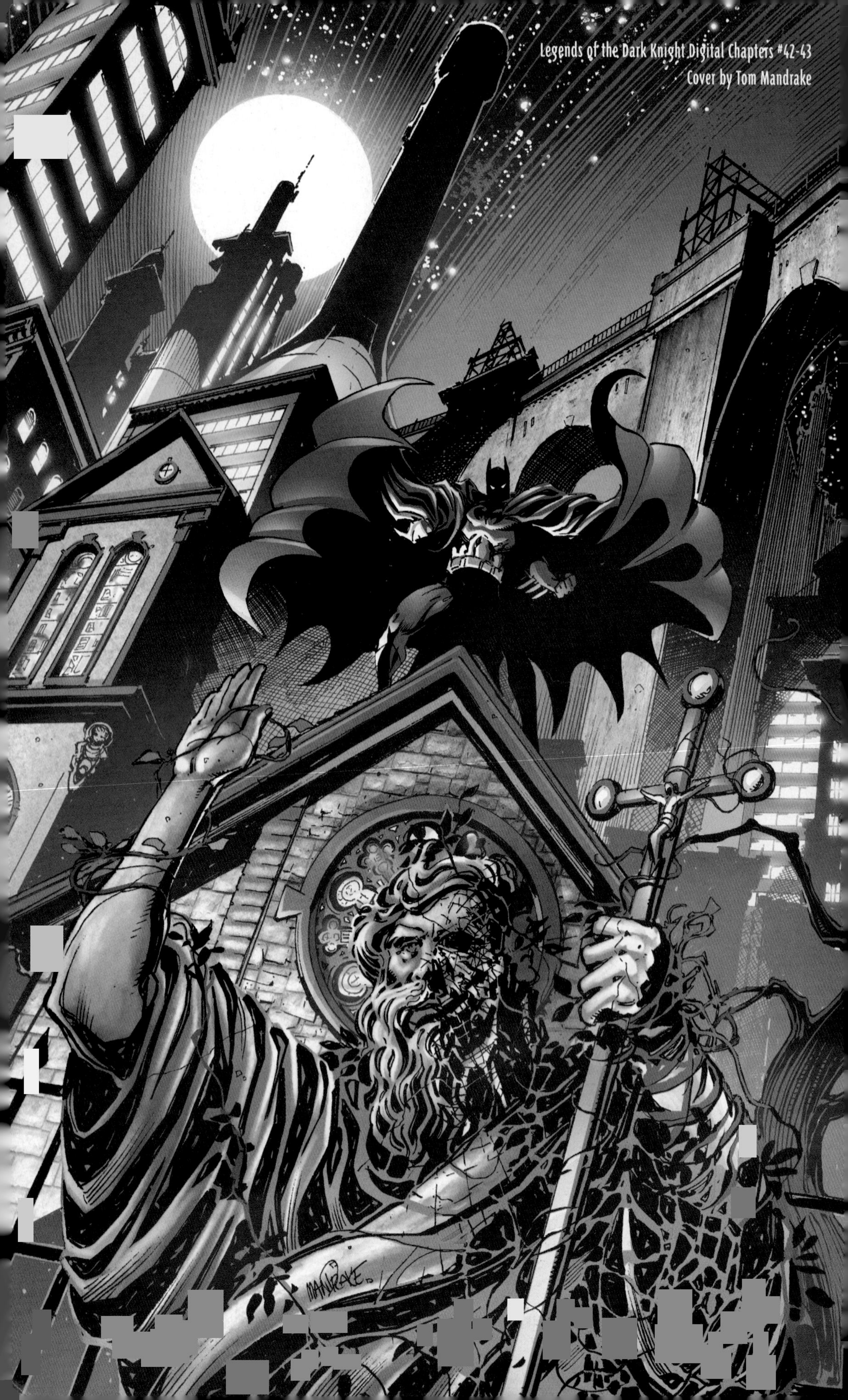
MANDRAKE

Legends of the Dark Knight Digital Chapters #42-43
Cover by Tom Mandrake

Legends of the Dark Knight Digital Chapters #44-45 Cover by Tom Mandrake

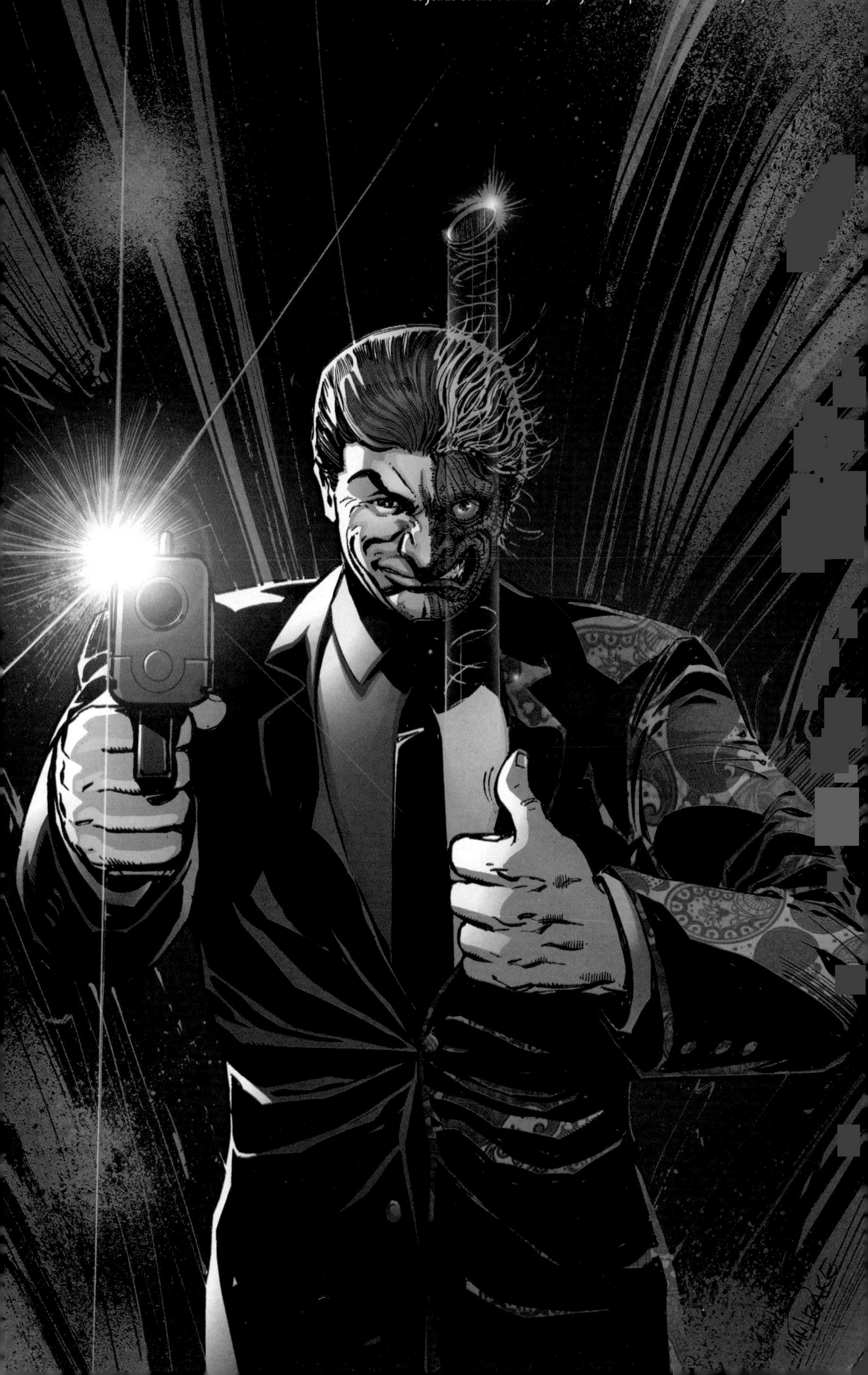

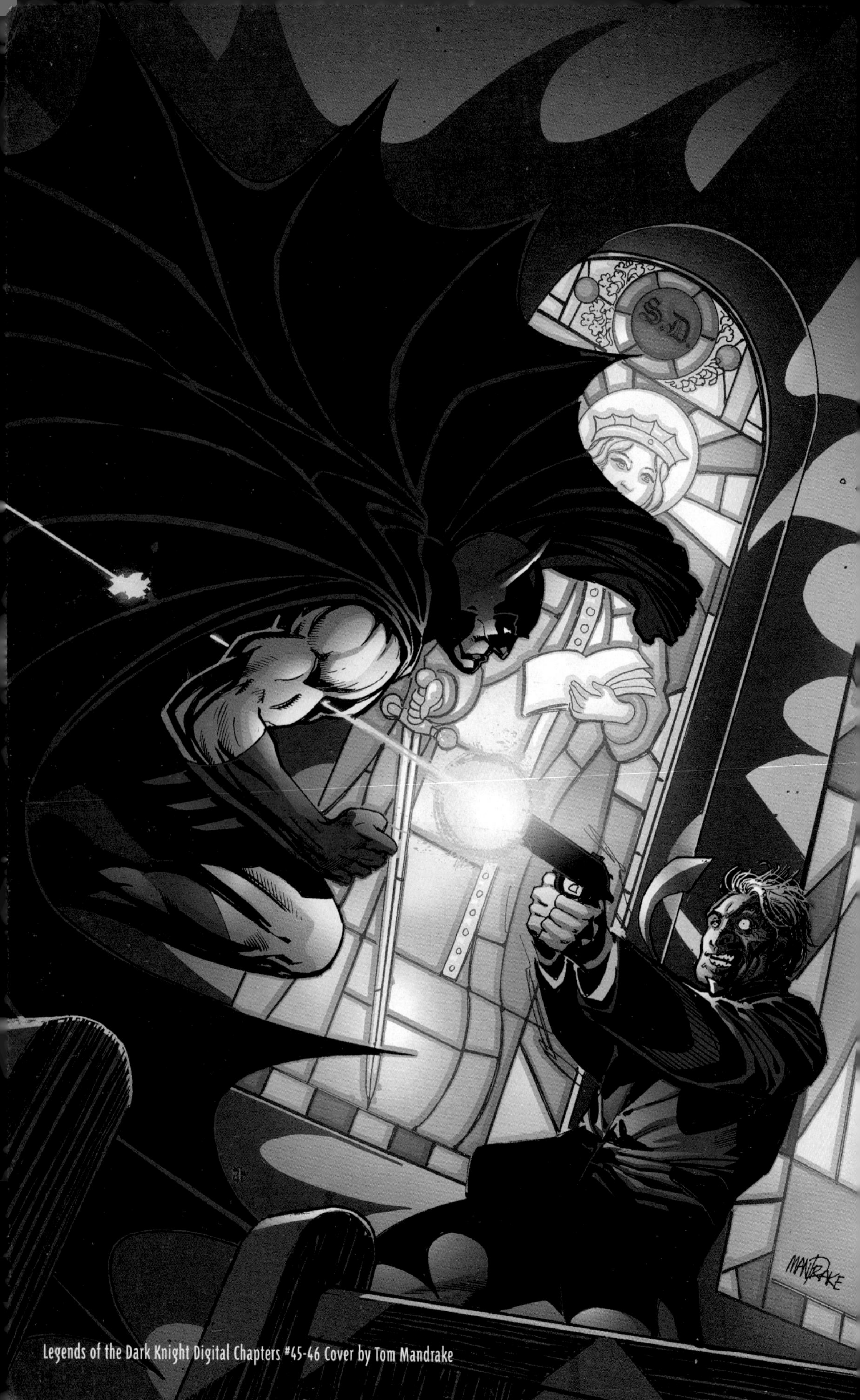
S.D.
MANDRAKE

Legends of the Dark Knight Digital Chapters #45-46 Cover by Tom Mandrake